# A Companion to
# the Study of History

*For my grandchildren –*
Anna, Laura, Michael, Alexandre,
Eleanor, Emma, Christopher,
Dominic, Victoria, Maria-Lluïsa and William
*– with love*

# A Companion to the Study of History

Michael Stanford

BLACKWELL
Oxford UK & Cambridge USA

First published 1994
Reprinted 1995

Blackwell Publishers, the publishing imprint of Basil Blackwell Ltd
108 Cowley Road
Oxford OX4 1JF, UK

Basil Blackwell Inc.
238 Main Street
Cambridge, Massachusetts 02142
USA

*British Library Cataloguing in Publication Data*
A CIP catalogue record for this book is available from the British Library.

*Library of Congress Cataloging-in-Publication Data*
Stanford, Michael, 1923–
    A companion to the study of history / Michael Stanford.
      p.      cm.
    Includes bibliographical references (p.) and index.
    ISBN 0–631–18158–X (hbk. : acid-free paper).
    – ISBN 0–631–18159–8 (pbk. : acid-free paper)
    1. History—Study and teaching (Higher)—United States.
    I. Title.
    D16.3.S74    1994
    907—dc20                                        93–33858
                                                       CIP

Typeset in 10½/12½ Sabon
by Photoprint, Torquay, Devon
Printed in Great Britain by T.J. Press Ltd, Padstow, Cornwall

This book is printed on acid-free paper

# Contents

# Introduction

In 1989 the states of central and eastern Europe threw off the Soviet yoke and declared themselves free and democratic republics. Among the jubilant reactions in the West there was one from Francis Fukuyama, a political theorist, who believed (like any true US citizen) that progress could go no further than freedom and democracy. He concluded, therefore, in a blaze of notoriety, that this was 'the end of history'; no further change could be expected. It was reported that a number of school students were hopefully asking whether the end of history would also mean the end of algebra.

This little story illustrates several points that will concern us in this book; for example, that history is about change, that the course of history may be seen as a progress towards better states of affairs, that history is enacted most obviously on the political scene, that history is concerned with the present as well as the past. But above all it illustrates the ambiguity of the word 'history'.

Before we go any further we should get clear in our minds this very important distinction between history-as-event and history-as-account. In the autumn of 1989 certain actions were taken by the people of East Germany, including the destruction of the Berlin Wall. These deeds were reported on television and in the press, were discussed by political commentators like Fukuyama, and have since found their place in the first of doubtless many history books. First came the actions, then came the representation of them in pictures and words, both spoken and written. If you are following what I am saying, you have in your mind a more or less clear picture of the destruction of the Wall. But you do not have the bricks and stones literally in your head. It is sometimes confusing that the same word 'history' is used both for the continuous series of events that happen in the world and for the ordered arrangements of words and ideas that give a more or less coherent account of those happenings. The distinction should now be clear enough. Some writers use 'history(e)' and 'history(n)' to mark the distinction – with (e) and (n) referring to event and narrative. Others use 'history(1)' and 'history(2)' where the numbers refer to what may be seen as first and second levels of reality. In this book I shall use the latter method where it is necessary.

Gibbon remarked that history 'is . . . little more than the register of the crimes, follies, and misfortunes of mankind'. Yet like many others, I have found a lifetime far too short for enjoying all the historians' accounts of the men and women who have lived before us on this earth. And it is not only historians who tell us. Wordsworth's great poem *The Prelude* relates how, as a young man, he went to France in July 1790 (just a year after the fall of the Bastille) and saw

> How bright a face is worn when joy of one
> Is joy of tens of millions,

and later

> Among sequestered villages we walked
> And found benevolence and blessedness
> Spread like a fragrance everywhere, like Spring.

Wouldn't it have been fun to be there and share in the feasting and dancing and singing that he goes on to describe? And, above all, the hope?

And yet, beyond all those particular occasions, my imagination has never lost hold of the vision that was set before me at the age of seventeen when I read H. G. Wells's *Outline of History*. When reading particular histories one tends to see Julius Caesar, Oliver Cromwell, Abraham Lincoln at the same distances, as it were, just as one sees the heroes and heroines of fiction. But Wells makes Man himself the hero, and the narrative is built around one obsessively interesting character. Since then, in addition to particular histories, there has always been for me one overriding single history that winds down through the ages from palaeolithic hunters, fashioning little figures of women and painting beasts on cave walls, to you and me today and our children and grandchildren and on and on . . . We have such a long ancestry, so many cousins and, we hope, many descendants who will be, perhaps, brighter and happier than we. History gives one a sense of family.

After these inspiring thoughts it comes as something of a shock to realize that our knowledge of the family is very inadequate. It is, perhaps, obvious that there is a great deal in our family history that we do not know. That might not matter so much if there were not a serious possibility that, if we did know more, we might change our ideas. It is as if we have always thought badly of Great-Uncle George because we know that he left his wife and disinherited his children. But if later on we learn more about his wife and children, we may understand why he did what he did and think rather more kindly of him. All our historical beliefs are similarly subject to possible revision, because if there is one thing we can be certain of in history, it is that there is a lot we do not know.

And our knowledge is seriously inadequate in another respect. This is due to the fact that we have no direct knowledge of the past; all that we claim to know is indirect knowledge. This means that we have to derive our beliefs from what we can *directly* know in the present – i.e. from what we call evidence. It is like boys in the woods who do not directly know that there is a bear in the cave (they cannot see or hear it), but they believe there is because they can see large paw-marks leading in and none coming out. They are probably right; but on the other hand we can think of ways in which they could be wrong; e.g. the bear might have left by the back entrance, he might have left walking on stones which would show no outgoing footprints, someone might have manufactured imitation bear-prints to play a trick on the boys, and so on. Their belief that the bear is in the cave is derived indirectly from evidence; they can never be so sure as they would be if they had dared to enter the cave and had met the bear. So it is with history – a cave that we can never enter.

Why, then, am I writing this book? My main purpose is to show that history, properly understood, is very important to us all; then to explain how it is properly understood.

First, why is it important? Because history, like politics, is an activity for free men and women in a free society. Just as eternal vigilance is the price of liberty, so is unceasing watchfulness of a different kind the price of knowledge. Neither in history nor in science can we expect perfect knowledge, but we can and should strive for the best knowledge available, together with the hope of improving on that. Neither freedom nor history can flourish in a closed society – one where minds are shut by ignorance and prejudice, and where government policy suppresses doubts and questions.

But history, like political activity, has no place for certainties and absolutes. In an open society we make our own politics and we make our own history; in neither case do we want them made for us. So what do I mean by saying that we make our own history?

I mean that we do it in both senses of the word – history(1) and history(2). It was in the former sense that Karl Marx made his famous remark, 'Men make their own history, but not of their own free will.' He goes on to explain that they do it, not in the ways they would wish, 'but under the given and inherited circumstances with which they are directly confronted.' And he seals it with the epigram, 'The tradition of the dead generations weighs like a nightmare on the minds of the living.[1] Now it is obvious that wherever we are going we have to start from here. But in considering what we intend to do and how we can best do it we take into account what we believe the circumstances to be. This assessment includes an understanding of the past right up to the present. But understanding the past does not mean being dominated by the past; in fact, quite the contrary. As J. H. Plumb has argued in his book, *The Death of the Past*,

[1] Marx (1973 b), p. 146.

the better we understand the past, the more we are free from its dead hand. The better historians we are, the less will Marx's words be true and the 'tradition of the dead generations' will no longer press 'like a nightmare' upon us. We can best make our own history (in this sense) by questioning and perhaps rejecting patterns and policies imposed on us by government, by church or by tradition. Instead we should realize that our future history is in the hands of us all, and that we must work together to make it, sharing and acknowledging each other's responsibility.

And now what about history in the other sense, history(2)? In what ways do we make that for ourselves?

The study of history today is a serious, a demanding and a respected search for truth; not less serious than the comparable search in physics or biology. Yet there is a difference. In the natural sciences a very large part is played by mathematics and by empirical observations, and a rather smaller part by the weighing of conflicting judgements and what may be called inspired guesses. In history, however, it is the other way round. Mathematics and empirical observation play a small part; problems of interpretation and influence and meaning, and the balancing of incalculable probabilities play the greater part. There is, therefore, a larger place for personal judgements and a wider scope for disagreement. In history we have no access to complete truth; so we must keep an open mind, recognize the fallibility of our beliefs, be always keen to widen our knowledge, and be ever ready to see the possibility of truth in an unwelcome fact or uncongenial opinion. If the study of history has anything of value to teach, it is the importance of seeing all sides of a question in order to understand it. In history, as in the sciences, understanding is reached by a careful and unprejudiced scrutiny of the evidence and by the formation of balanced judgements in the light of that evidence.

Since the evidence is always incomplete and often inadequate, it is not surprising that historians sometimes disagree. They disagree, not so much about the particulars of the evidence, as about the conclusions to be drawn from the whole mass of evidence: such large questions as, Why did the Roman Empire fall? Was either the USA or the USSR a potential aggressor in the years 1948–90, kept in check only by nuclear threats? If professionals cannot agree, it is even less surprising that non-historians differ even more over these large questions, especially when they involve the highly emotive issues of religion, race or nationality. Nevertheless, people in general do hold opinions about the past, opinions that influence their political actions and their everyday behaviour. Therefore, to be well-informed about the past is not only a right but a duty. Many political opinions are historical judgements, however crude, however ill-informed. In a sense, it is true that every man and woman is his/her own historian.[2]

I said above that history, properly understood, is important for us all. In

[2] See Stanford (1990), pp. 146–8, 157–71.

this book I hope to show in what ways it is important and how it is to be properly understood – using 'history' in both senses of the word.

## Historiography

Librarians will probably classify this book under 'Historiography'; this means 'the writing of history'. A few words of explanation may be useful. The word may refer to one (or more) of three aspects of history-writing. They can be distinguished as descriptive, historical and analytical.

Descriptive historiography accepts what historians normally do and describes the standard methods and procedures. This is what I attempted in Stanford (1990). Examples of this genre bulk large in Kitson Clark (1967), Elton (1967 and 1970), Marwick (1989, chapters 5 and 6), Seldon (1988), Shafer (1974) and Tosh (1984). For a general introduction to the study of historiography Marwick and Tosh are to be recommended.

Historical historiography traces the ways in which history has been written in the 2,500 years since Herodotus. Among the best surveys are Thompson (1942), Barnes (1962) and Fueter (1968). Like history itself, historical historiography is subdivided, often by periods, countries or issues, each providing a topic for the many books of this kind; there are also studies of individual historians. Among these are Blackwell's *Dictionary of Historians* (ed. Cannon et al., 1988), P. Burke (1990), Cannon (1980), Carbonell (1976), Ferro (1984), Higham (1963), Hofstadter (1968), Iggers (1983), Iggers and Parker (1980), Kaye (1984), Novick (1988), Parker (1990), Perrot (1992), Stoianovich (1976). Particularly to be recommended is the collection of historians' views of history down the ages in Kelley (1991). Not only does it illustrate how many different answers have been given to E. H. Carr's question, *What Is History?* It shows also how ancient are many of the issues of modern critical historiography.

Analytical or critical historiography discusses the concepts and philosophical problems arising from the writing of history. In practice it overlaps with the analytical or critical philosophy of history; the only difference, perhaps, is that the former approaches from the direction of the historian, the latter from the philosopher's. The present book attempts analytical historiography. Other examples are Collingwood (1961), E. H. Carr (1964), Butterfield (1960), Veyne (1984). From a more philosophical direction we have Collingwood (1961) – again, for he was both a historian and a philosopher, Atkinson (1978), Hayden White (1987), Olafson (1979) and, of course, Hegel (1975 or 1956).

In addition to these three categories we have that of the historiographical survey or guide. A book of this sort attempts to demonstrate some of the many fields or methods of history writing. One of the latest (P. Burke, 1991) includes chapters on women's history, microhistory, oral history,

history of reading, history of images, history of the body. Other examples of this genre are Finberg (1965), Dalzell (1976), Gilbert and Graubard (1972) and Rabb and Rotberg (1982). Useful and important though they are, such books usually omit more than they contain. For the topics available for the historian have proliferated almost without limit since the Second World War – partly, no doubt, under the influence of the *Annales* school and its concept of 'total or global history'.[3] There is virtually no human activity from astronomy or breast-freeding to yacht-racing or zither-playing that has not (or will not soon have) its own history. The same may be said of various human groups – from anglers or archimandrites to Zen Buddhists or Zionists.

As new topics or fresh definitions of groups arouse interest, so, we may be sure, someone will want to write their histories. Provided that strict canons of historical scholarship are observed, there is no reason why they should not – however bizarre or obscure the subject may at first sight appear. Indeed, there are good reasons why they should. Although writers of more conventional history may be supercilious, and although the pioneers may seem overenthusiastic, attaching too much importance to their pet projects, they must be taken seriously. This is because human life does not take place in the separate compartments of the historian: demographic facts can affect political history; religious beliefs can affect economic history; geography determines military campaigns. The *Annalistes'* project of global history did not envisage the compiling of innumerable separate histories; rather it called for the recognition of economic and social structures into which all historical phenomena could be fitted.[4] Their particular project may be unrealizable, but they were right in thinking that every history should be capable, in principle, of integration with every other history. Not only new historical facts, but also fresh historical insights and understandings can and must alter existing histories; that is why history is rewritten every generation.

So far I have spoken as if the only innovations in historiography were new subjects of study. A glance at the list of chapters in Burke (1991) cited above will show that this is not so. At least two of these (oral history and history of images) are concerned with the type of evidence used.[5] They are not divisions of the historical field, but distinct methods, remarkable in their difference from the conventional historians' material – texts and documents. Here again, there is no foreseeable limit to the methods that historians may find useful. Computers are already widely used, together with at least one appropriate learned journal, *History and Computing*.[6] Again it would be tedious to attempt to list all the

---

[3] See Stoianovich (1976), especially ch. 4.
[4] See Stoianovich (1976) and Braudel (1975; 1980; 1981–4).
[5] For oral history see below, ch. 6, pp. 163–5.
[6] Oxford University Press, 1989–.

auxiliary techniques that historians use – for example, sigillography, heraldry, chorography, diplomatic, palaeography, numismatics, statistics, etc. Since to these may be added many of the techniques of the social sciences, now also used by historians, the list would be out of date almost before it was completed.

A third area of innovation is that of the presentation of history. We tend to assume that the past is put before us largely by history books; this is less and less true. Traditionally it has also been presented (or represented) by paintings, carvings, statues, drama, pageantry, ritual. To these may now be added film, advertising, television, photo-journalism and that commercialized presentation of historical sites and buildings to the (mostly uninformed) public known as heritage history. It is only recently (1993) that the Tower of London, with its yeomen of the guard and headsmen's blocks, has ceased to be the most frequented tourist attraction in Britain. Vexed questions of historical truth, of historians' integrity and of the understanding of history are thereby raised.[7] Each case should be judged for itself. Perhaps, after reading this book, you will find it possible to see more clearly the validity and problems, not only of heritage history but of all these innovations, even if you cannot arrive at a definite conclusion.

## Gender and History

There remains for brief consideration the most significant of all historiographical innovations – those which have arisen in the last third of this century from the changing roles and perceptions of women. For a number of reasons these innovations are of greater consequence than the others we have been discussing. The chief reason is that they primarily concern not a minority group, but a majority of the human race. Another reason is that the chief subject of study (women) already includes a growing number of skilled and sophisticated practitioners. Indeed, women historians were well established in the profession long before women's history appeared. A third reason is that the matter raises interesting historiographical questions at a number of levels: at that of history-as-event, at that of sources, at that of evidence, at that of interpretation, at that of ideological stance, at that of presentation (in written, spoken or pictorial form), and at that of reverberation in the public consciousness – roughly, what we define as historicity.[8] The one possible disadvantage of this innovation is that it is linked with a lively contemporary debate about the changing perceptions of the functions and mutual relations of men and women in

---

[7] For more on this, see ch. 3, pp. 53–63. See also K. Walsh (1992).

[8] For 'historicity' see below, chapter 3, pp. 50–1. For the importance of their own history to women, see below, chapter 6, p. 165.

the world of today. While this ensures that a good deal of time and energy goes into both the reading and the writing of women's history and (as a development of that) the history of the relations between the sexes, there is still a danger in 'present-centred' history. Many historians have insisted that the past should be studied purely for its own sake, and that concern for present interests inevitably distorts it.

I know of no better advocate of the contrary case than the distinguished French historian, Michelle Perrot, who writes: 'Our goal is not to create a new territory called women's history ... but rather to change the direction of historical attention by posing the question of the relationship between the sexes as central. This is the inescapable price of women's history.' For an introduction to the subject, one can hardly do better than her own: *Writing Women's History*.[9]

I hope that the fundamental issues of the study of history will be made clear during the course of this book. I am sure that the intelligent student, once she has read it, will be able to work out for herself the arguments on both sides of the questions. History makes progress, not by substituting one fashion for another, but by steadily widening and deepening our understanding of the human condition.

## Use of this Book

To make reference easy each chapter is designed on the same pattern. The chapters are self-contained and need not be read in any particular order. Nevertheless there is a logical order to them and the book may be read as a structured whole, proceeding from the first chapter to the last.

Certain important terms are frequently used in historical literature without adequate definition. Indeed, the same writer will sometimes use a term in subtly different senses without giving any warning to the possibly confused reader. For this reason I have given my definition of a number of these terms – e.g. evidence, fact, event, cause, etc. I hope that I use them consistently throughout the book, and, if possible, consistently with accepted usage. Each definition is given in the most relevant chapter, and the index will show where it is to be found. In both cases this is indicated by **bold** type.

Please note that 'a' and 'b' are used in the bibliography suffixed to date of publication to denote two publications in the same year. In the index, if a name occurs in the text and in a footnote, the page number only is given; if the name occurs in the footnote only, the page number and the footnote number are given.

---

[9] See Perrot (1992), p. 8. See also Perrot and Duby (1990, 1992). The subject is pursued in the journal, *Gender and History*.

Like other authors, I have grappled with the problem of personal pronouns: what gender should I attribute to 'the historian', 'the student' and so on? I have considered and rejected the devices of writing 'he or she', 's/he', 'they' (after a singular noun), as well as the weary caveat that throughout the book 'he' must be taken as 'he or she'. I have preferred to assume that the historian, etc., is sometimes female, sometimes male, and so I use 'she' or 'he' quite indiscriminately. I hope nobody will do a word count, for I intend no favouritism. Whatever I do is likely to upset some people; I crave their indulgence and apologize in advance.

One last plea: if you become bored, then skip, but don't give up.

# 1

# History as Unity

One of the most important obligations of the historian is to keep good
faith with the dead and not to score cheap points off them.
John Cannon, *The Historian at Work*

## Introduction

What is this thing called 'history'? One answer is: 'The experience of
human life extended over time'. Life, as we all know, is full of ups and
downs, so one of the basic concepts of history is change. But our attention
is normally focused on what is happening at the moment, which we call
'the present'. If we concentrate on one experience at a time, we live in a
series of present moments. But we may also attend to experiences that
occurred once but are no longer with us. These we place in 'the past'. In
addition we can envisage possible happenings and experiences that have
not occurred and are not occurring, but may yet occur. These things are
hypothetical (i.e. possible in various ways of imagining), but we can
clearly distinguish them from fiction. The ability to make up stories, as
well as to follow those that others have made up, is a common feat of the
human imagination. At first sight it looks like the ability to envisage
hypothetical futures, but practically everyone is quite clear about the
difference, even from early childhood. Picturing a fictitious world and
picturing a possible future state of affairs are quite distinct. We know
what we mean by 'the future'.

Life is largely unpredictable. It is easy to think of things that may or
may not happen; it is much harder to list things that, though theoretically
possible, we can be sure *never will* happen. Human life would not be so
full of ups and downs if we could predict it. Just because it contains a
good deal of 'the contingent and the unforeseen', one of the key concepts
in history is 'experience'.

Lastly, we note that I have defined history as 'the experience' not 'the
experiences' of life. The reason for this is not that we all have the same
experience (though many of my pains and pleasures are similar to yours),

but that ultimately we all share a common experience of life. 'No man', said John Donne, 'is an Iland, intire of it selfe; every man is a peece of the Continent, a part of the maine.' We lead our lives in community, not in solitariness – the community of shared experience. No man or woman however distant – no Hottentot, no Patagonian – is excluded. And, what is more remarkable, that common experience extends from parent to child over many generations. The whole experience is what we call 'history' and history is a unity.

*Questions about the nature, types and methods of history*

1   What is this thing called 'history'?
2   Is it all about the past?
3   Has it anything to do with the present?
4   Why do we want history?
5   Is it an impossible demand?
6   Are there different sorts of history?
7   Are there many histories or, in the end, only one?
8   If history is one, what sort of unity has it?
9   Is history the story of progress?

The theme of this chapter is history as unity. It is divided into four parts as follows:

A   Experience – or the Concern of History
B   Time and Change – or the Essence of History
C   Cumulation – or the Sum of History
D   Process – or the March of History

## A.   Experience – or the Concern of History

1   *The common experience*

The other day a friend asked me about J. R. Green's *Short History of the English People*. 'It's very readable', I replied, 'but I must warn you that it's well over a hundred years old.' 'What does that matter?' she retorted. 'History's history, isn't it?' Clearly she was confusing history-as-event with history-as-account. The past cannot change; she was right about that. But Green's book is an example, not of history-as-event but of history-as-account. That certainly does change all the time.

Now, having carefully separated those two meanings of 'history', I want to show how they often come together. In spring 1991 the Baltic states of

Latvia, Lithuania and Estonia were claiming their independence from the Soviet Union. That summer the Iraqi government annexed Kuwait. Both sides in these disputes based their cases on certain beliefs about the past. Such beliefs are part of history(2) – that is, part of what is believed, said and written about the past. It is equally clear that these conflicts, resulting from history(2), were making history in 1991; they were history-as-event, part of history (1) of that year. By now these events are past history, but still live as part of history(2) in memory, in journalism and politics, and in the books and articles written about them. This is an example of the many ways in which what is written and believed about the past (history-as-account) brings about changes in history-as-event, and these in turn become part of a new history-as-account. It is all part of the common experience of mankind, and so both history (1) and history (2) have to be recognized as formative parts of history as a whole.

## 2   Community and imagination

The unity of history is also rooted in our imagination. We grow up in a particular community (village, city, state or nation) and often these communities are made the subjects of histories. Such works reflect the continuities of government and of economic and social life in one place. But some elements of society – language, trade, art, for example – have never been so confined; they cross boundaries. Hence, as well as histories of cities and states, we have histories of baroque music or the spice trade or political theory. Wanderers and conquerors, merchants and missionaries, scholars and artists have sewn mankind together. If we stay at home we can follow them in imagination, leaping over barriers of time as easily as of space. We not only read travellers' tales, but we can live vicariously in ancient Greece with Herodotus, in tenth-century Japan with *The Tale of Genji* or in medieval chivalry with Joinville and Froissart.

The imagination thus makes history possible. But it also makes difficult demands on the historian. We are material beings living in a material world, but much of the most important and interesting part of our lives is non-material: our ideas, our emotions, our reasoning. Unfortunately almost all the evidence of the past that remains for us is material. We can get at the minds of our predecessors only by their writings and, to a lesser extent, by their art and artefacts. These, however inadequate or unreliable, are almost the historian's only guide to the minds of men and women long ago. Yet it is just these that we want most to know.

We must not forget that a society may be materially poor, but culturally rich. Europeans, meeting Australian aborigines for the first time, were misled into supposing that people who went naked and who could carry all their worldly possessions in one hand were culturally impoverished. Not so: their religion, languages and art show a rich system of ideas. Can you think of the converse – a society choked with material goods but almost bereft of profound ideas?

## 3  Is history possible?

Are we engaged in an impossible enterprise, foredoomed to fail? Let us hear some arguments.

First, isn't it nonsense to try to reconstruct the past? Physically this can be done only on a small scale – a village or a fort at a fixed date. Does not the exclusion of the much larger area in which it was situated make it quite unreal? If we dress up modern people to inhabit our model, can we alter their minds? They have neither the brains nor the bodies of their ancestors. And what about hygiene? The germs and bacteria rampant in a medieval village would terrify a modern health authority. It would quickly ban any reproduction of them.

Mostly we confine ourselves to mental reconstructions – as when we read a history book. This work is based on evidence. But, as we shall see later, evidence can be distorted, false, misunderstood or completely absent. If knowledge is unobtainable, are we wise to replace ignorance with fantasy?

Even if both the evidence and the interpretation are reliable, can we hope to enter the minds of people long dead? When, on 15 July 1099, the Christian armies entered Jerusalem they slew every Muslim and every Jew – men, women and children. After wading knee-deep in blood and corpses they went 'to give thanks to God in the Church of the Holy Sepulchre'.[1] What did God mean to them?

As if these difficulties were not enough, there is also the deliberate manipulation of the historical record. Can we trust all that Sumerian kings or Egyptian pharaohs said of themselves in imprinted clay or carved stone? (Indeed, the ancient Egyptians used hammer and chisel to alter the records themselves – especially in connection with the religious revolution of Akhenaten and the subsequent restoration.) The 'Ministry of Truth' in Orwell's 1984 was only a reflection of the manufacture of lies by contemporary dictators. If democratic governments have now abjured such methods, they have found others. Many an investigative journalist or lawyer can witness that the old medieval crimes of suppressio veri and suggestio falsi (suppression of the truth and suggestion of the lie) are alive and well in modern government.

Finally there is the radical accusation of 'constructionism' – that historians do not discover the past but merely make up stories about it. We leave discussion of that to a later chapter.[2]

---

[1] Runciman (1965), vol. I, p. 287.
[2] See ch. 5, pp. 129–130.

## 4   How do we encounter history?

Possible or not, history holds a fascination. We meet it first in memory –
'written quite full with Annals', as Carlyle said. Then in family life. Marc
Bloch notices the influence of grandparents: 'With the moulding of each
new mind there is a backward step, joining the most malleable to the most
inflexible mentality, while skipping that generation which is the sponsor of
change.'[3] Children can hardly fail to notice that their grandparents knew a
different world. This growing sense of the past becomes a sense of history
when they go to school. There a good teacher will help them to relate their
experiences of old people, old things and old books to the structured texts
of the subject.[4]

Sometimes, however, the past is rejected. Young people often feel old
customs and moral attitudes as burdensome. They may be glad to
remember that many great moments of history were more or less
successful attempts to break with the past – the Renaissance, the
Reformation, the Enlightenment, the American and French revolutions.

Nor is the past always what it has seemed. History can reveal that
traditions (good and bad) may be quite recent – not so traditional after
all. When in 1836 Dickens described Mr Pickwick and his friends
celebrating Christmas at Dingley Dell, the Christmas tree was unknown in
England. Indeed, a good deal of 'tradition' has actually been invented.[5]

Yet however we encounter history we should respect the dignity of
those earlier men and women, and not fall into the vulgar error of supposing that they lived in order to prepare the way for us. E. P. Thompson
declared his purpose to rescue the poor men and women of the early
Industrial Revolution 'from the enormous condescension of posterity'.
Ranke, more ponderously, insisted that 'every epoch is immediate to God,
and its worth is not at all based on what derives from it but rests in its
own existence, its own self.'[6]

## 5   What do we make of history?

Certainly the past was different and in that difference lies interest.
Nevertheless, the lives of most people in the past were even more
humdrum than ours. Occasionally, however, they had the colour and
drama of a Hollywood movie. (Indeed, sometimes they became one.)
Hence to some, history always has a romantic appeal. For others, the
pursuit of history is an intellectual challenge – like chess or mathematics.
The skills demanded of a historian are various, according to whether he is

[3] Bloch (1954), p. 40).
[4] For more on history in education, see chapter 3, pp. 58–61.
[5] See Hobsbawm and Ranger (1984).
[6] See 'On the Epochs of Modern History', in Ranke (1973), p. 53.

studying diplomacy (the Congress of Vienna), trade (the East India Company), art (Mannerism in Italian painting) or religious emotions (early Methodism). All have to grapple with documents and other evidence, and all need insight into both their subject in particular and human nature in general. The exercise of this combination of skills is itself attractive.

Since the human race is not made up of clones or robots, it is hardly surprising that our historical sympathies should largely run along the lines of our national, religious, racial, sexual or ideological identities. It is a fact that we all see life differently; it should also be a fact that we can see other people's points of view. History can help us to do so. We are also fortunate in that, since history is written in so many modes for such varied interests, it has largely avoided a jargon of its own and is accessible to the common reader. History, in both senses of the word, concerns us all.

## B.   Time and Change – or the Essence of History

### 1   Fear of change

Unlike us, most animals seem to live in a perpetual present. It is because we know past and future that we notice change. In order to do so, we have to be aware that part of the present is the same as it was and part is different. Without novelty there would be only continuity; without continuity there would be only novelty. With both you have change. You also have history; the ever-shifting kaleidoscope of novelty and continuity in human affairs accounts for much of the fascination of the subject.

If changes never occurred the historian would be out of business, but few people in the past would have sympathized, for change was generally deplored. It tended to produce social unrest, as in south-west England in 1549. When Cranmer's magnificent English Prayer Book was introduced, the rebels declared, 'we will have the masse in Latten (Latin), as was before . . . we will not receyve the newe servye (service) because it is but lyke a Christmas game'. [7] The Cornish demanded the Latin mass on the grounds that they knew no English; this regardless of the fact that they knew even less Latin. Familiarity was all. Yet educated people were little different, for they looked back to a golden age of the past from which had come both the Scriptures and the classics. It was not until the seventeenth century that men began to think that modern civilization matched that of the ancients and so they looked forward to a future of progress instead of looking back on a past of degeneration. [8]

This deep-seated fear of change doubtless goes back beyond history. Many early peoples found psychological security in the belief that time

[7] See Fletcher (1968), p. 135.
[8] See Bury (1924), ch. IV.

runs round in circles and that extraordinary events – wars, famines – are irregularities. A modern scholar writes of their 'terror of history' and claims that 'archaic humanity ... defended itself, to the utmost of its powers, against all the novelty and irreversibility which history entails'.[9]

It is all the more surprising, then, that a few people in the past longed for the future. Most noteworthy are the prophets (and their followers) of the Old Testament, with their hopes of the 'Day of the Lord' and the coming of the Messiah. The establishment of Christianity tended to transfer such hopes out of this world into the next. But throughout the Middle Ages and beyond, a few heretics looked and lived for the Millennium – an age in which humanity would be 'at once perfectly good and perfectly happy'.[10]. The much more familiar teaching of Karl Marx is a modern secular version of this millenarism. On the whole, historical experience seems to show that it is even less wise to live for a promised future than to regret a vanished past.

## 2  Chronology and continuity

The fact of continuity, as opposed to change, is reflected in our measurement of time. If to us (as to most other animals) the world were to seem to be new every minute, there would be nothing to measure and no events to record. The ancient Egyptians were probably the first to record long periods, counting the years by the reigns and dynasties of their pharaohs from about 3000 BC. Innumerable chronological systems have since developed, but they can be reduced to three types. One, like the Egyptian, is based on rulers and royal houses; another, like the Roman, counted from a great event (in this case, the founding of the city); the third, like the Mayan and the Siamese, rested on cycles – in these cases, of 260 and 60 years respectively. The chronologies most familiar today – the Christian, the Muslim and the Jewish – are of the second type. Correlation of the many systems has been laborious, but behind them all lies the determination to fix the present to the past. (To do the converse – to fix the past to the present – has been the work of the historian.)

## 3  The rhythms of history

Continuity has a special aspect in the work of the French historians known as the *Annales* school.[11]. The flagship of this fleet is Braudel's *The Mediterranean and the Mediterranean World in the Age of Philip II*, first published (in French) in 1949. In this, as in later writings, Braudel plays down the importance of events in favour of *la longue durée* (the long time-span). The story is told in three speeds: geographical time, social time and

[9] Eliade (1989), p. 48.
[10] See Cohn (1952), p. xiii. For contrasting views of time, see Cohn (1993).
[11] For their stress on time, see Stoianovich (1976).

individual time. Many human concerns have moved so slowly (in geographical time – 'the slow unfolding of structural realities') that change is almost imperceptible to men, and it is hardly surprising that they should have taken cyclical views of history. Shorter, but still measured in decades and centuries, are the economic, political and cultural systems that he calls 'conjonctures' or trends. Only in the last quarter of this massive work does he consider events – 'surface disturbances, crests of foam that the tides of history carry on their strong backs.'[12]. It is the long-term rhythms that, for Braudel, are the shaping forces of history. We may think of it like this. Sailing in a small boat, the landsman is very conscious of the buffeting of the waves, the drenching spray and the rolling and pitching of the craft. These the sailor ignores; he is concerned with the powerful and potentially dangerous tides and currents, of which the landsman is quite oblivious. Hence the need to observe the *longues durées* of history.

That there is not one series of historical events but many, even at the same place; that historical phenomena occur in short, medium and long cycles, interweaving and overlapping like tunes in a Bach fugue – these are valuable insights. Old-fashioned narrative related one series of events along one time scale. Braudel is right to point out that history moves not at one pace, but at a thousand – all at the same time.[13]

## C.  Cumulation – or the Sum of History

### 1  Is history-as-account cumulative?

Another of Braudel's firm beliefs is that **historiography (the writing of history)** should be a co-operative enterprise; however, most historians work singly. Is history cumulative? Does it (in the dictionary's terms) increase 'by successive additions'? Is it like a heap of sand, to which anyone can add a spadeful to increase it? Are histories like this? Or are they works of art? (Would a Beethoven symphony be the better for someone else's addition of a few bars, or the *Mona Lisa* for a few brush-strokes?)

Not only Braudel believed in team-work in history. J. B. Bury, in his famous Inaugural Lecture at Cambridge in 1903, commended it. He spoke of 'armies of toiling students' and declared, 'We are heaping up material and arranging it, according to the best methods we know . . . Our work is to be used by future ages.'[14] Bury's actual use of the sand-heap metaphor suggests that he thinks history(2) can be literally cumulative, but one

---

[12] Braudel (1975) pp. 20–3.
[13] For further discussion of Braudel, see ch. 3, pp. 63–7.
[14] See Bury (1930), p. 17; also printed in Stern (1970), pp. 219–20.

cannot help feeling that the final writing, at least, should be the work of one hand.

## 2  Is history-as-event cumulative?

But what about history-as-event? If it is cyclical, then of course it cannot accumulate beyond the point where each cycle ends. But are there breaks in 'linear' history? The French philosopher Michel Foucault believed that he had found two such breaks, or 'discontinuities', in western thought – one in the mid-seventeenth century, the other at the beginning of the nineteenth.[15] Might the fall of Constantinople in 1453 have provided another? Thirdly, what of societies and civilizations that were mutually ignorant – like Europe and China before Marco Polo or America before Columbus? Were they not completely separate cumulations of history?

Finally, it can be asked whether the present is the sum of all that has gone before. Strictly, we cannot tell. I cannot point to anything in the past that contributed nothing to the present; my mere knowledge of it would make it a contribution. Yet we do not know all the past, so possibilities remain of unknown past events that shaped our present.

We may, for all we know, be in the position of the ancient Greeks. We now know, as they did not, that a great deal of their culture was a continuation of the Mycenaean (roughly that of the age of the Trojan War), and that Mycenae owed much to the Minoan cultures of Crete, and that the Minoans had derived some things from Egypt. And surely this is not the only example of people who did not know their origins, did not know why they behaved as they did. In terms of civilization it is the analogue of the Freudian unconscious, which is said to retain the shape of infancy. Sir Maurice Powicke rightly urged historians 'to retrieve the treasures that have been dropped on the way and lost, which, if restored, would enrich our civilization'.[16] Yet we cannot hope to recover them all, so our question must remain unanswered.

## D.  Process – or the March of History

### 1  What sort of process?

This chapter is about the unity of history, so we are led to ask what sort of unity is to be found in it. Is it some sort of process (and if so, of what sort?) or is it merely a random succession of one thing after another? The photographs on the film in your camera picture a succession of events, but they lack the unity of the frames of a cinematograph film. The latter may even be a work of art. To some people all history has seemed like this.

[15] See Foucault (1970), p. xxii.
[16] Powicke (1955), p. 95.

Could we all just be characters in a story that one supernatural being is telling to another? We can never know.

Supposing that history-as-event is neither a cosmic novel nor a random succession, what sort of process might it be? The dictionary definition of 'process' offers three characteristics – unity, regularity and sequence.

Clearly history does not have the unity given by regular procedure. History is a 'one-off'; it is unique. But uniqueness does not imply unity. We recall that many parts of the world have lived for millennia in mutual ignorance – hardly a historical unity, though perhaps a geographical one. But today all parts of the world are involved with one another, and they are aware of it. Is not world history (in both senses of the word) becoming a fact? So perhaps it does have a kind of unity – the unity of a river system, where many tributary streams flow into one.

Again, history is a sequence, but is it an ordered sequence? In spite of being unique (at least, it is the only one we know), it does seem to possess order – as in the apparent linkage of cause and effect.[17] This is because we find regularities within history, though never of history – except for those of us who believe in repetitive cycles of history.

## 2   Growth

We are most familiar with process in the form of growth – the characteristic of every form of life. The analogy has often been drawn between history and human life. But can it be taken seriously? (Are we now in the old age of the world? Or in its maturity? Or still in its childhood?) Yet the image is so strong that the hard-headed and rational Karl Marx was betrayed into appealing to it in order to explain the continuing popularity of Greek art and mythology long after (according to his own theories of culture's dependence on the economic base) they should have been discarded. For 'Where does Vulcan come in as against Roberts & Co.? Jupiter, as against the lightning conductor? and Hermes, as against the *Crédit Mobilier*?' he asks. And his answer is that the Greeks lived in the childhood of mankind. 'Why should the childhood of human society, where it had obtained its most beautiful development, not exert an eternal charm as an age that will never return?'[18]

More commonly, history is seen as a development. Now this concept implies the unfolding, or working out, of something that was present from the beginning. What might this be – charity, courage, intelligence, aesthetic sensibility? Were these always present in mankind? Are they noticeably more evident today than ever before? Not obviously so.

Since Darwin, development has frequently been understood in the form of evolution. The theory implies a process of increasing complexity,

---

[17] See ch. 8, 'History As Sequence'.
[18] Marx (1977), pp. 359–60. Also Prawer (1978), pp. 278–89.

together with inevitability and irreversibility. Many nineteenth-century thinkers hastened to apply Darwin's ideas to society, and to attempt to trace 'the survival of the fittest' in the story of mankind. Unfortunately this often led to a very inferior position being allotted to some (usually coloured) peoples and the top place awarded to the whites, or even only to Anglo-Saxons. The echoes of this racism long stained both literature and politics; nor was history free from shame.[19] In fact, there is little or no evidence of physical evolution since *homo sapiens* first appeared about 50,000 years ago. What has most conspicuously evolved is technology. As for 'the survival of the fittest', this notion should (as Karl Popper suggests) be applied to our ideas. Let them contend without privilege or prejudice in open and fair fight, and may the best one win. Thus we may hope to make progress and at the same time stop killing people.

## 3   *Progress*

But what is 'progress'? Is the story of mankind one of steady advance, as many have believed? Progress implies improvement – getting better. But 'better' in what sense? If history is the story of progress, does that mean that all things have improved? Or only some? If only some, have the improvements outweighed the deteriorations? Has the improvement been continuous, or in halts and leaps? Have there been backslidings? Has the improvement been everywhere, or only in some places? If the past is a progress, is that due to the efforts of man? Or to a supernatural force – God, Fate, the Absolute? Assuming progress does occur, is it inevitable? Or the result of good fortune? Above all, will it continue?

It is worth asking such questions because, as one historian believes, 'the idea of progress is, in this modern age, one of the most important ideas by which men live.' It is the 'modern religion, or the modern substitute for religion.'[20] Doubts are possible. What of the environment? Is that more or less polluted after fifty centuries of history? What of literature? Are Sophocles and Plato, Homer, Virgil and Dante, Augustine and Shakespeare overtopped by their modern counterparts? What of morality? Has there been notable advance upon the teachings of Christ, or even upon those of the Hebrew prophets, of Gautama Buddha, Zoroaster or Confucius several centuries before him?

Let us suppose that you wish to establish the fact of progress in one particular field over a stated period. These problems will confront you: an agreed interpretation of the evidence; the possibility of comparison; perhaps the establishment of valid statistical series; the determination of the beliefs, values and expectations of various groups of people; the evaluation of particular achievements and states of affairs; the balances of

[19] See, for example, C. Parker (1990), ch. 2.
[20] Pollard (1971) p. 13.

gains and losses. Progress cannot be taken for granted. On the other hand, is it worth all this effort to prove it? Most historians today (unlike their predecessors) rarely attempt it.

The processes that we have examined do not constitute the true unity of history. It has unity of a more subtle and tougher kind – as the following chapters, I hope, will show.

## Conclusion

History is a unity. First, it is like a family – a family of people connected by blood, by upbringing, by interdependence, and by common concern. We may not always like our parents, children, siblings and so on, but they are part of us. Moreover, although individuals come and go, the family continues.

Second, the word 'history' has two meanings – the deeds of that family and the record of those deeds. But the nature of that record helps to shape future deeds. Hence the unity is a continual interweaving of these two strands – deed and record.

Third, the points of intersection are most frequently the points of action. In the next chapter we look at actions – the growing-points of history where both record and deed come together. That chapter will be another step in exploring the subtle unities of history.

### Suggested Reading

Bloch 1954
Braudel 1975; 1980
Burke, P. 1969; 1990
Bury 1903 (in Stern 1970); 1924
Butterfield 1960
Carr, E. H. 1964
Hobsbawm and Ranger 1984

Nietzsche 1957
Nisbet 1969
Parker 1990
Plumb 1973
Pollard 1971
Renier 1965
Stern 1970

# 2

# History as Action

But yet the minds of men are the great wheels of things; thence come
changes and alterations in the world; teeming freedom exerts and puts
forth itself.

John Warr, 1659

## Introduction

In the last chapter we looked at history as changes within a unity. In this
one we consider how 'the minds of men' and women bring about those
'alterations in the world' which are the concern of the historian. As Warr
implies, it is in conditions of freedom that we are best inspired to great
efforts.

*Questions about the meaning of action; action in history; the use
and misuse of history*

1  What is the use of history?
2  In what ways is history misused?
3  Can we avoid history?
4  Can we learn from history?
5  How did people act in history?
6  What is meant by 'action'?
7  How do our actions acquire meaning?
8  Where does politics come in?

The theme of this chapter is 'History as Action'. It is divided into three
parts as follows:

A  The Analysis of Action
B  Contexts and Consequences of Action
C  Uses and Abuses of History

# A.   The Analysis of Action

## 1   *The past as present*

History is a study of the past, which we can do nothing to alter. What we *can* affect is the future. Even if we decide to do nothing at all, yet we still anticipate what it may bring. So, whether active or passive, human life is lived towards the future. We act to bring something about, or to prevent something from happening – like accelerator and brake in a motor car.

Since we often think before we act, a lot of thinking also is directed towards the future. But we never *know* the future. We always act in partial ignorance, with the possibility that we shall be pleasantly or unpleasantly surprised. (Bookmakers, stockbrokers and insurance companies thrive on this fact.)

These truths are often forgotten when we study the past. So we do well to remind ourselves that history consists chiefly of human actions. They may now be past, but they were performed in the present; more than that, those past actions looked towards the future just as ours do today. Our predecessors knew no more of their future than we know of ours. Like us, they could only hope or fear.

Like us, they saw their future as open, while we, looking back on that future, see it as closed. It may be that they saw choice and free will where we, with hindsight, see only necessity and fate. On the other hand, it may be that sometimes they had more choice than they thought and we are astonished at their blindness. Teaching international relations of the 1930s, I would sometimes be assailed by incredulous students (glad to be face to face with a survivor from that remote age) who would ask, 'Why didn't you stop Hitler when he occupied the Rhineland in 1936? Couldn't you all see what would happen if you didn't stand up to him?' Well, no, we couldn't (though a few guessed).

So we shall understand history better if we see it, not as the closed book of the past, but as a series of presents, each one as open, as pregnant with opportunity, as our present seems to us.

## 2   *Action and behaviour*

In studying history (as in other human affairs) it is helpful to distinguish action from behaviour. Both are what we do, but only the former is supposed to embody intention. Thus behaviour is what we see or hear people do; if we suppose that what they are doing is intended, then it counts as action. Only in the case of our own actions are we sure of the intention; with the actions of others intention has to be inferred. This is not always easy, but it is often important. Your stepping on my toe was your observable behaviour; only if you intended it was it your action. (It is thus held that only humans act; other animals behave. Most animals can walk; only humans go for a walk. Polo ponies gallop; their riders play polo.)

Since we humans are social creatures it is important to know one another's intentions. These, as we saw, have to be inferred from others' behaviour (including their behaviour of declaring their intentions). 'She summoned the waiter.' What was her behaviour – beckoning, shouting, sending a message by another waiter? 'He is moving his arm above his head.' What is his action? Greeting? Or calling for help? Is he waving or drowning?

Where the behaviour is ambiguous (capable of more than one meaning – as with the waving arm), the context usually makes the intention clear. But this is not so easy for the historian, who may not always know the context. In history (as in everyday life) it is important to remember that when agents acted, only their outward behaviour was observable. That could have been misinterpreted and the intention misunderstood. The famous charge of the Light Brigade at Balaclava in 1854 was the result of just such a misunderstanding. The commander-in-chief, Raglan, sent an unclear order to Lucan, the commander of the British cavalry. The latter asked the officer bearing the message, Nolan, which guns were to be attacked. 'Nolan threw back his head, and . . . with a furious gesture, pointed' to the wrong guns. ' "There, my lord, is your enemy, there are your guns". With those words and with that gesture the doom of the Light Brigade was sealed', writes the historian of the battle. 'What did Nolan mean?' she asks. '. . . The truth will never be known, because a few moments later Nolan was killed.'[1] Thus we can never know what Nolan intended, never know what his action was. But Lucan's interpretation (correct or incorrect) of Nolan's behaviour was 'the reason why' of Tennyson's poem – the death sentence for hundreds of men and horses.

We can now turn to action proper.

## 3    The analysis of action

It is convenient to distinguish five parts of an action. One we have already met is the *intention*. When we act we aim to bring about some change in the world or in ourselves. The second part is the *assessment* that we make of the present state of affairs. This state of affairs is not only relevant to why we want to act – our intention; it also helps us to weigh up our chances of success, and to decide how best to achieve our aim. The third, then, is the *means* that we adopt for our purpose. Next, we remember that to do anything at all requires energy, both mental and physical. Hence there has to be some emotion that drives us to act – love, hate, fear, ambition, and so on. (We can easily be mistaken about these.) So the *drive*, or the will, is the fourth element. The fifth contains them all; this is the *context*. By

---

[1] Woodham-Smith (1953), p. 239.

'context' we understand the whole environment – social, physical and cultural – within which the action occurs.

How does this analysis apply to history? In several ways, for the events of the past sometimes influence, sometimes constitute, each of these five elements. We can also see how our ideas about history affect these five. Thus an analysis of this kind can help the historian to a deeper understanding of those past events that she is studying.


## 4   The influence of the past, or history(1)

Let us take each of these in turn. We begin with the influence of the past. Any situation in which we find ourselves is the result of preceding events. Therefore, in order to understand our present situation, we should study history (i.e. the account of past events). Confusion arises from the use of the word 'history' in these two different senses. Let us show the difference between event and account in practice. By way of example we will look at the anti-communist revolutions in central and eastern Europe in the autumn of 1989.

The situation, of course, was the result of preceding events. But in it occurred deliberate actions on the part of hundreds of thousands of men, women and even children. To be sure, the historian of these events has to understand how this situation came about. He may well conclude that no such revolution could have succeeded had the USSR been willing to send its tanks in, as in East Berlin in 1953, in Budapest in 1956 and in Prague in 1968. But in 1989 it was not so willing. One may hazard that the reasons for this included the parlous state of the Soviet economy, internal weaknesses of the Soviet government, the consequent change in Soviet foreign policy, especially towards the USA, and, possibly, doubt about the Soviet army after its withdrawal from Afghanistan. These are the sorts of reasons that the historian is likely to give. They describe what Marxists call the 'objective situation'. But they would have been unknown to almost all of the crowds who filled the public places of capital cities and demanded the overthrow of the government.

People are moved to action, not by what is happening thousands of miles away (of which they are probably quite ignorant), but by what is going on in their own heads and hearts. This is the 'subjective situation'. The historian must take account of both. Let us concentrate on Prague, November 1989. Picking up our five elements of action, we start with *intention*. This was to put an end to a brutal and clumsy tyranny imposed by a foreign power. The rebels' *assessment* of the situation was that the Czech government was clearly worried about its great unpopularity, but mainly that communist governments had already fallen in Warsaw, Budapest and Berlin. Now it was their turn.

The *means* were, first, a student demonstration on Friday, 17 November, which was stopped by the police with much bloodshed. A strike of all students followed the next day (Saturday). On Sunday they were joined by actors and other theatre people, who declared a theatre strike and called for a general strike. Thus encouraged, students made more demands, including the most significant – the call for an end to the dominant role of the Communist Party. Following the initiative of the students and actors the chief existing opposition groups met in another theatre under the leadership of Vaclav Havel, the playwright. Days of mass demonstrations and negotiations ensued; on 20 December a new government was sworn in and on the 29th Havel became president.

Successful revolutions often grow confusedly. For instance, no one at the opening of the States-General at Versailles in 1789 foresaw, even less intended, the establishment of a French republic and the beheading of the king. In Prague, however, both the intention and the means to its fulfilment were clear to the leaders of the movement.[2]

## 5   Awareness of the past, or history (2)

We have seen the intention, the assessment, and the means adopted in the Prague revolution. Turning to the fourth element, the *drive*, we might suppose that a longing for freedom, a hope for better things, provided enough motivation. But it is here that history played a large part. The students' declaration of 19 November appealed 'especially to European states in the year of the two hundredth anniversary of the French revolution'. This, the first and greatest of modern European revolutions, has inspired many others. But the Czechs did not have to rely only on the French for historical inspiration. They remembered the birth of the first Czechoslovak republic in 1918 after the defeat of the Austro-Hungarian Empire, and, more recently, their earlier revolution in the 'Prague Spring' of 1968, which was finally crushed by Russian tanks. In that year, a Czech historian, Edo Fris, had written: 'The Czechs and the Slovaks . . . possess a national memory . . . History is omnipresent in our social consciousness, both as a warning and as a stimulus.'[3] The leader in 1968 had been Alexander Dubcek, who was recalled from internal exile twenty-one years later to join Havel as joint figurehead of the 1989 revolution. Three days later (1 January 1990) Havel as president addressed the nation: 'People, your government has returned to you.' He was quoting the words of Thomas Masaryk's inaugural address as first president of Czechoslovakia in 1918. But the words went back more than seventy-one years; they echoed a famous sentence of the great seventeenth-century Czech scholar, Comenius.[4]

Postponing consideration of the fifth element, the *context*, let us recall how ideas about the past influenced each of the four elements of action

[2] For details of the Prague revolution I have relied on Ash (1990).
[3] See Fejtö (1974), p. 213.
[4] See Ash (1990), p. 7.

that we have looked at. History helped to form the *intention*. The Czechs knew that unpopular governements had been overthrown before, both in Prague in 1618 and 1918, and elsewhere – especially in France. They also remembered their free, prosperous and democratic republic between 1918 and 1939. Their *assessment* of the situation in 1989 included both these considerations and, perhaps more important, their knowledge of recent events in Poland, Hungary and East Germany. Their methods (*means*), too, were based on their own and others' experiences: marches, demonstrations, proclamations, the organization of a rebel headquarters (in this case, the Civic Forum led by Havel), disciplined strikes of the workers, the massing of vast crowds in public places, the rapid and widespread circulation of broadsheets, pamphlets and newspapers. Fourthly, the appeal to history, by arousing the necessary determination, supplied much of the *drive*. It would not be difficult similarly to demonstrate the influence of England's Cromwellian revolution of the seventeenth century upon the American revolution under Jefferson and Washington a century later, nor the influence of ancient Rome upon the French revolutionaries of the 1790s. In all these cases, however, we must remember that the influence comes not from the objective facts of the past but from the participants' subjective beliefs about it – beliefs that in some cases we may now say were quite unhistorical.[5] However, such is not the case with the fifth element, the *context*, to which we now turn.

## B. Contexts and Consequences of Action

### 1 Three contexts

So much for the four components of action – intention, assessment, means and drive. But action is never isolated (like an asteroid free-floating in space). It takes place within a certain setting. The context of an action, then, is the whole environment – social, physical (or natural) and cultural – within which it occurs.

First, the social context. Most of the things we do affect other people, and we affect them in various ways – motivating, helping, frustrating, preventing. This gives significance to our actions.

Second, the physical or natural context. As Karl Marx wrote, 'Men . . . distinguish themselves from animals as soon as they begin to produce their means of subsistence.'[6] For food, shelter and clothing we have to work upon our natural environment. From these beginnings our technology has reached the point where it inflicts dangerous damage upon the planet –

---

[5] The idea of recurrence is explored at length in Trompf (1979). However, in my view he does not sufficiently emphasize the distinction between the historical agents' deliberate *imitation* of the past and the historian's observation of the *recurrence* of one period in another.

[6] See Marx (1977) p. 160.

not least in those very polities that were most inspired by Marx. This painfully reminds us that few human activities can ignore their natural context. One does not have to subscribe to the whole Marxist philosophy to agree that a large and necessary part of human activity has always been securing the physical necessities of life. From these basics we have gone on to produce greater and greater luxuries. As we now recognize, there are limits to the resources that we exploit. Here, as with the social context, acting upon the natural world may bring support and assistance (a good farmer co-operates with nature), or it may meet opposition (flood, fire, famine, storm, earthquake) or an exhaustion of supplies. A great deal of history, economic history, is concerned with human actions in their natural context – farming, mining, forestry, fishing, navigation, manufacture, etc. But, of course, it is not only so-called economic activities that are affected by the natural environment. We are reminded of this every time that a picnic or village fête is rained off. More seriously there is an intimate relationship between warfare and nature, whether we think of the stinking, lethal mud of Flanders in the 1914–18 war or the desert sands and burning oil-wells of the 1991 Gulf War. Indeed, there are few human activities that can ignore their natural context.

Third, the cultural context. **By 'culture' I understand 'language technology, the arts, religious and philosophic attitudes and beliefs, and whatever other objects, skills, habits, customs, explanatory system and the like are included in the social inheritance of various individuals living in a particular society'.**[7] Although culture is inherited, each generation can make some alteration. Much of it consists of ideas, rather than physical objects, so it is not surprising that we are hardly aware of them when they take the form of habits and customs. This is particularly true of the major part of any culture – its symbols.

**Symbols are conventional signs.** Natural signs are dark clouds (for rain), footprints (for an animal) and so on. But conventional signs (which may or may not have any natural connection) are peculiar to societies. A national flag, a set of traffic lights, a witch-doctor's mask are artificial, not natural signs. But the most important of symbols are words, for language is one of the oldest yet still one of the greatest of human creations. Like traffic lights, a language is not necessarily confined to one society, as English, Spanish and Arabic demonstrate. Among the many functions of language are: to facilitate communication, to recall and conserve the past, to convey information, to arouse emotion, to stimulate the imagination, to provoke to action, to perform a ritual or ceremony, to give a form and measure to life.

Yet, essential as it is for the historian, language holds many pitfalls. It contains, but conceals, many of the customs, beliefs and assumptions

[7] See Mandelbaum (1977), p. 12.

peculiar to one place or period. The historian, in some other time or place, may think he understands a text because he reads English, Spanish or Arabic. But he will not know the enveloping culture as the writer knew it. Reading the oldest Gospel (St Mark), one has to be aware that the words attributed to Jesus and the words written by Mark originated in different languages, in different generations, and very probably in different countries. Moreover, Jesus spoke in a wholly Jewish environment; Mark wrote in a context already Christian. Yet almost every reader of that gospel makes the assumptions of the latter context only.

## 2   Contexts: meanings

These, then, are the three contexts of action – social, physical and cultural – which the historian must take into account. The contexts shape and limit the action, but, above all, they help to give it meaning.

The word 'meaning' can be used in various ways. Here let us distinguish three of them. They are intention, social significance and historical significance. Since I am writing this on the Ides of March, let Julius Caesar's death furnish the examples. The *intention* of the conspirators was to preserve the Republic, which they thought to be threatened by Caesar's ambition. The *social significance* of the murder was how it was seen at the time. Political assassination was not uncommon in the Roman world, and educated Romans knew the praise in Greek literature for tyrannicides. Caesar had been a hero with the common people, but Suetonius says that he was beginning to lose favour with them, too. Unsurprising, therefore, and not indefensible. The *historical significance* is quite different. Caesar's death did not save the Republic. On the contrary, it led to a long line of emperors.

## 3   Contexts: axes of significance

No historian can ignore the first two uses, but there is more to be said about the third. Historical significance can be traced along two axes: the 'horizontal' (that is, contemporary) and the 'vertical' (that is, preceding and succeeding). Let the same month furnish another example, Hitler's occupation of the Rhineland in 1936. Along the horizontal axis the historian has to note conditions within Germany, the weakness of the French government, the British preoccupation with an expanding Japan, the prevalence of pacifist opinions, the isolationism of the USA, the embarrassment of the League of Nations caused by Italy's attack on Ethiopia, and the USSR's recent entry into power politics. The vertical context may be traced back through the Nazis' coming to power in 1933, through the Treaty of Versailles, the First World War and the nineteenth-century unification of Germany, with possible extensions to the history of the Rhine as a frontier disputed since Roman times. Going forward along the same axis, we meet 'Munich', the Second World War, and then the long 'Cold War' that followed from the defeat of the Third Reich. The historical significance is found at the junction of two axes.

## 4   Contexts: different meanings

The same event, however, can be given different significance in different national histories. Nelson's victory at Trafalgar in 1805 inaugurated a century of British maritime supremacy. The names of Nelson and Trafalgar are well known in England to this day. Spain's consequent naval weakness must have contributed to the almost immediate loss of her vast American empire, yet the battle has little place in Spanish histories or memories (nor in French ones – though sea power was never so important for France). Are these differences due merely to national pride, or do they reflect genuine divergences in judgements of cause and effect? And is 'significance' a quality conferred by the historian, or is it inherent in the events themselves?

## 5   Consequences: failures

Though not included in our analysis, the consequences of an action are of both practical and historical concern. Often they do not match the intention and the action fails. Why? Causes in general are to be discussed later (in chapter 8). Here a few remarks about failure are in order.

The arrival of the unexpected, first seen as a frustration, may well prove an opportunity for another success. The greatness of men like Cromwell or Napoleon consisted in part in their ability to do this. As Cromwell himself said, no man rises so high as he who does not know where he is going.

Genuine failure, however, is probably due to faulty assessments – of the present situation or of the immediate future: that is, of the contexts of the action. These boil down to nature or humanity. Our powers have been greatly increased by the natural sciences. Our ability to assess the human context is less remarkable, though the social sciences have made some progress. The historian aims to understand the past, but denies any pretensions to knowing the future. Yet readers of history cannot but feel that they are acquiring a deeper insight into human affairs and a sounder judgement. Is this so? Has the writing of history itself shown a deeper insight and a fuller understanding?

## 6   Avoiding failure: physical

Consider a peasant ploughing and sowing in order to feed his family. He may have a bumper harvest and rejoice. Very often he is disappointed, losing his crops to storms, insects, wild animals or armed men. He is helpless, and resorts to prayer, superstition or resignation. Others, however, with more leisure and resources tackle the problems. Strong governments deal with the armed men, foresters cull the wild animals, biologists and chemists fight the insects, and meteorologists warn of the storms. Now he is more certain of his harvest, but some things (weather, international markets) seem still beyond control.

In the twentieth century many historians, recognizing their importance, have paid more attention to such impersonal factors in the success or failure of human endeavour. Perhaps the leading proponents are those of the *Annales* school, though many others too have studied the histories of agriculture, industry, science and technology. Yet one cannot confine history to the impersonal factors. The greatest problems arise with the interaction of human and natural factors. The good historian must take both into account.

## 7   Avoiding failure: human

On the other hand, traditional history has dwelt too much on the human – and on only a few humans at that. Often it is more like interrelated biographies. Opening at random Joinville's *Chronicle of the Crusades*, I find:

> It was settled that the king should land on the Friday before Trinity and do battle with the Saracens, unless they refused to stand. The king ordered my Lord John of Beaumont to assign a galley to my Lord Everard of Brienne and to myself, so as that we might land, we and our knights, because the great ships could not get close up to the shore.
>
> As God so willed, when I returned to my ship, I found a little ship that my Lady of Beyrout, who was cousin-german to my Lord of Montbéliard and to myself, had given me, and that carried eight of my horses.[8]

Seven centuries later some historians still write like this (only in the third person, instead of the first). Like a soap opera, such history is no more than a series of personal interchanges. If most historians today place their narratives in richer and deeper contexts, that is a tribute, partly to the work of the natural sciences, but more to the social sciences. It is the task of the historian to show how all these many and varied strands weave together into the tapestry of life.

[8] Joinville (1908) p. 173. The scene is Cyprus in the year AD 1249.

## 8    *Cultural contexts*

It is, perhaps, here that the historian faces his greatest challenge. For the beliefs, attitudes, values, and so on, (cited in §1 above) that constitute a culture exist most of the time below the level of consciousness. We take them for granted. Now most history is based on documentary evidence: that is, on what men and women have thought necessary to record. This may be a royal charter, an act of parliament, a letter or a diary. In these are rarely stated explicitly the beliefs, the moral and social codes, that are shared with the rest of society. Such things are mentioned only when they become a matter of discussion, and therefore are not (or no longer) unquestioned assumptions. Thus a seventeenth-century parliamentarian protesting against the power of the king makes clear what assumptions he does *not* share. One could never tell from his speech that he believes (for example) in white magic, or that Adam and Eve in the Garden of Eden are historical fact.

Even today we do not and cannot make explicit all our assumptions. In the days before Marx and Frazer and Freud people were even less aware of such things. Thus it is difficult for the historian to reconstruct this important inner world of the very people he is concerned with. The problems are compounded by the fact that he is himself unaware of all his own assumptions and presuppositions, and may unintentionally be attributing them to his subjects.

But the best historians have not ignored this danger. Some three centuries ago an English scholar, Robert Brady, wrote of the ancient texts used in his *Introduction to the Old English History* (1694), 'Before the use of them I considered again and again whether I might not be mistaken in their true meaning and like wise considered all Circumstances.'[9]

The eighteenth-century Neapolitan lawyer, Giambattista Vico, made a great advance by showing that our language develops with our society; hence 'language, myths, antiquities directly reflect the various fashions in which social or economic or spiritual problems or realities were refracted in the minds of our ancestors.'[10] With all writings, but particularly with historical documents, we should ask, not, 'Are they true?' but, 'What do they mean?' The problem is to grasp not what they mean to us, but what they meant in the cultural context in which they were written. By his skill in teasing out the conditions of early medieval England from legal texts, Maitland (another lawyer) showed his pre-eminence among historians. He was well aware of the possible gap between language and meaning: 'When our kings of the eighth century set their hands to documents written in Latin and bristling with the technical terms of Roman law . . . we must

---

[9] See Douglas (1943), p. 158.
[10] Berlin (1980), p. 56. See also Collingwood (1961), pp. 63–71.

not at once assume that they have grasped these ideas.'[11] If you dip almost anywhere into his writings you will find him (perhaps unknowingly) following the precepts of Vico.

## 9  Mentalités

One particular aspect of cultural context has received a good deal of attention from (mostly French) historians since the 1960s. It was, however, about a quarter-century earlier that Lucien Febvre (one of the founders of the journal *Annales* that gave its name to a school of historians) called for the study of 'l'histoire des mentalités collectives'. What he meant by 'collective mentality' was the mental furniture that belongs to all, or most, members of a society. Just because everybody has it, people are normally unaware of it; the collective mentality is just the way that everybody reasons and the beliefs that everybody holds. If a farmer wishes to sell his bullocks well he fattens them and takes them to the market where he can expect the highest prices. This is common-sense. But in the days of Elizabeth I it was obvious common-sense for the farmers of Clynnog in Caernarvonshire to drive the bullocks into the churchyard to dedicate them to St Beuno to ensure high prices. The farmers had the same end as their modern counterparts (a high price); they just used different methods.[12] Today, if we have a fall, an illness, a loss of property, a fire, we accept it as bad luck and turn to the hospital, the doctor, the police, the insurance company for help. Four centuries ago we should have resorted to a 'wise man' or white witch to tell us what malign power or person had brought the misfortune upon us and how the evil influence could be countered. Do we laugh at these irrational beliefs? How many newspapers today find it profitable to print astrological predictions in a regular column?

This interest in collective mentalities has already brought a number of good books on the history of marriage and divorce, on attitudes to childhood and death, on magic and witchcraft, on carnivals and merry-making by Lawrence Stone, Philippe Ariès, Michel Vovelle, Georges Duby, Natalie Zemon Davis, Keith Thomas, Emmanuel Le Roy Ladurie, Peter Burke and many others.

The history of collective mentalities is, thus, a part of the history of culture. But unlike intellectual history or the history of ideas or the history of art (all of which form parts of the history of culture), the history of collective mentalities is not a study of deliberate actions, like writing a book or carving a statue. It is concerned with those parts of the cultural context which are largely assumed, unquestioned, uncriticized. They are much more difficult to unearth than the conscious ideas that shape a book

[11] See Maitland (1960a), p. 270.
[12] See Thomas (1978), p. 81.

or a statue. But they do form an unavoidable part of the context of any action, and in this respect their history is more like the history of the geography or the technology of a past society. For, like these, they both help to make possible and at the same time to limit any proposed course of action. When we find someone in the past failing to do what is (to us) the obvious thing, it is not that his social and cultural context forbids him to do what we would do; it is sometimes for him quite literally unthinkable. It is quite clear that we historians cannot hope to reach a fair understanding of what went on in the history of a people unless we have some grasp of how they thought both consciously and subconsciously, and of what sort of actions seemed open to them, and what not. And, if possible, we should like to penetrate to what it never occurred to them to think.[13]

## 10   Explaining consequences

To sum up, then, we see that a deeper understanding of the context – whether natural, social or cultural – is needed not only by the historical individual but also by the historian. It enables the former to predict the likely consequences of his proposed action; it enables the latter to explain the actual consequences. The historian seems to have the advantage over the agent in that he knows what the consequences were; the agent seems to have the advantage over the historian in that he knew (even if only subconsciously) the context better than the historian does.

There are two further points to be made. One is that we speak of the 'likely consequences' of an action. However great the advances in the natural and human sciences, we are never completely certain of the future. At best, we can deal only with probabilities. The second point is that the historian knows *what* the consequences were, but he may still not understand *why*. For example, he knows the consequences of the murder of the Archduke Franz Ferdinand at Sarajevo on 28 June 1914. But it is still by no means exactly clear why this one incident should have led to four years of appalling and uncivilized carnage.

## 11   Two ways of answering

In considering these problems historians tend to one or other of two attitudes. Some stress the unpredictability of human affairs and point to the play of sheer chance. If only the archduke's chauffeur had not missed his way and found it necessary to reverse in a side street, the assassin (who had already given up the attempt) would not have been presented with an unexpected second opportunity – one that he took with fatal consequences for all Europe. A. J. P. Taylor was one of many historians who

[13] See for example Febvre (1962), in which he attempted to demonstrate the impossibility of atheism in the sixteenth century.

insist on the role that chance plays in the affairs of nations. Others seek to emphasize the deep, underlying currents of human affairs. Marxist historians furnish the best examples, but many others take similar attitudes. Nationalist historians write of the steady advance to greatness of their own peoples. Religious historians discern the unbending will of God or Allah or Jehovah behind the progress of a religion or sect. Positivists make much of the advance of science. Scholars of today who are influenced by some theory of economics, anthropology, sociology tend to find hidden patterns and forces in history. Comparative historians look for them; many historians, especially the French, think they have found them . . . The common characteristic of all these theory-inspired writers is that they underplay the role of chance. They tend to believe that events follow a set course – a course that the application of their theory will enable them to determine. Thus they discount the chance event and argue that even if it had turned out otherwise, the long-term consequences would still have been much the same. As they put more science into history, so the mystery and excitement drop out of it. Which view is right?

## 12   Murphy's Law

One aspect of consequences should not be overlooked. This is the perverse fact that measures adopted to bring about a desired end are sometimes the very means that cause its opposite. The common example is that of a small bank in difficulties. Fearing a possible collapse, people begin to withdraw their savings. The resulting lack of funds causes the bank to crash. A little more trust would have kept it in business and everyone's money would have been safe. History furnishes many examples of this anomaly – like the murder of Julius Caesar. It has been remarked that the chief cause of problems is solutions.

Conrad Russell shows how Charles I's shortage of money in 1641 caused him to break his word to the Irish: 'So it appears, ironically, to have been Pym's success in preventing a regular grant of Tonnage and Poundage in England which contributed the final straw to driving Ireland into rebellion. There can hardly have been a more dramatic example of the law of unintended consequence, otherwise known as Murphy's Law.'[14]

## 13   Do we understand history?

The Viennese poet Grillparzer was sceptical of the historian's ability to grasp the realities of the past:

> History is nothing but the manner in which the spirit of man apprehends facts that are obscure to him, links things together whose

[14] See C. Russell (1990), p. 129.

connection heaven only knows, replaces the unintelligible by
something intelligible, puts his own ideas of causation into the
external world, which can perhaps be explained only from within;
and assumes the existence of chance where thousands of small causes
may be really at work.[15]


## C.   Uses and Abuses of History

### (i) THE USES OF HISTORY

### 1   *What is the use of you and me?*

It is sometimes asked, What is the use of history? How do you feel if it is
asked what is the use of you (or of someone you love)? Are you not
insulted? Surely everyone has intrinsic value, value in and for themselves?
If, as Kant insists, all humans should be treated as ends in themselves,
does this not apply to the dead as well as to the living?[16] We recall
Thompson's desire to rescue the poor 'from the enormous condescension
of posterity'.[17] The historian must not condescend. Nietzsche is rightly
scathing of those 'who write history in the naive faith that justice resides
in the popular view of their time'. They only 'adapt the past to the present
triviality'.[18] So what of that question about the use of history?

### 2   *What is the use of the historian?*

The answer is that it must not be asked of history(1), since that was made
up of men and women of worth and dignity like our own. It can be asked
only of the study of history – history(2). I have analysed above the actions
that we take to realize our ends, so now let us see what use history(2) may
be to each of the four elements of that action. (A brief illustration was
given on pp. 25–7 above in discussing the Czech revolution.)

### 3   *The uses of history for action: (a) the aim*

Since actions point forward, it does not often happen that history supplies
the aim. It does so only when one intends to reproduce something that
happened in the past. This can occur in two ways: either one intends to
continue a tradition, doing just what one did yesterday; or one intends to

[15] Quoted in Nietzsche (1957), p. 38.
[16] Kant (1956), p. 136 (Bk II, ch. 2, section v): also 'the humanity in our person must itself
be holy to us.'
[17] See above, p. 17.
[18] Nietzsche (1957), p. 37.

create anew something of the past. Of course, much traditional behaviour arises from indolence; one goes on doing the same thing because one cannot be bothered to do anything else. But this is not relevant, for history does not supply the aim of action here.

## 4  Aiming to preserve the past

Some people have a strong desire to preserve past ways of life. The Amish of Pennsylvania are an example. Their dark, plain old-fashioned clothing and their horse-drawn buggies so obviously belong to another age. However, their way of life, so different from that of the contemporary USA, is due not to a devotion to the past but to a devotion to their religion. If they reject the telephone or the television or the automobile, it is not because these are considered *intrinsically* evil; they can, however, be *instrumentally* evil in the way that they may lead members astray. Thus the intention of their actions is not to maintain the past, but to maintain a religion that is timeless.

## 5  Aiming to reproduce the past

If the intention so strictly to adhere to tradition is uncommon, still more rare are examples of the other kind of intention, that of reproducing anew some past state of affairs. Often history has supplied inspiration which we shall consider under the appropriate heading. What we are looking for here is examples of history providing the aim or intention. Perhaps we come nearest to it with that Roman Republic whose end was, paradoxically, brought about when defenders of tradition assassinated Julius Caesar in 44 BC. This attempt to preserve the Republic effectively destroyed it. Although Rome then passed for nineteen centuries under the rule of emperors and popes, the Republic was never forgotten.

Its memory inspired the Italian city-states of the twelfth and thirteenth centuries, it inspired the short-lived Roman revolution of Cola di Rienzo in 1347, it moved the political writers and historians of fifteenth- and early sixteenth-century Florence (Salutati, Bruni, Machiavelli, Guicciardini), and its very name was restored in Garibaldi and Mazzini's Roman Republic of 1848–9. But perhaps nowhere was it more ardently embraced than in the French revolution. This is seen in the paintings of David, the use of the title of First Consul by Napoleon and in the classical names given to the subordinate republics of the late 1790s – Batavian, Helvetic, Cisalpine, Ligurian, Roman and Parthenopean. But are not these all cases of the past as inspiration, not as aim? In none of these can we say that there was a clear intention to restore, actually to bring back, an earlier state of affairs. Indeed, one Renaissance historian specifically warned against any such attempt. 'How mistaken', wrote Guicciardini, 'are those who quote the Romans at every step. One would have to have a city with exactly the same conditions as theirs and then act according to their example.'[19] I think one must conclude that history rarely, if ever, provided a clear aim or intention for action.

## 6 The uses of history for action: (b) the assessment

Before acting we often examine the present state of affairs and, perhaps, calculate our chances of success. This appraisal of the situation is a necessary preliminary to any well-considered action. We need to ask: Where are we? How did we get here? Where are we going? What factors are relevant to our chances of getting there?

It is clear that some understanding of our past is essential to answer these questions. But not only that; we also need some grasp of the general course of affairs – political, economic, social, etc. – so that we can form some notion of likely events in the near future. Finally, we need to take into account the similar historical situations of those peoples, groups, armies, nations, etc. with whom we have to deal. For example, if we ask what role Britain should play in European affairs, we need to look not only at the history of Britain, but also that of other European countries. Suppose we are looking at the world role of the United States. We have to consider that country's experiences in the wars of the twentieth century, its conflicting traditions of isolationism, of support for justice and liberty, and of defence of American commercial interests. We also have to consider the American economy; its past development, its present form, and the common assumptions made about it by businessmen and economists.

There is no need to labour these points. Almost everyone who thinks or writes about public affairs is well aware of the need to bring some historical understanding to his task. Three points should be remembered, however. The first is the need for a broad view – for example, a survey of the economy of the USA requires some grasp of the history of the Middle East, of China and of Japan. The second is that historians ought to study contemporary history – something that many have rejected. Admittedly it is difficult to gain a balanced view of world events without the benefit of a decade or so of hindsight, yet the historian's ability to bring many different sorts of evidence together (political, economic, cultural, linguistic, etc.), as well as his ability to see the past in the present and the present in the past, is uniquely valuable here. If he shuns the task, that does not mean it will not be done: it means that it will be done by others less equipped to perform it. The third point is a warning from Nietzsche. 'For as we are merely the resultant of previous generations, we are also the resultant of their errors, passions, and crimes; it is impossible to shake off

[19] See P. Burke (1974), p. 225

this chain. Though we condemn the errors and think we have escaped them, we cannot escape the fact that we spring from them.'[20]

## 7   The uses of history for action: (c) the means

It is no less clear that when we look for the best means to employ to gain our end, we do well to consult history. The whole of English Common Law used to rest on the use of precedent, and it still plays an important part. Precedent, too, is a basic feature (sometimes too prominent) of every bureaucracy. However, as we noted above when discussing tradition, the mere repetition of action hardly counts as a use of history. A better example occurred in 1642 when, before the English Civil War broke out, Parliamentary leaders were discussing how restraint could be put upon the king, Charles I, by separating the authority of the Crown from the king's person. They looked back in medieval history to groups of peers who had done just this: the Lords Appellant of 1388 under Richard II, the Lords Ordainers under Edward II earlier in that century and Simon de Montfort in 1258 under Henry III.[21]

That this was not a development of constitutional theory, but a genuine search for a means to a particular end, is clear from Conrad Russell's comment: 'they were, like their medieval predecessors, *ad hoc* ideas constructed out of any materials ready to hand, to serve the immediate purpose of clipping the wings of a king with whom they simply could not cope.'[22] To take a modern example, when Iraq invaded Kuwait in August 1990, the Security Council of the United Nations decreed that economic sanctions be applied by the international community to compel Iraq to withdraw. This provoked considerable debate about the likely effectiveness of such measures, into which were drawn discussions of the alleged success or failure of similar sanctions against Italy in the 1930s, Rhodesia in the 1960s and 1970s, and South Africa in the 1980s.

## 8   The uses of history for action: (d) the drive

In this respect the chief function of history is to supply inspiration for action. 'History', writes Nietzsche, 'is necessary above all to the man of action and power who fights a great fight and needs examples, teachers, and comforters; he cannot find them among his contemporaries.' But the need is felt not only by heroes. Anyone can benefit from 'the knowledge that the great thing existed and was therefore possible, and so may be possible again'.[23] One of the earliest functions of history was to record

---

[20] Nietzsche (1957), p. 21
[21] See C. Russell (1990), p. 159.
[22] Ibid., p. 160.
[23] Nietzsche (1957), p. 12.

great deeds for the encouragement of later generations. Indeed, long before written history, oral traditions did this. A young Greek was taught the exploits of Hercules, Theseus, Jason, Themistocles without distinguishing the mythical, the legendary and the historical. Similarly, in Chaucer's *Canterbury Tales*, the Man of Law heaps up higgledy-piggledy Achilles, Hector, Pompey, Julius Caesar, Samson, Hercules and Socrates – all to him perhaps equally historical characters.[24] Unlike the other three applications of history (as aim, as assessment, as means), history as drive does not demand much in the way of accuracy. Indeed, if a historical character is to be held up as a hero or a battle claimed as a triumph (e.g. the Falklands War of 1982 or the Gulf War of 1991), then admiration and patriotism (or other desired emotions) are more easily aroused by an account that is oversimplified, biassed and highly coloured.

## 9   *Exemplars as inspiration*

A distinction should here be noted in what is called exemplary history. Much of traditional historiography was intended to provide suitable examples (or 'exemplars') for the benefit of later generations. This is true not only of the ancient Greek historians, Herodotus, Thucydides, Polybius, and of the Romans, Livy, Cicero (though not a historian, he made much use of history), Suetonius and Ammianus. It is also true of the leading humanist historians of early modern Europe, for example Coluccio Salutati, Leonardo Bruni, Robert Gaguin, Erasmus, Machiavelli, Guicciardini, Ralegh, Bodin, Bacon. (Like Cicero, not all of these were historians, but they drew examples from the past.) The distinction I wish to make is that some of this exemplary history is intended for inspiration, and some of it is to show what can be done in a particular situation. The former serves the *drive*, being a stimulus to action, while the latter serves the *means* by way of offering practical suggestions.

This useful distinction is not often made. Yet it should be, for it is relevant to the question of good history. Where history is to be put to practical use it is important that the suggested example be studied carefully; that is, with close attention to detail and with a broad and balanced view of the context. Otherwise the wrong lesson may be drawn and the remedy misapplied. Where history is to supply inspiration, however, such careful study might only blur the picture. Not only would the detailed scholarly account confuse the unscholarly viewer; it is also likely that an accurate account of the exemplary hero or victory would reveal details that marred the glorious vision. As Nietzsche puts it (with very uncharacteristic understatement): 'as long as the past is principally

---

[24] G. Chaucer, *The Canterbury Tales: The Man of Law's Tale*, 197–201. For the medieval failure to distinguish history and fiction, see Levine (1987), ch. 1.

used as a model for imitation, it is always in danger of being a little altered and touched up and brought nearer to fiction.'[25] To a civilized nineteenth-century scholar the depths of barbarism of the twentieth century were inconceivable, even to a radical iconoclast like Nietzsche. In the compulsory worship of the great dictators – Lenin, Stalin, Hitler, Mao Tse-Tung – and of a host of lesser imitators, history has not merely been 'touched up'; it has been perverted and distorted, wrenched out of all semblance either to truth or to decency. The politicians rightly fear that an accurate historical account would reveal much about even the greatest hero or triumph that is not at all inspiring. Nietzsche again:

'(Man) must bring the past to the bar of judgment, interrogate it remorselessly, and finally condemn it. Every past is worth condemning; this is the rule in mortal affairs, which always contain a large measure of human power and human weakness.'[26] Any critical and honest history must reveal the errors, failures, weaknesses and crimes that accompany even the greatest actions. If history is to supply inspiration these should not be stressed.

## 10 Dare we omit the bad in exemplars?

But should they be omitted altogether? One of the benefits of a serious study of history is to learn that human affairs are an inextricable mixture of good and bad. To a disinterested public the cruder representations of past heroisms and triumphs are not inspiring at all; they are recognized as travesties tricked out in tinsel. It is harder when the exemplars offered support one's own convictions. It may be difficult for a Protestant to dismiss the sufferings of Mary Tudor's fiery victims, whose memory was so long preserved in millions of English homes by Foxe's Book of Martyrs, just as a Catholic cannot help but sympathize with Thomas More, John Fisher and the other Catholics who died at the hands of the Tudors. Patriotic Americans or Britons may not easily accept that the excellences of George Washington or Winston Churchill may have been greatly exaggerated. The millions of constitutionalists, liberals, republicans and democrats who have drawn encouragement and determination down the ages from Periclean Athens or republican Rome have ignored or forgotten the brutality, corruption and slavery that marred those ideal states. If you favour the parliamentary side in the English Civil War, it is hard to realize that 'the good old cause' was often narrow, intolerant and illegal. As students of history we can learn to honour great men and women without shutting our eyes to their faults. Perhaps these human imperfections make their achievements all the more heroic.

[25] Nietzsche (1957), p. 15.
[26] Ibid., p. 21.

## (ii)   THE ABUSES OF HISTORY

### 11   *An anatomy of abuses*

We should now consider how history may be abused. On this subject historians tend to get warm, but in their heat they sometimes fail to distinguish the different kinds of misuse and the reasons for them. (Knowing the reasons for a bad practice makes it easier to avoid it.) It may help to list various kinds of misuse.

### 12   *Can we have too much history?*

*First*, we may ask whether it is possible to have too much history. For history is knowledge of life at secondhand. Should one first practise living before trying to understand how other people lived? I have quoted Nietzsche on the uses of history. Now let us hear him on its abuse. Under the educational system of his Germany of the 1870s the student had to

> begin with a knowledge of culture, . . . (which) is forced into the young mind in the form of historical knowledge; . . . his head is filled with an enormous mass of ideas, taken second-hand . . . He desires to experience something for himself . . . But his desire is drowned and dizzied in the sea of shams, as if it were possible to sum up in a few years the highest and most notable experiences of ancient times, and the greatest times, too.[27]

It is, perhaps, for educationists rather than historians to decide this issue. But it is worth remembering that even second-hand knowledge of life is not without value. Perhaps no one can appreciate love poetry who has never been in love. But it is also true that the experience of being in love is deepened and enhanced by love poetry. And so for other emotions, experiences and activities; words do not merely echo life, they also help to make it.

### 13   *Is it better to forget the past?*

Is it good for a nation to be much concerned with its past? For many years Northern Ireland has been plagued with marches, demonstrations, crime, bloodshed and sudden murderous violence. Political and economic stresses are exacerbated by a perpetuation of religious rivalries. If only they could forget Oliver Cromwell and 'King Billy' and subsequent centuries, they could make a clean and clear-eyed start upon the twenty-first. Ireland, one could argue, has too much of history.

[27] Ibid., p. 67.

And is this not also true of England? In 1945 the British emerged victorious from a long and painful war which, at the beginning, they could hardly have hoped to win. The relief was enormous and justifiable. The consequences were less happy. Because the English way of life had emerged from the war untouched by invasion or defeat, it was largely immune from criticism. Governments and people were content to retain the old world dominance, the old industries, the old class-ridden social forms. Many of the problems of Britain in the 1990s stem from an inability to forget the triumph of the forties. By contrast the defeated nations (West Germany and Japan) lost no time after the war in putting a discredited past behind them and making a fresh start that soon brought them many of the successes that eluded the British. Here, again, one can have too much history.[28]

## 14   The tyranny of theory

Second, it is an abuse of history to subordinate it to a theory, however brilliant. The great German philosopher, Georg Wilhelm Friedrich Hegel (1770–1831), is a notable culprit here. Many thinkers have tried to blend the course of human history with a philosophical theory; Hegel did it best. His abuse of history is the more seductive because it is the most brilliant.

Why is Hegel's philosophy an abuse? The first reason relates to what was said at the beginning of this section about the intrinsic value of a human life. Hegel, however, is dismissive of all 'non-historical' peoples, and among historical nations he singles out for praise 'World-Historical Individuals' whose aims are those of creative Spirit.[29] Theory, even more than knowledge, must serve life, not be subservient to it.

Lives, as we saw, constitute history(1). But if we pass on to history(2), from history lived to history told, can that be made part of a theory? We have to be careful here. There are bluff, no-nonsense empirical historians (as G. R. Elton claims to be in The Practice of History) who deal only with the facts and have no truck with theory. It is not quite so simple. As we see elsewhere in this book (chapter 5, pp. 124–5, below), so-called historical facts are what historians agree to make of the existing evidence. And in interpreting the evidence their minds work along the prevailing lines; some of the lines are peculiar to the individual historian, some to his profession or to his age. Even the language in which he expresses his conclusions is, like all human language, theory-laden, for language is a

---

[28] In justice, one should remember J. H. Plumb's argument in The Death of the Past, that a sound knowledge of history is an effective antidote to such mistaken attitudes (see Introduction and p. 15 above). Unfortunately the public and the politicians rarely possess a sound historical education.

[29] Hegel (1956), pp. 59–61, 29–32.

construct of human societies. That is why it is often said that history should be rewritten every generation.

But if our common stock of words is theory-laden, it is not the product of any one theory. The ideas that are hidden in our ways of thinking and of speaking are more in the nature of subconscious and inarticulate assumptions than fully developed philosophical theories. They are a miscellaneous rag-bag of notions, got from diverse sources and, many of them, mutually inconsistent. Thus, while it seems true that we can understand the world only by means of our concepts, those concepts are independent of any overarching theory. To reduce this rag-bag to one theory would inevitably be to impoverish it. It would also place restrictions on our freedom to apply the contents of the rag-bag, (that is, our existing set of concepts). Thus, in history as in daily life, we feel that we are free to think empirically; not theoretically, but in accordance with our experience. For the historian, the relevant experiences are his readings of the evidence. Thus, to conclude, most practising historians would claim that their allegiance is to the truth revealed by the evidence, rather than to any one theory of history, however persuasive. Marxist historians are a partial exception. But most of them, if pressed, would say that they use Marx's theory as a guide to what to look for (e.g. class conflicts) and as a help to understanding the evidence that they find, but they would deny that they shape their findings to conform to Marxist theory. One has only to compare the writings of a Christopher Hill or an Eric Hobsbawm with the products of Soviet historians under Stalin or Brezhnev to see the justice of their claim.[30]

## 15   *The tyranny of politics*

*Third*, history must not be subordinated to politics. Here, again, we must blame Hegel. 'The State,' he wrote, 'is the Divine Idea as it exists on earth.'[31] In an unforgettable phrase he came close to stating that whatever is, is right: 'the history of the world . . . is the world's court of justice.'[32]

History must not be subordinated to politics because the two things serve quite different ends: politics is about the distribution of power within a community; history is an attempt to get at the truth about the past. Power and truth do not go well together. Hegel's pronouncements tend to confuse them. But indeed most people who wield power think that truth should be on their side. This is as true of priests, soldiers and administrators as it is of politicians. They easily convince themselves that

[30] For more on Hegel and Marx, see ch. 10, pp. 262–75, below.
[31] Hegel, (1956), p. 39.
[32] It is even more impressive in the original: 'Die Weltgeschichte ist das Weltgericht' (*The Philosophy of Right*, para. 340) in Hegel (1967), p. 216.

there is some necessary connection between truth and power (for example, that our party must be right because we won the election). But this is false. It is purely contingent whether truth happens to be on the side of power or on the opposite side. Whether it is or not, on any particular occasion, is a matter for impartial judgement. And that must be disinterested judgement. It cannot be entrusted to the wielders of power for they have an obvious interest in the decision. History, defined as the pursuit of truth, must therefore be kept remote from power. Any history told by the wielders of power, or by seekers after power or by their friends, must be regarded with the utmost suspicion.

This danger, like all dangers, is greatest when it is hidden. Power resides not only in governments and churches and institutions, but also in public opinion. Complacent views about the achievements and almost inevitable triumphal progress of the British were widely held in nineteenth-century England; Whig history was written (e.g. by Macaulay) to justify it. Exploration and imperialism brought increased contact with other races later in the century. Public opinion took a racist tinge, and Freeman and Stubbs wrote history slanted to racism.[33] The American victory over Germany and Japan in the Second World War brought a widespread conviction that the USA was dedicated to the defence of the free world against totalitarianism. American historians obliged. 'Intellect has associated itself with power as perhaps never before in history', wrote Lionel Trilling in 1952; on which Peter Novick commented, 'With the exception of physics, it would be difficult to think of any academic discipline which, during World War II and the cold war, participated more wholeheartedly in that association than did history.' The result was 'a substantial shift in historians' capacity for identifying with those who exercise power'[34].

It would be easy, but tedious, to demonstrate the corruption of history by power under every dictatorial regime – Fascist, Nazi, Marxist-Leninist. It is more important to see how power can abuse history in our own more open societies of the West, where the very fact of so much openness can blind us to corruption. Whenever strong feelings of nationalism, racism or religious prejudice seize the public mind, it becomes less easy to see the bias in histories written in accordance with such prejudices. I will cite one example only, but this is a prejudice of very long standing.

There is the male prejudice that women are (a) inferior and (b) comparatively unimportant. The result is that for centuries historians have almost ignored women (with a few exceptions, mostly rulers like Cleopatra or Catherine the Great). In a very understandable attempt to rectify this error recent historians have tried to write histories of women.[35] In spite of some good results, this has not been as successful as

---

[33] See Christopher Parker (1990), pp. 43–5.
[34] Novick (1988) pp. 301, 304.
[35] See for example Perrot and Duby (1990).

might be hoped, for the simple reason that there is not a lot of evidence. Women, for most of history, have not held the positions of power which have been, until recently, the subjects of most historical records and of historical interest. For that reason, to mention no other, this bias in history will not be easily corrected.

## 16  *The danger of prejudice*

*Fourth*, it is possible for even sound and accurate history to be misused. For example, Steven Runciman's three-volume *History of the Crusades* (1965) is technically good history. It is good, in the sense that it exhibits thorough research, use of a wide range of sources, scrupulous accuracy of detail, perceptive descriptions of character, narrative tension, and so on. Yet it is still written from a European perspective; one empathizes even if one cannot sympathize with the Christians. I cannot think that it would appeal as history to a Muslim Arab. Similarly one could write a scholarly account of the Third Reich that left the reader with anti-German sympathies. Accurate accounts of the British in India, of the English in Ireland, of the French in North Africa, of the white Americans in conflict with the native Americans ('Red Indians') would all leave a distaste for, even a prejudice against these peoples. A truthful account of the working of the Inquisition hardly endears the Catholic Church. Fortunately, present relations between these groups (Poles and Germans, say, or English and Indians) are not at all bad. Is it because most people have not read history, or at least ignore what they have read? I suspect so. Yet if these works are technically sound historical works, what is wrong? Why do I mention them under the heading of the abuses of history? It seems they are not quite satisfactory. Should history, however technically correct, leave the reader with a rooted prejudice for or against a particular group or nation? On the other hand, can this be avoided without doing violence to the truth?

## 17  *Bad history*

*Fifth and last*, any history that is bad history, i.e. that falls short in one way or another of the canons of proper historical study, is an abuse of history, in the same way that false coinage is an abuse of money. It is not only a cheat and a deception; Gresham's Law of money applies here. When standards are lowered the bad drives out the good. Just what the canons of good history are should become clear during the course of this book. Here I may suggest three cardinal sins to be avoided at all costs: (1) subordinating history to any non-historical theory or ideology, whether it be religious, economic, philosophical, sociological or political; (2) neglecting breadth (i.e. failing to take all considerations into account) and failing to do justice to all concerned; (3) ignoring or suppressing evidence.

* American historians (and teachers) ignoring Stalin's crimes.

This last is a crime committed by governments of all complexions. That some historians connive at it even in the most open of societies is regrettable. Novick reports of American historians in the years after the Second World War: 'Special access to (government) materials not otherwise available was frequently extended to those who were well connected and could be depended upon to use the data in question with discretion.'[36] To get this into proportion just imagine that it is spoken of a communist state, not of the USA. The situation in Britain is worse. Many will still remember the British government's futile attempts in 1985–7 to suppress the world-wide publication of Peter Wright's book *Spycatcher*.

## Conclusion

Since human activity is the subject matter of history, it is appropriate to begin with a discussion of what is involved in human actions. It is helpful first to distinguish these from behaviour, bearing in mind that the behaviour is all that is observable. The agent's intentions, which mark the distinction between behaviour and action, are *not* to be observed. They have to be inferred – probably on the basis of our familiarity with the way in which our own intentions inform our own actions.

These considerations are important for the historian, for most of his knowledge is based upon what contemporaries understood, and then reported, of others' behaviour. Misinterpretation is always possible, both by contemporaries and by historians; for this the student of history must always be on his guard.

The analysis of action into its various constituent parts makes it possible to identify the part that each plays in history, as well as the part that history plays in each of those parts. This was illustrated by the Czech revolution of 1989. A discussion of the contexts of action and of its consequences showed the importance of these aspects of this central idea.

The chapter concludes with an account of some of the uses and abuses of the study of history. We have seen that history can be put to bad ends by being made a substitute for living, by imposing the evils of the past upon the present, by forcing it to serve a theory, a government or a prejudice. Finally it is abused when bad history (like false money) is passed off for good. Both use and abuse, but especially the abuse, show that history has two faces that constantly interact. Just as the historical deeds shape the historical account, so the account (true, false or twisted) shapes a further set of historical deeds. The interplay between history (1) and history (2) never ceases. In the next chapter we see what all this brings to our understanding of life in general.

[36] See Novick (1988) p. 305, n. 42.

## Suggested Reading

Ash 1990
Baron 1966
Berlin 1980, part 1
Burke, P. 1990; 1991
Collingwood 1961, pp. 63–71,
    249–71
Febvre 1962
Gardiner 1974
Levine 1987, chapter 1
Maitland 1960a, pp. 23–32,
    264–71
Mandelbaum 1977, chapter 1

Nietzsche 1957
Novick 1988, chapter 10
Olafson 1979
Parker, C. 1990, chapter 2
Plumb 1973
Skinner 1974
Thomas 1978
Trompf 1979
White, A. R 1968 (for those with a
    taste for philosophy)
Winch 1958 (for those with a taste
    for philosophy)

# 3

# History as Outlook

*On the past*
You think that just because it's already happened, the past is finished and unchangeable? Oh no, the past is cloaked in multi-coloured taffeta and every time we look at it we can see a different hue.

Milan Kundera

*On the present*
What romance means is the capacity for a true conception of history, a power of making the past part of the present.

William Morris

History is the life of the mind itself, which is not mind except so far as it both lives in the historical process and knows itself as so living.

R. G. Collingwood

*On the future*
a universe seen . . . as a Great Opportunity rather than as any kind of a Great System.

John Wren Lewis

Not what thou art, nor what thou hast been, does God regard with His merciful eyes, but what thou wouldst be.

*The Cloud of Unknowing*

## Introduction

In the last chapter we looked at actions, how 'the minds of men and women' make 'alterations in the world'. In this one we look at how history helps them to perceive and to understand that world.

*Questions about the importance of the past; history in modern society; history and the social sciences*

1  Why do people bother so much about the past?
2  Why are so many novels and films set in the past, not today?
3  Why do teachers, politicians, journalists want to tell us so much about the past?

4   Why are so many people (usually after their school-days) fascinated by history?
5   Is history any help in knowing what to do in the future?
6   Is there any point in knowing about the past? Surely what's done is done?
7   What is the social role of history?
8   Is history one of the social sciences? If not, should it be?
9   Does knowledge of history make one see the world differently?

The theme of this chapter is *History as Outlook*. It is divided into three sections as follows:

A   Personal Attitudes to History
B   Public Attitudes to History
C   History and the Social Sciences

## A.   Personal Attitudes to History

### 1   *Historicity*

'Consider the herds that are feeding yonder', wrote Nietzsche: 'They know not the meaning of yesterday or today . . .'[1] Whether we are better or worse off for knowing 'yesterday and today' is a moot point. Nevertheless we are all – whether philosophers, oxen or dinosaurs – creatures of time.

But are we all creatures of history? In some sense we are, for history has its effect upon us, whether we know it or not. But in another sense we are not, for not all human beings are aware of being situated in history; still less does everyone know what that history is. This awareness is called 'historicity.'[2] Some writers use this word to refer to our awareness of the passage of time, but this, though necessary for historicity, is not sufficient for it.

Consider a people who make no record of events, but know only the alternation of day and night, the phases of the moon, the circuit of the seasons. They are certainly aware of time, but not of history. They do not, as it were, 'nail down' events to a particular occasion, never to be repeated. Whatever has happened will, for them, happen again and again as the carousel comes round. Such people, whether real or imaginary, have neither history nor historicity.

Many illiterate peoples have tribal memories, long and detailed accounts of past but significant events. To us such oral histories may not

---

[1] So Nietzsche begins his essay, 'The Use and Abuse of History' (1957), p. 5.
[2] For discussion of this term, see Eagleton (1983) pp. 64–6; Olafson, (1979) pp. 93ff; Collingwood (1961), p. 227.

seem very plausible (some of the occurrences being highly unlikely), and they may well lack a chronology. Still, if they caused their people to believe that the past was different from the present (and perhaps they inspired people to further great deeds in the future, deeds to be recorded in the same way), then these people had a history and (because they were aware of living in it), they also had a historicity. **Thus the concept of historicity links together both meanings of 'history', for it calls on both history-as-account and history-as-event.**

These two meanings constantly intertwine. Suppose that we had no memory at all, no sense of the past, then we should be like Nietzsche's oxen. History-as-event would roll on, but only in that sense would there be history. Clearly we are not in that situation; we remember events and sometimes record them. In our actions we employ memories and ideas of the past, on which we base hopes and plans for the future. Thus at all times history-as-account forms part of history-as-event. This is most obvious when we deliberately dwell on the past to shape our present actions (as when the revolutionaries in Paris in 1848 or 1871 were guided by the first French Revolution), but it is not confined to such occasions.

## 2   *Private attitudes* . . .

'The secret of our emotions', said George Eliot, 'never lies in the bare object, but in its subtle relations to our own past.'[3] We are drawn to the past not by visions and memories so much as by emotions. It is these that make vivid both the recollections of our own pasts and the visions of history – for example, my wedding day and the fall of the Bastille or of the Berlin Wall. An old letter or photograph can release a flood of recollections. It is personal memories that first give us our sense of the past. These are extended by older members of our families. Conrad Russell, a distinguished living historian, is the son of Bertrand Russell, the philosopher. The later well remembered his grandfather, Lord John Russell, describing a visit paid to Napoleon on Elba. Thus, at two removes, the family memories of today can go back nearly two centuries.[4]

## 3   *. . . acquired in three ways*

In what ways do most men and women build up their picture of history? The first way, as I have suggested, is by memory; first one's own, then that of a parent or grandparent. Such recollections may be naive, narrow, unreliable and selective. But they have the virtue of vividness and authenticity: 'I was there!' They hardly constitute historical knowledge, but they do make one aware that once there was a past when the world was very different from what it is now.

[3] *Adam Bede*, ch. 18, p. 191 (Zodiac edn. 1952).
[4] B. Russell (1978), p. 14.

Personal memories are chancy things, and in any case are very restricted in range, both of time and space. Hence education requires some more formal, ordered and extensive knowledge of the past. School history lacks the authenticity and vividness of personal memory, but it is (or should be) clearly explained, coherent and reliable. Alas, it often seems dull, and after school-days most of it is forgotten. Only a minority pursue the subject into higher education.

The third way in which we gain our ideas about the past is much less organized. It is the casual snowfall of information fluttering into our lives from many sources. These include the writings of historians (especially about war or recent history); historical fiction in a variety of media – novel, film, radio, television; guide books, exhibition catalogues and theatre programmes; journalism – again in several media; the spoken word of politicians, preachers and publicists; and many wordless witnesses of the past – cathedrals, castles, paintings, statues, Roman roads, mills, canals, steam engines and even commonplace household objects like thimbles or tables. (Such is the rage for antiques in the richer countries that a dealer in a small New England town told me that he can sell any object, no matter how cheap and paltry, if it is more than thirty years old.) From all these we pick out what arouse our interest, and perhaps try to find out more.

If the first way to knowledge rests on the authenticity of experience, the second on the intellectual development of a formal education, this third way depends upon emotions. Such emotions include patriotism (Bunker Hill), revulsion (Auschwitz), wonder (the Parthenon or the Taj Mahal), sympathy (Mary Queen of Scots), sadness (the battlefields of the American Civil War), or admiration (Mahatma Gandhi). Curiosity may be aroused by artefacts (a soldier's cap or an old gun) or by people's memories of battles, air-raids, demonstrations or celebrations. Such enthusiasms can give an appetite for history that formal education never aroused.

## 4   A sense of continuity

There are, however, deeper reasons for this appetite than curiosity or admiration. A knowledge of history brings a sense of historicity, a feeling that we are part of a fellowship that runs through the ages from long before our birth to long after our death. This sense of continuity is part of the deep-seated protest against time and death. It is also an affirmation of our common humanity. Unfortunately it is often abused and exploited in ways which deny that very humanity by racial, national or religious exclusiveness.

Genealogical research is a hobby for the many people who like to trace their ancestry; it has produced societies, journals and full-time paid researchers. Arthur Haley's *Roots* (both book and film) was a bold attempt to do this for a whole people. In North America and Europe local history societies proliferate; thus historical curiosity goes along with a desire to establish the identity of the community. This, again, gives more meaning to individual lives.

However, neither family history nor local history has the same hold on the imagination as national history. This is not merely a question of size. Speaking personally, I am a Stanford, a Bristolian and an Englishman. Obviously the third may be a greater source of pride than the first two: there are a lot more things to be proud of (even if there are many more things to be ashamed of). More revealing is the fact that being English is more interesting than being a Bristolian or a Stanford. I think one reason is that England has, until recently, been a more or less self-contained historical unit, as my city and family have not. **A historical unit contains a sequence of events that is intelligible in itself.** Of course, England has been part of Britain, part of Europe, part of the British Empire, part of a world community. It remains true, however, as countless books testify, that a great deal of the history of England can be told with little reference to what was going on elsewhere. The causes and effects of the actions studied are largely to be found here. This means that the plot of the story has a unity. Neither my city nor my family was ever self-sufficient to any such extent. Thus, as I follow the news (i.e. contemporary history), I find a continuity of narrative and a coherence of plot in national events far more than in family or local affairs. And other people likewise. Thus it is in our national identity, rather than in our family or local identity, that we may feel ourselves characters in an ongoing drama.[5] Of course, I am not arguing that a sense of national identity ought to be greater than any other. I merely observe that for most people today it is. And one of the most cogent reasons why it is so is that the work of historians (who write mostly on the national scale) has made us familiar with this continuing drama of history. That is largely what 'historicity' means: being both a player in and a spectator of that drama.

Thus we are led from private to public attitudes to history.

## B.   Public Attitudes to History

### 1   An honest approach

There is one important difference between private and public attitudes. Private attitudes to history spring from personal experiences and memories, from one's own peculiar interest aroused by these experiences and powered by personal emotions. Public attitudes to history, however, do not arise from what an individual finds good. They arise from what other people think one ought to believe. Public attitudes are imposed by

[5] A striking application of modern ideas and techniques in historiography is David Harris Sacks's study of the city of Bristol in an Atlantic context. See Sacks (1991).

politicians, publicists and educators. This may be done from the best of motives, but the difference remains – like that between enjoying a peach that you picked yourself and eating up your greens because they are good for you. Such 'public benefactors' wish to increase our historicity by increasing our awareness of the past. The trouble is that they know best. Whether or not they actually possess greater historical knowledge (and often they don't), they are quite convinced that they know better than we do what our attitudes to history should be. My advice is to distrust all politicians, publicists and professional educators who attempt to shape your attitude to history. The only people to trust in this respect are those who are concerned with the past rather than the present, who have no purpose to which history can be put, and who are motivated only by an open-minded search for the truth, wherever that search may lead and whatever convictions its results may overthrow. Do not, therefore, study history so that you may be more patriotic, nor that you may be a more convinced socialist or conservative, Catholic or Protestant, Muslim or Jew. Do not study it, even, in order to become wiser or more tolerant – though that may well be the result. Study it only because you want to know the truth. Anything less is a prostitution of Clio, the Muse of History.

## 2  Historicity of the community

How is it, then, that public attitudes to history can get such a purchase on us? Perhaps (as I have already hinted) because we are all participants in a common national drama. How does this come about? First, we each remember something of our own pasts – which, incidentally helps to form our sense of self. Many of these memories are shared with family or friends. We did things together – got married, celebrated Christmas, went on holiday. Getting together later we remind each other: 'Do you remember when . . .?' And we all enjoy it. This is not only fun; it reinforces for each of us our sense of self and of family.

Beyond this there may come formal instruction in the history of our own community – a community that may be local, religious, or political, but is usually national. In many communities some member is authorized to make decisions on behalf of the whole – typically a government decides to take a nation to war. Such decisions may involve most or all of the members of the community. Later they may be remembered not as deeds of the impersonal state ('The US declared war'), but as our deeds ('We went to war'). As we have seen, it may be that one's sense of self is the result of the stories that one tells about oneself to oneself.[6] Similarly members of a family, a club, a school, a regiment create that sense of communal identity by the stories that they share about that community.

[6] See Dennett (1991), pp. 410–18.

So with national identity. Not only formal history, but myths, legends, folk-tales of all kinds make up the stories of what we English (or Spanish or Japanese) did, saw and suffered in the past. Thus our own self-identity is linked to, and enlarged by, the identity of the larger group. Our placing of ourselves in time, with our own personal past, present and future, is fused with the communal or national placing in time; that is, with the history and the sense of history (historicity) of our community.

### 3   Sinister manipulation

This fusing of identities by means of the fusing of historicities shows the importance of history to any community, and accounts for much of its use and abuse. Indeed, it is precisely why I uttered that warning on p. 54 above. For it is an old truth that he who controls public history goes a long way to controlling the public mind. To this day in Northern Ireland most Protestant and Catholic children are taught in separate schools. Totalitarian governments of both the right and the left have gone to excessive lengths to ensure that only a history favourable to them should be available to the public. Trotsky, for example, second only to Lenin in making the Russian revolution, was later systematically obliterated not only from all history books, but also from encyclopaedias and even from photographs. Nor are only totalitarian governments guilty. Few governments of any kind – religious or political – can resist the urge to shape our attitudes to history.[7] Historians have a public duty to expose these attempts.

Since public attitudes are so important that politicians and churchmen try to manipulate them, it is unfortunate that history is a subject so easily open to abuse. But why *is* history so important to society?

### 4   Plotting the course of change

Let us separate history(1) from history(2). If we ask what is the role of history(1) in society, the answer is obvious: the present is largely shaped by the past; today is largely a consequence of yesterday. The clear role of history(2) is to make us aware of this. It is useful to know *that* the past shapes the present, more useful to know exactly *how* the past shapes the present, but most important of all is to know how much of the present has *not* been shaped by the past but remains open as a field of choice. Without taking a determinist line, we must remember that once a certain course of action has been adopted (and human and material resources committed to it), then other options are largely foreclosed. If we suddenly ran out of oil we could not easily go back to a transport system based on horse- and steam-power. Yet we managed perfectly well a century ago. To put it

---

[7] See remarks above on heritage history in the Introduction p. 7. Also p. 47 above and below in ch. 6, p. 164, for governmental manipulation.

briefly, in a world of rapid changes we need history to plot for us the course of those changes.

## 5   Finding alternatives

Other advantages flow from plotting that course. One is that it accustoms us to the idea of change; indeed, it teaches us to expect it.

Another is that it reveals to us other ways of conducting affairs, and so helps us to be healthily critical of our present ways. Moreover, in paying more attention to the past, we may come across 'jewels dropped by the wayside' – i.e. works of art, old recipes, songs, poems and stories, and (more subtle) forgotten values. I will mention two examples of this last. The first comes from the opening lines of the medieval poem of *Tristan*, written (probably soon after the year 1200) by Gottfried von Strassburg. The poet remarks of Tristan's father that 'to those whom it was his duty to make happy, this lord all his days was a joy-giving sun'.[8] Is it not good to recognize that, to certain people around us – family, friends, colleagues, and especially dependants – we have a positive duty to make them happy, even, if possible, to be 'a joy-giving sun' to them? And the second example comes from the civic humanism of fifteenth-century Florence. It is derived from Aristotle and continues through to seventeenth-century England and eighteenth-century America, since when politicians have rather lost sight of it. Briefly, it is that the excellence of a republic consists in the fact that all men (and nowadays women) share in the common business and participate in the government. If any one group is so disadvantaged that it falls under the power of another, there are three losers (not one only). The victims, of course, lose, but so, too, do the overpowering group *and* the republic as a whole. 'To lose one's due share of authority, or to have more than one's due, amounted to a loss of virtue . . . The republic could persist only if all its citizens were so far autonomous that they could be equally and immediately participant in the pursuit of the universal good.'[9] One can hardly fail to note the contrast between this view of society and that of many governments to-day.

## 6   Learning from history?

Are there practical lessons to be learned from history? Hegel said that the only thing to be learned from history is that men learn nothing from history.[10] I do not think that history teaches many practical lessons that common-sense would not suggest: for example, 'Do not start a fight with a more powerful enemy'; 'do not show bad faith to a person with whom

[8] Von Strassburg (1960), p. 45.
[9] See 'Civic Humanism and Its Role in Anglo-American Thought', in Pocock (1972), p. 87. The idea is fully developed in Pocock (1975).
[10] Hegel (1956), p. 6.

you expect to deal again.' Such lessons might be learned from history, but there is no need to bother to seek them there. You can see them around you. The illusion that we draw lessons from history is usually due to history books written so as to suggest them. We find lessons in history because we put them there first.

History was long written in an exemplary mode – 'philosophy teaching by example'. Unfortunately, for almost any example cited, history can somewhere produce a counter-example. We forget this when we meet a striking historical parallel. In the fifth century BC Thucydides claimed to be explaining 'the events which happened in the past and which (human nature being what it is) will, at some time or other and in much the same ways, be repeated in the future'.[11] He was right: anyone reading his account of the revolution in Corcyra in book III, will recognize that it could almost be a description of many a revolution in the modern world. To take another case, there was a close parallel between the United States just before the Civil War and that of the Soviet Union in 1991. In December 1860 the retiring President, James Buchanan, warned that if secession was legitimate, the Union became 'a rope of sand' and 'our thirty-three States may resolve themselves into as many petty, jarring, and hostile republics.'[12] Apart from the number of states, the words might almost have been spoken of the Soviet Union 130 years later. It is tempting to make such comparisons, and, for historians, interesting and harmless. But practising politicians should resist them; there are too many occasions when it proved wrong to apply 'the lessons of history'. (Is this itself a lesson of history?)

## 7   History should not serve a cause

A few pages back we noted that sharing a common history gives a people a sense of common identity – and this can enrich their lives with greater meaning. But is this particular function of history to be commended? Recognizing a common identity means recognizing that people of your group are different from those of other groups. From this it is but a short step to feeling the superiority of your own (more familiar) group – as happened long ago with Greeks and barbarians (people who didn't speak Greek but spoke 'Bar-bar'). In a world drawn ever closer together by economics, by communications, by weaponry and by ecological dangers, we cannot afford to be exclusive. History has often been written deliberately to create or enhance a sense of nationality, as by Michelet for the French, Palacky for the Czechs or Bancroft for the USA. But we do not need such history today.

Another social role of history is that of reconciling the people to their

---

[11] See *History of the Peloponnesian War* (1954), I, 22 (p. 24).
[12] See McPherson (1990), p. 246.

government. It is, of course, possible to write history in a mode of radical criticism as A. J. P. Taylor, Christopher Hill and Eric Hobsbawm have done in England and William A. Williams, Eugene Genovese and Howard Zinn in the USA. On the whole, however, the slant of historical writing has been conformist, if not conservative. It is always comforting to believe that ours was the right side in past struggles or that on the whole things have turned out as well as could be expected.[13] But here, again, this particular role of history is hardly to be commended. History should not be committed to the opposition any more than to the Establishment; it should be critical and impartial. It must point out that right did not always triumph, that history is usually written by the victors, that rejected ways of acting might have been better, and that 'our side' was sometimes in the wrong. History should not be the servant of any cause.[14]

We should remember also that history at its most austere has a social role as a body of knowledge on a par with, say, zoology, engineering, medicine, anthropology or nuclear physics. All such disciplines pursue the truth and do so by different methods. Although none have exhausted their sphere of potential knowledge, nevertheless the most advanced findings of any intellectual discipline should be available to those whose interest or concern it is to know them. History, like zoology and the rest, forms part of the intellectual resources of society.

## 8   History in education

Finally, what is the role of history in one very important function of society, education? There are one or two problems about this. One is that to be able to appreciate history you need to have some experience of the world of men and women. Children, of course, lack this; hence the common observation that many people find the subject fascinating in adult life who found it uninteresting at school. One solution is to remember that everyone loves a good story; history can be entertainingly taught to any age as narrative. Another problem is that, like all good things, history is more attractive if you find it for yourself – as many do in later life. Fortunately school children are remarkably resilient and often find it possible to enjoy a subject even if it *is* prescribed in the curriculum.

As to why history should be in the curriculum, the reasons offered are legion. They range from a blatantly nationalist plea that every child should know the 'great deeds' of her fellow countrymen ('drum-and-trumpet history') to pleas from the teaching profession that she should be acquainted with the distinctive methodology of the historian. Education has two aspects – the personal and the social. Studying history for oneself (discussed on pp. 50–3 above) is part of the personal aspect. A govern-

[13] See the chapter on late nineteenth-century American historians, entitled 'Consensus and Legitimation' in Novick (1988), pp. 61–85.
[14] See also ch. 2, pp. 46–7 above.

ment's insistence on a certain curriculum in its schools is part of the public aspect of historical education. But what about parents? They wish their child to gain certain information and skills as part of her personal development. But they also want her to grow up as part of a wider community, and to share its historical knowledge. This presents a particular problem to immigrants. They want their child to enjoy the public education of their new home, but at the same time they want her to carry on the social, moral and religious traditions of her family. Hence in many countries there arise pressures upon the curriculum and lively, even embittered, debates.

Leaving on one side these problems of a mixed community, there remain others about a public education in history. The education authorities, local or national, both pay the piper and call the tune. What sort of return should the community look for from its investment in the historical education of its future citizens? Setting aside all personal and family considerations, what is it *in the public interest* that a child should know? The answer can be given in terms of certain facts, certain abilities and certain attitudes.

## 9   What should a child know?

Traditional education in history was to drive into children's memories a number of 'facts' that were held to be the backbone of a nation's history – sometimes little more than a list of kings, heroes and battles.[15] Should such things represent a nations's history? Is it not more important, one politician has recently argued, that English children should learn about the match-girls' strike in 1888 than the Battle of Waterloo in 1815? He need not have worried. Unless historical 'facts' are embedded in a wide and deep context they become meaningless and are soon forgotten. When conscientious teachers try to provide such a context, two problems immediately present themselves. The first is that the context is very demanding of time and other resources. Either it is fully explained and the teacher has to leave out most out of the other 'facts' that it would be desirable for children to know, or it is severely restricted at the expense of interest and understanding. The second problem is that to weave the whole tapestry of the detailed course of history – political, administrative, legal, economic, religious, social, cultural – in which these important events occurred is to make demands on children's understanding far in advance of their intellectual development. Thus there are severe limitations both upon the number of 'facts' that a child will long remember and upon the degree of comprehension of those 'facts'.[16]

Nevertheless, the second approach has proved the more rewarding. For

[15] Cf. Sellar and Yeatman (1931).
[16] Sellar and Yeatman's classic work admirably illustrates this.

in trying to understand the context in which things occur – the 'how' and the 'why' – children do learn more than the bare facts. They learn something about the world – about power, wealth, status, tradition, and about the functioning of institutions (courts, parliaments, armies). Thus history may be described as education through vicarious experience. The student gains insight into other modes of living, other ways of thinking, other solutions to common problems. She encounters unfamiliar but still human situations, emotions, and behaviour. She becomes acquainted with strange and wonderful personalities, more entrancing than any in fiction: Hannibal, the Emperor Frederick II ('Stupor Mundi'), Catherine the Great or Benjamin Franklin.

All this knowledge comes with a historical education. Unfortunately it is occasional and unorganized. For it to be of useful application outside particular contexts it needs to be generalized. Now there is no reason why learned studies should not be made of such things as human emotions, or armies, or how wealth is created and channelled. Indeed, they are made. But they are considered to be parts of the social sciences rather than history. And no one has suggested that the school student of history should absorb massive textbooks of psychology, government, economics, military organization and so on before she can come to terms with a passage of history. Nor is this how historians themselves work.

So perhaps the most rewarding way to teach history, at least to younger children, is to encourage them to find out for themselves in a simplified model of historical research. A good deal of ingenuity has gone into the development of so-called 'historical skills'. This has involved allowing children to handle and examine some of the exhibits in museums; encouraging them to act out historical events; printing facsimiles of historical documents for scrutiny, collation and incorporation in a coherent historical account. Imagination is stirred, understanding is deepened, and certain skills are acquired. But might equally valuable results have been attained in ways less demanding of time, energy and other resources? And how far are the knowledge gained and the skills acquired transferable to other situations? Possibly they can be employed in further historical study, and for this they will be useful. But the function of a child's education is not to make her a historian; it is (from the public perspective) to make her a useful and responsible citizen. If, however, what has been acquired in learning history can be applied elsewhere – to management, to politics, to literary expression, for example – then such methods are justified. How far skills so gained *can* be transferred to other activities is not yet clear. We may be more confident that if interest and enthusiasm are aroused in the primary school child, such seeds will come to flower in later life – even much later.

Such methods are hardly possible for children in secondary schools, where the curriculum is dominated by examination requirements. We have to face two questions here: (1) does the very fact of examination not quench, for many children, their growing enthusiasm for history? And (2) does not the method of examining, with its emphasis on 'right' and 'wrong' answers, militate against the nature of the subject? Nevertheless the advantages of education through vicarious experience of humanity can hardly fail to be valuable in any future calling that involves understanding people.

## 10   *No laws of history*

One thing that history lacks for educational purposes is a set of laws or principles. The chief aim of an education in chemistry, for example, is to inculcate a knowledge and understanding of the laws, theories and hypotheses of the science. It is, of course, useful to know how to handle a test-tube or Bunsen burner, to be able to identify certain chemical substances, and even more useful in practice to know some of their qualities. But the main thrust of the science is theoretical. Now this is not so in history. There is factual knowledge – to which the chemical counterpart would be that the stuff I heated in a test-tube this morning evaporated; there is general knowledge – comparable to 'sodium chloride dissolves in water'; there are skills – comparable to knowing how to use a pipette. But in history there are no laws. So an education in history can have none of the theoretical advantages and few of the practical ones of a scientific education.

The comparison with chemistry reminds us of the attractions of a theory-based science. Once one has mastered a law or principle one has mastered an indefinite number of instances. This gives a sense of power and saves effort. Moreover, there is the excitement of seeing how a fact can be explained by more fundamental, underlying laws – like those of valency, of molecular structures and of atoms. There is intellectual satisfaction in perceiving that a particular phenomenon must always occur because it is determined by deep universal laws. I remember the excitement with which, in my early twenties, I read Toynbee's *A Study of History*. The broad sweep of historical information, together with certain simple generalizations that were applied to twenty-one civilizations was quite intoxicating. Now at last, I felt, history was making sense. Later, reading Toynbee's many critics as well as extending my own knowledge, I came to see that his was a brilliant but still inevitably unsuccessful attempt to find a general theory of history. One advantage remained, however: this experience taught me how great an intellectual excitement Marxism must have always held for many people. Some were moved by sympathy with the underdogs, others by the vision of a better future, but there was always the intellectual glamour of a well-wrought theory. This attraction is, paradoxically, especially powerful in history – an extensive and confusing subject that cries out for theoretical ordering, yet obstinately resists anything of the kind.

## 11   *Is it rational?*

One can well understand the determination of two great German philosophers to conquer this obstinacy. In 1784 Kant wrote in his *Idea for a Universal History with a Cosmopolitan Purpose*:

> The only way out for the philosopher, since he cannot assume that mankind follows any rational *purpose of its own* in its collective actions, is for him to attempt to discover *a purpose in nature* behind this senseless course of human events, and decide whether it is after all possible to formulate in terms of a definite plan of nature a history of creatures who act without a plan of their own. – Let us now see if we can succeed in finding a guiding principle for such a history, and then leave it to nature to produce someone capable of writing it along the lines suggested.[17]

A generation later nature did produce someone – Georg Wilhelm Friedrich Hegel, perhaps the greatest philosopher to tackle the problem of history. (One cannot but feel that if Hegel failed – as he did – no one else is likely to succeed.) In the Introduction to his *Philosophy of History* (1831) he wrote: 'The only Thought which Philosophy brings with it to the contemplation of History, is the simple conception of *Reason*; that Reason is the Sovereign of the World; that the history of the world, therefore, presents us with a rational process.'[18] Such confidence in the powers of reason over history are a far cry from Gibbon's famous remark that 'history . . . is indeed, little more than the register of the crimes, follies, and misfortunes of mankind.'[19]

While Gibbon was unduly pessimistic about the experiences of history, he was nearer the truth than Hegel about its inscrutability. Surely, if Hegel is right in asserting that the history of the world presents us with a rational process, that process has escaped our notice. It is much more likely that any traces of a rational process – the subject of various theories of history – have been put there by the philosophers. 'Of course they have!' chortle the historians. But wait! Are the historians entirely innocent of the same offence? To be precise, have they been putting things into history(2) that were not there in history(1)?

## 12   *Do we find only what we have put in?*

This reminds us that the most rewarding way to teach history is to make comprehensible that deep and wide context in which historical events

---

[17] See Reiss (1977), p. 42.
[18] See Hegel (1956), p. 9.
[19] Gibbon (1910), vol. I, p. 77.

occur. Nevertheless, in offering explanations it is all too easy for the teacher to assume (or, worse, to state explicitly) certain generalizations – e.g. that all bureaucracies tend to become obsessed with precedent. But is this not imposing a pattern that was not inherent in the events? The fact that one historian's patterns of explanation differ from another's, and both of them from the way that the actual historical agents saw it, must give us pause. Yet how can we do our duty to our students and our public if we abstain from any kind of generalization? And if we are to be permitted some, then where is the line to be drawn? And if we draw no line, shall we find ourselves committed to some speculative philosophy of history?[20]

These questions, which have arisen in the context of history as education, lead us on to the next section on history and social science.

## C.  History and the Social Sciences

### 1  History and sociology

Out at dinner once I asked my neighbour what he did. He was a sociologist, I a historian. 'So you are one of the fellows who are trying to take us over', I quipped. 'Too late', he replied. 'We've taken you over.' But neither discipline has yet swallowed the other, and rivalry persists. Yet perhaps it is no longer quite a 'dialogue of the deaf', as Fernand Braudel described it.

Once the subjects could be distinguished by their matter: historians were concerned with the actions of a few great men – kings, ministers, popes, generals, while the social sciences were concerned with society at large, the multitudes who hardly figured in the history books except as 'the people', 'the commons' or 'the mob'. But by the twentieth century historians had begun to study whole groups: Puritans, nobles, seamen, working women, settlers and so on. Thus history and the social sciences cannot be distinguished by their subject.

Another distinction has been drawn between their attitudes to time. Social science is said to emulate physical science in trying to establish laws (or at least theories) that are valid for all times and places – like the law of gravity. This is manifestly not true of history which gives a particular date to the facts that it records and is very well aware of chronology. 'Social science has almost . . . a horror of the event', says Braudel.[21] In the Enlightenment it was often held that timeless generalizations could be made about human nature. In a philosophical classic, An Enquiry Concerning Human Understanding (1748), David Hume wrote:

[20] For these, see chs 9 and 10 below.
[21] Braudel (1980), p. 28 See also Cipolla's discussion of the 'short run' and the 'long run' in Cipolla (1991), pp. 10–11.

It is universally acknowledged, that there is a great uniformity
among the actions of men ... Would you know the sentiments,
inclinations, and course of life of the Greeks and Romans? Study
well the temper and actions of the French and English ... Mankind
are so much the same, in all times and places, that history informs us
of nothing new or strange in this particular.[22]

Such an outlook, almost incredible to us, formed once the basic
assumption of the social sciences. Indeed, some of the acclaimed founders
of sociology, Montesquieu (1689–1755), Adam Ferguson (1723–1816)
and John Millar (1735–1801), might equally well be considered as
analytical or 'philosophical' historians.[23] As the nineteenth-century was
the great century of historical study (rendering attitudes like that of Hume
virtually impossible), sociologists drew much of their material from
history. In the twentieth century, however, particularly through the
influence of anthropologists, most of sociology became concerned only
with the present. By thus losing sight of history it was all the easier to
restore (nearly two centuries later) the old illusion that human phenomena
can be described without reference to the date, just like the phenomena of
the natural sciences. (We do not record that hydrogen combined with
oxygen to form water at such and such a date; it always does.) Much
sociological writing was not devoted to building or testing theories, but
merely to employing existing theories in description. Such studies are of
little use without historical context.[24] It is unfortunate that, at times,
psychology, anthropology and sociology have been 'trapped in a wholly
static vision of society'.[25]

## 2   Social change

Since the Second World War, however, and partly as a result of that
experience, social scientists have taken note that societies do not continue
the same, nor does human nature. Hence there developed theories of
social change. This enabled them to acknowledge changes over time while
they formulated theories to account for them. Thus they kept the prestige
of a science. This, it must be stressed, is only a compromise: although the
content of the theories takes account of time, the theories themselves are
assumed to be timeless – no date is attached to them, nor place of origin.
Cipolla considers the attempt a 'total failure'.[26]

Moreover, such theories of change are open to all the important doubts
about theorizing from history discussed below. The true historian, on the

[22] See Hume (1975), p. 83.
[23] See P. Burke (1980), p. 15.
[24] See Braudel (1980), pp. 37–8.
[25] See Stone (1987), pp. 8–9.
[26] (1991), pp. 10–11.

other hand, is well aware that, however scrupulously careful she may be, she is writing history from the point of view of a certain person in a certain place at a certain time. Hers is emphatically not 'the view from nowhere'.[27]

## 3  *A plurality of times*

In several of his books Fernand Braudel introduces yet another aspect of time. This is that history has a plurality of times, ranging in length from the instantaneous (the shot that killed Kennedy) to the almost everlasting (the 3,000 years of ancient Egypt). 'Social time does not flow at one even rate, but goes at a thousand different paces, swift or slow, which bear almost no relation to the day-to-day rhythm of a chronicle or of traditional history.'[28] Braudel stresses the 'long time-span' (*la longue durée*). He points out that in economic and social history one has to observe a phenomenon – a price curve or the growth of a population – over a series of years before one can have a clear picture of what was going on. This is the usual pattern of quantitative history. But he is not concerned only with things that can be counted. Geographical facts – climate, vegetation, land contours – all closely restrict human activity. Thus the lives of the inhabitants run for centuries along the same economic channels. There are also examples in the history of culture; he cites Latin literature in medieval Europe, the crusading spirit, or the Aristotelian concept of the universe.[29] All of these endured for many centuries. A striking example is that of the trade-based capitalistic economy of the period *c.* 1350–*c.* 1750. It was dominated by water and ships – hence almost all economic growth took place on rivers or coasts; merchants and precious metals played a leading part, the underlying agricultural economy was subject to sharp seasonal crises. Braudel described this in a three-volume work, *Civilization and Capitalism, 15th–18th Century* (1979, English translation 1981–4). His earlier and better-known masterpiece, *The Mediterranean and the Mediterranean World in the Age of Philip II* (1949, English translation 1972) was constructed around three time scales – **the structural (roughly, the 'long time-span'), the conjunctural (roughly, trends or series over shorter spans – say, 20–50 years) and the history of events.**

Braudel reminds us that as well as the fixed time of the traditional historian's event and the disregard of time in most of the products of the social sciences, there are stretches of time of very varying lengths that all have to be woven together (whether by scientists or historians) if they are to give an accurate account of social reality. In short, traditional history is

---

[27] See T. Nagel's study of subjectivity and objectivity under this title (1986).
[28] Braudel (1980), p. 12.
[29] Ibid., pp. 31–2.

concerned with *some* time, the social scientist with *no* time, and Braudel with *long* time.[30]

## 4   *Is history a social science?*

For Braudel there is no important distinction between history and the social sciences. They study the same field of social reality – that is, societies in the round, embracing all aspects of life. Braudel also points out that both historians and social scientists are engaged in reconstructing the social reality that they study. A sociological description of a mid-West town is no less a reconstruction than a historian's account of a Crusade. 'Ah, yes', you may say, 'but the historian traces events through time as he recounts the story of that Crusade, while the sociologist describes the town at one point in time. There is a difference.' That might have been so two or three generations ago, but the distinction hardly stands today. Many historical accounts are set at one time and trace no process, tell no story. Think of Burckhardt's *The Civilization of the Renaissance in Italy*, Maitland's *Domesday Book and Beyond*, Namier's *The Structure of Politics on the Accession of George III*, or Le Roy Ladurie's *Montaillou*. Equally there are works in the social sciences which do take account of the passage of time: Barrington Moore's *Social Origins of Dictatorship and Democracy*, Michel Foucault's *The Order of Things*, J. G. A. Pocock's *The Machiavellian Moment*, or, of course, a good deal of the writing of Karl Marx. Therefore we may conclude that the presence or absence of the dimension of time does not constitute a distinction between history and social science.

Can it be that they reconstruct social reality upon different lines? It used to be claimed (by Windelband and Rickert in the late nineteenth-century) that history was *ideographic* (i.e. described particulars), while science was *nomothetic* (i.e. strove to find, or to fashion, laws). Convincing as this may seem (it is, after all, very like Aristotle's reason for preferring poetry to history) it will not do. Sometimes science is concerned with a particular event – a volcanic eruption, for example; and sometimes historians like Braudel are concerned to establish general truths. On the whole, however, historians are very much at home with the concrete and the particular, even if they do make use of the abstract and the general; while, by contrast, scientists, however absorbed in any single phenomenon, tend to go beyond that into the realm of theory. Historians are shy of generalizations, while scientists (if they have not quite the horror of the particular event that Braudel attributes to them) feel that they are fulfilling their role best when they are formulating, testing, refuting, or, at least,

---

[30] The dimension of time in the social sciences remains to be fully explored. A start may be made with Bendix in Burns and Saul (1967), Bock (1979), Nisbet (1969), Floud (1974) and Skocpol (1984), together with the works they cite.

employing some general law. Different tendencies, then, but no exclusive distinction yet.

## 5   Knowing from the inside

A greater contrast between science and history is made by thinkers of an Idealist tendency, like R. G. Collingwood. Their argument is that scientists of nature have developed methods for studying what is other than themselves; they have no experience of what it is to be a star, a crystal, an earthworm or even a dog.[31] They have to rely solely on observation, i.e. on the evidence of their senses, mediated at times by instruments. On the other hand, in dealing with men and women one does not have to rely on sensory observation alone; one knows what it is to be human. In understanding one's fellows there is the 'rediscovery of the I in the Thou', as the German philosopher Wilhelm Dilthey put it.[32] Moreover, not only mankind is understood from the inside; one also has an insight into the works of man – laws, cities, languages, arts – that one does not have into the works of nature, like thunderstorms or trees. A Neapolitan lawyer, Giambattista Vico (1668–1774) said this long ago. He maintained that whatever man had made, man could understand. This, in a double sense, lightens the work of the historian.

> But in the night of thick darkness enveloping the earliest antiquity, ... there shines the eternal ... light of a truth beyond all question: that the world of civil society has certainly been made by men, and that its principles are therefore to be found within ... our own human mind. Whoever reflects on this cannot but marvel that the philosophers should have bent all their energies to the study of the world of nature, which, since God made it, He alone knows; and that they should have neglected the study of the world of nations, or civil world, which, since men had made it, men could come to know.[33]

The distinction between the natural and the human sciences could hardly have been put more clearly.

Such considerations led R. G. Collingwood to his famous assertion that 'the historian must re-enact the past in his own mind.' Collingwood argues, correctly, that the past 'is never a given fact which he can apprehend empirically by perception'. He goes on to argue that 'the historian does not know the past by simply believing a witness who saw the events in question and has left his evidence on record.' This would

---

[31] For a profound but entertaining study of the problem, see Thomas Nagel, 'What is it like to be a bat?' in Nagel (1979).
[32] See Dilthey (1976), p. 208.
[33] See Vico (1970), pp. 52–3, 331.

furnish grounds for, at best, a shaky belief, not knowledge. Here, again, it is difficult to disagree, but one must remember that such an account does form part of the evidence on which the historian must rely. But, rejecting both fact and witness, Collingwood leaps to the conclusion that historical knowledge must be a re-enactment of past thoughts. Indeed, he insists that 'of everything other than thought, there can be no history.' Going further than Vico or Dilthey, he says, 'Historical knowledge, then, has for its proper object thought: not things thought about, but the act of thinking itself.'[34]

This is probably the best-known expression of non-positivist views of historical knowledge, but one must not reject them all just because Collingwood goes too far. Vico's distinction between the works of man and the works of nature, and Dilthey's insistence that in human affairs we find ourselves in others, are more convincing. Please note, though, that while Collingwood uses his view of historical knowledge to make a sharp division between history and science, Dilthey's point has been used to make a division *within* the human sciences.

## 6   Meaning

Some practitioners of the human sciences hold that the same disinterested attitude that a chemist has to a chemical, or a biologist to a bacillus, should inform any scientific study of human beings. This is, roughly, **the behaviourist school of thought, so called because human beings are studied solely through external observation of their behaviour.** Other practitioners argue that, whatever the merits of this approach, there are additional ways of learning about human beings. In particular, the behaviourists ignore something very important: they ignore meanings. Almost every human action – what we say, what we write, what we paint, what we build etc. – has a meaning. Indeed, it usually has **meaning in a double sense: one meaning is our intention, what we *mean* by saying or doing something; the other is what others understand by it.** These two aspects of meaning do not always coincide. But meanings in either sense of the word play no part in behaviourist methods. By contrast, the method that does take meanings into account goes by the name of 'hermeneutics'. It may help to remember that the word is derived from Hermes, the mythical messenger of the gods (known to the Romans as Mercury), a swift figure with winged helmet and winged heels. Thus **hermeneutics may be thought of as the study of messages in a broad sense.** Since to act with meaning is typically human, a social scientist of the hermeneutic persuasion would consider that the behaviourist approach to human beings is like studying birds only when they are not flying or fish only

---

[34] See Collingwood (1961), pp. 282, 304, 305.

when they are not swimming. (For a fuller discussion of meaning, see chapter 10 below.)

## 7 Explaining and understanding

Sometimes the debate between these two schools of thought is described as between 'explanation' and 'understanding'. As von Wright points out, 'Ordinary usage does not make a sharp distinction between the words "explain" and "understand".' For this reason I have preferred the terms 'behaviourism' and 'hermeneutics'.[35] The difficulty with the more familiar terms is partly due to the fact that any explanation *does* increase understanding. Nevertheless, 'understanding is . . . connected with *intentionality* in a way explanation is not', says von Wright. He goes on: 'One understands the aims and purposes of an agent, the meaning of a sign or symbol, and the significance of a social institution or religious rite.'[36]

Perhaps the leading figure in the hermeneutic approach to the social sciences is the great German sociologist, Max Weber (1864–1920). He defined sociology as 'a science which attempts the interpretive understanding of social action in order thereby to arrive at a causal explanation of its course and effects. In "action" is included all human behaviour when and in so far as the acting individual attaches a subjective meaning to it.'[37] Please note the words 'subjective meaning' and 'interpretive', and remember that **'hermeneutics' is normally defined as 'the science of interpretation'.** Not surprisingly he was also a historian and conceived of the social sciences as historical sciences. For him 'all human reality is to be understood in the dimension of time and by the methods of the historian.'[38] The debate continues in the human sciences.

Our concern here, though, is with history. We were asking whether any clear distinction can be drawn between history and the social sciences. At first it seemed that the behaviourist/hermeneutical divide was just such a distinction, but then we found that the dividing line is not, as Collingwood supposed, between science and history, but between two schools of thought in the social sciences. Strangely enough, the debate has also been found within history. It has been much debated whether or not this subject should employ the same methods of explanation as the sciences. This is treated in a later chapter. Here we must observe that the dividing line of this debate (as to whether history uses scientific methods

[35] See von Wright (1971), pp. 5, 6 and 29ff. See also the discussion in Bauman (1978).
[36] Von Wright (1971), p. 6.
[37] See Weber (1947), p. 88.
[38] See MacRae (1974), p. 63. For further reading, see Bottomore (1971), pp. 31ff; Bock (1979), pp. 39–79; Coser and Rosenberg (1969), pp. 243ff; Ryan (1973), pp. 7ff; for a more philosophical discussion, see Winch (1958) and Ryan (1970), pp. 127ff. Gadamer (1979), is a thorough study of hermeneutics, and Schutz (1972) takes further Weber's notion of subjective meaning in social actions.

of explanation or methods of explanation peculiar to itself) is a line that runs *through* history, not between history and science.[39]

## 8   *Quantitative explanation*

But the debate is not confined to philosophers of history. It tends to arise whenever (as is increasingly the case) statistical methods are used in what is known as 'quantitative history' or 'cliometrics'. As economic history lends itself most readily to these methods, there has arisen a type of quantitative economic history (known as 'new' economic history or econometrics) which is derived from economics rather than history. This has been defined as 'the exploration and testing of hypotheses about historical events, hypotheses which have been framed on the basis of established economic theory'.[40] Such work is normally regarded as the province of the scientist: testing hypotheses based on pre-existing theories. It is not, as Floud recognizes, the usual way historians work. 'The "new" economic historian', he goes on, 'concentrates on measurable economic phenomena, and uses economic theory linking those phenomena, specifically because he wishes to cut through the complexity of history and to concentrate on those phenomena which best explain the events he is studying.'[41]

Let us note the assumptions made here. The econometrician concentrates on what can be measured, assuming that what cannot be measured will be largely irrelevant to his purposes. Again, he wishes to cut through the complexity of history, assuming that he knows which way such risky short cuts are to be made. To be fair, any historian would admit that short cuts do have to be made – no historian can put everything in. What is questionable is whether those cuts should be determined by the established theories of another discipline. But the third assumption is the most doubtful: namely, that the 'new' economic historian can identify those phenomena which offer the best explanation. Again, any historian would grant that this search for explanatory factors is common practice. What many would *not* grant is that it can be known in advance that these explanatory factors are quantifiable – the first assumption.

## 9   *'Cliometrics'*

Another 'new' economic historian, Peter Temin, describes 'new' economic history as 'a form of applied neo-classical economics'. Hence the method is to 'start with a formal model of some aspect of economic behaviour, assemble data for use in the model, and draw conclusions by joining the

[39] See Skinner (1990), p. 6.
[40] Floud (1974), p. 2.
[41] Ibid.

data and the model'.[42] Here again the procedure is scientific not historical; and here again we notice that the pre-existing model is brought to the data, and that only data suitable for use in the model are sought. But what if some of the data (religious or political opinions, for example) cannot be fitted into an economic model? Must they then be ignored or rejected?

Another American economic historian, R. W. Fogel, describes 'cliometrics' as 'the new brand of "scientific history".' He goes on: 'The common characteristic of cliometricians is that they apply the quantitative methods and behavioral models of the social sciences to the study of history . . . Cliometricians want the study of history to be based on explicit models of human behavior.'[43] As he makes clear, cliometrics applies not only to economic history, but also to 'population and family history'.[44]

Here again, the question is whether the behavioural models and the quantitative methods used in the social sciences can be imported into history without some distortion of typical historical methods and understandings. One must also point out that, as we have seen, by no means all social scientists are agreed about the value of quantitative methods and behavioural models. The Italian economic historian Carlo Cipolla rejects this 'new' economic history. He finds that it has the defects of oversimplification, *ex post* reasoning, and subjectivism. Moreover, it rests on 'very shallow philosophical and epistemological foundations'. It runs the danger of reducing ends to means and according means the status of ends.[45] On the whole, though, the historian does not reject outright any methods that may help him towards the truth. But he prefers not to have his methods prescribed for him, his data chosen in advance or his explanations fashioned by some extraneous theory. He wishes to be free to choose all these for himself. Historians suspect theory-based approaches. From the experience of many generations they are aware of the danger of importing into one's researches the very things one hopes to find. Crudely, that is why the kings and generals of one's own nation have mostly been heroic, those of other nations less so.

Of course, we all think we have outgrown that kind of self-deception. But the danger does not cease there. Economists have surveyed the economic problems of a Third World country, confidently specified the appropriate remedies, and then have been surprised at their failure. The reason so often has been some social or cultural element in the situation whose impact on the economy has been ignored because it had no place in their theories. Similar mistakes can as easily be made in history, though

[42] See Temin (1973), p. 8.
[43] See Fogel and Elton (1983), pp. 24–5.
[44] Ibid.
[45] Cipolla (1991), pp. 59, 69.

not so easily discovered. As G. R. Elton remarks, 'there is some evidence somewhere for just about every interpretation of the past, provided other evidence is ignored.'[46] It is easy for both scientists and historians to carry some assumption of their own age or society into another.

## 10   *A dividing line?*

It seems there is no simple answer to the question of where, if anywhere, to draw the dividing line between social science and history. One's answer depends very much on how one sees these disciplines: Braudel has quite a different conception of history from Collingwood, and so finds no difficulty in counting history among the social sciences. This would be anathema to Collingwood, as it is to the French historian, Paul Veyne: 'History is not a science; it has no less rigor, but that rigor applies to the level of criticism.'[47] Similarly, when social scientists claim that their methods are applicable to history, we must first ask what methods these are. The claims I have quoted above from Fogel or Temin or Floud are not those that would be made by social scientists of the hermeneutic persuasion.

## 11   *Comparative studies*

But there are further aspects of the history/social science question. The first of these is that of comparative studies. Every empirical science makes comparisons, observing similarities and differences. This is as true of the sciences of societies as it is of those of corals or butterflies. How far is comparison valid for the historian? Well, why does the ornithologist compare birds? First he does it in order to classify them into orders, families, genera and species. In doing so he will have observed that certain characteristics go together: a stubby beak with eating grains, webbed feet with swimming, and so on. This is the second stage. Thirdly, on the basis of such connections he may go on to draw general conclusions, such as that all sea-birds have oily skins.

How far can the historian proceed along these lines when he compares societies, states, institutions, economic systems, and so on? Strangely enough, very few people, whether social scientists or historians, have attempted a full classification, or taxonomy, of the social phenomena that they both study. To be sure, Aristotle compiled a list of the constitutions of 158 Greek cities. Toynbee made a table of twenty-one civilizations. At least one sociologist has attempted a taxonomy of all societies.[48] Nevertheless, there is no recognised taxonomy of social entities as there is of birds, beasts and flowers. The social sciences lack their Linnaeus. Most

---

[46] Fogel and Elton (1983), p. 99.
[47] Veyne (1984), p. 14.
[48] See Marsh (1967).

of the work in comparative history is done at the second stage, that of making connections between two observed characteristics. Herodotus, the 'Father of History', is full of them; Bishop Stubbs lectured in the nineteenth-century on 'The Comparative Constitutional History of Medieval Europe'; Marc Bloch in 1928 urged upon historians the comparative history of European societies, and in 1959 a learned journal for this purpose was founded: *Comparative Studies in Society and History*.[49] Doubts about the validity of comparisons in history apply particularly to Marx. He believed that all societies pass through similar stages of development and so can be compared at all points. 'The country', wrote Marx in 1867, 'that is more developed industrially only shows, to the less developed, the image of its own future.' He warned his German readers not to ignore the fate of the English workers in the Industrial Revolution; it would soon happen in Germany, too, because of the 'natural laws of capitalist production'. These laws were 'winning their way through and working themselves out with iron necessity'.[50] It is clear that Marx had moved to the third stage, that of formulating general laws from the comparison of certain phenomena. (For more on Marx, see chapter 10 below.) However, he was a philosopher by training, not a historian. Few historians have been prepared to move from the second stage of comparison (that of making connections between two observed characteristics) to the third stage, that of making general rules, let alone 'natural laws' that work with 'iron necessity'. An English historian (in controversy with the American 'cliometrician', R. W. Fogel) says of this second stage: 'The point is that no amount of analogy can prove anything in history . . . Analogy has its place in true (traditional) history, but it is a very minor one. It can prove a stimulus to thought and enquiry . . . But that is all: such similarities *prove* nothing.'[51]

## 12    *Similarity proves nothing*

In strict logic Elton is undoubtedly correct. Let us suppose a number of similar but unconnected events (say, successful revolutions) which we will number $R_1$, $R_2$, $R_3$ and so on. Let us also suppose that $R_1$ appears to have been brought about by a social group that is upwardly mobile, not by the destitute poor. Let us call this origin $O_1$. Then we look at $R_2$ and $R_3$ and find that they have similar origins, $O_2$ and $O_3$. We should then be justified in looking at a fourth example, $R_4$, to see if that, too, had a similar origin, $O_4$. But should we be justified in making a general rule that all successful revolutions originate with an upwardly mobile group? Clearly not, for $R_5$ might have a different origin and so disprove the rule. But supposing we

[49] See Stubbs (1906); Bloch (1967). See also 'Comparative History in Theory and Practice', *American Historical Review* 85, 4 (October 1980).
[50] Marx (1976), p. 91.
[51] See Elton in Fogel and Elton (1983) p. 96.

find ten more favourable instances would the rule be proved? Strictly, no. Suppose we went still further and examined all the Rs and found that each one was preceded by an O, would the rule be proved? No, because there remains the possibility that the next revolution to occur in the future (or even an as yet undiscovered revolution in the past) lacked this kind of origin. So however many examples of $O_1R_1$, $O_2R_2$ ... and so on we found, we could never logically conclude that the occurrence of O must lead to the occurrence of R, or, conversely, that every R must be preceded by O. This is known as the problem of induction.

Now this logical difficulty is not peculiar to history; it is common to all sciences. How do they tackle it? Well, there at least two ways. One way is that made famous by Sir Karl Popper. He argues that, since (as we have seen) not even a very large number of confirmations of a rule will ever *prove* it, the scientist must seek to *disprove* his hypothesis. One counter-example will suffice to do that. But the more people try to disprove a rule and yet it stands, then the greater the likelihood that it approximates to the truth.[52]

Another way is to show that the two things that repeatedly occur together do not do so by chance, but because they are linked by a third factor. It is not chance that all mammals, birds and reptiles have four limbs (even if, as with whales and snakes, the limbs are only rudimentary). It is because they are all descended from common four-limbed amphibian ancestors.

## 13  Historians suspect generalizations

Now both of these methods are, in fact, employed by social scientists. Many historians do so also, though unlike the social scientists they are usually reluctant to form general conclusions. Why? Sometimes they argue that there are not enough examples of the phenomenon to justify making a general rule.[53] But there are as many examples available to historians as there are to social scientists: they have the same potential field of work – the known facts about human life in society. And social scientists are far from shy of making generalizations. I think the reluctance of historians (ignoring the sheer prejudice present in some cases) rests on two kinds of well-founded doubt. One is doubt whether they know enough about each instance in a possibly wide range of phenomena. (Successful revolutions, for example, range from that in Corcyra in 427 BC to those in eastern Europe in AD 1989.) The other is doubt about correctly identifying which phenomena fall under the suggested classification. The American and French revolutions of the eighteenth century were certainly examples of successful revolutions. But was the English revolution of the seventeeth

[52] See Popper (1972 a), p. 33 and passim.
[53] 'For statistical generalization . . . history is likely to be forever handicapped by the smallness of the sample' (Elton, 1969, p. 41).

century successful? It could be argued either way. Was it even a revolution at all? Many historians would deny it. If there can be strong doubts about a historical phenomenon so long and carefully studied as this, can we be confident that we can correctly characterize every change of power in all the states of Asia over the past 2,000 years or more? Hence, probably, the lack of taxonomy (referred to above). The historian is perhaps more conscious than the social scientist of how vast is our ignorance of the greater part of human affairs.

One aspect of this ignorance makes clear why historians are more doubtful than social scientists of being able to find a third, underlying, factor that explains the connection between two characteristics that repeatedly occur together. In the example of four-limbed beasts the third, explanatory, factor is the common descent from amphibians.[54] But if one seeks for a similar explanation in history (as in our example of upwardly mobile groups and successful revolutions) one immediately finds the lack of anything to correspond to the theory of evolution. We believe we know how animals have evolved – that is, we understand the genetic mechanism. But we are very far from understanding the mechanism (if there is one) that determines the succession and the shape of events in history. (For a further and fuller discussion of cause in history, see chapter 8 below.)

## 14   *The answer of the social sciences*

So how do the social sciences tackle this problem? How do they account for the way things are? Broadly, the answers fall into two categories; those that ignore the dimension of time and those that don't. In the first category we find some equilibrium model, such as the theory of functionalism which explains a social phenomenon by the function that it fulfils in maintaining society as a whole. Typical of the second category is some theory of the development of societies (or of some part of a society) along lines similar to Darwinian evolution. This idea has become widely accepted, as can be seen in such phrases as 'underdeveloped nations'. The general expectation, as much in Africa and Asia as in Europe and North America, is that all nations are destined to go through a similar process of economic and social development – the same assumption that Karl Marx made in *Capital* quoted above. Whether they will or not remains to be seen, but there is no necessity about it. Such theories cannot be proved.[55] Nevertheless, since the Second World War few social scientists have been able altogether to ignore the problems of changing societies, in Asia, Africa and Latin America. The literature on various forms of development theory, especially in economics, is extensive. Most historians, however,

[54] See also remarks on chemistry, p. 61 above.
[55] For a good account see Nisbet (1969).

are very sceptical of any such theories of the natural development of societies.[56] None appears to have the validity of Darwin's original theory of animal evolution. But even if as convincing a theory of social evolution were developed, we should still lack the detailed understanding of the mechanism by which change is brought about – something that modern genetic theory has brought to the support of Darwin.[57] It is this close understanding of how change has occurred that history can offer. Unfortunately for the hopeful scientist, such understanding is only of individual instances in different contexts and so offers little help towards a general theory.

## 15   Social sciences help history

Before leaving history and the social sciences we should ask what benefit each can bring to the other.

In the last fifty years or so the study of history has been extended to all kinds of men, women and children, however humble, and to every part of human life, however bizarre. Everything from sanitation to sexuality, from banditry to breast-feeding, has its history today. Almost every aspect of society has become a subject of historical as well as scientific study. Inevitably the social scientists have influenced historians in methods as well as subject matter. The major points are listed by Lawrence Stone.

1   Historians were encouraged to make their thinking – assumptions, presuppositions, models of causation or social structure – more explicit and more precise.

2   Historians were urged to define and use their terms more carefully – for example, 'feudalism', 'bureaucracy', 'court'.

3   The social sciences helped historians to refine their research strategies and to define problems: in particular to make comparisons careful and systematic, and to adopt sampling techniques.

4   Quantitative methods were to be used wherever appropriate. This is particularly necessary where the subject matter is a group rather than a few individuals. (We know little or nothing about any one seventeenth-century peasant, but the researches of Pierre Goubert or Emmanuel Le Roy Ladurie have taught us much about the inhabitants of the Beauvaisis or Languedoc.)

5   The fifth contribution is to provide hypotheses to be tested against the evidence of the past.[58]

As I have indicated, such methods appropriate to the social sciences cannot be taken over lock, stock and barrel and applied uncritically to

[56] See Cipolla, pp. 63–4 above.
[57] See, for example, the writings of Richard Dawkins: *The Selfish Gene* (1986), *The Blind Watchmaker* (1986), and *The Extended Phenotype* (1983).
[58] For the foregoing, see Stone (1987), pp. 17–19.

historical research. The historian, while struggling to understand unfamiliar procedures like statistical methods, must at the same time preserve his own standards and principles and be wary that he does not become a worse historian in the attempt to become a better social scientist. With this in mind, however, he can profitably learn a great deal. Indeed, he is likely to find support for some of his doubts within the social sciences. These are, in many ways, becoming less positivistic. A leading sociologist insists that the social sciences have to link their frames of meaning with the meanings that already make up social life. 'Sociology, unlike natural sciences, stands in a subject–subject relation to its "field of study", not a subject – object relation; it deals with a pre-interpreted world, in which the meanings developed by active subjects actually enter into the actual constitution or production of that world.'[59] **The 'subject – subject relation' is Dilthey's notion of 'the rediscovery of the I in the Thou'.** As I have suggested above, the great divide does not run so much between the historians and the social scientists. Rather it lies between those historians and social scientists who adopt a 'behaviourist' or 'subject–object' attitude to humanity, and the other historians and social scientists who adopt the hermeneutic or 'subject–subject' approach.

## 16   History helps the social sciences

Now what can historians offer to social scientists? For those on the behaviourist (or positivist) side of the divide there is an easy answer: history has a large body of facts to be made available for digestion by the methods of social science – especially those facts like the records of births and deaths or of imports and exports which readily lend themselves to quantification. Those on the hermeneutic side of the divide will not find this sort of co-operation available, for both the historians and the social scientists of this persuasion realize that history does not consist of a lot of discrete facts to be handed about like the ingredients of a cake, or chemicals in a laboratory.

A more promising area of co-operation is that of development studies. As we have seen, the social sciences have been obliged, in the modern world of rapid change, to pay attention to social processess. So far this has largely been done on the basis of an evolutionary approach which turns out to be not entirely satisfactory.[60] Historians, however, have always been familiar with change as fundamental to their studies. Historical causation, how one set of circumstances leads on to another, is central to their thinking without the dominance of a particular theory. Surely, scientists have something to learn here?

But if historians are more accustomed than scientists to working along

[59] Giddens (1976), p. 146.
[60] See Nisbet (1969), chs 4, 5, 6. Also Cipolla, p. 64 above.

the 'vertical' axis of time, they are also experienced in working along the horizontal axis. That is to say, they often have an ability to grasp an age as a whole, to understand how the various parts interact. Of course, social scientists do this with their models of society, but often the sixth sense of an experienced historian can suspect where a formal model does not fit historical reality. But, whatever the problems and difficulties, an atmosphere of mutual understanding and co-operation is to be desired. Each has much to learn from the other, but this can most profitably be done if neither party lose sight of their own particular, hard-won insights.

## Conclusion

This chapter has looked first at the role of history(2) in our private and public lives. In both we have found the importance of 'historicity' – the awareness of living in history. This helps to define both personal and group identities. We have seen the various ways in which this awareness is acquired and have given some thought to the place of history in formal education. These considerations brought us to ask how far history is a law-governed, rational activity, and so we were led on to its relation to the social sciences. Similarities and differences were found between them, but, interestingly, one of the most marked divides was found to lie not *between* history and social science, but *within* each of them. They can help each other in many ways and so co-operation is to be encouraged. Much of the impact of history, however, lies not in its rational structures and methods (as is the case with a science), but in the mode of its communication – how it is conveyed. Thus we need to examine how history is written and presented. This is the subject of the next chapter.

### Suggested Reading

Blackburn 1972
Bock 1979
Bottomore 1971
Bottomore and Nisbet 1979
Braudel 1975, especially pp. 13–24,
    892–900, 1238–44; 1980
Burke, P. 1980; 1992
Cipolla 1991, part I
Clark, S. 1990
Collingwood 1961, especially part V,
    §i
Elton 1969
Floud 1974, especially Introduction
    and chapter II
Furet 1981

Gilbert and Graubard 1972
Iggers 1975
Jones 1972
Lipset and Hofstadter 1968
Marwick 1989
Nietzsche 1957
Nisbet 1969
Rabb and Rotberg 1982
Ryan 1970
Skinner 1990, Introduction
Skocpol 1984
Stanford 1990
Stern 1970
Stone 1987, part I
Veyne 1984

# 4

# History as Discourse

> It was, after all, Greeks who pioneered the writing of history as what it has so largely remained, an exercise in political ironics – an intelligible story of how men's actions produce results other than those they intended.
>
> J. G. A. Pocock

> Consider history with the beginnings of it stretching dimly into the remote time; emerging darkly out of the mysterious eternity: the true epic poem and universal divine scripture.
>
> Thomas Carlyle

## Introduction

The 'true epic poem' that, according to Carlyle, history is – this 'divine scripture' – must, nevertheless, be written by man. And the writing of history (what we call 'historiography') has been going on for a long time, as we shall see. In the last chapter we discussed how history helps to shape the ways in which people see the world. In this one we look at the ways in which that history is written.

*Questions about how and why people write history, and what is good history*

1  What makes a good history book?
2  Is good history nearer to science or to literature?
3  Why are so many works of history produced and read – much more, say, than other subjects, like mathematics, zoology, economics?
4  Do old history books go out of date and become useless?
5  Why do people write history?
6  Should history be a story?

We began by making a clear distinction between history-as-event and history-as-account. We also saw in subsequent chapters that, in practice, these two aspects of history could not be completely separated because they interacted in so many ways. In this chapter we shall be concentrating on the second of these two meanings – the writing of history. Since this has been going on for nearly 3,000 years, we cannot entirely ignore all the changes in human life and society that have occurred over that stretch of time. Nor must we forget that the writing of history has sometimes influenced non-literary events. These influences we looked at in chapter 2. Here we shall stick to the writing of history.

This chapter is divided into four sections, as follows:

A   Communication
B   Narrative
C   Non-narrative History
D   Other Relevant Topics

## A.   Communication

### 1   *Communication shares something*

It is notorious that the study of history involves a lot of reading. All this reading can be seen as the receiving of communications. In the same way every document and every book can be seen as the sending out of a communication. The very word 'communication' implies that something is made the common property of two or more people. In the case of historical communications, what is this 'something'?

The first thing to notice is the occasional mismatch between what is sent out and what is received. When the sender and receiver are fairly close in time and share common interests, understandings and purposes, then there is better communication – better in the sense that what is received is not too different from what is sent. This is largely the case with modern readers and modern historians. But when historians read ancient writings (i.e. the documents that furnish their evidence), then what they receive may be quite different from what the writer sends. (Think, for example, of reading Domesday Book). And this may be so in two ways, one in their favour, the other less so.

The point in their favour is that, by bringing their superior knowledge to the document (i.e. knowledge greater than the sender's of both what came after and what was going on at the time), they can read in it (i.e. receive from it) more than the writer intended to convey. This is particularly important when the document was written with the intention to influence, bias or deceive some future reader.[1]

The second point, however, is that, living as we do in a different world with a different set of ideas, it is unlikely that we can grasp the full

---

[1] See below, ch. 6, pp. 146–7

meaning of a writer of an earlier age. As we saw, it was once generally supposed that men and their cultures have always been much the same.[2] But as history has progressed (not to mention other subjects like anthropology), we have come to realize the great mental gaps between us and people of an earlier age. Paradoxically, knowing them better has made them more remote. We laugh at medieval artists who portrayed classical and biblical figures in medieval garments, but do we always avoid dressing the minds of men and women of past ages in our own mental clothes? Less confident than our predecessors that we understand the mentalities of earlier times, we suspect that the message we receive is *less* than what the writer intended to convey.

## 2 What makes a good history book?

Now let us turn from historical evidence to historical discourse; that is, to the writing of history or writing about history. (Notice the two meanings of 'history' in the previous sentence.) Here the act of communication is clear: the historian knows (or believes he knows) something about the past which he wants to tell other people – namely, his readers.

One of the first questions to ask is: What makes a good history book? There are, perhaps, three ways of answering this. First, it is a good book if it is true. Is it a reliable record or reconstruction of some part of the past? Second, we judge it good if it succeeds in conveying this to its readers. Third, it may be good if it can be judged as a work of art in its own right. In brief, is it true? is it clear? is it fine (as in 'fine arts')? This does not often happen, but there are a few historical 'classics' which are thought to have great and abiding literary merit, and as such are read not primarily for historical information.

We leave aside the first criterion, that of truth. This belongs to the next chapter. Nor can we yet be clear about the third criterion.

But what of the second? What makes a history book a successful communication? The short answer is that it succeeds if it conveys to the reader what the writer wants it to convey. Splendid! But as a matter of fact few history books register 100 per cent success with every reader. So what can go wrong?

## 3 What can go wrong

If we think about this sort of verbal communication more carefully we see that the something made common between writer and reader is not a set of words but a set of ideas. In history books this set of ideas is usually some knowledge of the past. This knowledge is conveyed mainly in words, though often accompanied by pictures, diagrams, tables, statistics and so on. All these may be considered as the code by which one set of ideas (the

[2] See above, ch. 3, pp. 63–4

message) is conveyed from writer to reader. The pattern of communication looks something like this:

Sender —— Encoding —— Coded message —— Decoding —— Receiver.

It will help if you think of the code, not as ordinary language, but something like a cipher, or Morse code or a foreign language. Now it becomes easier to see where communication may fall short of 100 per cent success.

The first place is the encoding. Through carelessness or ignorance the sender may misuse the symbols of the code and send a message that he does not intend to convey. Similar errors in decoding can lead to the reader misunderstanding the message. The third possibility of failure is more subtle. Many literary critics believe that a text has a life of its own, quite distinct from both what the writer intended and what the reader thought he had understood by it.[3]

This should alert us to the fact that no text, however long or elaborate, can articulate all that the writer thinks, all the unconscious assumptions, the overtones, the nuances, the hints, the shadings of ideas. Equally, it cannot contain all the thoughts that the reader drew from it. You will, perhaps, most easily see what I mean if you take a dictionary and try to translate a good poem from one language to another. Word for word (with the help of the dictionary) the encoding may be technically correct, but if the poem has all the meaning in the second language that it had in the original you have performed a work of rare genius.

## 4   *How do words convey meaning?*

There are, moreover, further aspects of successful communication. So far we have considered only a historian's attempt to put his knowledge into words and other symbols, and thus to make a verbal representation of the past. But remember that words cannot represent a battle or a sea-voyage or a revolution in the way that a brush and a palette of paints can. Words do not *resemble* blood or rough seas or angry men. So a *verbal* representation calls for a good deal of work on the part of the reader. At a minimum she has to have learnt to read. Yet a seven-year-old child could spell out the words. What more is needed to be able to follow an account of, say, the taking of the Bastille? The writer has to assume that his readers can bring enough extraneous knowledge to the decoding of his text to enable them to follow what he is talking about: some knowledge of cities and fortresses and weapons and crowds and politics and, above all,

---

[3] As Foucault put it: 'Expressing their thoughts in words of which they are not the masters, enclosing them in verbal forms whose historical dimensions they are unaware of, men believe that their speech is their servant and do not realize that they are submitting themselves to its demands.' See Foucault (1970), p. 297.

of the psychology of men and women. Nor are these contemporary cities and people; they are people, weapons, etc., as they were over 200 years ago in Paris. Yet how does one know what they were like without reading about the French revolution? We can know history only if we have read history already. Is the whole thing a vicious circle? Actually, no, but the explanation of it must wait for the next chapter. The point here is to stress that for the reader to be able properly to decode the historian's message she must bring to the task a good deal of knowledge. If this knowledge is in any way inadequate the decoding will to that extent fail.

Another difficulty arises from the encoding. Briefly, the writer must ensure, once he has encoded his message into a text, that *the* meaning of the text coincides with *his* meaning. That is, would any impartial reader gain the same message from the text that he intended it to convey? For example, one historian has remarked, 'Henry VIII was a real killer.' Did he mean that the king slaughtered people personally? Or did he mean that Henry had no qualms of conscience in ordering the deaths of those he disliked? In a conversation it is easy to ask the speaker which he means. But a writer's meaning has to be inferred with the aid of extraneous knowledge and of the surrounding context. Even so, misunderstanding is still possible. That is why the writer must take great pains to ensure that *the* meaning of his text corresponds with his meaning. (For further discussion of meaning, see chapter 10, pp. 280–5.)

## 5   What is the historian trying to do?

So much for historical writing as the communication of knowledge. This is nearly always the ostensible purpose of writing history. But the writer often has other purposes also. Let us consider what some of these may be.

First, we have to recognize that the reading of history will always have an effect upon the reader other than simply increasing her store of information. For example, she may well enjoy reading history. Accordingly the writer may compose his work in such as way as to give pleasure. To amuse while instructing has been the aim of some historians from Herodotus to A. J. P. Taylor. Then again, the writer may wish to share with his reader not only his knowledge but also his enthusiasm. He may wish to provoke or inspire greater efforts of the imagination or of the intellect. He may wish to help her to pass examinations or to inspire her to carry out her own research projects. These, too, are laudable intentions for the writer of history.

Rarely indeed are the effects confined to a simple increase of information. The reading of history usually makes subtle alterations in the beliefs, the values, the outlook and the understanding of the reader. To revert to an earlier example, it is not comfortable for an Anglican (like myself) to recall that the originator of our church was a killer. Since the sixteenth century, I comfort myself, the Anglican record has been rather

less sanguinary. Nevertheless, my knowledge of that king makes it easier
to understand the attitude of my Roman Catholic friends.

Thus knowledge of the history of the Reformation can affect one's
religious beliefs. Yet perhaps no historiography has been so powerful in its
effects as the Bible itself. 'But', you may exclaim, 'that is not a history
book; it is religious.' Yes, it is primarily religious, for the clear aim of the
writers was to proclaim God. But what was the means that they chose for
this proclamation? It was to show the actions of God *in history*. Whether
it is the freeing of the Hebrews from Egyptian captivity, the exile in
Babylon, the life and death of Jesus or the spread of Christianity through
the Roman Empire, the purpose of the writers of both Testaments was to
convey knowledge of history – God in history. Hence Judaeo-Christian
tradition differs from other traditions in the importance it attaches to
history.

## 6   Improper uses of history

But is it proper for a modern historian to write history with the intent to
alter the moral, political or religious attitudes of his reader? Many
consider this a pointless question. Proper or not, it is impossible to write
history in such a way that it does not somehow affect these attitudes, they
say. But even if the historian cannot altogether avoid having some such
effect should he try to avoid doing so? Surely history written as a form of
moral, political or religious propaganda is distasteful and probably
distorted? Do we not want to make up our own minds about our moral,
political and religious convictions?

Yet the answer is not so simple. By insisting that the historian should
make every effort to avoid influencing our opinions, are we not putting
too much restriction upon him? Considering some of the methods that he
may legitimately employ to increase our understanding of the past,
perhaps we are. The reason lies in one word: emotion. If his writing
arouses no emotions, we shall neither learn nor remember nor understand.
Communication – in any sense beyond that of spelling out words like a
young child – will fail. There must be some emotional response. And if
emotions are aroused about human affairs, then it is almost impossible
that they should not affect our moral, political or religious convictions,
however subtly. This will become even clearer when we look at how the
historian may realize his intentions.

## 7   Communication requires keeping hold of the other end

If the historian is to achieve any of his purposes he must arouse and retain
the attention of his readers. There are several ways of doing so. He may
tell a story, put forward an explanation, illustrate a theme, construct a
logical argument, or even simply offer a description. Let me illustrate

these by titles from my shelves: *The English Civil War* tells a story; *The Causes of the Industrial Revolution in England* puts forward an explanation; *Religion and the Decline of Magic* illustrates a theme; *The Myth of the Great Depression 1873–1896* constructs an argument (that there was no such thing), and *The World We Have Lost* is a description.

Another way of keeping hold of the reader is the writer's style. One cannot prescribe style to an historian. But most studies of the great historians have something to say about their style of writing. Peter Gay's *Style in History* (1975) compares four historians and makes some useful general remarks. John Clive's *Not by Fact Alone: Essays on the Writing and Reading of History* (1989) has several discussions of styles. More profoundly, Hayden White's *Metahistory* (1973) examines four historians and four philosophers of history from the point of view of literary theory. Yet it is not easy to say in general what is a good style, for the style is personal to the writer. (The style is the man himself, as Buffon said.) And one's appreciation depends on the rapport established between oneself and the writer – just as the idiosyncrasies of a person's character may be endearing to some and irritating to others. It is easier to say what a historian should avoid. Among these faults are confused thinking, failure to express himself clearly, the lack of a firm structure to the work, the use of jargon, an excess of abstraction in place of concrete statements, and vagueness and imprecision. Beyond these it is probably not possible to say in advance what constitutes a good style; one can only recognize it when it is there. It is like goodness or beauty in a person; something we cannot prescribe, but which we recognize when we meet it. I will now give a hostage to my readers and quote one of my favourite historical stylists, Edward Gibbon, explaining why the Roman Empire stopped at Hadrian's Wall:

> The native Caledonians preserved in the northern extremity of the island their wild independence, for which they were not less indebted to their poverty than to their valour. Their incursions were frequently repelled and chastised; but their country was never subdued. The masters of the fairest and most wealthy climates of the globe turned with contempt from gloomy hills assailed by the winter tempest, from lakes concealed in a blue mist, and from cold and lonely heaths, over which the deer of the forest were chased by a troop of naked barbarians. (*The Decline and Fall of the Roman Empire*, chapter 1 (1910), p. 5.)

## 8   Should history be relevant?

A third way of retaining interest is by making history 'relevant'. The idea that we should study the past only because it relates to our present concerns has been much attacked. In 1931 the historian Herbert

Butterfield launched his attack upon the Whig interpretation of history: 'It is part and parcel of the whig interpretation of history that it studies the past with reference to the present . . . Through this system of immediate reference to the present-day, historical personages can easily and irresistibly be classed into the men who furthered progress and the men who tried to hinder it.'[4] On this interpretation, 'progress' is understood as 'whatever led to the present state of affairs', with the implied judgement that the existing outcome of things is the best possible. Butterfield probably had Lord Macaulay in mind here.

Two years later, a young philosopher, Michael Oakeshott drew a firm distinction between the 'practical past' and the 'historical past'. Only the latter is a proper subject for the historian – the past for its own sake. He wrote: 'Wherever the past is merely that which preceded the present, that from which the present has grown, wherever the significance of the past lies in the fact that it has been influential in deciding the present and future fortunes of man . . . the past involved is a practical, and not an historical past' (Oakeshott, 1933, p. 103). One takes the point. Nevertheless, not only the readers of history but also its writers tend to prefer those periods that, through resemblance or through causal chains, seem to be particularly related to the present. Indeed, E. H. Carr insisted that the historian cannot divorce himself from the outlook and interests of his age. As he points out, 'Over the last hundred years the changed balance of power in Europe has reversed the attitude of British historians to Frederick the Great'.[5] He sees history as a 'moving procession', where the historian is not on the saluting base, but 'just another dim figure trudging along in another part of the procession'. As the procession winds along, even doubling back, the relations between the different parts are constantly changing. Thus 'it may make perfectly good sense to say . . . that the age of Caesar is nearer to us than the age of Dante.' And he concludes: 'The historian is part of history. The point in the procession at which he finds himself determines his angle of vision over the past.'[6]

## 9   Should history follow our interests?

Carr's observation was not original. A great German historian and sociologist remarked that we consider some past events worthy of history (e.g. wars between European nations), but others not (e.g. fights between African tribes or North American Indians).[7] This is not Hegel's reason for rejecting peoples without history.[8] Weber makes a different point. He thinks that what peoples, events or problems we choose to study vary

[4] Butterfield (1950), p. 11.
[5] E. H. Carr (1964), p. 25.
[6] Ibid., p. 36.
[7] See Weber (1949), p. 172. Also pp. 156–7.
[8] See below, ch. 7, p. 181.

from time to time and from place to place. And this is surely true. Weber says that history is related to our values; we study only those bits of history in which we find them.

The subsequent course of historiography would seem to give the lie to Weber. For since the rise of the *Annales* school almost every aspect of life of every people is grist to the historian's mill. One avowed aim of that school is the writing of total history.

Weber still has a point, however, with respect to the readers of history, if not to its writers. Most people who read history choose books that (not surprisingly) link with their own interests. These interests cannot be ignored by historians and their publishers, who have an eye on the market; hence the flood of books on war or women or sex or racial oppression in history. Thus to link his writings to his readers' interest is a perfectly proper way for the historian to engage and to retain their attention.

## 10   Unsolved problems

All history involves communication – the sharing of an idea, or a complex of ideas. This sharing has at least two stages; the transition from the historical agent to the historical scholar – a leap that may cross great divides of time, space and culture – and the subsequent transition from the scholar to his public. It is not surprising that what is conveyed often changes its form and even its nature in transit. In the light of this, what are we to make of Collingwood's insistence that history is 'the re-enactment of past experience'?[9] We seem to be left with two troubling questions: is it ever possible to do this? and, if we can sometimes succeed in doing it, how can we know that we are doing it? Some of the greatest unanswered problems of history centre around this fact of communication. Communication is absolutely essential to history, yet we must always be in doubt how far communication has been achieved.

## B.   Narrative

Most men, you may observe, speak only to narrate.
Thomas Carlyle, 'On History'

'History', wrote the Dutch historian, G. J. Renier, 'is the story of the experiences of men living in societies.'[10] Notice that he defines 'history' as a 'story', and then recall that a similar identification is made by language: story–history; histoire–histoire; Geschichte–Geschichte; storia–storia; historia–historia (though other words are also used).

[9] See Collingwood (1961), pp. 282, 288. Also ch. 3 above, pp. 67–8.
[10] Renier (1965), p. 33.

## 1    *What is a story?*

Aristotle says that a story is a representation of action with a plot. A story, like a history, is concerned with action. It represents that action through a particular medium, which may consist of words, spoken or written. But the medium of representation may also be pictures – as in paintings, comic strips, cartoons, films and television. Or the medium may be statues, puppets or, finally, living actors on a stage – the form of representation that Aristotle probably had in mind. Whatever the medium, a narrative represents action – a word that includes what people suffer, or experience, as well as what they do. As Aristotle put it, history is about 'what, say, Alcibiades did or what happened to him'.[11] But what is it for this representation to have a plot? Aristotle defines plot as 'the ordered arrangement of the incidents'.[12] This definition leaves two important questions for the composer of the story: which incidents are to be selected and which omitted? And what is the order in which they are to be arranged? It would help our understanding of 'plot' to bear in mind that it involves the two concepts of coherence and of meaning. A plot must have a unity, as Aristotle observes. The story must hang together. The story-teller should not wander from the point and bring in irrelevancies. But the story must also have some significance; it must find some echo in our minds; otherwise, we ask, what is the point of it? So, to repeat, any story (whether a tragedy of Shakespeare, a massive work of history or an anecdote told in a bar) is a representation of action with a plot. But there is something more. We have forgotten the audience. Narration (the telling of a story) implies one or more persons to whom the story is told. And, as any practised raconteur knows, the nature of the audience influences the story, in respect both of what incidents are selected and of how they are told.

Clearly history and narrative have much in common. But, in spite of the implications of language, they are not the same thing: many narratives are fictitious, therefore not historical; many histories claim to be true but are not stories. Let us see how they differ.

## 2    *How fictional and historical narratives differ*

In order to make a systematic comparison it will be convenient to deal with the essential elements of narrative separately. In what follows I mostly use the novel as the representative type of fiction. But my remarks apply to all types of fictional narrative.

---

[11] See Aristotle (1965), p. 44.
[12] Ibid., p. 39.

(a) *Beginning*    To find a starting-point the narrator frequently selects a person or event significant for what follows. 'It was Apollo, son of Zeus and Leto, who started the feud . . .' is how Homer begins the *Iliad*. But how can the historian start without breaking the continuity of history? The great narrative historians, Thucydides, Gibbon, Prescott, mention the war, the Empire, and Mexico in their opening sentences.

(b) *Subject*    The role of the subject in fiction is to focus the action. The narrative centres on him, both for his deeds and for his awareness: Hamlet, Tom Sawyer, Elizabeth Bennet. But history lacks such a central subject. A few attempts to write history around one man (e.g. Carlyle's *Frederick the Great* or Schlesinger's *The First Thousand Days*) have tried to supply the missing subject, but for most history it is hardly worth trying.

The hero or heroine in fiction is not only a centre of interest for the reader. He or she also supplies a 'single temporally continuous conscious-ness' – i.e. an awareness of most of the action.[13] To be sure, such a central consciousness is not always that of the hero. Sometimes (as with Mr Lockwood in Emily Brontë's *Wuthering Heights*) it is that of the observer. The point for us is that in history it is lacking. In fiction the period of action can be contained in one lifetime – and usually much less. Thus the reader can identify himself with this central consciousness – and temporarily forget his real life. I spent many happy hours of boyhood being d'Artagnan or Jim Hawkins. But whoever felt that he was the American Constitution or the peasants of Languedoc?

(c) *Events*    These are significant happenings of long or short duration. The novelist may invent them as required; the historian may not. The latter has to ask what real events are significant for her narrative. And if she is a conscientious historian she must be sure that what are significant for her narrative were actually significant for the course of history.[14]

(d) *Characters*    These are the participants in the action, 'who', as Aristotle says, 'necessarily display certain distinctive qualities both of character and of thought.'[15] Much of the interest of a story comes from the interplay and contrasts between well-defined characters. History, however, does not afford its narrator such luxuries. He has to deal not only with individuals as he finds them – by no means always well defined or conveniently contrasted – but also with large groups of people or, worse, institutions and organizations that are not people at all. How is he

---

[13] Olafson (1979), p. 79. I am indebted to Olafson for several points here.
[14] For a fuller discussion of events in history, see ch. 7, below.
[15] Aristotle (1965), p. 39.

to characterize them? The narrator of fiction rarely attempts such a task, and even more rarely does he succeed.

*(e) Setting*   The setting forms the background – human, artificial, or natural – against which the characters stand out. Sometimes the setting sets the mood of the story – *Wuthering Heights* again. For the historical narrator, however, the setting is less of a foil to the characters than a continuation of them. Even kings are part of the scene in which they act. And when historians extend the setting to the geographical, economic, social and cultural circumstances, these form part of the story, not merely a stage for the actors. Moreover, there is the difference that, in fiction, the setting tends to remain unchanged (as in the theatre, at least for long periods), while the historian knows, even if he ignores it, that the setting is constantly changing. In non-narrative histories, as we shall see, the setting can replace the story and its characters.

*(f) Sequence*   Events in the story succeed one another, arousing expectation. 'What did she say to that?' asks the eager listener. 'Then what happened?' Such questions, apparently about mere sequence, are actually about stronger ties in the narrative. They are about cause and effect, driving the story from one event to the next. In fiction the causal connections have to be made clear to the reader – if not at once, then later, as in detective stories. They usually consist of human intentions or reactions. A novelist is little concerned with the sort of causes and effects that interest a scientist. Nor can the novelist introduce sheer chance if he wishes to write a convincing tale. Of a strange coincidence occurring in real life it is often remarked that no novelist would dare to use it. The historian has different problems. First, he has to determine (not invent) the sequence of events. Next, he has to establish, to his own and his readers' satisfaction, which sequences are merely chronological and which are causal. Thirdly, he has to go beyond the easily understood actions and responses of our everyday personal exchanges to the deeper and less understood causal forces of psychology and society. It is often in such as these, obscure as they may be, that he has to seek for explanation. Finally, and unlike the novelist, he is at liberty to admit the force of coincidence, of sheer chance.[16]

*(g) Plot*   Such entailments of actions are not the plot of the story, though they may form part of it. Plot, as we have seen, is the 'ordered arrangement of the incidents', though they do not have to be related in the order in which they happen.[17] They are arranged in a way that best allows the reader to grasp the story as a whole. Now a plot is a whole in several

[16] For fuller discussion of causation, see ch. 8, pp. 194–204 below.
[17] Aristotle (1965), p. 39. The *Odyssey* admirably illustrates the point.

senses. First, it is greater than the sum of its parts. Next, each part is integrally related to the whole. Thirdly, it is complete: nothing essential has been omitted. Lastly, it has a meaning: it makes an impression that lingers in the mind. All these requirements present great problems for the narrative historian. If he does succeed in meeting them all it is almost certain that he has done it at the expense of truth – or, at any rate, of historical validity. How, for example, can he be sure that nothing essential has been omitted, or that he has correctly discerned the meaning of the events he has related?

*(h) Perspective*  With fiction the narrator may place himself inside or outside the story, close to or remote from the action in time or space; he may adopt any attitude, from warm sympathy to cold distaste. This the reader is subtly invited to share. The opening words of a novel not only start the action; they often show the reader where to stand in order to view it. The historian, however, has only one place to stand – his own. He is permitted only one attitude – that of the impartial observer, unmoved equally by admiration or repugnance. Nor does he presume to dictate the reader's response; he simply relates the facts.

*(i) Verisimilitude*  A fiction cannot be truth. But, to be convincing, it must be like the truth. However marvellous the tale (e.g. *The Thousand and One Nights* or science fiction), the characters and at least some of the events should be so credible that we may willingly suspend our disbelief. The author of a historical narrative cannot shape the events or the personages to suit our credulity. He must tell the truth, however strange. But he may use his skill in description and explanation so that we can understand and appreciate what people did and why they did it.

*(j) Internal time*  Every story has its own time – the period of hours, days or years that is supposed to elapse between the beginning and end. It is quite distinct from the real time that we spend in reading it. In the case of historical narrative it is a more complex question how 'story time' relates to 'real time'. Unlike fiction, the case here is that the 'story time' and 'real time' all belong to the same time sequence. Moreover, both the agents in the story and the writer and readers outside it are conscious of their places in that time sequence – i.e. they possess 'historicity'.[18] Indeed, they may all be aware of the same past. For example, the subjects of the Roman Empire, Edmund Gibbon who related the collapse of that empire, and we who read his history over two centuries later were and are quite aware of the origins of that empire in the Roman Republic and its overthrow by Julius and Augustus Caesar. For over 2,000 years Europeans have known a common past.

---

[18] The theme is pursued further in Olafson (1979).

*(k) Ending*   A good story does not just stop; it comes to a conclusion. The ending, like the beginning, is chosen for its significance. In the best stories we feel that the end was entailed by all that went before, and sometimes that it explains all that. The historian cannot be so fortunate. Wherever he chooses to end his narrative, he knows that it is not a conclusion; life goes on. His stopping-place cannot have been entailed by all that went before; there are too many threads in history. Worst of all, it cannot be a full explanation, if only because he has not been able to give a full description of the events in his narrative. As Danto has pointed out, we cannot properly describe any historical event until we know its consequences – and that will not be before the end of time.[19] For this reason alone all historiography is merely an interim report.

*(l) Truth*   This is, of course, the fundamental difference; history purports to be true; fiction does not. Yet we have seen that this is only one of many aspects of narrative where history and fiction differ.


## 3   The development of narrative history

Narrative was the common mode of the earliest forms of historiography (Thucydides, Polybius, Livy, Tacitus). Since their revival in the Renaissance the skills of the narrative historian have been progressively developed. This may be conveniently illustrated from the writing of history in England.

In the sixteenth century appeared many of the first printed histories of England. These often consisted of little more than 'scissors-and-paste' work – snippets abstracted from medieval chronicles arranged in order. Such a work was less a story than 'a rope of sand'.[20] When historians learned to trace cause and effect the 'rope' gained more substance and the narrative more continuity; there was now something like a story to follow. This lesson appears to have been learnt from chronicles. So-called 'contemporary history' has often been called into question. History, it is argued, needs to be written long after the events so that they may be seen in perspective and their significance understood in the light of their consequences. Nevertheless it seems clear that chroniclers, writing about the events they lived through, were for long superior in method to historians. For while the latter simply raided old writings to make a mere collage, the former tried to explain the reasons for the actions they related. For example, the Anglo-Saxon Chronicle for AD 1100 reads: 'Then before Michaelmas, Anselm, archbishop of Canterbury, returned to this country, *since* King Henry had sent for him, *following* the advice of his councillors, for he had left the country *on account* of the great injustice which king

---

[19] See Danto (1965), pp. 61 ff. See also Kermode (1967).
[20] Butterfield (1968), p. 167. I owe much of this section to Butterfield.

William had done to him.'[21] Note how an explanatory reason is given three times in one sentence. In addition, such contemporary writers often inquired into various sources of information, both oral and documentary, that were available to them, and even compared them in search of the most truthful account. Such advances in explanation, in research and in criticism were first practised in contemporary history and then brought to the more conventional history about the remote past. As Butterfield remarks, a contemporary who had lived through the events, 'would have a feeling for the flow of things.'[22]

In historians of the seventeenth century – Bacon, Ralegh, Clarendon, Burnet – may be found other signs of progress. Ralegh added political maxims, Clarendon and Burnet vivid personal portraits, and Clarendon, writing of his own experience, could explain the controversial and crucially important Grand Remonstrance of 1641 by a detailed narrative. This is a good example of Oakeshott's dictum that 'history accounts *for* change by means of a full account *of* change.'[23] A more important and subtle change also appears in the writing of Bacon and (in the eighteenth century) Hume. This is the view of history as a process, involving both human and non-human causes – a process that has a driving force of its own. This view contrasts with the earlier understanding of history where everything is attributed (as in the above example) to either human or divine will. Thus there comes into historiography, perhaps as a result of the Scientific Revolution of the seventeenth century and of the eighteenth-century Enlightenment, a recognition of the role played by the background or setting of the story. This may easily be seen in Macaulay's justly popular *History of England* (1849–61). He begins by announcing that he will not write only of politics: 'It will be my endeavour to relate the history of the people as well as the history of the government, to trace the progress of useful and ornamental arts . . .'[24] Then he devotes a very long third chapter to a description of England in 1685. This was, perhaps, the first attempt by a major historian to write economic and social history as part of his narrative. Both historical research and historiography made great advances in the succeeding century and a half, and Macaulay is no longer an authority, but it is to be doubted whether, in English at least, he has ever been matched as a narrative historian.

## 4  *The Eclipse of Narrative*

Surprisingly enough, some of the merits of good narrative were to develop in a way that nearly put paid to narrative as a mode of history. One of them is the use of selection. Any history, of course, has to be selective, for

---

[21] Anglo-Saxon Chronicle (1953), p. 235 (my italics).
[22] Butterfield (1968), p. 170.
[23] See Oakeshott (1933), p. 143.
[24] Macaulay (1931), vol. I, p. 2.

not every event can be described. Yet there remains the doubt that this may be done at the expense of strict truth. Are there not relevant facts which the narrator has, perhaps half-unconsciously, omitted because they would bend the direction or halt the flow of his tale? And even the most scrupulous historian may, with a good conscience, omit details which *she* thinks unimportant or irrelevant but which we, if we knew of them, would not. Then there is the question of certainty. Since all history rests on whatever evidence happens to remain, it is rarely possible for the historian to be certain that she fully comprehends a past situation or set of actions. For this reason Bismarck opposed the keeping of diplomatic archives. 'As for using them some day as material of history, nothing of any value will be found in them . . . Even the despatches which do contain information are scarcely intelligible to those who do not know the people and their relations to one another.'[25] One can see his point. So often the honest researcher has to admit that, bearing in mind this inevitable ignorance, the existing evidence does not point totally and absolutely to any one conclusion. She must judge on a balance of probabilities. History has none of the certainty of mathematics. But one can hardly build a gripping story where almost every statement is qualified with 'it seems', 'perhaps', 'the probability is', and suchlike. Did Macaulay ever feel such doubts? 'I wish', his friend Melbourne once remarked, 'that I was so cocksure of anything as Tom Macaulay is of everything.' Thus we may suspect that the most scrupulously accurate of histories is not the most readable.

But there is a greater difficulty. This arises from the distinction between men and circumstances (or characters and setting). Early historians used to focus almost exclusively upon a few main characters, with occasional scattered references to the common people. But as historical understanding developed historians felt it necessary to paint in more of the circumstances. This was not merely to make the story more realistic; it was also to achieve deeper insights. For not even kings and heroes can ignore the weather, finance, the willingness of men to leave home and fight, or the growth of grass essential for mounted warriors. But as historians recognized the importance of geographical, technical, religious, social, fiscal, psychological elements in human affairs, so it became less and less possible to tell a straightforward story.

Thus the circumstances of the story came more and more to crowd in upon the actions of men and women. The problem they posed was twofold: How were ever longer and more elaborate descriptions and analyses of these elements to be woven into the narrative without breaking the thread? More fundamentally, exactly what part did this or that circumstance play in the action? And, most difficult of all, how did

[25] See E. L. Woodward, in Sutherland (1966), p. 303.

the circumstances combine with the actions of men and women to weave the complicated web we call history?

This last is a question that few historians have attempted to answer in general. However, the necessity of bringing men and circumstances together was recognized and was tackled in different ways. Perhaps one of the commonest, though also one of the lamest, was to write chapters of political narrative interrupted from time by quite separate chapters dealing with economic or religious or social or cultural 'background'. Little attempt was made to integrate this material with the main narrative, and one sometimes finds that these subsidiary chapters are not themselves integrated, but contain little more than a disconnected series of topics. As one critic has put it, 'History may be either narrated or expounded: but there are forms of itemization which are neither story nor explanation, and it is difficult to discover the purpose of these.'[26]

## 5   Can we get rid of narrative?

As a result some historians decided to break away from narrative and construct their studies on a different pattern. (Non-narrative history is discussed in Section C below). For history does not have to be narrative history. But can history be completely separated from story – 'histoire' from 'histoire', 'Geschichte' from 'Geschichte'? What lies behind Gallie's assertion that 'historical understanding is the exercise of the capacity to follow a story'?[27] Is Ricoeur right when he says: 'If history were to break every connection to *our basic competence for following a story . . .* it would . . . cease to be historical'?[28]

If there is indeed an irreducible element of narrative in our understanding of history, where does it come from? Is it to be found in the course of history itself – history(1)? Or is it written in by the historian – history(2)? Do historical events shape themselves in the form of a story? Or is a story a construct of the narrator who assembles his material into an attractive form, just as Velasquez assembled the colours on a palette to paint the Rokeby Venus? I will now review some of the different positions taken on this question of where the narrative in history comes from.

## 6   Narrative is found in the events

The first position is that narrative is inherent in history. Tell what happened and there you have a story. This is the common-sense view which is reflected in the similarity of the words in many languages for 'story' and 'history'. The man in the street takes it for granted that the story he reads in history books (books sometimes entitled *The Story of*

---

[26] Butterfield (1968), pp. 172–3.
[27] Gallie (1964), p. 105.
[28] Ricoeur (1984), p. 91.

. . .) is the true story, or as near as may be. He assumes that events bore the shape of the narrative he reads. And not only the common reader takes this view. Gallie's opinion (quoted above) is well known. Less well-known is the rest of the sentence: 'where the story is known to be based on evidence and is put forward as a sincere effort to get at *the* story so far as the evidence and the writer's general knowledge and intelligence allow' (the italics are Gallie's).[29] The reference to '*the story*' implies that there exists one true story in, and of, the events. This is the common-sense view.

Another well-known writer on history is the historian E. H. Carr. He confesses: 'For myself, as soon as I have got going on a few of what I take to be the capital sources, the itch becomes too strong and I begin to write.'[30] I think we may assume that in writing his long, multi-volume history of Soviet Russia he had no doubt that the narrative he wrote was a story that bore the shape of events. And is it not the attitude of all sincere historians?

Gallie says that to understand history is simply to be able to follow a story. We all acquire this ability in childhood – much to our delight. Since he makes no distinction here between history(1) and history(2), we may assume that he believes that in following the historian's narrative – history(2), the reader is understanding the events – history(1). For him, as for the common man, the course of history and the course of the narrative bear nearly enough the same shape.

## 7    Narrative is made up by the historian: (a) Veyne's view

The second position is the direct contrary. This is the view that the events of history – history(1) – have no shape in themselves and do not naturally form a narrative. The story-shape that they appear to have in a work of history is given them by the narrator. For such a view we may first look at the French historian Paul Veyne who writes, 'The field of history is thus completely undetermined – with one exception: everything in it must really have taken place.'[31] For Veyne facts do not become material for history until they have been ordered by some organizing narrator or reader. So where does the story come from? It comes, says Veyne, from the plot. A plot he defines as 'a very human and not very "scientific" mixture of material causes, aims, and chances – a slice of life, in short, that the historian cuts as he wills and in which facts have their objective connections and their relative importance . . .'[32] He sees the plot as a route or itinerary traced by the historian across the field of events. The latter is perfectly free to choose his own route and all routes are equally

[29] See Gallie (1964), p. 105.
[30] E. H. Carr (1964), p. 28.
[31] Veyne (1984), p. 15.
[32] Ibid., p. 32.

legitimate – though they are not all equally interesting.[33] No historian can describe the totality of the field, for a route has to make choices and cannot go everywhere. None of these routes is the Truth, nor is it History. Nor does the field contain places which the historian's routes can visit and call events; an event is not a thing, it is an intersection of possible routes.[34] As Paul Ricoeur aptly puts it, 'The force of Paul Veyne's book is . . . the idea that history is only the construction and understanding of plots.'[35]

## 8   Narrative is made up by the historian: (b) Mink's view

A similar, but slightly different, view has been put forward by the American philosopher, Louis O. Mink. He, too, sees narratives as artificial but he does not use the idea of plot. Instead he has the notion of an overall view of the relevant facts. It is, he says, 'the problem of comprehending them (the constituent events) in an act of judgement which manages to hold them together', rather than reviewing them one by one. While Veyne sees the historian tracing his way laboriously along a particular route through the 'field of events', Mink sees him as standing above that field and perceiving (rightly or wrongly) a certain pattern within that field. He calls it 'synoptic judgement'.[36] It is a sort of bird's eye view.

## 9   Narrative is made up by the historian: (c) White's view

Another American philosopher, Hayden White, is more forthright. He denies that history itself is story-shaped. He dismisses as palpably untrue the view that 'history itself was a congeries of lived stories awaiting only the historian to turn them into prose equivalents.'[37] Historical narratives are not copies of story-shaped history, but are 'verbal fictions, the contents of which are as much invented as found, and the forms of which have more in common with their counterparts in literature than they have with those in the sciences'.[38] The element of fiction comes in because the historical narrative is 'a verbal artifact that purports to be a model of structures and processes that are long past and cannot therefore be subjected to either experimental or observational controls'.[39] To put it simply, the historian does not make up facts; in this way he tells the truth. But he makes up the story. It is in this sense that historical narratives are

[33] Ibid., p. 36.
[34] Ibid.
[35] See Ricoeur (1984), vol. I, p. 174.
[36] See Mink, in Dray (1966), pp. 178, 191.
[37] See H. White (1987), p. 170.
[38] See H. White, 'Historical Text as Literary Artifact', in Canary and Kozicki (1978), p. 42.
[39] Ibid.

'verbal fictions'. Historical evidence does not give us any story at all; at most it gives us story-elements which can be put together in various ways.

## 10   Different stories of the same events

If we consider, for example, the hundreds of books about the French or the American revolution, we find very considerable differences among them. Some of these differences are due to the different evidence at the disposal of the historian, but not very much. The salient facts (the surrender at Saratoga, the fall of the Bastille, and so on) were known to all of them. Further differences are due to selection; one historian will include events that another will omit. But even this does not account for the fact that we seem to be reading quite different stories that have, and are intended to have, quite different effects upon us. At the end of the story we ask, 'What does it all add up to?' 'What is the point of it all?' This is distinct from Gallie's assertion that in order to understand history we have to be able to follow a story. We have, let us suppose, done this; we have followed and understood the sequence of events (the What? and the How?) from beginning to end. But we have now to consider the story as a whole. Here we perceive the plot of the story, by which the story makes sense.

## 11   Methods of Emplotment

A Canadian literary critic, Northrop Frye, has explained that the plots of stories make sense to us because (throughout our lives and throughout nearly 3,000 years of literary tradition) we have become familiar with a few basic kinds of plot: Romance, Tragedy, Comedy and Satire.[40] As White says, 'Providing the "meaning" of a story by identifying the *kind of story* that has been told is called explanation by emplotment. If in the course of narrating his story, the historian provides it with the plot structure of a Tragedy, he has 'explained' it in one way; if he has structured it as a Comedy, he has 'explained' it in another way.[41] Historians provide 'sets of past events with meanings' using the 'similarities between sets of real events and the conventional structures of our fictions.'[42] In this analysis of historiography White argues that the shape and meaning of historical narratives are not in history at all, but in the historian. He insists that history benefits from his approach in two ways: one is that this intimate connection between literature and history is not a

[40] For his explanation and examples of these, see Frye (1971), especially pp. 162–3, 186, 206, 223.
[41] See H. White, (1973), p. 7.
[42] H. White, 'The Historical Text as Literary Artifact', in Canary and Kozicki (1978), p. 53.

weakness but one of history's strengths; the other is that history thrives upon the discovery of all the plot-structures possible for a given set of events – though all may not be equally suitable for any one set.[43]

## 12   *Narrative form is in the action – Olafson*

The third position is different again. Unlike the second (pp. 96–8 above), it does not hold that history is written according to recognized literary conventions – Tragedy, Satire, etc. But unlike the first position, it does not insist that there is *one* (and by implication the only true) story to be told of a set of events. Position 3 insists that *narrative form* is found in history itself, but there may be more than one story to be told of it. Thus history is always *story-shaped*, though not necessarily in the shape of only one story. This argument rests on human experience and human action, something that we have already looked at in previous chapters. In support of this thesis are two American philosophers, Frederick A. Olafson and David Carr. Olafson puts it crisply: 'The rational structure of action is the structure of narrative.'[44] Of this structure of narrative Olafson makes several general arguments, two of which are relevant here. The first is 'that human actions are the primary events with which the historian deals and that the historical narrative is to be understood as the reconstruction of a sequence of human actions within which one action and its consequences become the premise for a succeeding action and so on.' As we know, the fundamental work of the historian is always to say *what* happened and *how* it came about. Olafson is here claiming that the 'Whats' of history are human actions. Every action brings about results, intended or unintended. These results form part of the people's reasons for the next actions. The 'Hows', then, are human motivation and decision, not impersonal 'laws' of history. Olafson's second point is 'that it is a condition of grasping this kind of action-based continuity of historical narrative that the actions themselves be identified by the historian under the descriptions which the agent may be supposed to have used as well as those used by those who were in some way affected by those actions'.[45] This is to say that the actions are to be described as the agents saw them. For example, the panic-stricken Commune of Paris in September 1792 permitted 'citizens' courts' to kill without trial hundreds of prisoners. History knows this as 'the September Massacres'. But to the killers these were acts of justice and of patriotism. Olafson's point is that we shall not understand these actions if we describe them as we see them – as massacres. We must identify them – odious as this may seem – 'under the descriptions which the agents may be supposed to have used', i.e. as acts of patriotism and justice. Of course, we must also see them under the

[43] Ibid., pp. 53, 62. Cf. Veyne's view of the plot as itinerary quoted on pp. 96–7 above.
[44] See Olafson (1979), p. 151.
[45] Ibid.

descriptions 'used by those who were in some way affected by those actions'. For the friends of the victims the actions were indeed 'massacres', but Olafson's point stands. One must understand how all those concerned saw the actions, and in what terms they described them, in order to understand what people did next. For a person's actions rest commonly on a practical inference: there is something that I want to bring about; I see that my present situation offers either an opportunity or an obstacle to this; I act accordingly. This brings about a new situation, which offers to me and my contemporaries goals, opportunities or obstacles, means and meanings. We again act accordingly. So human life goes on. It is these practical inferences, made by the agent about what to do in a given situation, that the historian must understand. For these link the sequence of events that he is describing and explaining.[46]

This continuity of action, essential for the historian, is well understood by children. They will interrupt a story to ask, 'But why did he do that?' All the elements of a story; goal, opportunity or obstacle, means to end, opinion of others, assessment of situation are clearly grasped by quite young children. This is the pattern equally of human action and of narrative – or so it is argued by those who maintain this third position.

## 13   Narrative form is in the action: Carr and individuals

This link between life and story is drawn even more closely by David Carr, who believes that we each see our own life as a story.[47] It may help here to recapitulate the positions. Position 1 held that history is in itself a story; we have only to tell the events in order and there we have it. Position 2 denies that historical events have any inherent shape at all; the form of the story is one chosen and given by the historian. Now Carr argues that there *is* a similarity of shape between narrative and reality – a 'community of form', as he puts it. He meets the objections of Position 2 by asserting that the historical reality he is talking about is life experience, what people think and feel about their lives. This is the 'What' of history, for action is what happens and this is what history(2) is about. This view of historical reality is not unlike Collingwood's view that all history is, and must be, the history of thought.[48] In Carr's own words 'Narrative is not merely a possibly successful way of describing events; its structure inheres in the events themselves. Far from being a formal distortion of the events it relates, a narrative account is an extension of their primary features.'[49] Opposing the second position (§§6–10 above), he denies that life is a structureless sequence of isolated events. But, unlike the first position (§5 above), he does not think that a sequence of events forms a

---

[46] Ibid., p. 165. See also the analysis of action in ch. 2, pp. 24–5 above.
[47] See D. Carr (1986a), pp. 117–131. For a fuller statement of his views, see (1986b).
[48] See Collingwood (1961), p. 215.
[49] D. Carr (1986a), p. 117.

story merely by being related in chronological order. The structure that he believes to lie in the events themselves is the structure of action. It is our actions that link events. We find ourselves in a certain situation; we have a goal in view; we take certain steps to attain it. These correspond to the beginning, end and middle of a narrative. We may not attain our goal; unexpected events may prevent it. Both life and stories involve contingency, suspense and uncertainty. But that is how we think and act. We, as it were, throw ourselves forward in thought. We adopt what he calls 'a future retrospective point of view on the present.'[50] This means that, in thinking about our action, we 'throw ourselves forward' into the future to the point where the action will have been completed and we can look back on how we did it. This, Carr says, amounts to telling ourselves a story about it. Often we answer the question 'What are you doing?' by telling a story – a story that identifies the situation, the goal and the means to it. For example, one answer to that question might be: 'I am making some bookshelves. You see, I found I hadn't room for all my books, and I wanted somewhere to keep them.' You will perceive in this reply the situation, the goal and the means, corresponding to the beginning, end and middle of a story. Narrative, therefore (says Carr), does not occur *after* the action; it occurs *with* the action. But after the action we often extend and refine (and perhaps subtly alter) the original story – that is, the story that we told about what we were doing while we were doing it.

Let us remember that the action of story-telling normally involves three roles: those of the narrator (who tells the story), the character(s) (about whom the story is told), and the audience (to whom the story is told). In the 'bookshelf' example above, the first two roles are played by the person who answers; the third role is played by the enquirer. When we tell ourselves a story about what we are doing, we are playing all three roles.[51] This business of constantly telling ourselves the story of our lives as we live them is believed by some philosophers and psychologists to be the very thing that constitutes our sense of self.[52]

## 14   Narrative form is in the action: Carr and societies

But Carr does not stop here, for history is more concerned with groups of people than with individuals. A typical national historian (like Michelet, Macaulay or Bancroft) was a member of a nation telling a story *about* that nation. In such cases the three roles of narrator, characters and audience are played by different individuals, but all within the same

[50] Ibid., p. 125.
[51] See MacIntyre (1981), p. 197: 'It is because we all live out narratives in our lives, and because we understand our own lives in terms of the narratives that we live out, that the form of narrative is appropriate for understanding the actions of others. Stories are lived before they are told – except in the case of fiction.'
[52] Cf. Dennett (1991), pp. 410–18.

group. The parallel with the self telling stories about itself to itself is obvious. It seems that the individual telling his life story to himself as he lives it is what helps to constitute his sense of himself. In the same way a group of people – a nation, a class, a church, a profession – can build a sense of communal identity by, first, sharing in common actions and experiences, and then telling themselves the story of these actions and experiences. We recall Carr's insistence that we do not have to wait until after the events for the story to be told. Journalists and historians only extend and refine the story that we have been telling ourselves as we *live* the events. Those who were in England in the summer of 1940 can recall their sense of living a story as they determined to follow Churchill's lead and to fight on after the fall of France. They did not need to wait for some historian after the war to make a meaningful narrative out of what they were doing. Many young Europeans – in Berlin, Prague or Bucharest – will have similar memories of what they were doing in the dramatic months of 1989. Carr puts it like this: '*We* have an experience in common when *we* grasp a sequence of events as a temporal configuration such that its present phase derives its significance from its relation to a common past and future.'[53]

We saw earlier (chapter 2, p. 24 above) that an action contains the elements of goal, assessment of situation, means to the end and driving force. When we share these elements with others in common experiences and common actions – as at the fall of the Berlin Wall in 1989 or of the Bastille in 1789, then we have a sense of community. '*Then*', the participants might declare, 'we really knew what it was to be German (or French).'

The link with historiography is that the subsequent narratives of journalists, autobiographers and historians do not merely reproduce the stories that we simultaneously live and tell ourselves in the course of the action; they change and improve on the story. But these later literary genres do not produce narrative form and impose it on non-narrative reality. (This is Position 2.) Narrative form, Carr insists, is there already.[54]

## C.  Non-narrative History

### 1  *Why write non-narrative history?*

I have said a good deal about narrative history for two reasons: (1) that narrative is the most familiar form of history (as the name implies and as Gallie argues); (2) that there is an irreducible element of narrative in all history. Nevertheless, most academic works of history are not written in the narrative mode. Why is this?

[53] D. Carr (1986a), p. 127.
[54] Ibid., p. 131.

First, we note that description plays a large part in many narrative histories. The *Histories* of Herodotus (written about 440 BC) contain the most entertaining accounts of life in Egypt and the Near East. Similar rich descriptions adorn the writings of the great Arab historian, Ibn Khaldun (1332–1406). Gibbon and Macaulay took great pains over their 'set pieces'. Voltaire's *The Age of Louis XIV* (1751) was perhaps the first wholly descriptive work of history. Since description has a part in almost any narrative, it is not surprising that eventually it came, in some cases, to take over the whole work. Both Voltaire and Burckhardt showed that history can be written on the 'horizontal' plane of time instead of the traditional 'vertical' plane. In all narratives there is an essential background that has to be described and explained (unless it is immediately obvious) for the reader to be able to follow the tale. This is all the more necessary when elements of the background (a natural catastrophe or a peasant revolt) come into the foreground and play a major part in the story. Thus, while political narrative is the typical form of traditional history, sometimes economic and social circumstances so far obtrude into the story that they have to be recognized as causal factors of some importance. Writers of the eighteenth-century Enlightenment – Voltaire, Vico, Montesquieu, Adam Smith, Adam Ferguson – explored the important place in human life of geographical, economic, social and cultural elements. From then on, although narrative history continued to be written, no conscientious historian could ignore these factors.

## 2   A broader view required

But why should historians take account of them? Why not leave them to the social scientists? For many reasons history has to go beyond the limits of the political narrative. Human life is like a multicoloured tapestry, in which threads of many different kinds are interwoven. The historian cannot confine himself to one type of phenomenon (religious, literary, demographic, fiscal, etc.) if he is to tell a coherent story. This is as true of the economic historian as of the political or social. Economics itself is an austere and abstract discipline. As such it can remain highly theoretical, but once the economic historian descends from these heights to everyday life he finds all sorts of non-economic factors (religious beliefs, social customs, political loyalties) cutting right across his calculations.[55] People just will not behave in an economically rational way. This, in itself, does not make a purely political or economic or religious narrative impossible. But it does show that the life of a society is so complex that it has to be unravelled thread by thread. To speak less metaphorically, it needs to be analysed.

[55] The essays in Cipolla (1991), Floud (1974) or Tenim (1973) afford ample illustration of the point. See above, ch. 3, pp. 70–2.

104 A COMPANION TO THE STUDY OF HISTORY

These 'threads' – economic, geographical, cultural, religious, demographic etc. – need to be understood in their own terms. These 'terms' are often the concepts, language, methods, values of other academic disciplines. It is characteristic of such disciplines (roughly, the social or human sciences) that the dimension of time does not play anything like the essential part that it does in history. Indeed, much of the work done there pays no attention to time at all, any more than in most of the natural sciences. The narrative historian runs through the tapestry of human affairs at speed and with striking effect. The non-narrative historian analyses it, examining it piece by piece and thread by thread. In doing so he is much guided by the relevant social science, which, however, takes little account of time. How is he to integrate these concepts into a history?

## 3 How does a static account deal with change?

The solution usually adopted is to assume that the piece of history he is concerned with (Italy in the age of the Renaissance, England in the Victorian era) can be divided up into several categories (economic, social, religious) or themes ('The state as a work of art'), which are then described in successive chapters. In such cases, unlike narratives, the sequence of reading does not follow the sequence of events.[56]

Two problems are skated over here. One is that of time. The historian in such cases fixes the limits of the age to be described and then draws his material from any point within these limits. This involves the tacit assumption that the phenomena described have undergone no change within that space of time – an assumption that is almost certainly false. Sometimes, the historian divides his book into two or three stages and describes his subject at each of these. In so doing he acknowledges the passage of time between one stage and another but still ignores it within those stages. This is the problem that Braudel saw and to which he proposed the method of his *Mediterranean* – he told the same story three times over at different speeds (see chapter 3, pp. 65–6 above). But, as Hexter pointed out, this does not solve the problem, for history moves at a hundred speeds.[57] The problem, I believe, remains unsolved. Time, which is the very backbone of narrative history, is a real puzzle for the non-narrative historian.

## 4 Problems of analysis

The other problem frequently skated over is that of analysis. As we can easily see from books that describe an age, the society so described can be divided up in many different ways. Does the division of the book into

---

[56] Two noteworthy examples provide fascinating reading: Hale (1971) and Zeldin (1973).
[57] See Hexter (1979), p. 137. Braudel elsewhere acknowledged thousands. See below, ch. 7, p. 172.

chapters coincide with the division of society into its constituent elements? And does every one agree what those elements are? Let us take a famous work of political analysis, Sir Lewis Namier's *England in the Age of the American Revolution*. The divisions are labelled 'The Unreformed House of Commons', 'The Social Structure', 'The Land as Basis of Citizenship', 'The House of Commons and America', and so on. These can hardly claim to be an exhaustive list of the constituent parts even of political England. Are they more than the topics that the author wishes to write about, perhaps because of these he has ample evidence?[58]

It is clear how one thing is related to another in a narrative: it is the plot that holds them together. But by what principle is the subject of non-narrative history (typically a country, a city, an organization or a group of people within the limits of an era) analysed into its constituent parts? And when the parts have been examined, how can they be shown to fit together into the living whole that constitutes history?[59]

These problems have accompanied the broadening of the historical field in the twentieth century. Whereas earlier centuries concentrated largely on politics and religion, the twentieth has seen a vast expansion of subject matter to the point where almost no human activity lacks its historian. There has been a corresponding expansion of admissible evidence, to the point where almost anything can be called upon to tell us about the past. Thus there have arisen many sub-disciplines of history – not only the familiar political, economic and social forms, but also histories of population, of manners, of family, of science, of ideas and so on. These are listed and described in a number of useful volumes.[60]

Each sub-discipline is sustained by one or more learned journals. All have their own attractions and their enthusiastic followers. But the problems about time and about analysis/synthesis that I have sketched above still apply to these sub-disciplines. Even if the problems should prove insoluble they ought still to be faced. Too often they are simply ignored – to the confusion of the enquiring student.

## 5  *Marxists and* Annalistes

Fortunately there are two very active schools of historiography which do not ignore these problems – though their practitioners are not always sufficiently explicit about them. One is Marxist, the other is *Annaliste* – based on the distinguished French journal *Annales: Économies, Sociétés, Civilisations*, founded in 1929 by Lucien Febvre and Marc Bloch. At the risk of oversimplification one can, perhaps, draw a useful contrast between the approaches of these two schools. The *Annalistes* tend

[58] For further discussion see Stanford (1990), pp. 19–20.
[59] For a brief discussion see Hobsbawm in Gilbert and Graubard (1972), pp. 12–13.
[60] Examples are Burke (1991), Rabb and Rotberg (1982), Iggers (1975), Gilbert and Graubard (1972) and Finberg (1962).

towards a structural-functional attitude to society.[61] To elucidate: the structuralist 'aims to discover universal elements in human society'; the functionalist directs 'attention to the actual working of social institutions ... in particular societies'.[62] One might say that the *Annalistes* have tackled problems of analysis/synthesis, especially with their concept of total history or *histoire globale*, but have not fully come to terms with the problems of time. Although the chief exponent of this problem, Fernand Braudel, was the leader of this school for many years, none of his colleagues followed him in his particular form of solution.[63]

On the other hand, the philosophy of Marx centres on the concept of historical development through time by the process of conflict. It has been aptly described as 'a general theory of societies in movement'.[64] But Marxist historiography is weak on the analysis/synthesis problem. Marx's own substructure/superstructure theory is quite inadequate (see chapter 10, p. 270 below.) The best of Marxist historians are not unaware of this. Eric Hobsbawm argues that 'the theoretical constructions of sociology (or social anthropology) have been most successful by excluding history, that is, directional or oriented change.'[65]

But though many historians of both schools use each others' ideas – to their common and mutual benefit – the main problems remain. They are: first, how to make accurate and exhaustive analyses; and second, how to relate the analysed elements to the unceasing flow of historical change.

## D.   Other Relevant Topics

Some may be indicated here, and a few useful books are listed in the bibliography on p. 108.

### 1   *Style*

One subject relevant to communication in history is that of the historian's style. When we read a great writer (Shakespeare, Milton, Pope) we may be struck by the way that the words so closely fit the thoughts. Indeed, it is more than this. The thoughts, given flesh and blood by the words, flow freely, lucidly and attractively. How far can the historian achieve this? Which historians are most successful?

Another aspect of style is that it reflects the personality of the author; in particular, his orientation to the world. The greater his comprehension of life – its joys, its tragedies, its meanings – the more profound his style.

---

[61] See Stoianovich (1976), p. 25.
[62] Bottomore (1971), p. 62.
[63] See Hexter (1979), p. 137. For more on the *Annales* school see Stoianovich (1976) and Burke (1990).
[64] Pierre Vilar, quoted in Stoianovich (1976), p. 131.
[65] Hobsbawm in Gilbert and Graubard (1972), p. 9.

Greatness in the writer calls for greatness in the reader. That is why we can return again and again to the masters and find something more each time. It is not they that are changing; they are maturing us as they deepen our responses.

These two aspects of style do not always come together. In my opinion Edward Gibbon had a superb style that fitted his thoughts and mirrored his personality exactly. If he is compared to his contemporary and acquaintance, Samuel Johnson, I should say that Johnson had the profounder mind and the larger comprehension. But as a stylist he was inferior to Gibbon. A truly great historian (who has, perhaps, never yet appeared) would match both Gibbon and Johnson. Yet they afford us criteria for judging historical writing, past, present and future.

## 2   Narrative

There is a case (as we have seen) for regarding narrative as, in some sense, basic not only to history but to life itself. This theme may be followed up both in the fields of literary studies and in those of philosophy and psychology. It is clear that such writers as Paul Ricoeur, Louis O. Mink, Frederick A. Olafson, Hayden White, David Carr and Noël Carroll have made only a beginning in the applications of narrative theory to the writing of history. There is much more fruitful work yet to be done.

## 3   Non-narrative

Apart from the *Annalistes* and Marxists there are the point-centred approach of Roland Mousnier's *The Assassination of Henri IV*, the prosopographical approach of Simon Schama's *Citizens* and of many business historians, and the *mentalité* studies of Robert Mandrou, Natalie Zemon Davies or Keith Thomas, not to mention the massive development of quantitative history through the use of computers.[66] Guides to some contemporary modes of writing are given in the bibliography. Pertinent is Roland Barthes's remark on the predominance of non-narrative history among contemporary historians 'who deal in structures rather than chronologies'. 'Historical narrative', he declares, 'is dying: from now on the touchstone of history is not so much reality as intelligibility.'[67]

## Conclusion

This chapter has been concerned with the writing of history – historiography. But we must remember that a good deal of historical knowledge is

---

[66] For prosopography a useful introduction is Lawrence Stone's article of that name in Stone (1987).
[67] See Barthes, 'Historical Discourse', in Lane (1970). There is no foreseeable limit to potential subjects for non-narrative history.

conveyed by word of mouth, especially in lectures. More and more, in an increasingly sub-literate world, it is conveyed also through the medium of drama, film, television and other images. That is why I have used the word 'discourse' in the title of this chapter. Theorists of narrative distinguish between 'story' – that which is to be conveyed, and 'discourse' – the process of conveying it. The former is, as it were, an object that could be put on the table and looked at; the latter is extended through a time sequence and has to be followed. It is like the difference between a painting and a piece of music. From the 'process' we now turn to the 'product' – that which historical discourse conveys. This brings us to the subject of what we know, or think we know, about the past. The next chapter is about that sort of knowledge.

## Suggested Reading

Aristotle 1965

Auerbach 1968

Barthes, 1970; 1984

Burke, P. 1991

Butterfield 1950; 1960; 1968

Canary and Kozicki 1978

Cannon 1980

Carlyle 1899

Carr, D. 1986a; 1986b

Carr, E. H. 1964

Carroll 1990

Chatman 1980

Cherry 1966

Cipolla 1991

Clive 1990

Collingwood 1961

Danto 1965

Dennett 1991

Dray 1959; 1974; 1966

Floud 1979

Frye 1971

Gallie 1964

Gay 1975

Gilbert and Graubard 1972

Harte 1971

Hegel 1956

Hexter 1972

Iggers 1975

Iggers and Parker 1980

Kann 1968

Kenyon 1983

Lane 1970

MacIntyre 1981

Mink 1966; 1978

Munz 1977

Norman 1991

Novick 1988

Oakeshott 1967; 1983

Olafson 1979

Parker, C. 1990

Rabb and Rotberg 1982

Ricoeur 1984

Rigney 1990

Stanford 1990

Stoianovich 1976

Stone 1987

White, H., 1973; 1975; 1978a; 1978b; 1987

White, M. 1965

# 5

# History as Knowledge

Historical knowledge is no luxury, or mere amusement of a mind at leisure from more pressing occupations, but a prime duty whose discharge is essential to the maintenance, not only of any particular form or type of reason, but of reason itself.

R. G. Collingwood

For as time lengthens truth is known.

Aeschylus

## Introduction

But is this true? Do we know more or less about the past as time goes on? There is no simple answer, but historians clearly believe that 'as time lengthens' their labours bring us nearer to the truth about the past. What sort of knowledge is it that historical study produces? In the last chapter we looked at how history is written. In this one we discuss the reliability of what historians write.

*Questions about historical knowledge; historical truth; reconstructing the past*

1 How do we know that we are being told the truth?
2 Are all historians biased?
3 Is it possible to write unbiased, objective history?
4 How is it possible to know the past?
5 Do we reconstruct the past, or only construct versions of it?
6 What is the place of imagination in history?
7 What are historical facts?
8 Do historians ever know the exact truth?
9 What precisely do historians know?

We all believe that a good deal is known about the past. States, nations and religions largely justify their existence and authority by certain claims about the past. Art and literature and (perhaps to a lesser extent) science and technology rely upon knowledge of the past. Journalists, politicians, bureaucrats, economists and, finally, historians themselves all base their words and their careers on what they believe is known about the past. But how reliable is historical knowledge?

This chapter is divided into four parts:

A    What is Historical Knowledge?
B    Construction or Reconstruction?
C    Fact, Truth and Objectivity.
D    Imagination.

## A.   What is Historical Knowledge?

### 1    *Knowledge defined*

What is it to know something? **A philosopher might reply that a person, A, can claim to know a proposition, p, if, and only if, the following conditions are satisfied:**

1    **A believes p;**
2    **A has good grounds for believing p;**
3    **p is actually the case.**

Thus, Mary Smith could claim to *know* that the North won the American Civil War because

1    she believes that the North won;
2    she has spent a whole term in college studying the war;
3    the North did actually win.

Here, it seems, is a good case of historical knowledge. But let us take John Brown who claims to know that Luther purified the Christian religion in the sixteenth century. We may grant (1), that he believes it; we may even grant (2), since he has made deep but one-sided researches into the Germany of Luther's time. But we might not be prepared to grant (3), that Luther actually did what John claimed. Or let us take Horatio Walde-grave, a classical scholar, who claims that King Agamemnon of Mycenae led a great naval expedition and captured Troy. Here, again, we might grant that he has satisfied conditions (1) and (2) about believing and having good grounds. But we cannot grant condition (3), because, here again, there is no certainty of it.

### 2    *Historical knowledge must rest on evidence*

The strength of John's and Horatio's claims does not rest on condition (1) – for belief is not enough to justify knowledge. (Some of us, like the White

Queen in *Alice Through the Looking Glass*, can believe six impossible things before breakfast.) Nor do they rest on condition (3), for these are highly disputable propositions. Any validity for John's and Horatio's knowledge-claims must rest on condition (2); that is, upon historical evidence. But Mary Smith, who has been to a good college, is quick to point out to them that they should make a more thorough study of the evidence. If they did so, they would find that there was also evidence *against* their beliefs. Thus, on the philosopher's criteria, they cannot claim to *know* the propositions about Luther and Agamemnon. The most they can claim is that the balance of evidence tilts in their favour. They then round upon Mary. She claims that her belief about the Civil War is real knowledge, unlike theirs. 'Real knowledge!' they exclaim. 'How do you make that out?' 'Because I, unlike you, claim to know something that really happened', she retorts smugly. 'How do you know it happened?' 'Because all the evidence is in favour', she replies. 'All? Have you examined all possible evidence for that war?' 'Well, no. But all that I have examined points my way.' 'Exactly the same with us', John and Horatio reply. 'You claim that the balance of historical evidence tilts in your favour. We admit that the tilt is more marked in your case than in ours, but what, in principle, is the difference? You cannot satisfy all three conditions any more than we can. For, although we all agree that the North won the Civil War, there are no grounds for that other than condition (2), the historical evidence. We cannot, therefore, grant that your belief is, in fact, the case (condition 3); but only that there are good grounds for it.'

From the above conversation we may conclude that there is something slightly odd about historical knowledge, for it cannot, in principle, satisfy all three of the philosopher's requirements. In the case of historical knowledge it seems that the third condition always boils down to the second one. This seems not to be the case in ordinary everyday examples of knowledge, as in 'I know that I am typing this sentence.'

## 3  Three presuppositions of historical knowledge

So now let us see what we *can* be sure of.

First, history claims to be concerned with what has really taken place.[1] There are difficulties about what, exactly, did and what did not happen. But once we have decided that something did *not* happen, that something is cast out of history and relegated to the realms of fiction or of error. We cannot admit make-believe.

Second, historical knowledge rests upon the interpretation of evidence. There is no way of getting at the past but by what remains in the present. This includes ruins, documents, memories, and other things. Further, since

[1] See pp. 129–30 below.

we can never be sure that we have all the relevant evidence, and since people often disagree about how to interpret what evidence we have, it must be concluded that in many cases historical knowledge is no more than a balance of probabilities. Of course, in many other cases historical knowledge amounts to near certainty, but with history even certainty rests on no other basis than the interpretation of evidence.

Third, at the root of so many difficulties lies time. Historical knowledge is not about present truths (as in the example above of my typing), nor is it about supposedly timeless truths like 'Water is composed of oxygen and hydrogen.' Historical knowledge always involves time, because it involves the distance in time between the present and some point in the past – a distance of minutes or of thousands of years. But time is usually involved in a second way too. The event or state of affairs that we are interested in (for example the assassination of Abraham Lincoln or the institution of feudalism in medieval Europe) has also an extension in time, be it of micro-seconds or of centuries. And time itself is something of a mystery. It is nearly 1,600 years since St Augustine confessed his ignorance.[2] Of course, we are much wiser nowadays. Anyone can explain time. Just try . . .

## 4    *The dimension of time*

**Perhaps those three presuppositions are all that we need for a definition of history. Provided that reality, interpretation of remains, and time are involved, we have history.** Thus, with these three, anything can be treated historically; we can have histories of limestone or earthworms or chairs or cheese or banking or opera. History, as has been abundantly demonstrated in this century, need not be confined to kings and battles and great men. Perhaps history is to be regarded not so much as a discipline with a particular subject matter (like botany, for example), but rather as a *way* of knowing, or a mode of knowledge. The world can be treated in various ways. We can treat it practically, using it for our purposes, like making a rabbit hutch or arranging a foreign holiday. It can be treated scientifically and theoretically, trying to establish general laws about the formation of crystals or the direction-finding of migrating birds. It can be treated mathematically – the realm of statistics and computers. But it can also be treated historically, and seen as a series of phenomena extended in the dimension of time.[3]

Not every one would agree with this view of history, though it is found in that remarkable best-seller, Stephen Hawking's *A Brief History of Time*. No one could take a larger view of time than Hawking, going back, as he does, to the moment of the origin of the universe and even

[2] See below, ch. 7, p. 182.
[3] For further discussion of time, see ch. 7, pp. 182–92, below.

speculating about the contraction of the universe so that time ran backwards. Yet other definitions of history would restrict it to human life only, which would take it back no further than 50,000 or 5 million years, according to how one defines 'human'. The definition favoured by most historians would commence history about 5,000 years ago.[4] Hegel, more restrictive still, believed that only those peoples who were themselves conscious of having a history, of living in history, could be regarded as historical peoples.[5]

## 5   Knowledge in three forms

History, however we define it, seems to entail knowledge of the past.[6] I said earlier that we need only three things for history: past reality, interpretation of remains, and time. How do we build historical knowledge out of these?

(i)   Let us consider the main forms that knowledge takes. The first is that of direct experience, mostly through the senses. (Some people would claim that *all* direct experience is sensory; this question need not detain us here.) In my daily life I am well aware of what is around me: the people, the house, the traffic, and so on. I am very certain of these. Yet so far I am little more than an intelligent animal − like a dog or a chimpanzee.

(ii)   But my knowledge extends further. I have received a good deal of information beyond my direct experience − from books, newspapers, television, photographs and word of mouth. Thus I know quite a lot about Japan or the Moon in spite of never having been there. Such secondary, or indirect, knowledge is often confirmed by direct experience, or primary knowledge. Thus when I visited New York for the first time I was not surprised to see skyscrapers, nor to find that Manhattan was surrounded by water. I had little difficulty in making my way around because I already knew the numbering of the streets and avenues. Such advance information came in several forms. Some of it (for example, photographs of skyscrapers) was a copy or representation of a sense experience. When I saw a skyscraper it was instantly recognizable from pictures I had seen. My knowledge that Manhattan was an island came from a map. From a third source (word of mouth) I knew that the roads were named by consecutive numbers, with the avenues running north–south and the streets east–west. In making my way around the city I had to use a fourth source of knowledge, my reason. No photograph, map or remark had told me that, as I walked up Fifth Avenue, 45th Street would be three blocks up from 42nd Street. I worked that out.

(iii)   This application of reason to secondary knowledge opens up a

---

[4] See below, ch. 7, p. 176. Also G. J. Renier quoted on p. 87 above.
[5] See ch. 7, p. 181.
[6] For the view that we cannot know the past, see below, pp. 129–30.

whole world of generalized knowledge. That objects in a vacuum fall with an acceleration of 32 ft per second per second, that water freezes at 0°C, that birds come from eggs – these are examples of generalized (or tertiary) knowledge. Most scientific knowledge takes this form. Reason plays a large part in both the building up of such knowledge (for example, by forming and testing hypotheses) and in applying it – as I did in finding 45th Street. The great advantages of this kind of knowledge are that it comes in very concentrated form (which makes it easy to convey and to retain) and yet it can be used on a large number of occasions.

## 6   Knowledge of the past: an example

Now what about knowledge of the past? In various ways it seems to share in all these kinds of knowledge. Yet there is something puzzling about the past. It's not there. My typewriter and Manhattan and birds' eggs and freezing water and even the moon are all part of the world as we see it. But Alexander the Great and the American Civil War and my grandmother seem not to be around. Where are they? How can I claim to know them?

Well, take my grandmother. Her photograph looks at me as I write. I remember her very well. There are other mementoes of her – letters, books, personal possessions. But if I claim to know her it is largely on the grounds of memory. This, I think, is the nearest I can come to direct experience of her. But I know more about her than this. There is also what others have told me about her, there are photographs, writings etc. These constitute indirect knowledge of her, corresponding to the indirect knowledge of Manhattan before I went there. So much for primary and secondary knowledge.

What can I learn from generalized knowledge – the third kind? She ate and drank and wore clothes; she married and had children, lived to a good age, and so on. All this could be inferred from the fact that I knew my grandmother. But the really interesting things about her cannot be deduced from such generalities; that she was a vegetarian and refused to wear leather shoes; that she educated all her children personally; that she would go out in the middle of the night to help a sick neighbour. From all these it may be inferred that she was a woman of strong character. The inference goes like this: England in her day was a conventional society, and women in particular were expected to adhere to conventions. Any woman who went against them and yet kept the good opinion of her neighbours must have had a strong character. This looks like a deduction from one of Hempel's covering laws. How much help is such a deduction?

Does it tell us anything new about her? Anyone who had not known her directly might have recognized her strong character from secondary information about her without the help of a covering law. Nor does the covering law explain *why* she had a strong character, though this would be interesting to know. Thus knowledge of the generalized (tertiary) kind is of limited use in history. It only comes into play when a good deal of such knowledge has already been acquired by primary and secondary methods. This includes knowing how far and in what circumstances any general law is applicable to a particular occasion. By the time all that has been ascertained the general law may have little more to tell us. But a greater weakness of generalized knowledge is that, by its very nature, it overlooks the exceptional and unexpected. These are just the cases that interest us.[7]

## 7   Primary knowledge of the past

I have dwelt at some length on my grandmother because knowledge of a close relative is fairly easy to come to terms with. But what about Alexander the Great and the American Civil War? It is rather these that are considered the stuff of historical knowledge. How can we claim to know them, and the rest of history?

At first we are inclined to rule out primary knowledge at once. No one now alive can remember the American Civil War, much less the Battle of Hastings or Alexander the Great. It looks as if we are reduced to secondary and tertiary knowledge only. But has memory no part to play? Perhaps it has at least in folk memory. In this, certain ideas, beliefs and attitudes are handed down from one generation to the next, often in an unformulated way quite distinct from explicit information. For example, though I was born after the First World War, I have a very clear impression of my parents' and grandparents' feelings about it. This was distinct from, and more powerful than, any information I had about the war. Possibly it was because, as a child, I was old enough to be much impressed by their emotions but not old enough to understand factual information. I can understand the generations after Alexander or Hastings or Appomattox handing on in a similar way the deep impressions these had made upon them.

There is another way that memory helps our historical knowledge. Any one of mature years can remember the world of twenty or thirty years back, a world very like that of today, but yet notably different in some respects. It requires no great effort to go further and create a mental picture (a process very similar to remembering, as psychologists tell us) of the same world at a slightly earlier date. A few more adjustments would have to be made (in respect of clothes or motor traffic or entertainment), but it is not too difficult to form a picture of the world in our grandparents' day. We read with ease the fiction of those days. This imaginative creation of an earlier world is what history also is about. The

[7] For Hempel and covering laws, see ch. 8, pp. 214–22 below.

ability to do this seems an extension of the faculty of memory. Imagine a race of beings like ourselves but with no powers of memory, people who lived solely in the present. Would they not find it more difficult to create the picture of an earlier age? They would have no idea, as we have, of how to distinguish the more permanent from the ephemeral, for example. Nor could they enjoy Dickens or Jane Austen.[8]

## 8   Secondary knowledge of the past

But, whatever memory may contribute, there is little doubt that most of our historical knowledge must be of the secondary and tertiary kinds. These we now examine. It will be recalled that my secondary knowledge of Manhattan was of four kinds. First, I had seen pictures of it. Here is an immediate analogy with one kind of historical knowledge. Photographs, paintings, carvings and so on show today what a person or place or object looked like in the past. If you met George Washington you might very well recognize him. Second, I had seen a map. To this correspond not only historical maps (as it might be a street plan of London in the mid-eighteenth century), but also explanatory diagrams of all kinds. Some show the structure of government of, say, Philip II or of Napoleon. Others the organization of the East India Company or the Roman Catholic Church or the Constitution of the USA. But by far the most important for historical knowledge are diagrams of time – lists of kings or presidents, chronological tables of all kinds. Third, I was told about the streets in New York. This is like the chief source of all information for the historian – what comes to him in verbal form. It is not true, as it was once taught, that without documents there can be no history, but it is certainly true that most of our knowledge of the past has come to us in the form of words – some spoken, but the greater part written. Finally, there is what I discovered about Manhattan by my own reasoning powers. Sometimes (as in my example) the reasoning employed is mathematical. This is pretty reliable, provided that the calculations are correct. The increasing use of statistics and computers in historical research shows the efficacy of this method.[9] But reasoning is used (though with less certainty) in other ways, too. This brings us to tertiary or generalized knowledge.

## 9   Tertiary knowledge of the past

Generalized knowledge can take two forms, *a priori* knowledge and empirical knowledge. **The former is defined as that which can be known**

---

[8] For narrative in fiction and history, see ch. 4, pp. 87–102 above.
[9] For the latter, see, for example, Denley and Hopkin (1987), and the journal *History and Computing* (1989–).

**without reference to experience.** The two standard cases of a *priori* knowledge are mathematics and logic. **Empirical knowledge, on the other hand, is derived from experience.** This is the usual kind. Indeed, most of the generalized knowledge that applies to history is empirical.

## 10   *Deduction and induction*

To put it simply, two logical processes are involved in generalizations – **deduction and induction. A deductive argument is one in which it is impossible to assert the premises and deny the conclusion without contradicting oneself.** For example:

> All the squares on this chessboard are either black or white.
> The bottom right-hand square is not black. [These are the premises.]
> Therefore, the bottom right-hand square is white. [Conclusion]

Here it is clear that if you don't accept the conclusion you will have to deny one of the premises. What you cannot do (without self-contradiction) is accept the premises but not the conclusion. The latter inevitably follows from the former. Deductive arguments are pretty certain.

Uncertainty, however, creeps in with induction. To take a well-known example, until about two hundred years ago the swan was the very type of a white bird. Everyone would have agreed that all swans are white, for every swan that had ever been seen was white. The general law 'All swans are white' was inferred from a large number of particular instances: 'This swan is white', and 'This swan is white', and so on. **No exception had ever been found, so the general law was established by what is called 'induction'.** Then black swans were discovered in Australia; the general law was clearly wrong. The procedure of induction was at fault. You may make a generalization from a number of observed particular instances, only to meet one counter-example that disproves it. You may believe, on the basis of your experience, that all Germans are efficient or all Welshmen can sing. Meeting a muddle-headed and incompetent German or a Welshman with a voice like a corncrake would invalidate your inductions. The trouble is that from 'All A's *that I have examined* are p' one cannot conclude that 'All A's are p.' For there is always the possibility that somewhere there is an exception to your generalization, no matter how many observations seem to confirm it.

Nevertheless, though not perfectly reliable, generalizations are very useful. Every car that I have met will turn to the right when the steering wheel is turned to the right. Whenever I drive a car I rely on the general law 'All cars turn right when the steering wheel is turned to the right.' Indeed, I risk my life on it. Yet a friend of mine can tell a hilarious story of collecting his car (faultily repaired) from a closed garage and driving it home with reversed steering; it turned *left* when he turned the wheel to the right. You can never be certain.

## 11   *Generalization in history*

It is clear how this difficulty in logic casts doubt upon the use of generalizations in history. It is possible to make generalizations that are quite sound in the present world, but would be misleading in the past. In Britain today child labour is illegal. It is regarded as morally reprehensible and a sign of acute poverty. Yet in the 1720s the public-spirited Daniel Defoe in his *Tour through the Whole Island of Great Britain* rejoiced to see so many children at work in Yorkshire. It was a sign that there was work for all; therefore the whole family would be properly fed and clothed.

Any student of history can supply examples like this of generalizations, apparently well substantiated, that yet fail at a particular time or place. On the other hand, just as we could not live our daily lives without relying on countless useful (but not infallible) generalizations, so we could not hope to understand the worlds of the past without them. In spite of Waterloo (see below, ch. 8, pp. 220–1), we have to go on assuming that the larger and better army or the more experienced general will win, unless we have evidence to the contrary. This is the case with all generalizations about the past: we have to assume that they apply unless we have good evidence that they do not on any particular occasion. The problem is that the generalization will not tell us which are the particular occasions when it fails to apply. The conclusion is that we have to rely on other types of knowledge to confirm or disconfirm the generalization. It is obvious that we cannot rely on generalizations alone – unless they are of the *a priori* kind, as in mathematics. We must use generalizations only in close co-operation with particular knowledge. Such particular knowledge must, therefore, be of the primary or secondary kind. For events beyond the reach of memory we have little but the secondary kind.

## 12   *The importance of secondary knowledge*

Knowledge of the secondary kind is particular, empirical and indirect. As we saw in the Manhattan instance, it is usually based on visual representation (pictures), structural representation (diagrams and tables) or verbal representation (documents or speech). In addition to representations, historical knowledge may be based on survivals. The special case of survival that we call memory has already been dealt with. Other cases are old buildings and other physical objects; various kinds of institutions, organizations, customs and habits, things that are partly physical and partly ideal (like governments); and languages and ideas and idea systems, which are wholly ideal, that is, non-material. All these sources of knowledge may constitute evidence for the historian, but only after they have been interpreted. The discussion of evidence belongs to the next chapter. Here we will consider the nature of the knowledge that arises from these sources.

## B.  Construction or Reconstruction?

### 1  *Representations of the past*

Bad teaching, it is said, occurs when a flow of words goes from the teacher's lecture notes to the student's writing pad without passing through the brains of either party. What happens in good history teaching? This begins with a mental picture or construct in the teacher's mind of some period or aspect of the past. By means of words or pictures this representation of the past is conveyed to the student's mind. Sometimes it comes as a completely new occupant to that mind. More often the student already has some picture (more or less rough, more or less adequate) of this bit of the past. The teacher's words supplement, reinforce, correct, and generally improve the student's understanding. By further reading, research, conversation, and general intellectual maturing her understanding is still further improved until she emerges from the course with a brillant degree.

But let us go back to the teacher. What is the nature of the knowledge that she so successfully imparts to her students? Is it a faithful reconstruction of the past? Or is it something that she herself has made, one that may or may not represent the past? In short, is our knowledge of the past a reconstruction or a new construction?

### 2  *Reconstruction of the past*

People sometimes talk of reconstructing the past. Yet it is quite impossible literally to repeat the past. A few years ago a group of volunteers undertook to live for twelve months in Iron Age conditions. They faithfully built the huts, wove the coarse cloth for their garments, tilled the fields, kept animals and in every way depended only on the resources that would have been available to them in south-western England 2,000 years ago. They and their archaeologist sponsors learned many things from the experiment. Yet all their efforts could not make a complete reconstruction of the past. They could emulate the physical life of their ancestors, but not the mental world. These young men and women of the twentieth century were ignorant of many things that their predecessors had known; nor could they empty their minds of modern attitudes – especially to the natural world, to religion, and to relations between the sexes. This fascinating experiment taught the lesson, above all others, that the past cannot be fully reconstructed. It might have required R. G. Collingwood to modify his theory that historical knowledge is gained by a mental re-enactment of the past.[10]

## 3   *The value of models*

We need not give up hope, however. The word 'experiment' reminds us of scientific laboratories, where chemicals are treated in test-tubes, micro-organisms are grown in glass dishes, or model ships are subjected to artificial winds and waves in tanks of water. These experiments have one thing in common. They are working with models of the world, not the real world itself. In order to make the experiment all the inessentials (of industrial processes, of human illness, of Atlantic storms) are stripped away. The experimenter admits only those factors – chemical, biological, physical – whose actions and interactions he wishes to examine. Every model represents the real world, but not the whole of the real world. Each is specifically designed for a particular purpose; thus what is stripped away and what is admitted differ in each case.

The analogy with historical knowledge should now be clear. No historian can hope to reconstruct the past (or any portion of it) in its entirety. The Iron Age experiment demonstrated that. Nor can the historian represent the past in all its richness and variety. Modern historians, perhaps more conscious than their predecessors of how very different the past was, rarely attempt a full-scale description. Possibly they are aware that this sort of thing is done more convincingly in fiction. It is interesting that a dramatist or novelist is more likely to give one the temporary illusion of looking at – even living in – the past than is a historian.

More and more, historians today proceed like scientists. They try to abstract from the complexities of the real world certain characteristics only, the irrelevant ones being omitted. The question whether these models are constructions or reconstructions turns out to be of little consequence. They are constructions in the sense that they have been built for particular purposes. They are re-constructions in the sense that they attempt to reproduce certain aspects of the real world – as a chemist does in a test-tube. His experiment is both real and artificial.

## 4   *Problems of models in history*

There is one big difference, however. The scientist is usually free to examine the 'real world' situation (e.g. the tanning of leather, the ship at sea) before he decides which factors he wishes to incorporate in his model and which to exclude. The historian is not so fortunate. Let us suppose that he is examining the functioning of the port of Bristol in the fifteenth century or that of agriculture in colonial Massachusetts. He has two

---

[10] See above, ch. 4, pp. 87, 100.

major handicaps as compared to the scientist. One is that he cannot examine the real world situation; it disappeared long ago. The second handicap is worse. Ideally, he would wish to admit all the relevant facts and exclude all the irrelevant. In practice he cannot do this; the selection of facts is made for him by the sparseness of the evidence. Very little remains today of fifteenth-century Bristol or eighteenth-century Massachusetts. Most of what is lacking from his model is omitted not because it has been examined and judged irrelevant, but because he simply does not know it. He has to make a rough guess (based on other knowledge) at how either of these systems functioned. In the light of that he has to seek for evidence that may possibly be relevant, and then admit or discard it in accordance with his guesses. Gradually a firmer picture will be built up in his mind, and he will admit or reject evidence with more confidence as the model takes shape. He must always remember, however, that most of what he needs is missing. He cannot be sure that he has put in all the relevant facts. Nor can he be sure, either, that all the facts he has put in are relevant, or that all the facts he has excluded are irrelevant. Thus the more evidence he examines, the more his work progresses, the more firmly his model takes shape . . . then the greater is the likelihood that that model follows the bent of his own convictions rather than the original 'real world' situation.

## 5   Improving the model

This is a very worrying conclusion. Are we to assume that all histories are deceptions – perhaps, worse, self-deceptions? Fortunately the experience of scientists is again a help to the historians. For in spite of having the advantage of being able to examine the 'real world' situation, scientists have not escaped similar pitfalls. Before the work of Copernicus and Kepler the model of the solar system was a series of cycles and epicycles with the earth at the centre. Before Harvey the blood was thought to flow back and forth from the heart like tides. The history of science is littered with models of reality like these – false models that yet became more and more convincing as men worked at them. How, then do the sciences progress? There are only two ways, the keys to progress in both science and history. One is further investigation in search of more evidence. Admittedly, there is the danger that the investigator, besotted with her so-far-successful model, will always interpret new evidence in a way that supports her theory. This kind of mistake has been pointed out by such philosophers of science as Karl Popper, N. R. Hanson and Thomas Kuhn, and among historians by Herbert Butterfield. Yet in spite of this real danger, progress, we believe, must eventually result from experience, the discovery of awkward facts and the elucidation of the problems to which they give rise.

The other resource for both scientists and historians is their colleagues.

Scholars in a particular field are concerned not only with their own researches but also with each other's. Through collaboration, discussion, seminars, conferences, learned journals, book reviews and so on, a scholar's work is subjected to continuous criticism from those who are in the best position for it. Here, again, there is the danger that new facts will be put into existing pigeon-holes, and that new theories will be rejected just because they clash with the old. Kuhn's account of how this occurs in science is well known; Butterfield's in history perhaps less so.[11] But the tendency to twist or reject new ideas because they do not conform to old ones is not a fault peculiar to scientists and historians. It is common to the human race and is found in every walk of life – not least the military and the religious. It would be fairer to say that scientists and historians are more alert to these dangers than most other people, and, though doubtless often guilty, are less prone to these faults than the rest of us. In science and history humility is as necessary a virtue as in morals.

## C.   Fact, Truth and Objectivity?

### 1   *How do we know it's right?*

The central problems of historical knowledge have been put in a nutshell by the historian of Germany Hajo Holborn, who said that they 'hinge upon the fact that an objective knowledge of the past can only be obtained through the subjective experience of the scholar.'[12] Such an 'objective knowledge of the past' was defined in 1824 by the great German historian Leopold von Ranke. Disclaiming any desire to judge the past in his *Histories of the Latin and Germanic Nations*, he wanted only to show 'how it actually was'.[13] That phrase – a rendering of the original *wie es eigentlich gewesen* – has haunted historians ever since. Clearly this is what they should be describing: but how can they be sure that they are doing it? And for the rest of us the problem is even more worrying: apart from what historians tell us, what means have we of knowing what actually happened? In theory, anyone can examine the evidence for himself in order to check up on the historians. This is sometimes attempted, and in very rare cases may succeed. The difficulty is that a thorough examination of all the relevant evidence requires intelligence, general historical knowledge and specialized historical skills. It also requires access to the sources (which are often closed to all but already accredited historians) and the investment of large amounts of time, energy and money. By the time one has (improbably) satisfied all these requirements one has become

[11] See Kuhn (1970); Butterfield (1960) pp. 142–70.
[12] Holborn (1972), p. 79.
[13] See Stern (1970), p. 56.

a historian oneself. This leaves all the non-historians (i.e. the vast majority of the human race) still wholly dependent on what the historians tell them.

It would seem, then, that once we have got beyond the reach of memory, we must depend for our knowledge of the past almost entirely upon historians. But this is not disastrous. Are we not dependent upon astronomers, nuclear physicists, geologists and so on in the same way?

Well, no. Not in the same way. The reason is to be found in Holborn's phrase 'the subjective experience of the scholar'. Our knowledge of the natural world (though admittedly much dependent on the work of natural scientists) does not have to be filtered through anyone's subjective experience – or, at any rate, to nothing like the same extent.[14] But there is little to be gained for history by pointing out that even the 'pure' natural sciences are not so pure as had been commonly supposed.

## 2  'Objective' and 'subjective' defined

What can we mean by 'objective' and 'subjective'? Imagine a group of people sitting round a table on which is a large Dutch cheese. This is the object at which they, the subjects, are looking and about which they are talking. Some remark that the cheese is large, is round, is red, rests on the table, weighs so many kilos. All these statements are said to be objective because they refer to qualities of the cheese. Then one remarks that it looks mouth-wateringly tempting, another that it nauseates him, a third that it reminds her of a holiday in Alkmaar, a fourth that it looks like a full moon rising on an autumn evening. These statements (though provoked by the cheese) are about the different tastes, associations and memories of the individual subjects, and hence are said to be subjective. So 'objective' is about the object, and 'subjective' is about the subject. What Holborn means is that objective knowledge of an event in the past (say, the surrender at Yorktown) is possible only through the subjective (i.e. private and personal) experience of the historian.

In fact, the historian's knowledge of Yorktown is likely to be subjective in more than one way. First, she will have formed her own conception of the event from various books and paintings (secondary sources) as well as from sundry letters, military and political reports, diaries, memoirs and newspapers more or less contemporary with the event (primary sources). These data she will have supplemented and enriched with her own more general knowledge of politics, armies, governments, sea power and other relevant considerations. This composite conception, or construction, is her subjective experience. Moreover, in another sense of 'subjective', it would have a different *meaning* for her according to whether she is French,

[14] For suggestions that the natural sciences are to some degree affected by the subjective experience of the scientists, see, for example, James Watson's account of the discovery of the structure of the DNA molecule (1970). See also O'Hear (1988) for further discussion.

American or British, whether she is a military or a diplomatic or a social historian, and so on.

And there is a further consideration. The primary sources describe what the writers saw and heard (or believed they saw and heard) of the event itself. These, too, are subjective experiences. We might say that only when certain movements of men and material were perceived in a certain way did an event occur. It was the subjective experiences and understanding of what was going on, by both participants and spectators, that constituted an event in the first place.[15] To an Indian from the Amazonian jungle suddenly transported to Yorktown, the whole scene might have been totally bewildering and inexplicable. Thus there are at least three levels of subjective experience in turn: those of the participants and spectators: those of the reporters – military, diplomatic, journalistic; and finally those of the historian. When you read the historian's book about the surrender of Yorktown your comprehension will constitute a fourth level of subjective experience.

### 3   *Words and objective knowledge*

So how do we obtain objective knowledge? Or, rather, what can 'objective knowledge' mean in history? Clearly it cannot be direct, sensory knowledge of the object – like looking at the cheese. It has to be indirect knowledge acquired almost entirely through the medium of words. (I do not forget that there may also be drawings or diagrams or material relics of the event, but most of these are likely to be accompanied and explained by words. Undoubtedly the bulk of historical evidence is in verbal form.) Words bring us to language and all its problems. Do my words mean the same to me as they do to you? Not exactly. Especially not if we are separated by barriers of time, class, nationality, culture, even context. There is a vast literature on the problems of language and meaning. Here it is sufficient to note that any so-called 'objective' knowledge in history has to be put in words in order to be stated. To agree in our descriptions of the world (as Wittgenstein pointed out), it is necessary that we agree both how the world is and how we use words: we have to agree both in judgements and in definitions.[16] In the circumstances that I have outlined, **objective knowledge in history can mean no more than that there is a consensus among historians to agree in certain descriptions.**

### 4   *Facts*

So what about facts? Does not history pride itself on being factual rather than fictional? For me, **a historical fact accords with a judgement about the past in which historians agree:** e.g that Constantinople fell to the

---

[15] For further discussion of this point, see ch. 7 below.
[16] See Wittgenstein (1968), I, 242, p. 88.

Turks in 1453, or that Abraham Lincoln was shot in Ford's Theatre, Washington. That the Roman Empire fell because its leaders gave themselves to decadence and luxury, or that Lee Harvey Oswald shot Kennedy are not facts I can affirm with confidence. They may be true statements. But they may also be false. What gives the status of historical fact is the consensus of historical judgements. There is as yet no consensus about the second pair of statements. '**Facts are what statements (when true) state; they are not what statements are about.**'[17] Facts are what the first pair of statements state; Constantinople and Ford's Theatre are what they are about. If (as we believe) the statements are true, then facts are what they state and what they state are facts. If they are or may be untrue, then they do not state facts (as with the second pair). Thus the whole question turns on truth. If and when we have settled the question of truth we have also settled the question of fact. Not before.[18]

## 5   Truth in History

The question of truth in history is what we have to face; the concept of 'fact' is dependent upon it. The concept of 'truth' in history may be seen in two ways, neither entirely without problems. **The first way is to regard truth as a property of a true statement** – telling the truth, as we say. **The second way is to regard truth as a goal**, something at which all scholarly disciplines aim. When we say that we wish to know *the* truth about the fall of the Roman Empire we imply all that could possibly be known. This amounts to something like a huge mass of true statements, after which there remains nothing more to be said. It has an air of completeness, of finality about it. On this way of looking at it, there is a suggestion of convergence, like all the paths up a mountain meeting at the summit. (Then where do you go?)

Coming back for a moment to the first way (truth as the property of a true statement), what can we mean by a true historical statement? Let us suppose you were present in Ford's Theatre on that evening in April 1865. Witnessing the assassination as you did, you had direct, or primary, knowledge of it. Later you would have told your friends about it, perhaps describing it so graphically that they felt they were there. Their knowledge, however vivid, would be only indirect or secondary knowledge, conveyed to them by your words and gestures. Were their beliefs about it true? When they told *their* friends, were their statements true? And so on until, over a century later and by many channels, the news comes to me. Still exactly true? What do we mean here by 'true'? I think we mean that the account I receive in the 1990s is true if it agrees exactly

---

[17] See P. F. Strawson, 'Truth', in Pitcher (1964), p. 38.
[18] For further discussion of facts in history, see Stanford (1990), pp. 71–4, 79–81.

with what you saw in the theatre that evening. It is true if my secondary knowledge agrees with your primary knowledge. (You will remember how my secondary knowledge of New York was confirmed on my first visit.) At any rate, that is the least we mean.

## 6    The whole truth?

Perhaps we mean more than that. We may mean that a true account of the assassination must be a full account. It must agree not only with what you saw and heard, but with what everyone present (including Booth and Lincoln) experienced. That is more difficult, for not everyone either remembered or recounted their experiences as graphically as you did. But perhaps we want more yet: facts (to use the term loosely) about nineteenth-century guns, the trajectory of bullets, the state of medical knowledge at the time, even the subconscious urges that took both Lincoln and Booth to the theatre. These were part of no one's experiences, yet they are very relevant parts of historical knowledge. And, of course, we don't stop here. I doubt whether any one is satisfied that there is no more to be known about the death of Lincoln. It is a safe bet that historical research will continue and more books and articles will appear on it.[19]

It looks as if we are moving from the first to the second way of looking at truth. We are being led from the truth contained in the true statements of an eye-witness to *the* truth ('the whole truth and nothing but the truth') about the death of Lincoln. Supposing for a moment that this is a meaningful and attainable goal, what are the problems? You will have guessed one already: that not all the eye-witnesses agree. That is one reason why researches continue. For a true account must be self-consistent. Until all the disagreements and contradictions are ironed out we cannot be satisfied that we have the truth. Let us suppose that that has been done, that we now have a number of statements that agree, or at least are not inconsistent. Then there is the problem raised by Danto: briefly, that we cannot give a full account of any historical event until the end of history.[20] Next is a third problem. Either 'the truth about Lincoln's death' is the same thing as a collection of true statements or it is not. In support of the second alternative one cannot but feel that the truth amounts to more than this. After all, we say, these statements are true only because they state what happened. So the truth is not true statements: it is more like 'how it actually was' (as von Ranke said in 1824). *What actually happened* is the criterion for the truth or falsity of the statements about Lincoln's death.

---

[19] By 1962 the American Civil War had produced nearly 100,000 volumes. See Don E. Fehrenbacker, 'Disunion and Reunion', in Higham (1962), p. 98.
[20] See ch. 4, p. 92.

## 7    Meaning

Let us look at the other alternative: that the truth we are after amounts to no more than a number of statements. Now statements are couched in words. Words are symbols, arbitrary and merely conventional symbols for pieces of reality. You and I know that the Stars and Stripes represents the United States of America. But it is perfectly possible for an intelligent person not to know that and to see only a piece of coloured cloth; he just does not know the convention. The link between the flag and the country is purely a matter of human decision; there is no necessary connection. Similarly there is no necessary connection between the words 'Booth shot Lincoln' and certain human actions and certain movements of matter. It is just a useful convention that one should represent the other. It is a matter of the *meaning* of the symbols, whether flags or words.

Now there is a difference between the meaning of a statement and its truth. 'Abraham Lincoln died in 1870' is a statement that has meaning but not truth. 'Iso-leucrine is an amino-acid present in vasopressin' is, to me, meaningless, though I believe it to be true. If *the* truth about Lincoln's death (or anything else in the past) is no more than a collection of statements, then we have to be sure of the meaning of those statements, as well as of their truth. There is not a lot of doubt about the meaning of the simple statement 'Booth shot Lincoln', but if *the* truth consists of *all* the true statements, think of the problems of meaning that may be involved in some of them. Who can be sure he understands them all? Can we be sure that we all agree in our use of words?[21] Does the phrase 'the United States of America' mean the same to me as it does to you?

To sum up, then, it seems that we have been led from 'fact' on to 'truth', and from 'truth' on to 'what actually happened' and to 'meaning'. And although there is more to be said about both truth and meaning (in chapter 10), for the moment we can accept that historical knowledge is knowledge of 'what actually happened'. Now there remain only the two questions: What is it that we know? and: How do we know it?

## 8    Doubts to be dispelled

These two questions, which seem perhaps deceptively simple, will be discussed in later chapters. Here, before concluding this section, it is worth making a few comments to pull us back from the brink of total scepticism. Such scepticism commonly expresses two doubts. The first is whether it is possible to have any particular knowledge of the past – i.e. whether any particular statement about the past (like 'Abraham Lincoln died in 1865') can be known to be true or false. The second is whether it is possible to have any knowledge of the past at all.

[21] See Wittgenstein (1968) and the discussion above p. 124.

In respect of the first of these, it is possible that such a doubt can arise from the various difficulties I have pointed out in relation to sources, direct and indirect knowledge, transmission of evidence, representation, and language as a system of symbols and meanings. I cite these in order to discredit the naive, positivistic view of historiography: a view that endows the words in a history book with the same inerrancy that a devout fundamentalist gives to the Bible or the Koran. Such a notion of history belongs more to the nineteenth than to our more disillusioned century. A hundred years ago even one of the most learned of historians, Lord Acton, believed that he and his colleagues were about to write a final, definitive and wholly unbiased history of Europe.[22] No reputable historian believes in the possibility today.

## 9    A hint from Karl Popper

However, a sense of perspective is restored if one takes a leaf out of the book of Karl Popper, the philosopher of science. His theory of falsifiability, as we have seen, argues that no observations, however numerous, can prove the truth of a hypothesis, but only one will suffice to falsify it.[23] The task of the scientist, therefore, is to formulate a general hypothesis, then to seek to refute it. The more attempts at refutation that it withstands, the nearer to the truth it is likely to be. On the other hand, if observation does refute it, then the hypothesis is altered to take account of this observation so that the new hypothesis is closer to the truth. Thus hypotheses, which are always mental constructs, are shaped and reshaped by contact with reality to bring them nearer to the truth: reality, we might say, licks them into shape.[24]

## 10    Closing in on the truth

There is considerable similarity between Popper's approach to scientific truth and the historian's approach to historical truth. This similarity does not lie in the use of general hypotheses, but in the same method of coming closer and closer to the truth by eliminating what is false. In both cases progress is made not so much by being sure of what we know as by being sure of what we do *not* know, and by drawing ever closer limits to our ignorance.

For example, the great national survey of 1085–6 known as Domesday Book is a major source for the history of medieval England. But we cannot be quite sure that we understand it aright unless we know for what purpose it was drawn up. Was it for the benefit of future generations, like

[22] See Acton's letter to the contributors to the *Cambridge Modern History*, in Stern (1970), pp. 246–50.
[23] See ch. 3, p. 74 above.
[24] See Popper (1959), p. 33 and passim.

that other great contemporary source, the Anglo-Saxon Chronicle? Was it a legal record, showing who held what land? Was it an administrative survey of all the shires, towns and villages in England? Was it a record of feudal obligations? Was it a head count of population? Was it a register of wealth for the convenience of taxation? These and other suggestions have been made, each with some plausibility. By closer examination some of these have been eliminated, others retained as possibilities. It is now agreed that it was no more than three of these: a feudal record, a register for taxation and a statement of land-holding.

To take another example, historical statistics are usually incapable of precise determination. But after much research and ingenious calculation it now seems likely that the troops who fought for the South in the American Civil War (more difficult to calculate than for the North where better records survive) were between 850,000 and 900,000 men, although earlier estimates have ranged from 600,000 to 1,400,000.[25] Again, medieval inquiries into land-holding may show that a certain man held an estate in 1350 and his son held it in 1375. From this it may be reckoned that he was born probably after 1300 but before 1329, was married before 1354 and died before 1375. Later evidence may bring us to more accurate knowledge in each of these cases. We are, however, unlikely ever to know the exact truth.

A good historian is less concerned with trying to state the exact truth (usually a forlorn hope anyway) than with establishing the limits within which the truth must fall. She is much more certain of what must be false (e.g. that Lincoln was dead in 1864 or alive in 1866) than with what is exactly true (e.g. the precise second that the fatal shot was fired.) Historical knowledge does not consist of a set of exactly and unquestionably true statements. Rather it is a web of mutually limiting statements or beliefs, few if any of which are absolutely certain. Yet, taken together they form a consistent and very probable whole. It is like trying to arrive at a point by a number of intersecting loops. Although we sometimes stress the differences among historians, it is surprising how very much they agree.

## 11   Can we know the past?

This brings us to the second of the doubts: whether it is possible to have any knowledge of the past at all. People who argue this usually take what is called a 'confrontational' view of knowledge: unless they can be confronted (at least in principle) with the object of knowledge they see no reason to recognize it as possible. They insist that knowledge must be always what I have called direct knowledge.

In history this view is called 'constructionism': historians do not *discover* what happened in the past, but *construct* stories according to

[25] See McPherson (1990), p. 306, n. 41.

certain rules. The term was coined by an American philosopher, Jack W, Meiland. He defined it as '(1) **a claim that the historian should not be regarded as trying to discover facts about an independently existing realm of past events; (2) a claim that history is nevertheless important and significant because it attempts to deal with a certain class of present entities . . .'**[26] The 'present entities' are documents and other kinds of what are normally considered historical evidence. For Meiland, these are to form part of a 'coherent account of the *present* world', not the past. Much of this argument is based (with whatever justification) on two Idealist philosophers of history, Benedetto Croce and Michael Oakeshott. Constructionism (which no serious historian can accept) is still occasionally put forward, though it has been refuted in philosophy.[27]

Two observations seem called for. One is that it is very difficult to account for so much agreement about the past unless it all refers to the same objects. The other is that it is just common-sense, just the way humanity is constituted, to suppose that what occurred five seconds or five centuries ago can still be known – at least, in principle. We do not suppose that the resort where we spent our holiday has gone out of existence and beyond all knowledge just because we have returned home. We must not restrict reality to the contents of consciousness.

I began this chapter by citing the usual philosophers' criteria for claiming knowledge. It may appear that historical knowledge has some difficulty in meeting these criteria. On the other hand, history is a discipline as old, as reputable and as diligently pursued as philosophy. If it should happen that what is claimed as historical knowledge fails to meet the demands of philosophers, it must be asked who should give way. Whose position should be rethought? Many philosophers can and do read history. Fewer historians can or do read philosophy. But this fact gives philosophy no intellectual authority over the other discipline. Both would benefit from greater efforts to understand each other. That is one reason for this book.

## D.   Another Relevant Topic: Imagination

*Imagination*

One important topic that this chapter has left untouched is the part played by imagination. It is a commonplace that the historian, like the historical novelist, should be able to picture his characters in their actions – their clothes, habits, beliefs, etc. But this is merely the ornamental use of imagination. More important is the structural use. This use of imagination

---

[26] Meiland (1965), p. 192.
[27] See Atkinson (1978), pp. 40–55.

appears in the web of story that the historian weaves between the fixed points of his apparent data. 'Apparent' because, as Collingwood observes, there are no data, no fixed points. What appear to be data are certain historical problems which, for the present, the historian 'proposes to treat as settled' until someone decides to reopen them.[28]

Briefly put, imagination is needed by the historian in five ways: (1) for visualizing the past scene; (2) for inference from fixed points (as Collingwood describes); (3) for positing counter-factuals, which involves envisaging what might have happened, and so estimating the significance (or insignificance) of what *did* happen; (4) for interpretation, when one surveys a whole course of action (for example, the career of Adolf Hitler) and gives it a particular meaning; and (5) for insight. 'It is the imagination of the historian', said Trevor-Roper . . . 'which will discern the hidden forces of change.'[29]

## Conclusion

We began this chapter with a standard definition of knowledge. We identified three kinds of knowledge: direct, indirect and generalized. History employs all three, but mainly the second. It appears that any historical account must be a construction, not a reconstruction, of the past. It is best understood as a model; that is, helpful, but not to be confused with reality. Holborn's dictum led us to consider the meanings of 'objective' and 'subjective' in history. Historical truth may be seen either as 'in accordance with what happened', or as 'consistent in meaning'. (These are roughly the 'correspondence' and 'coherence' discussed below in chapter 10, pp. 279–80). Historical knowledge may, perhaps, best be seen as convergent on the truth; that is, with increasing certainty of what did *not* happen. Meeting the sceptic's doubts of whether we can know the past at all, we urge that the philosopher has no necessary superiority over the historian in questions of knowledge. The part that imagination plays in historical knowledge is outlined on pp. 130–1, but not fully explored.

It should be observed that philosophers of history are no longer almost exclusively concerned with history as knowledge. Recently they have come also to debate history as meaning – in other words, they have moved from epistemological to interpretative concerns. This chapter looks at the former, chapter 10, at the latter. But both knowledge and meaning in history depend upon what remains of the past, without which nothing can be said. So in the next chapter we look at what the past has left behind.

---

[28] Collingwood (1961), pp. 243–4.
[29] Trevor-Roper, 'History and Imagination', in Lloyd-Jones et al. (1981), p. 368. For further discussion of imagination, see Stanford (1990), pp. 80–3.

## Suggested Reading

Atkinson 1978
Ayer 1956
Collingwood 1961
Chisholm 1966
Danto 1965
Danto 1968
Goldstein 1976

Hamlyn 1971
McCullagh 1984
Marrou 1966
Nagel 1979, chapter 14
Novick 1988
Stanford 1990
Stern 1970

# 6

# History as Relic

Faith is . . . the evidence of things not seen.

St Paul

Some circumstantial evidence is very strong, as when you find a trout
in the milk.

Henry D. Thoreau

## Introduction

From our discussion of the kind of knowledge that we have of history one
thing is very clear. That is that we know the past only by means of
something that is present to us. We infer past events and past states of
affairs from whatever has survived into the present. Such survivors may be
people, physical objects or ideas. Having been 'left behind' by the past
they can be designated 'relics'. There is nothing pejorative about this term.
In this sense you can be regarded as a 'relic' of your former self and some
of your present knowledge a 'relic' of what you learned at school. All such
survivors into the present are evidence of the past. How present evidence
is used to gain knowledge of the past is no simple matter. In this chapter
we discuss the concept and nature of evidence, its use by historians, and
the ways in which evidence originally came into being.

*Questions about historical relics, the use of evidence, fact and
interpretation*

1 How can we hope to know the lives of people long dead?
2 What links are there between us and them?
3 Is history concerned only with old books and papers?
4 What materials do historians use for their histories?
5 How do they use them?
6 Where do they find them?
7 What is 'evidence'?
8 What sort of things are evidence for the past?

9    How does evidence work?
10    Where does historical evidence come from in the first place?
11    What are historical facts?
12    What do we mean by 'interpretation'?

The theme of this chapter is 'History as Relic'. Enthusiasts for a less blinkered view of history often call us from our books and point to old houses, old roads, old fields and hedges, old customs and habits, exclaiming, 'History is all around us!' Strictly, however, this is not true, if by 'history' they mean the past (as they usually do). For the past is gone; it is *not* around us. What is around us is the world of today which may be seen as a relic of the past. Only in that sense of relic, something left behind, is it true that history is all around us. In this chapter we shall discuss in turn:

A.    The Concept of Evidence
B    The Nature of Historical Evidence
C    The Use of Historical Evidence
D    The Origins of Historical Evidence
E    Oral History

## A.    The Concept of Evidence

### 1    *Tending to prove*

Let us consider the following propositions:

1    No bachelor is married.
2    $349 \times 113 = 39{,}437$.
3    Water is a combination of oxygen and hydrogen.
4    The sun is about 93 million miles from the earth.
5    Blockade by the US Navy brought about the defeat of the South in the American Civil War.
6    The prisoner at the bar is guilty of murder.
7    Liberal democracy is preferable to Communism.
8    It is raining.

Of these, nos. 1 and 8 are clearly true (or clearly false). They need no evidence to support them: they are themselves evident, the sort of things that might be evidence for other propositions. No. 2 is not evident, though it is necessarily true; it needs demonstration, not evidence. No. 3 is universally, but not necessarily, true. Few would dispute it, yet it rests on experimental evidence. No. 4 is a truth neither universal nor necessary; it also needs evidence, but its truth is generally accepted. The remaining propositions, nos. 5, 6 and 7, are unlike the others. They are certainly not necessary truths; but neither do they rest on experimental evidence. What experiments would analyse or measure them? They cannot be conclusively proved; they remain debatable. They are historical, legal or political judgements. As such they are likely to lead to important actions: to a government's policy of maintaining a costly navy, to sentencing a man to death or long imprisonment, to risking one's life in the streets against a dictatorship. As so often, people have to act as they think best, because no certainty is to be had. They simply have to weigh up the arguments for and against their decision. One dictionary definition of '**evidence**' is '**Ground for belief; that which tends to prove or disprove any conclusion**'. Please note the phrase '*tends* to prove'; most judgements that need evidence are not susceptible of absolute proof.

## 2   *Judging evidence*

So what, exactly, is evidence? Let us start with the adjective 'evident'. **Something that is evident is obvious,** it stands out. A dictionary defines it as '**clear to the senses, especially the sight, or clear to the mind**'. In my examples above, no. 8 is clear to the senses, no. 1 to the mind; they are evident. The other propositions are not clear or evident. Except for no. 2 which is an *a priori* truth, they all stand in need of evidence. So we may say that **propositions that are not themselves evi*dent* need to be supported by evi*dence*.** If they are not obvious they need the backing of something else that is. Let us note, in particular, the historical judgement, no. (5). Unlike the other seven, its truth cannot be established by logic, by calculation, by experiment, by measurement, by confession, by public opinion, or by observation. Any of these may play *some* part in the historical judgement, they may provide some evidence for or against, but essentially such **a historical judgement is a considered conclusion when all arguments have been carefully weighed.**

## 3   *Adequate evidence*

That is how good historians answer historical questions. But not all questions are capable of a firm answer. Lord Acton tells the story of two famous London doctors who could not make up their minds on a case, and said so. The head of the family insisted on a positive opinion. They replied that they were unable to give one, but he might easily find fifty doctors who would.[1] This raises the notion of '**adequate evidence**'. There are two points here. One is the question of whether the evidence is adequate for the conclusion drawn from it; the other is that of who is best qualified to draw a conclusion.

Several travellers in the high Himalayas have seen indentations in the snow which locals allege to be the footprints of a large man-like creature,

[1] See his Inaugural Lecture at Cambridge, 1895, in Acton, (1960), p. 33.

the yeti or Abominable Snowman. Since no large anthropoid is known outside the tropics, such evidence (however well-attested in itself) is commonly judged inadequate for the conclusion that such a creature exists.

Who should draw conclusions from evidence? Surely the recognized experts in the field. To settle whether a painting is a Giorgione or a Titian we ask an art historian; to determine whether a child has chickenpox or scarlet fever we call in a doctor; to decide which way the lion went we ask a hunter. But to settle whether a prisoner is guilty we ask a jury of twelve ordinary men and women. In matters of history the answer is not so obvious. This is because, as we shall see, judgement in history calls for at least two different sorts of ability: one is technical expertise; the other is that practical wisdom in human affairs and human nature that usually comes from long and wide experience. The two are not often found in the same person.

## 4    Four questions about evidence

These issues have not always been as clear as they are today. In particular there are four questions: What sort of problem requires evidence for its solution? What sort of evidence is appropriate to a particular problem? What weight of evidence is adequate for a decision? For whom must it be adequate? These questions are of central importance to history, but they are equally important to law, to religion and to science. The sort of answers that we should give to them began to come into focus in England in the seventeenth century. Briefly, what happened was that a traditional view of knowledge gave way to something like our modern view. In this change the concept of evidence played a vital part.

The traditional view, which went back to the ancient Greeks, made a clear distinction between 'science', 'knowledge', 'certainty' and 'philosophy' on the one hand, and 'opinion', 'probability', 'appearance' and 'rhetoric' on the other.[2] The distinction was based on the belief that science belonged to the heavenly sphere, the realm of Being, but human affairs to the sublunary sphere ('under the moon'), the realm of Becoming. In the seventeenth century this contrast was gradually replaced by a spectrum of factual knowledge that stretched from 'fiction' and 'opinion' at one end, through 'probable' and 'highly probable' to the 'morally certain' at the other. In the gap between demonstrable certainty and mere opinion there was developing a wide range of knowledge – legal, historical, religious and scientific – that was much surer than mere opinion but fell well short of the sort of demonstrable certainty that had formally been demanded of 'science'. This was part of the famous 'rise of

[2] See Shapiro (1983), p. 3. The next few paragraphs are based largely on Dr Shapiro's work.

modern science'.[3] In particular, this enormous leap in knowledge depended on a new understanding of the role of evidence. Lawyers, scientists, theologians and historians all began to search for evidence to resolve their problems. Interestingly enough, they were all involved in the question of witchcraft, one that conveniently illustrates our four issues.

## 5   Witchcraft in seventeenth-century England

**Witches (people who can effect good or evil by occult powers – spells, magic potions and the like)** have been known in almost every society. But the great witch-craze of the sixteenth and seventeenth centuries was something special. It was largely due to a reversal of attitude by the Church, supplemented by the late Renaissance revival of Neo-Platonism with its doctrine of immaterial spirits – a doctrine that was reconciled with Christianity by many good and learned men. For most of its existence the Christian Church had condemned belief in witches as a relic of paganism. It denied the reality of witches and condemned their persecution.[4] Only in the late Middle Ages (the fourteenth and fifteenth centuries) was a new notion added to belief in witches – namely, the idea that they owed their powers to an explicit compact with the Devil. This made them heretics, enemies of God and of Christian society. The Church condemned them and official persecution began. It is notable that from the late fifteenth century a belief in witches was held by learned men – a cultural elite who in former times had been as scornful of witchcraft as today they are of popular astrology.[5] There was a delay of about a century before supposed pacts with the Devil were taken seriously in England in late Elizabethan times, and not until 1604 were they condemned by Act of Parliament. Earlier Acts (1542 and 1563) had recognized witchcraft as a felony. Now it became a statutory offence and carried the death penalty.[6] Law courts and officers of justice thus had to take the crime more seriously. To their credit they all began to demand stricter standards of proof. This is where our concern with evidence comes in. On the Continent methods of prosecution were so fierce that, once accused, a man or women had virtually no chance of acquittal. In these courts, it would appear, evidence carried little weight.[7] In England things were not quite so bad, though bad enough: at the very worst of times (the 1640's) an accused stood a two-in-five chance of acquittal.[8] For a number of reasons witchcraft trials fell rapidly in number towards the end of the century. Though the belief lingered on among the common people, the

[3] See, for example, Butterfield (1957b).
[4] See Trevor-Roper (1967) pp. 91, 103.
[5] See Thomas (1978), p. 521.
[6] Ibid., p. 525.
[7] Ibid., p. 687.
[8] Shapiro (1983), p. 206.

French government put a stop to witchcraft trials in 1682. Executions ceased in England in the same year, though the Witchcraft Act was not repealed till 1736.[9]

## 6   The four questions illustrated

Each of our four issues can be seen in this story. The first question is whether this is the sort of problem that requires evidence for its solution. Here two problems need to be distinguished: one is the possibility of witchcraft, the other is the guilt of the accused. The first was a matter of theology, philosophy and science. It was theoretical, and for long learned men did not see how or what evidence could apply.[10] The second was a matter of law, where evidence was customarily required. (Fortunately for the accused, English law forbade the use of torture; otherwise confessions and convictions might have been as common as on the Continent.) It was this emphasis on legal evidence that saved many a poor man or woman's life, for judges who themselves believed in witchcraft were still scrupulous to see that no one was condemned without good evidence. It was the increasing difficulty of finding convincing evidence of a compact with the Devil that led to the gradual abandonment of witchcraft trials. The steady decline in belief in witchcraft itself was an effect rather than a cause of this abandonment.

Our second question (what sort of evidence is appropriate to the problem?) now comes to the fore. This problem also had two parts: Was this a case of witchcraft? Who was the witch? Responsible authorities pointed out that alternative explanations had to be considered. The misfortune suffered supposedly at the hands of a witch might have been an act of God, or a direct act of the Devil without the intervention of a witch, or the result of an imposture or of natural causes.[11] This made it difficult enough for a firm decision to be reached at any of the three stages of inquiry that English law at that time required: examination and collection of evidence by a justice of the peace; consideration of evidence by a grand jury to determine whether the case should be sent for trial; and finally the trial by petty jury in a king's court presided over by a judge. To decide whether the illness or death of an animal or a person was due to witchcraft and not to one of the other possibilities tested the scientific, medical and theological learning of the day. As for the second problem – who was the offending witch? – that was usually alleged to be some lonely, poor and eccentric man or woman unpopular with the neighbours. The justices, however, were less easily convinced. To establish that the accused had made a compact with the Devil (as the 1604 act stipulated)

[9] Ibid., pp. 208, 211, 224.
[10] See the quotation from 1712 on p. 139 below.
[11] Thomas (1978), p. 685.

required stricter standards of evidence – usually one of three things: the presence of a familiar spirit (often in the form of an animal), the Devil's mark upon the body, or the confession of the accused. None of these was easy to establish: the familiar spirit might be a harmless pet; the devil's mark a natural excrescence, and even the confession the muddled utterance of a crazed old woman, frightened and deprived of sleep. One writer noted in 1665 that the 'truth of Witches Confessions themselves hath been often doubted'.[12]

## 7   The adequacy of the evidence – our third and fourth questions

It is interesting that *historical* evidence (our own concern in this chapter) was called into question during the debate on adequate evidence for witchcraft. The existence of records of past convictions did not, according to one writer, offer satisfactory proof; this was not, as we might suppose, because judges and juries could have made wrong decisions, but because we cannot rely on records. There were, he said, records of such strange creatures as 'Antipodes' (presumably dwellers on the other side of the globe), and these, he affirmed, were no longer believed to exist.[13] This brings us to our third question: is the evidence adequate for a decision? It was increasingly accepted by law courts in the course of the seventeenth century that the evidence for particular cases of witchcraft was never sufficient for the death penalty. As one statesman wrote in 1697, 'the Parlements of France and other judicatories who are persuaded of the being of witches never try them now, because of the experience they have had that it is impossible to distinguish possession from nature in disorder; and they choose rather to let the guilty escape than to punish the innocent.'[14].

Another writer in 1712 made the point (familiar to us from discussion of the criteria for knowledge in the last chapter) that nothing can be the object of a wise man's faith without the evidence to weigh with a reasonable man. He clinches it thus: 'For our belief in anything does not depend on the intrinsick Certainty and Reality of the Thing itself, but upon the Evidence it carries with it.'[15]

Our fourth question asks for whom the evidence must be adequate. While there is plenty of evidence that the uneducated were more prone to belief in witchcraft (and they even unlawfully hanged or 'lynched' supposed witches who had been acquitted in the courts), yet many of the

[12] Shapiro (1983) p. 205.
[13] Ibid., p. 209. As I hope my book will find some readers in the Antipodes I can only apologize for this ignorance of the voyages of Captain Abel Tasman.
[14] Thomas (1978), p. 686.
[15] Shapiro (1983), p. 209.

educated shared that belief.[16] On the whole, however, and increasingly as the century went on, the experience by judges and justices of the difficulties involved in anyone's proving a charge of witchcraft led them to reject any such charge. The experience of king James I is illuminating. In 1597 he wrote one of the leading works on witchcraft, his *Daemonologie*. Then, becoming king of England in 1603, he took a keen interest in English witchcraft trials. This experience of 'justice' in action disillusioned him. On one occasion he stopped a trial, and on another he sharply rebuked two judges for condemning witches on inadequate evidence.[17] It seems that it was an increasing regard for evidence rather than sheer disbelief in the possibility of witchcraft that put a stop to the prosecution of witches. As Dr Shapiro demonstrates, the problems of witchcraft brings together questions of evidence in several different areas at the same time: 'Precisely because witchcraft raised problems of fact finding within a practical area and within the interlocking contexts of historical authority, religious belief, and legal technology, it was a forcing ground for working out the implications of the new approach to evidence.'[18].

Thus the concept of evidence appears at first to be merely a philosophical question, but in the seventeenth century a closer examination and a more rational view of that concept spared many lives.

American readers may be interested to compare the foregoing with the notorious witchcraft affair in Salem, Massachusetts, in 1692. It must be remembered that these trials were quite untypical of New England, for they provided nineteen of the total of twenty-four executions for witchcraft in the whole of that century in Massachusetts. They were also unusual in respect of the age, wealth and status of the accused and in the nature of the proceedings, as well as in the subsequent confession of error by the state and the voluntary payment of compensations.[19] After 1692 there were no more witchcraft trials in Massachusetts, though popular belief in witchcraft lingered on. Thus in America, as in Europe, it was the cessation of prosecution that led to the cessation of belief, not the other way round. Subsequent writing on the subject by scholarly ministers, such as Increase and Cotton Mather and John Hale, as well as the reactions of the legal authorities, show their different doubts about evidence and proof. The difficulty of securing evidence which could, at the same time, satisfy the lawyers, the ministers and the populace nurtured these doubts; it was not disbelief in the possibility of witchcraft.[20] Thus on both sides of the Atlantic the problem of adequate evidence played a large part in putting an end to the murderous persecution of witches.

[16] Ibid., pp. 208–11.
[17] Ibid., p. 199.
[18] Ibid., p. 226.
[19] Weisman (1984) pp. 17, 135–6, 174–6. For comparisons with the situations in England and on the Continent, see pp. 11–14, 120–3, 187.
[20] Ibid., pp. 176–83.

## B.   The Nature of Historical Evidence

### 1   *The limits of observation*

In the summer of 1991 a mild sensation was caused in astronomical circles by the supposed discovery of a planet circling a star in a remote part of the galaxy. This was said to be the first planet known to exist outside the Solar System. Unfortunately it was too far away to be examined by the most powerful telescope, optical or radio. So we were unlikely ever to know more about it. Months later, the observation was discredited and the 'planet' joined the 'canals' of Mars among figments of astronomical imagination: a disappointment.

Statements about the past are like statements about distant stars – or perhaps about the centre of the earth. These, too, are places quite beyond our observation. We cannot experience them directly, so anything we know about them has to be established indirectly. Yet it is not inconceivable that one day men or women may be able to reach such a remote planet, or even the centre of the earth. Unlikely as it is, either is more likely than the frank impossibility of returning to the past to verify historical statements by direct observation.

### 2   *Indirect knowledge*

Since all knowledge about the past is indirect knowledge, it has to be mediated to us by what we call 'evidence'. We can have no more evidence for the past than what is now in existence, though it is not yet all known. (In this connection an interesting problem is raised by memory – the most familiar form of evidence for the past. Suppose that tomorrow I shall remember something about yesterday that I have forgotten now – that I arranged a meeting today, for example. Can I argue that this evidence for yesterday exists at this moment? I think so, for many things are buried in our memories of which we are not all the time aware. The alternative is to suppose that tomorrow's memory of yesterday will be a new creation, which seems very odd.) Here there is a clear contrast between knowledge and evidence. We are told by archaeologists that there is almost certainly more of Roman Britain still under the soil than has yet been excavated. Thus we may look forward to having far greater knowledge of that era in 100 years' time than we have now. The evidence, on the contrary, will not have increased one jot. We can never have more evidence of Roman Britain than exists now, but we can have much more knowledge.

### 3   *Everything is evidence*

If this seems rather disappointing, let us look at the other, more cheerful, side of the coin. This is that every single thing now in existence can be used as evidence for the past. Historical evidence is not confined to old stones and old documents. As we see below (pp. 145–6), historians and archaeologists have been learning to use kinds of evidence that were previously ignored. The fact is that any remains (whether material or ideal) can provide evidence for the lives of past men and women. Every working historian is hungry for more evidence. Although exactly what she wants may not be available, there remain many riches yet. To put it briefly: **all evidence is here; all here is evidence.**

### 4   *What the historian uses*

Turning now to the evidence that the historian may use, we consider in turn primary and secondary evidence, types of evidence, hard and soft evidence, and intentional and non-intentional evidence.

### 5   *Primary and secondary sources*

**A primary source is a piece of evidence whose origin is contemporary with the period in question** – thus the Domesday Book for the Norman Conquest, or Wellington's dispatches for the Peninsular War. **A secondary source is a study, usually by a historian, of the period under review,** or some aspect of it. This is written after (often long after) the period. All reputable historical research must be based on primary sources. Work in the archives is as essential to the historian as laboratory work to the scientist. A scientist does not spend all his time in the laboratory, nor a historian in the archives, but the experience acquired there is essential to both professions, and their conclusions must be open to verification in both places. In addition no historian should venture to set pen to paper until he or she has read widely and deeply in what others have had to say on the subject. Indeed she can hardly get her bearings at all or find out what questions are to be asked until she has read her predecessors. To the study of secondary sources we may apply Pope's advice:

> A little learning is a dang'rous thing;
> Drink deep, or taste not the Pierian spring:
> There shallow draughts intoxicate the brain,
> And drinking largely sobers us again.

### 6   *Primary or secondary?*

Primary and secondary sources cannot always be easily distinguished, however. We observed that two things characterize primary material: that it is contemporary and that it is unprocessed. If, as is commonly done, we use the first criterion alone to distinguish primary from secondary, then problems arise in relation to the other one.

To begin with, what of the editions of printed documents? A large proportion of the relevant papers for medieval and early modern history have been collected, transcribed, ordered and published. This is a great convenience for the historian, who would otherwise not be able to consult more than a fraction of these materials. A visit to a university or large reference library will show these volumes (Calendars of Close and Patent Rolls, Letters and Papers of Henry VIII, State Papers Venetian, etc.) marching side by side for yard after of yard of shelving. There are drawbacks, however. One is that the very quantity conceals the fact that not all the relevant documents may be there. Moreover, some of them are only partially transcribed. Also there is the possibility that errors have crept into the transcription or the printing. And finally the historian is denied the clues that the original document may afford by way of ink, handwriting, paper or vellum, format, etc. Nevertheless, the printing of sources is invaluable. This becomes even more apparent in European history. Four well-known histories in paperback will illustrate the point: Steven Runciman's *History of the Crusades*; Geoffrey Parker's *The Dutch Revolt* – a book whose bibliography contains particularly interesting discussions of evidence; R. J. W. Evans's *The Making of the Habsburg Monarchy*; and J. H. Elliott's *The Count-Duke of Olivares*. These authors have each read source materials in five, six or more languages, including Czech and Hungarian (Evans), Greek (Runciman) and Dutch (Parker). A facility in French, German, Italian, Spanish and Latin is common to them all – probably as a matter of course. Although they studied some original documents, much of their work was based on printed sources (as their bibliographies indicate). The twin difficulties of frequent access to distant repositories and of deciphering a foreign language in a foreign hand for every document would have been costly in time and labour. Nevertheless, necessary as they are, such printed sources cannot be considered completely unprocessed raw material.

## 7   Contemporary opinion

A second problem arises with pamphlets (from the sixteenth century on) and with newspapers (from the seventeenth century on). These, being strictly contemporary, show what some people at the time thought of the events in question. As such, they are good primary sources. But when you consider how ill-informed, biased and even unscrupulous the writers and printers are likely to have been, you realize that they are not good evidence for the events themselves.

Then there are contemporary chronicles and histories. Such works (even the apparently simple Anglo-Saxon Chronicle) at least provide a skeleton chronology for ordering events in time. Some venture upon cause and explanation. The more informed discuss motive and the interplay of personality. The more educated (profiting from the humanism of the

Italian Renaissance) consciously model themselves upon classical authors and attempt to write political or 'philosophical' histories – for example, Machiavelli and Guicciardini in Florence, Polydore Vergil and Thomas More in England, Philippe de Commynes in France. These can be very useful. In an appendix to his *Edward IV* Charles Ross laments the lack of such contemporary historians for that reign, and he quotes G. R. Elton: 'it is because no sound contemporary history exists for this age that its shape and meaning are so much in dispute now.'[21]

And what are we to make of those histories written while the events recounted are still in train? Geoffrey Parker records thirty-four contemporary histories of the revolt of the Netherlands.[22] Before we dismiss all these as too premature to be worth serious consideration – for they must be lacking both in essential information and in the perspective given by distance, we should remember that one of the acknowledged masterpieces of the historian's art, Thucydides's *History of the Peloponnesian War*, is just such a 'premature' effort. Contemporary, yes. But unprocessed raw material? Hardly. Yet it is almost all we have to go on for our knowledge of that great conflict.

Finally, and most problematic of all, is the evidence of the imaginative literature of an age. It is easy to sneer at the facile attempts, fashionable in the first half of this century, to write social histories of 'The World of Chaucer', 'The England of Shakespeare' or 'The London of Dickens' based largely upon supposed facts drawn from the poetry, plays and novels of these writers. These fictions supply no hard evidence; yet it is difficult to believe that one could have as deep an insight into the England of Edward III, Elizabeth I or Victoria if Chaucer, Shakespeare and Dickens had never written. They give contemporary evidence without a doubt, but it is difficult to state precisely evidence for what.

## 8   Types of evidence

About 100 years ago two French scholars, C. V. Langlois and C. Seignobos, wrote an *Introduction to the Study of History* in which they ruled that history essentially depended on documentary evidence – 'no documents, no history'.[23] If this was an attempt to rule out other sources of history (for example, architecture, art or archaeology, of which historians had long been making use) it was a spectacular failure. Within a few years the American James Harvey Robinson opened his *The New History* thus: 'In its amplest meaning History includes every trace and vestige of everything that man has done or thought since first he appeared on the earth . . . Its sources of information extend from the rude flint hatchets of

---

[21] Ross (1975), p. 429.
[22] See his *The Dutch Revolt* (1979), p. 277.
[23] Langlois and Seignobos (1898), p. 17.

Chelles to this morning's newspaper.'[24] Nowadays we observe that historians employ an ever-widening range of material to furnish evidence of the past – not only the flints and potsherds of the archaeologist, but crop patterns, hedgerows, ruined and rejected machinery, folk-songs, myths, memories, blood-groups, speech patterns, parish registers, land surveys, account books, place-names, sunken wrecks and much more. It seems that now all is grist that comes to the historian's mill. What is required is the ability to read that evidence aright.

## 9    Hard and soft evidence

One important element in this explosion of historical sources is statistical evidence. While some kinds of evidence are fairly sparse (for example, for ancient Greek cities other than Athens, or eleventh-century charters) other kinds are voluminous – for example, the births, deaths and marriages recorded in thousands of parishes in this and other countries. From these has arisen a whole new science of **historical demography: that is, the statistical study of populations in the past.** A good short introduction to this important subject is E. A. Wrigley's *Population and History* (1969), which is based on the much larger work under Wrigley's editorship, *An Introduction to English Historical Demography* (1966). Of great value to historians is the massive work that he produced with R. S. Schofield, *The Population History of England 1541–1871: A Reconstruction* (1981). The pioneer work in this field was, of course, Thomas Malthus's *First Essay on Population* (1789), but a full development of the theory had to wait until A. Sauvy's *Théorie générale de la population* (1952–4).

Two modern advances have made possible the extension of historical research into areas where vast amounts of data present hitherto insoluble problems: these are the development of statistical theory and the invention of the micro-chip leading to ever more powerful computers. Economic historians have thus been able to measure populations, land-holdings, imports and exports, rents, profits, exchange rates, yields of fields and mines, profitability, investment and economic growth. Two useful introductions to quantitative history are Michael Drake (ed.), *Applied Historical Studies* (1973) and Roderick Floud (ed.), *Essays in Quantitative Economic History* (1974), especially the cautionary essay in the latter by G. Ohlin, 'No Safety in Numbers: Some Pitfalls of Historical Statistics'.[25] A French approach to quantitative history is found in the work of the *Annales* school of historians, of which a good example is E. Le Roy Ladurie, *The Territory of the Historian* (1979). **Such historical evidence, processed by statistics and embodied in computer print-outs, is expressed in numbers and symbols rather than words and sentences.** Such measure-

---

[24] Robinson (1965), p. 1.
[25] See also above, ch. 3, pp. 70–2.

ments carry great authority in the eyes of econometric and 'cliometric' historians — perhaps all the more because expressions like

$$\frac{\Delta y}{\gamma} = \frac{\Delta Kph}{\gamma py} \times \frac{\Delta y}{\Delta K} \times \frac{ph}{ph}$$

(as in Floud, 1979, p. 236) daunt and baffle the innumerate reader. **This is known as 'hard' evidence.**

By contrast, **'soft' evidence** is found in more conventional historical documents, where it **is couched in words not figures, and** where it **often expresses ideas rather than quantities.** (Think, for example, of political and constitutional documents — Magna Carta, the Act in Restraint of Appeals of 1533 or the Constitution of the United States of America.) The epithet 'soft' suggests that the material is disputable, qualifiable, even malleable. It is open to more than one interpretation; people argue endlessly about what exactly it means. 'Not so with our hard evidence', boast the cliometricians. 'Ours is quantifiable and unambiguous.' But not everything is quantifiable. For example, sociologists insist that our social reality consists of beliefs, conventions, customs, institutions — which boil down to ideas. But how do you write the history of ideas? Many people try, but, as one political historian said, that is like nailing jelly to the wall.[26] R. G. Collingwood has argued that history can only be the history of thought. Material objects are not self-explanatory. Their meanings are not borne on their faces — not even coins or monuments if we cannot read the language or reconstruct the social conventions, as many a baffled archaeologist has discovered. Because soft evidence is in words, not numbers, there arise all the problems of language — of translation, of intention, of comprehension. Notoriously, one can never be sure that a string of words means the same to the hearer or reader as to the speaker or writer — or even to another hearer or reader. With numbers there is little doubt. There is less ambiguity in '10' or '365' than in words like 'crown' or 'Vaterland'. But we must still ask in the former case, What has been counted? How correctly? And by whom? When? and Where?

There is no need here to argue the respective merits and demerits of hard and soft evidence. The intelligent reader can think of some of them for herself. The working historian has to use both kinds, if possible, and know how to evaluate them for her purpose.

## 10  *Intentional and non-intentional evidence*

The last distinction to be made is between evidence which is intended for the eyes of some future inquirer and that which is not so intended. Marc Bloch in his sadly uncompleted work, *The Historian's Craft*, makes the

---

[26] See Novick (1988), p. 7.

distinction admirably clear. When we read histories or memoirs or battle reports 'we are only doing exactly what the writers expected us to do.' But the prehistoric woman who threw her garbage into a lake or river, the medieval businessman who wrote up his accounts had not 'the least desire to influence the opinions either of contemporaries or of future historians.'[27] Although the historian cannot do without evidence of the first kind, she is rightly distrustful of it – as if she were buying a second-hand car or a middle-aged horse. Evidence of the second kind has no intention to mislead her, but it presents problems of understanding. It does not come out to meet her, as it were. What exactly is meant by this sentence in a politician's letter? What was the function of this peculiar piece of metal or that hole in the wall? As with hard and soft evidence, the historian must use, but not confuse, both intentional and unintentional evidence.

## C.   The Use of Evidence

### 1   *How the historian works*

'It was at Rome, on the 15th of October 1764, as I sat musing amidst the ruins of the Capitol, while the barefooted friars were singing vespers in the temple of Jupiter, that the idea of writing the decline and fall of the city first started to my mind.' These words from the *Autobiography* of Edward Gibbon stir the imagination. (No matter that later scholars have pointed out the inaccuracy of one or two of the details.) In my turn I have stood on the same spot, looked out over the ruins of ancient Rome to the Renaissance domes and roofs still rising above the modern city – nearly 3,000 years of greatness at my feet. And I thought of Gibbon there, more than two centuries before me, contrasting in his mind the majesty of imperial Rome with the triumphant humility of its successor, the Christian Church.

Thus, one feels, should historical enterprises be conceived. Of course, few are. Yet if the historian has never been seized by the drama of his subject, never had his imagination stretched far beyond the commonplace and the everyday, then he would do well to seek another trade. For without imagination or sense of drama he will bore his readers. Worse, he will eventually bore himself. The illuminating inspiration in which the work is conceived must be followed by laborious months and years before the book comes to birth.

So where does evidence come in? Let us look at the stages of historical composition. Most works develop like this, though we must remember that the historian goes back and forth between the stages as he works.

---

[27] Bloch (1954), pp. 60–1.

## 2   The development of the work

Listed in logical (not chronological) order, the stages are:

1   The choice of subject.
2   The selection and, where necessary, the preparation of the evidence.
3   An alert and thorough reading, or other study, of the sources.
4   The tentative construction of a mental picture or model to fit the subject.
5   A firm version of this construction in a way that is fit to be made public.

Let us consider each stage in turn.

## 3   Choice of subject

Here several influences operate. If he writes history for a living, the historian is likely to choose a topic that has public appeal – often to national pride or the excitements of war. Writers with a private income (that is, almost all historians before the twentieth century) are free, like Gibbon, to choose whatever inspires them. That other works already exist on the subject need not deter them, provided that they have something new to say. The academic historian, by contrast, who is part teacher, part student, is not wholly free in his choice. He has invested a good deal of capital (in his case, labour) in his area of teaching; thus he is unlikely to go outside this area for his book.

More often than might be supposed, the historian does not first select a topic and then look for evidence; he is struck by the evidence and sees that this can yield a book. Using sixteenth-century records of the High Court of Admiralty for another purpose, I was struck many years ago by the frequency of the name 'Ralegh' in the proceedings of that court. This moved me to write the history of the family of that seaman, courtier and colonizer. Much better known is *Montaillou*, the vivid study of a medieval village by Emmanuel Le Roy Ladurie. Using the Inquisition Register of a French bishop, Ladurie achieved something very rare: the direct testimony of medieval peasants, describing their life in their own words.[28]

The exigencies of war sometimes produce books under stranger circumstances. It was partly in the concentration camp of Buchenwald and partly in German-occupied Holland from 1940 to 1944 that the Dutch historian, Pieter Geyl, wrote a masterly study of the historiography of Bonaparte, *Napoleon: For and Against*.[29] After fighting for his country in two world wars, the French historian Marc Bloch meditated upon the

[28] Le Roy Ladurie (1978).
[29] Geyl (1965).

collapse of Frence in 1940, wrote his poignant and searching explanation of that collapse, joined the Resistance and was shot by the Germans in 1944.[30] It is unusual for a historian to be able to supply almost all his evidence from his own experience. Yet in 1945 a British intelligence officer was commanded to investigate the end of Hitler's life. Two years later this officer, Hugh Trevor-Roper, produced a small masterpiece, *The Last Days of Hitler*.[31]

## 4  Selection of evidence

As we have seen, in some cases the availability of the evidence precedes the choice of the topic. But even when this happens there is always more evidence to be sought. Modern archivists and librarians have to find space every year for yards and yards of files and books that are added to their stores. One might be forgiven for supposing that historical studies suffer from a surfeit of evidence. Occasionally this is true, but in the majority of cases the historian finds himself frustrated by the lack of relevant material. Generally, though not always, the further one goes back in time, the sparser is the evidence. The Roman Empire is fairly well documented, but comparatively little remains for the history of Europe between 500 and 1000 AD. The documentation for the twentieth century, on the other hand, is voluminous. This is deceptive, however. Since the advent of the telephone many important conversations take place of which no record remains. In this respect the previous centuries – when people even in the same building sent written notes to each other – were kinder to historians. Perhaps nothing gives a better idea of the difficulties of finding suitable evidence than to try to write the history of your own family over the past hundred years. Some of the evidence consists of memories, some of photographs, letters and diaries, some of accidentally preserved theatre programmes, rail tickets and so on. Most of what you can put together will be found to rest on the support of a single source – one person's recollections, a single diary or letter. Yet the historian knows that all such evidence is unreliable unless supported by at least one other piece of independent evidence. How much of your evidence can you check in this way? Of course, the historian has to examine all possibly relevant evidence, picking out the more from the less useful. He does not complain about that. What irks him is that most of his evidence has already been sorted for him – sorted by blind chance which has left him much that is useless while bearing into oblivion just what he wanted to know. Nor is his judgement of relevance always infallible. Most historians have had the experience of spending days in reading, noting and transcribing material that later turned out to be of little value to the enterprise. The converse is

---

[30] Bloch (1968).
[31] Trevor-Roper (1947).

just as frustrating. Often, at a later stage, one needs to go back for a second look at the documents that one thought had been thoroughly explored. This may not be too difficult if the archive is in one's home town. Frequently it is in another city and sometimes in another country, even nowadays in a distant continent. E. H. Carr speaks of history being 'a continuous process of interaction between the historian and his facts'.[32] The interaction is not so easy when one component is three or four thousand miles away.

Languages, too, act as a filter for the evidence. Any historian of Europe needs to be able to read several languages.[33] Indeed, it is often necessary even for one's own country. The history of the port of Bristol (a modest piece of local history, one might suppose) calls for, at least, English, French, Latin and Spanish. However linguistically gifted, few people can read several other languages as easily as their own. Reading speed (or rather the lack of it) reduces the number of documents that a researcher can peruse in a given time. Moreover, it is easy to miss the subtle nuances of a foreign style. This, too, obscures some of the evidence. To pay to have the documents translated is usually too costly. There is some relief to be found in the fact that calendars and collections of documents have been published in translation. But these are, inevitably, only a very small part of what the researching historian wishes to consult. In any case, the conscientious historian prefers to study the original of a document rather than a version of it that has passed through several hands before it comes to him. In all these ways language reduces and selects the evidence available to the historian regardless of his particular needs.

Similar arguments apply to other sources of historical evidence that often require him to call on the expert in one or more of the so-called 'auxiliary' sciences: handwriting, legal forms, heraldry, the arts of the book and the picture, linguistics, place-names, seals and medals. All these yield historical evidence, but it is evidence that calls for rare skills laboriously acquired.

## 5    A reading of the sources

Although he may have been initially inspired by the primary evidence, the historian must make a thorough perusal of the secondary sources – all that has been written on the subject by earlier historians. One reason is to ensure that he does not merely repeat them. A. J. P. Taylor quipped, 'History does not repeat itself; historians repeat each other.' Like many jokes, this one had a serious message. It is that one's predecessors may well not be the best guides. They can mislead you. Taylor himself believed this when he wrote his radical revision of the history of the foreign

[32] E. H. Carr (1964), p. 30.
[33] As we noted above in this chapter, p. 143.

relations of Germany.[34] In *Man On His Past* (1960) Herbert Butterfield demonstrated how historians of the Seven Years War had been misled into following the erroneous assumptions of their predecessors.[35] In 1913 Charles A. Beard published *An Economic Interpretation of the Constitution of the United States*. This produced cries of rage, both academic and popular. A newspaper headline of the day read: 'SCAVENGERS, HYENA-LIKE, DESECRATE THE GRAVES OF THE DEAD PATRIOTS WE REVERE.'[36] Clearly Beard was, to say the least, taking a different line from his predecessors. In the 1960s and 1970s a number of economic historians in America tried to overthrow the traditional view of the economics of slavery in the American South. As one review of their work stated, 'Indications are that on the eve of the Civil War slavery was profitable to the planters, viable, and consistent with a growing economy.'[37] Along with the secondary sources the historian will immerse himself in the primary sources – reading and reading until he can almost hear the voices. The fascination here is that, with certain exceptions that we have noted, what he is reading is communications that were never intended for him. He is like an eavesdropper secretly overhearing important or fascinating conversations. As the ball of talk is tossed to and fro he swoops in like a footballer intercepting a pass and carries off his prize. (This romanticized but strictly truthful view of historical research may help the scholar through a weary hour.)

## 6   Constructing a model

From the very beginning of the enterprise the historian has had some vague idea of what he was going to find out. Now, as he researches and reads and reflects on what he has learned, a picture, or rather a representation, of the past is taking a firmer and firmer shape in his mind. As yet, only parts of the whole are fairly clear; other parts are still hazy or unresolved and call for more work. As he goes back and forth between his primary evidence, his secondary sources, perhaps also the opinions of colleagues and friends, and lastly the constructions growing in his mind and in his writing, he may alter his conception of the finished work. For example, the French historian Pierre Goubert tells us that at first he aspired to write a total history of the people of the Beauvaisis (a small region to the north of Paris) in the seventeenth century. As he worked on he found the evidence so abundant that he had to abandon the military, juridical, religious, moral and even agrarian aspects. He was yet able to build up a fascinatingly detailed demographic and social picture of some

[34] See A. J. P. Taylor (1964).
[35] See chapter 5.3, 'The Fallacies of the Historians'.
[36] See Novick (1988), p. 96.
[37] S. L. Engerman, 'The Effects of Slavery upon the Southern Economy: A Review of the Recent Debate' 1967 reprinted in Temin (1973), pp. 398–428.

two hundred parishes.[38] Such a representation is, as we have seen, a model of part of the past rather than a complete copy. The model may be colourful and dramatic in the manner of old-fashioned historians like G. M. Trevelyan or George Bancroft; or it may be an austere framework of girders made by an economic historian out of statistical series and algebraic equations. But whatever form it takes, it will still be the subjective experience of that historian, as Holborn has warned us. And no two historians have the same subjective experiences because no two men (still less women) have the same minds.

## 7   Publication

Finally all this subjective experience has to be put into public form; it has to be published. The thoughts have to be made objective in words and diagrams that the historian's readers and hearers will understand.

## 8   Placing the evidence

We may now see more clearly the essential part played by evidence. To the historian evidence is as necessary as flour to the baker – though neither of them is confined to that particular ingredient. Two things need to be remembered about evidence in history; one is that evidence is something *evident*; it is something that has survived into the light of the present from the darkness of the past. The other is that historical evidence may be sparse or it may be plentiful, but it is always inadequate, falling far short of the richness of the original reality. Moreover, exactly what survives is rarely just what the historian wishes; it is largely a matter of chance.

The historian, therefore, has a problem: just where should she fit a particular piece of evidence into the self-consistent whole that she is constructing as a model or representation of the past? Pieces of evidence do not appear before her in isolation. Sometimes it seems it might be better if they did. Then the assemblage of evidence into a finished historical work would be like putting together a jigsaw puzzle or a mosaic. But nearly always one piece of evidence is found in proximity to another. Documents are found in bundles; in an archaeological dig objects lie near one another and the exact location of an artefact is often more revealing to the scholar than the object itself. In a published work one text (in a collection of documents) or one fact (in a narrative history) is placed next to another. Thus the researcher can hardly avoid the psychological jump from physical proximity to material relevance. But she must beware; there may be no connection at all. Just as a careless librarian may shelve *The Golden Bough* under Forestry, so a document may (as I have sometimes found in my own researches) be put in the wrong place in a series simply on grounds of apparent similarity of name or topic. Sometimes it is

[38] See Goubert (1968), pp. 10, 15.

impossible to be certain whether or not the John Smith referred to in it is the same man as the subject of the rest of the bundle. Similar problems arise in a narrative. When we are told that a certain person did A, and then B, and proceeded to do C, we are likely to suppose that there was a continuing purpose here; that he did B because of A, and then found himself in circumstances that led him to do C. Why else should the narrator bother to mention these things? But we may be jumping to unwarranted conclusions. There may be no connection whatever. Sheer proximity in time or place does not entail relevance or cause and effect or, indeed, any relationship other than itself.

## 9  Horizontal and vertical knowledge

Evidence, then, has to be 'placed'; the historian has to put it where it belongs. This requires what may be called both **'horizontal'** and **'vertical'** **knowledge.**[39] **By the former I mean knowledge of what was going on at about the same time; by the latter I mean knowledge of what happened before and after.** I will illustrate horizontal knowledge first.

Suppose that a plough has turned up a quantity of what appear to be musket balls, rusty swords, buckles etc. 'Ah, a battle!' we exclaim. But these never constituted a battle. That consisted of large bodies of men, filled with varying emotions of hatred, loyalty or fear, engaged in slaughtering one another, or in avoiding being slaughtered. These scraps of metal were only a small part of what had been a phenomenon of blood, flame, smoke, noise, terror and death. But to the trained imagination of the historian they suggest the events that occurred at the time when they were scattered on the ground. It is quite a salutary exercise to take a famous text such as Magna Carta, the American Declaration of Independence, the Communist Manifesto or Lincoln's Gettysburg speech and to try to make the appropriate 'horizontal' connections with the surrounding events; to work out how the evidence that *has* remained was once connected with the simultaneously existing things that have not remained. For every timeless classic was a product of history.

Turning to vertical knowledge, we have now to consider where to locate our piece of evidence in the long flow of time. Immediately a difficulty appears. For in one sense our piece of evidence is located here and now, in the present; otherwise it would not be evident. But, as we have seen, it also survives from the past; otherwise it would not constitute evidence for that. From exactly what point in the past did it originate? For exactly what event in the past is it evidence? Many of the special skills or 'auxiliary sciences' of history are devoted to this problem of exact dating. Boring as it may seem to the layman, its vital importance is recognized by

---

[39] See ch. 2, pp. 29–30 above for vertical and horizontal contexts.

every serious historian. All these many and varied skills have three imperatives in common: first, it is necessary to be sure exactly what is before one now; second, to trace its course from its origin to its present lying before one's eyes; and third, to establish how and why it came into existence, as well as where and, finally, when. Each needs a few words of comment.

## 10   Identifying the evidence

On first sight of a document one is inclined to say. 'This is a letter from A (the signatory) to B (the recipient).' But that is jumping to the task of the third imperative. One's first duty is to establish what is there now. Is it written on paper, parchment or vellum? What is the constitution of the ink in which it is written? Whose or what is the handwriting? And so on. We must not be deceived by a forgery. As for the second imperative, much of the evidence that influences a historian's thinking is found in books – either secondary works or collections of primary sources. These latter have been through the hands of transcriber (and possibly translator), printer and editor. For much of the time the historian has to rely on the work of other historians; she cannot do over again everything that her predecessors did. Nevertheless, whenever she has any doubt about their reliability she goes to where they got the information – 'What was their evidence for saying this?' The inquiry may take her to a modern edition of an older text – let us say, Machiavelli's *The Prince* or a Leveller tract of the 1640s. She may rest content with the scholarship of this modern edition. On the other hand she may recognize that the supposedly accurate text before her has passed through many hands and, to set her doubts at rest, she may pursue the original document. This is not likely to be easily secured, but if she can lay hands on it (and if her linguistic skills are up to it) she may feel that she has succeeded in going behind the backs of many intermediaries and has come as close to the original as she can. (In fact, unless she is as good as the highly specialized scholar who produced the modern edition she may have gone too far and led herself into the possibility of error, but we will leave this on one side.) Even so, the task is not finished. The original document she now has in her hands is kept in some archive or repository. How did it get there? Where was it before that? What happened to it through all those centuries? (For example, what are the implications of the fact that *The Prince* was published nineteen years after it was written?) This inquiry (similar to those undertaken by art dealers with paintings) is called tracing the provenance of the document. In effect, it is a matter of tracing history backwards. As Kitson Clark explained: 'The questions "through whose hands has this evidence passed and what have they done to it" cannot be confined to those who have had documents in their charge. They must be asked of everyone else who has transmitted the evidence upon which the history which men and women are going to use is based.'[40] The third imperative is to establish the reason for the creation of the document in the first place. Was it really a letter from A to B? Or was it written for purposes of publicity or deception? If a genuine personal letter, was it ever sent? Did B ever receive it? If so, did he read it? If he did, did he act on it or ignore it? The questions are almost endless. Perhaps the document is part of the ledger of a customs officer. Is he faithfully recording the goods? Or is he presenting an account that will satisfy his superiors? Even if he is scrupulously honest, can he have been mistaken about some of the quantities? Here again many questions remain.

But when our three imperatives have been obeyed to the best of anyone's ability (and not before) we can turn to the other half of vertical knowledge. You may have forgotten that we have so far considered only the second phase of vertical knowledge – i.e. the stretch of time between the origin of the evidence and the present. But what of the earlier phase – that which came before the creation of the evidence? What were the antecedent causes and reasons for it? These questions, too, have to be asked. But we shall not look at them here. Cause and effect are a topic for a later chapter.

## 11   *Relics do not speak*

All this, then, is involved in the correct 'placing' and identifying of the evidence. But that is not enough. You could supply all that information to the untutored inquirer and he would be baffled. 'But what does it all *mean*?' he will cry in desperation. He's quite right. The really important thing about evidence is that it should be correctly interpreted, that we should know *for what* it is evidence. Now here we note an important distinction – between evidence-as-relic and evidence-as-argument. Let us recall that this chapter is entitled 'History as Relic'. Some events in the past have left traces in the present: they are all we have to go on. But these traces are mute: whether bones, castles or documents, they wait silently *for us* to make something of them, *for us* to make them speak, *for us* to determine what they mean. Only when we understand them (or believe that we do) can they be considered as *evidence for* something. And, as the traditional detective story demonstrates, a trace from the past (a footprint, a hair, a written note) can be understood in more than one way. To put it in a nutshell, evidence-as-relic is silent. It is we who interpret it as evidence for this or that and thus make it evidence-as-argument.

## 12   *Three interpretations*

Thus, just as the baker's art consists in what he does with the flour, so the historian's lies in what she does with the evidence. Interpretation is not, of

---

[40] G. Kitson Clark (1967), p. 82.

course, totally distinct from the identifying and placing that we have already discussed. Indeed, it can be held that they are the same thing. 'It is impossible', wrote Oakeshott, '. . . to "fix" a text before we begin to interpret it. To "fix" a text involves an interpretation; the text is the interpretation and the interpretation is the text.'[41] Be that as it may, it will be convenient here to treat them separately.

When we read a text for the first time – be it a modern novel, a poem or a historical document – it reverberates in our experience. Indeed, we have to bring to it whatever we have learned from life – our reading, our conversations, our deeds and feelings and sufferings. If we had not these to go on, we should not be able to make sense of it. In short, the first and most natural interpretation is what meaning it has for us, here and now, in the context of our present moment in life.

This is as true for the historian as anyone else, but she (unlike the rest) does not stop there. She goes on to look for a second interpretation. She asks of a historical document (or other relic of the past) what it meant for the person or persons who produced it and for their contemporaries. 'We hold these truths to be self evident', wrote Thomas Jefferson, a slave-owner, 'that all men are created equal . . .' Thousands were inspired by these words. Did they then free their own slaves? Did they expect Jefferson to free his? It is too easy to dismiss Jefferson as a liar or a hypocrite. It is better to ask what those words meant to the men of 1776. And to the women. Their interpretation, it seems, was not ours.

Much has been written on this laborious task for the historian, trying to determine the second interpretation. But the task does not stop there either. There is a third interpretation, one that is to be reached only after we have made the first two. This is the meaning that the text has *for us* in full recognition of what it meant *for them*. In one sense every such relic of the *past* has this third meaning for the historian in the *present* simply because it acts as evidence for her. Thus it links her present thoughts and writings about the past with that very, once-living, past that is her subject. But some relics, especially some texts, have a further meaning in the present, and the Declaration of Independence is a good example. This text, like Magna Carta (1215) or the Declaration of the Rights of Man and the Citizen (1789) or the Communist Manifesto (1848), is important for people today not only for what it says to us now but because of what it meant at the time – and hence it says even more to us; it has a triple reverberation.

## 13   Variety in interpretation

Because of this plurality of echoes (as it were), the accepted interpretation of the same evidence can vary from time to time as well as from country to

---

[41] Oakeshott, (1933), p. 113.

country or from one school of historians to another. The first reading has different meanings for different people because they have different life experiences. Approaching the past with different presumptions they may well attribute different contemporary meanings in the second interpretation. Finally all these differences cross-multiply to lead to even wider variation in the third interpretation. Surprisingly there is, nevertheless, a great deal of agreement among historians. We may speculate on the various social forces that influence such agreement. We may even speculate about what would be the ideally correct interpretation were one to exist. We are content to agree about some things (like dates); it would be sad if we all agreed about everything. Could we really desire that the ringing words of Jefferson had nothing to say to coming generations other than what has already been said?

But let us return to the historian and her evidence. This, I repeat, is the indispensable link between her subject in the past and her ideas about it in the present. Without evidence she would be writing fiction. If she is a good historian she will have gone through the first and second interpretations to arrive at the third – the meaning that the text now has for her in the light of what it meant for people in the past. This interpretation will cohere with the rest of that picture of the past that she has been carefully building up – though it may well require some modification of that picture. This I take to be the process that E. H. Carr refers to when he speaks of the historian as 'engaged on a continuous process of moulding his facts to his interpretation and his interpretation to his facts'.[42]

In this coherence there lurks a danger, however. While it is quite proper that her tentative reconstruction of the past should be modified in the light of new evidence (this happens in the course of almost every detective story), it is not desirable that she should modify her evidence to fit her reconstruction. (Is this what Carr means by 'moulding his facts'?) The temptation is all the greater since she can recognize the full meaning of the evidence only in the light of its various contexts.[43] And she will have assembled these contexts in her mind, and perhaps even put them in her reconstruction. Nevertheless, she must never forget that the context of the evidence is events in the past, not her ideas and writings in the present. In all fairness, however, one must admit that it is difficult for a working historian to distinguish the two. Her critics may disagree with her interpretation of certain evidence, but if it has been well woven into her reconstruction they may find that they have to challenge her whole book. Since they may well not have the time to go over all the evidence themselves her work may stand for some years. But eventually it is likely to be challenged and replaced. Sir Geoffrey Elton is perfectly correct when he insists that two questions only are fundamental to historical method:

[42] E. H. Carr (1964), p. 29.
[43] See pp. 152–3 above.

'exactly what evidence is there, and exactly what does it mean?'[44] Yet it is not always a simple matter to determine the meaning of evidence, still less the 'exact' meaning. It is, I conclude, important to realize that for some questions (like 'When was the Battle of Waterloo fought?' and 'Who won?') it is desirable to secure agreement among the historians; for others (such as 'What is the significance of the Italian Renaissance of the fifteenth century?') it is not desirable. Whether any such agreement is *possible* in any particular case is another matter altogether.

## 14   Fact and interpretation

Among all this talk about 'fact' and 'interpretation', we should remind ourselves that in history we have only evidence and judgements about the evidence. Neither 'fact' nor 'interpretation' is a solid, determinate object to be unearthed like a dinosaur's bones. Neither is more than an agreed judgement. The degree of acceptance accorded to these judgements ranges from the virtually certain (e.g. that Napoleon was emperor of France) to the highly disputable (e.g. that Napoleon was a true son of the Revolution who found himself obliged to conquer Europe in self-defence). Unless we bear this in mind we are in danger of wasting a lot of energy arguing about what is and what is not a fact, or in searching for the one exact interpretation of every piece of evidence. We must not be misled by the word 'fact'. If Napoleon was emperor, then it is a fact that he was emperor. If Napoleon was not a true son, etc., then it is a fact that he was not a true son, etc. The historical question turns on the 'if'. Thus the concept of 'fact' does not help either way, though 'fact' is a useful shorthand term for agreed judgements. 'But if it is a fact it must be true!' you will exclaim. 'Surely we are concerned with what is true, not just with what learned professors think!' Precisely. But let me remind you that truth lies at the end of our researches. It is our goal. We must not claim to have arrived while we are still on the journey. For the time being the consensus of learned minds is the best guarantee of the truth that we have. Scholars are not infallible, but where, this side of Judgement Day, shall we find a better guide to historical truth than historical scholarship?

## 15   Relevance of evidence

Two small points remain before we leave the subject of the historian's use of evidence. One is the question of relevance. In her excitement at a new discovery – perhaps a series of very revealing documents – or in fascination with an intriguing story, the historian may be led astray from her strict purpose. It is a weakness of all but the most disciplined of historians to recount what seems important, amusing, interesting, salacious or exciting, but which is not strictly relevant to the matter in hand.

[44] Elton (1969), p. 87.

How often in reading history does one want to challenge the author: 'Yes, but what is the point of telling me this?' Historians should never cease to question themselves: 'Have I ignored nothing that is relevant? Have I included nothing that is irrelevant?'

## 16  Quoting evidence

The other warning relates to the use of quotation. In history we are trying to get at 'what actually happened'. In most cases, though certainly not in all, our evidence for this is what somebody said happened. Even as dull a source as a column of figures in an Exchequer account, a list of cases heard in a law court, or a page of customs receipts is what someone thought happened – or pretended to think. Thus even the most original of sources has already arranged things in a comprehensible way. They have observed what was going on and made sense of it. In literary terms they have *prefigured* the events. Perhaps for a truly unbiased and objective account we should have a highly observant Martian who could see everything and understand nothing. (But how would he describe it?)

Let us consider a particular case. To give authenticity and vividness to his account a historian will often quote part of his evidence: 'John Rawley and his adherents . . . commaundyd . . . to strieke downe all the sailles or elles thei sayd thay wolde sinke the . . . shipp . . . whiche was a verie old shipp and wolde be soone enforsed to sinke, and therfore for feare (they) dyd striek downe all the sailes . . .'[45] Retaining the original spelling increases the sense of a sixteenth-century voice. Nevertheless, although this is as near as we are likely to get to 'what actually happened', the veracity is something of an illusion. The words quoted are the clerk's copy (partly in Latin) of the evidence submitted to the High Court of Admiralty by the Spaniard's attorney – evidence that may have had to pass through a translator between the Spaniard and the attorney. Nor is it likely that the aggrieved captain was giving a complete and unbiased account of the events. But even if he was, and even if his words, passing through several intermediaries, give us a fair description, the account still prefigures the happenings and circumstances in terms of human actions. Movements, we could say, have already been interpreted as actions. That this is largely how we see life all the time is illustrated by the fact that a fictional narrative could use exactly the same words. Thus the historian's quotations, though justified on literary grounds by giving colour to the story, are suspect on epistemological grounds – they are rarely the guarantees of truth that they appear to be. They tell us what people said or thought happened, rather than 'what actually occurred'.

However, lest I be thought to be too dismissive of the participant's

---

[45] This is part of the description of the attack on a Spanish ship in 1549 by a half-brother of Sir Walter Ralegh. See Stanford (1962), p. 24.

version of events, let me close this section with what Carlyle had to say of his collection of Cromwell's letters and speeches: 'These are the words this man found suitablest to represent the Things themselves, around him, and in him, of which we seek a History. The newborn Things and Events, as they bodied themselves forth to Oliver Cromwell from the Whirlwind of the passing Time, – this is the name and definition he saw good to give of them.'[46]

# D.   The Origins of Evidence

## 1   *The bridge of evidence*

In this chapter ('History as Relic') we have been looking at historical evidence as something that makes the essential bridge between a moment in the past and that moment that we call the present. Every schoolchild knows the story of George Washington's axe – 'This is the very axe that he used to chop down the cherry tree – though it has had three new heads and two new handles.' Clearly that axe was no sort of evidence, for it did not stretch far enough back – i.e. to the boyhood of Washington. In the last section we looked at the near end of this 'bridge' – the evidence that the historian uses. Now we look at the far end of the 'bridge' – at the evidence in its origins.

## 2   *Four kinds of bridge*

Such 'bridges' from the past to the present may be put into four categories: natural, artificial, communicative and processive.

(i)   Natural evidence calls for little explanation. To the geologist the rocks tell the earth's history. For the palaeontologist those same rocks reveal in fossil form the story of life on earth. Historical geography is a fascinating study of past landscapes and of how man has changed them. But here we are approaching the second category.

(ii)   Artificial evidence consists of artefacts – the results of human efforts to transform the natural environment to our own purposes. A tilled field, a cleared forest, a bridged river, a goose-quill pen, a house, a bottle of wine or a laser are all relics that bear witness of the earlier times from which they came. Of particular interest are those artefacts that meet familiar household purposes – old furniture, bicycles, pans, garden tools etc. These bring home the fact of change with particular force even to the most unimaginative.

(iii)   From the last category I have separated that class of artefacts that

[46] Carlyle (1893) p. 10.

gives us most of our historical knowledge. Communicative evidence reveals the intention to communicate. It includes songs, cave and rock paintings, inscriptions on weapons or stones, statues in temples, and many other (though not all) forms of art. Most communicative artefacts, however, bear some sort of writing – from Egyptian hieroglyphics to electronic tapes and floppy disks. Yet with written evidence there is the important distinction to be made that some was intended for the eyes of contemporaries only and some was intended for posterity.[47] Even so honest a man as Samuel Johnson insisted that in the writing of epitaphs no man was upon oath. Kings and tyrants raised monuments and struck medals to impress posterity as well as their subjects – like Shelley's Ozymandias. Politicians and generals keep diaries and publish memoirs with more of a view to their own reputation than to historical accuracy. Many a forgotten cause is still pleaded from the grave. Historians, therefore, prefer the intimate letter meant for no eyes but the recipient's. It is not intended to influence them.

(iv) 'Processive' evidence is less common, but must not be overlooked. It can happen that what has endured from past to present is not one thing, but a process. For example, a field of wheat is evidence of the earlier activities of ploughing and sowing, though these themselves have not survived. The evidence lies in the process of growth. So a community may be law-abiding or law-rejecting; the relations between a married couple may be harmonious or fractious; this person may be polite and well-informed; that one may be ignorant and boorish. Social development, married life and upbringing, are processes. All these furnish indirect evidence of past happenings, which are not themselves surviving objects. What remains is simply the conclusion of a process.

The question of 'processive' evidence as such must be distinguished from another question which has to be asked about any evidence whatsoever. This is the question of what processes the relic has suffered since its origin. Documents may be altered or defaced; edifices may crumble, be demolished or be restored. Few relics come down the ages to us in their pristine condition. We have to try to discover what has happened to them in the meantime – sometimes a very long 'meantime' of a thousand years or more. The historian must grasp the processes by which anything originating in the past has come to the condition in which it presents itself to us now. Otherwise he can grossly misread the evidence – like believing that Norman architects built Windsor Castle, or medieval Germans Neu Schwanstein.

## 3   What does not survive

One can become so engrossed with the evidence that has survived from an

[47] See also ch. 6, pp. 146–7 above.

earlier age that one forgets how rare and unusual this is. Most of what makes up our lives – natural objects, artefacts, thoughts and conversations (even we human beings ourselves) – do not survive. Just look around you and ask yourself how much of what gives meaning to your life this week will still be around in a hundred years' time. Sir Walter Ralegh wrote:

> Even such is Time, which takes in trust
> Our youth, our joys, and all we have.
> And pays us but with age and dust . . .

Indeed very few things are capable of surviving that long. Hence our evidence is very selective. This fact is more obvious in archaeology – where the bowl (but not the soup in it) may remain, or in palaeontology – where bones (but not hearts or lungs) may be found. So in history: most of the things that most concern us are not capable of surviving for a hundred years or more; of the few classes of things that are so capable, only a tiny proportion in fact do so.

## 4    *Context of origin*

Hence we have to supply the context in which our (unusual) piece of surviving evidence came into existence. What was the intention of the writer of this document? What were the social and official conventions within which he wrote? What were the social and political forces that were playing upon him at that time? What were the psychological urges that led him to see the situation and to react to it in the ways that he did? What was the intended reader of the document likely to understand by it? What unspoken assumptions were shared by both writer and reader? I do not say that these questions can be answered in any particular case. But I do insist that we should ask them (and others like them) or we are likely to fall victim to our own assumptions.[48]

As we have remarked, the historian must never forget that the document before her was not meant for *her* eyes, but for someone else's – at least in most cases. Paradoxically, it is just on the occasions when she suspects that it *was* written for her eyes that she must doubt it.[49] Above all, she must remember that the document records the contemporary situation not only in the ways that the writer saw and understood it, but also in the words that he used to describe it. What she has before her is *his* verbal representation: the same words might represent a different reality

[48] See ch. 2, pp. 33–4 above.
[49] See p. 147 above.

to her. All these things have be to borne in mind when she evaluates her source. She is forced to consider problems of reliability whenever two or more sources are in conflict. This does not, however, absolve her from such questioning when she has only one, or when she has more than one but they do *not* conflict. Historical evidence is our only witness to the past. Therefore the historian must interrogate it ruthlessly like a prosecuting lawyer.

## E.   Another Relevant Topic: Oral History

As I suggested in the Introduction, there seems no limit to the ingenuity of researchers in finding evidence for the past. While it would be impossible to list them all (for the number grows daily), yet one type is of particular interest – the evidence of the spoken word. One reason for this is the fact that the researcher can generate this kind of evidence for herself. Most historical evidence, as we have seen, is derived from relics of paper, parchment, stone etc., left behind by earlier ages. Spoken evidence, however, appears in response to the researcher's questions. It is made to order – something of which the dangers are as obvious as the advantages are real.

Another reason for the importance of oral history is that it is a novelty at several levels. Not only does it introduce evidence of an unusual kind; it also opens up different sources, it makes available different (and often otherwise hidden) parts of the historical field, and it often suggests new angles of interpretation.

Like many other historiographical innovations, oral history grew into prominence as a result of technical advances; in particular, the microphone and the tape recorder. These make it comparatively easy for the researcher to interview the informant. The latter can talk freely, often forgetting the purpose of the interview. The former can concentrate on her subject and what he says, and leave until later the business of transcribing, sorting, selecting and editing the material. Moreover, the nuances of utterance are recorded, as they would not be in a written document.

Of course, the basic technique of historical research in this way is far from new. Thucydides, at the beginning of his history of the Peloponnesian War, wrote: 'Either I was present myself at the events I have described or else I heard them from eye-witnesses whose reports I have checked with as much thoroughness as possible. Not that even so the truth was easy to discover: different eye-witnesses give different accounts of the same events . . .'[50] Doubtless it was oral research of this contemporary kind that alerted historians to the need for a critical approach to their

[50] Thucydides (1954), p. 24.

evidence – a need that was long neglected by those 'scissors-and-paste' historians so justly pilloried by Collingwood.[51] But the microphone and tape recorder have many advantages over the wax tablet and stylus or the notebook and pencil.

New techniques, once perfected, opened new sources. They have been widely employed (as Vansina describes) to research the history of illiterate peoples – peoples who could not record their history in writing, but who preserved it in often remarkably accurate memories. Even among literate nations like ourselves there are many who, from age or lack of education, cannot write their memoirs, but who have important things to relate of their experiences over sixty, seventy or eighty years. Thus new parts of the historical field, especially in social history, are opened up to the historian's survey.

But not only the old and the poor can provide important historical evidence. For all governments, not only dictatorships, are reluctant to make their archives available to the historian. As a result important happenings are concealed from public knowledge. Where such attempts have been unsuccessful (as, for example, the mutinies in the British army in 1917), it is memories and oral research, not written documents, that have made them known.[52]

Thus 'the history of the present cannot be written without oral sources.'[53] That there is a case for not restricting this approach to the poor, the illiterate and the downtrodden has been powerfully made by Anthony Seldon and Joanna Pappworth. They have seen the importance of 'gathering information from those who forged or witnessed events in history' – that is, the leaders rather than the led. It is not just that the leaders have seen more of the game. It is also that they are likely to be articulate and complex characters – though their evidence is, for those reasons, more likely to need checking and counter-checking. Seldon and Pappworth quote a business historian saying that such spoken sources reveal 'the complexity of human motive, the fugitive nature of historical "truth", the gaps in the evidence, the sometimes tenuous relationship of word and deed'.[54] This accords with Bismarck's insistence on the uselessness of documentary sources.[55]

Of course, oral history has the disadvantage that in most cases it cannot reach further back than one lifetime.[56] Nevertheless it plays an important part in contemporary history. And the study of contemporary history

---

[51] Collingwood (1961), pp. 257–66.
[52] For further examples of British and American government's attempts to distort history, see Gwyn Prins, 'Oral History', in P. Burke (1991), pp. 127–8, 131–2, 135–6.
[53] Vandecasteele-Schweitzer and Voldman in Perrot (1992) p. 41.
[54] See Seldon and Pappworth (1983), p. 156.
[55] See above, p. 94.
[56] The study of oral tradition is another matter. See Vansina (1973).

(roughly that of the last half-century) is valuable not only for what it tells us, but also for the excellent training it gives the historian – training that he may then employ upon earlier periods.[57] A further advantage is recognized in women's history: 'In the field of women's history, however, the problem of memory is central, because women still remain an oppressed group, whose history is denied. To give them back their memory is to give them back their past, their history . . .'[58] Thus oral history can help in the important task of increasing a people's historicity – that is, their awareness of their place in history.[59]

These remarks are all too brief. To pursue oral history further, you may look at the classic works by Jan Vansina and Paul Thompson, at Henige (1982), at Gwyn Prins, 'Oral History', in Burke (1991), at Seldon (1988), at Seldon and Pappworth (1983), and at the journals, *Oral History* and *Oral History Review*. All these are in the bibliography at the back of this book.

## Conclusion

Historical knowledge, various aspects of which were discussed in the previous chapter, is now seen to rest upon historical evidence. Such evidence consists of relics of the past which form a bridge between those days and these. Our knowledge of that past is derived from a correct understanding of the nature of such 'bridges' – of what they actually are, and of what they imply about the world from which they came. Both 'fact' and 'interpretation' (often the subjects of dispute) are seen to be no more than judgements (more or less consensual) about such nature and such implications. To grasp that historical knowledge must be based on evidence, and to be able to estimate the reliability of such evidence are fairly sophisticated and fairly recent achievements, roughly contemporary with the beginnings of modern scientific thinking. The techniques required in the handling and understanding of historical evidence have largely developed only since the days of Leopold von Ranke and the opening of state archives to historians in the first half of the nineteenth century. However, a full understanding of the manifold nature of historical evidence and of the many disparate objects that may be exploited to yield such evidence hardly emerged before the twentieth century. The pitfalls in using any kind of historical evidence are many and are often well concealed. The price of historical knowledge, no less than that of liberty, is eternal vigilance.

---

[57] See Butterfield's remarks, p. 93 above. See also Seldon (1988).
[58] Vandecasteele-Schweitzer and Voldman in Perrot (1992), p. 43.
[59] For 'historicity' see pp. 50–1 above.

## Suggested Reading

Bloch 1954

Butterfield 1957

Butterfield 1960

Carr, E. H. 1964

Cipolla 1991

Clark G. K. 1967

Collingwood 1961

Elton 1969; 1970; 1983

Finberg 1965

Floud 1979; 1974

Fogel and Elton 1983

Gilbert and Graubard 1972

Hoskins, 1955; 1959

Maitland, 1960a; 1960b

Mandelbaum 1977

Marrou 1966

Marwick 1989

Momigliano 1966

Renier 1965

Rogers 1977

Shapiro 1983

Stanford 1990

Temin 1973

Tosh 1984

Trevor-Roper 1967

Wainwright 1962

Weisman 1984

# 7

# History as Event

What seest thou else
In the dark backward and abysm of time?

Shakespeare, *The Tempest*

What's past is prologue.

Shakespeare, *The Tempest*

Such is the unity of history that anyone who endeavours to tell a piece
of it must feel that his first sentence tears a seamless web.

F. W. Maitland

Le temps ne s'en va pas, mais nous nous en allons (Time does not go
from us, but we from it).

Source unknown

All only constant is in constant change;
What done is, is undone, and when undone,
Into some other fashion doth it range:
Thus goes the floating world beneath the moon.

William Drummond of Hawthornden

## Introduction

In the last three chapters we have been looking at history(2) – that is,
what people say and think and write about the past. In this chapter we
will consider the past itself and some of the problems that arise from it.
We do not overlook the fact that some writers have asserted that it is
virtually impossible to know the past, and therefore that the writings of
historians are little more than figments of their imagination to suit the
ideological demands of their age or social milieu.[1]

Let there be no confusion here: whether and how far our knowledge of
the past is accurate is one question; whether there is or was a past to be
known is quite another. All that we have discussed in previous chapters

---

[1] See Atkinson (1978), pp. 40–4; Ricoeur (1984), p. 98. For a lengthy discussion, see
Novick (1988), ch 15 and 16. For a popular statement of the extreme relativism of (so-
called) post-modernism, see Jenkins (1991). For a fierce rebuttal of these views, see Elton
(1991). See also above, ch. 1, p. 13.

warns us to be very critical of the accuracy of our claims to such knowledge. Nothing that we have said implies that there is nothing to be known. The past, after all, began only a second ago, and who doubts our knowledge of that? It is true that, with both time and space, we are less *aware* of what is remote than of what is at hand. But we must not suppose that it is our consciousness that endows things with their reality. I do not doubt that a great war was fought from 1914 to 1918 though I was not then born. Likewise I do not doubt that the Himalayas exist though I cannot see them from my study window. The *accuracy* of my knowledge of both that war and those mountains is, of course, quite another matter.

What, then, can be said of that ever-receding landscape that stretches from right under our nose (five seconds ago) to the remote tracts far beyond the horizon (5,000 years ago)?

*Questions about what happened in the past; the pattern of events; time*

1    What actually happened in the past?
2    What is an event?
3    Can we discern any shapes or patterns in the events?
4    If history is a 'seamless web', where and how can it best be cut up?
5    What connections (if any) are there between the pieces?
6    Is it structured (as distinct from merely shaped) in any way?
7    If so, are the structures always imposed by historians, or are at least some genuinely there in the events?
8    How far does history go back?
9    Do all nations have histories?
10    Do the various national histories make up one history?
11    Are there real eras that have beginnings and endings?
12    What is time?
13    Does it always pass at the same speed?
14    Does it move in a straight line or in circles?
15    How do we measure it?

The theme of this chapter is 'History as Event'. We are looking at what may be called the 'historical field' – the temporal space in which things happen. We shall look first at the constituents of the field – that is, what is in it. Then we shall look at the various ways in which the constituents are arranged – shapes and patterns and structures. Thirdly we look at time, the dimension in which events are ordered.

A    What Is an Event?
B    The Forms and Structures of History.
C    Time.

# A.    What is an event?

## 1    *What has changed?*

There's a sudden, unusual noise. A crowd gathers. 'What's happened?' we ask. The task of historians, we might say, is to answer that question about the last 5,000 years. But what do we mean by 'happen'? We mean that things 'occur', 'come about', 'take place'. What sort of things? Things like tables and chairs or dogs and cats? No, not those. Rather, things like occurrences, happenings, events. So an event is something that happens? We seem to be talking in a circle.

Yet events, we might say, are what history is all about. We must, surely, be able to say what they are. Traditional history is about kings and queens, presidents and generals, wars and treaties. More fashionable history is about populations and poverty and marriage customs and field systems and trade cycles. Are these things events? Some are: wars, treaties and trade cycles. But kings and poverty and field systems are not. We could say that members of the second group do not happen, whereas those of the first group do. We are back to the same problem: what is it to 'happen' or 'to take place'?

There is a clue in our opening sentence: the noise was described as 'sudden', 'unusual'. Does this not suggest that we were alerted by a change? And doesn't the phrase 'to take place' also suggest a change, the notion of one thing taking the place of another? So perhaps we have an answer. Can we add to what was said in chapter 1 (see pp. 11–12), and say that **an event (or a happening or an occurrence) is a change in a state of affairs?**

But notice that it is the change that we remark; it is the *difference* that is to be explained. This suggests that so long as things remain the same we are not bothered. It is changes that wake us up, that make us ask questions. That is why history records the changes in human affairs and, if possible, accounts for them.

## 2    *Noticing change*

Yet is it not surprising that we should be surprised by change? 'All things flow', said Heraclitus. Modern science confirms this. Whether we examine the universe at the microcosmic level of sub-atomic particles or at the macrocosmic level of whirling galaxies, we find that everything is in ceaseless motion. If motion is the norm, why is change unexpected?

Not long ago I visited the World Trade Center in New York, where an express lift whisked us up to the 107th storey in less than a minute. There was no sensation of movement; only the light on the indicator showed our rapid ascent. Nor do astronauts have any sense of speed as they whirl round the earth. This suggests that change of position (however rapid) means little if we are not aware of it. So it is not change in itself that surprises us, but *perceived* change. To perceive change is to be simultaneously aware of two states of affairs, one before and one after the alteration.

## 3   The definition of 'event'

So now we have a clearer idea of our keyword: **an event is a perceived change in a given state of affairs**; a change that we notice because we are simultaneously aware (whether by visual nerves, memory, documentation or other source of information) of both the earlier and the later states of affairs. Note, however, that the word 'event' has a public rather than a private connotation. Little, everyday changes – my shoe-lace is undone, my coffee has grown cold – hardly count as 'events'; rather they are 'happenings'. An event is a happening out of the normal run of things that is worth people's attention. It becomes a topic of conversation and is worth recording – as in a diary, a newspaper, a chronicle. Often, too, some anticipated future occasion is called an event – a concert or a football match.

Now we are approaching the sort of events that get into history books. We are talking about alterations in the normal states of affairs that arouse attention and so are remembered and recorded. For example: '1048. In this year there was a severe earthquake far and wide in England. In this same year Sandwich and the Isle of Wight were harried, and the best men that were there were slain; and king Edward and the earls put out to sea in their ships in pursuit of them.'[2]

## 4   Events in History

Events, then, at the most basic level, are simply changes. But changes go on all the time. An event has to be something that people take notice of. How many people, though, and how much notice? As to the first, we can reply: as many people as it concerns. A village fête will count as an event for the villagers, but for few outside the village, while a war will concern whole nations or even continents. That much is fairly obvious. How much notice has to be taken of an occurrence for it to count as an event depends very much on the context. We can see the sort of things that the English monks thought were events in 1048 – earthquakes and Viking raids. But what of all the other happenings in that year? Were there not more events than were recorded in the Chronicle? On the other hand, for a general history of England (still less one of Europe) that earthquake and those raids would not merit a mention. Would they count as events at all?

It seems, then, here is another way in which 'men make their own

[2] Anglo-Saxon Chronicle (1953), p. 166.

history.'[3] We have made the distinction between history(1) – history-as-event – and history(2) – history-as-account. This chapter is about the former. Since events are changes in states of affairs they clearly belong to history(1). But from the myriad changes taking place in the universe every second of its existence, we pick out and notice and record a few changes and call them events – whether it be the explosion of a supernova in the heavens or a fight on the coast of Kent. This up-grading from 'change' to 'happening' to 'event' is human work; it illustrates at a quite basic level how our minds transform history(1) into history(2); most of this is done before we ever start to write history proper. Changes take place all the time; only those that particularly concern us do we call events. And since *what* concerns us and *how many* of us and *how much* can vary from situation to situation and from context to context, there is no hard and fast rule as to what is or what is not an event – except that all events are perceived changes.

## 5    How long is an event?

What is the length of an event? In some contexts whole wars can count as events, like the Peloponnesian War in Greece (431–404 BC), or the Gulf War in Arabia in 1991. Thus an event can last months, years or decades – perhaps centuries. Was not the (probably lengthy) invention of agriculture one of the most important events in the long history of mankind? Equally an event can last a split second, like the shot that kills a head of state. And of course a war can be divided into smaller events like the Gallipoli campaign, the defence of Verdun, or the Battle of the Somme in the First World War. These, too, can be subdivided into various stages of the battle. However, contrary to what is sometimes asserted, an event is not capable of unlimited subdivision. If one proceeds in this way one will come down to the brief skirmish of a couple of platoons or even the individual shots from a gun. These, since they were perceived, can at least count as occurrences, but unless they were regarded as particularly noteworthy by several people they hardly count as events. Yet even a skirmish might be remembered if it involved the death of the colonel of the regiment. Thus it is not easy to draw an exact line between an event and a mere occurrence; so much depends on the context and the interests of the people concerned. After all, the death of the humblest private is an important event for his family and friends, though not for the history books.

The dimensions of any particular event are not always easy to determine. Some, like volcanic eruptions or earthquakes, have a definite centre but an indefinite extent as the shock-waves move outwards. For example, in 1992 was celebrated the quincentenary of the discovery of

---

[3] See Marx (1973b), p. 146.

America – the discovery for Europeans, that is. The key point of that protracted business may well have been the sighting of an island of the Bahamas. But the discovery must have been more than that, for if Columbus had then turned back to Spain, Europe would have been little the wiser. There had been reports before of islands across the Atlantic. Nor did the discovery of the mainland by John Cabot in 1497 or by Columbus on his third voyagle in 1498 properly constitute that discovery. For it was believed that they had found the coast of Asia. It was probably not before Balboa's sighting of the Pacific in 1513 and perhaps not until Magellan's expedition of circumnavigation in 1519–22 that it was perfectly clear that a whole new continent had been found. The discovery of America was a matter of years rather than of moments.

## 6    The various speeds of history

So far we have assumed that events are what history is about – which has long been accepted. This was forcibly challenged, however, in 1949 by Fernand Braudel in *The Mediterranean and the Mediterranean World in the Reign of Philip II*.[4] He had little patience with event-based history (*l'histoire événementielle*). Events for Braudel are only 'the ephemera of history; they pass across its stage like fire-flies, hardly glimpsed before they settle back into darkness and as often as not into oblivion.' Nevertheless, he admits, 'every event, however brief, has to be sure a contribution to make, lights up some dark corner or even some wide vista of history.'[5]

Abandoning the traditional style of event-based history, Braudel concentrates his attention on continuities rather than on changes. (Change, we recall, is the essence of event.) The idea stems from the cycles that are familiar to any student of economics. Economic phenomena (such as food prices) fluctuate in swings that may be measured in years (like the current booms and depressions of our own day) or in decades (like the long price rise of the sixteenth century). Braudel is surely right to assert that these are more than a backcloth to historical events; they actually constitute history, of which they form perhaps a more important part than the ephemeral events that make up traditional history. Social phenomena, too – systems of law and administration, of religion and of education; customs of marriage and burial, of inheritance and exchange, of feasting and fasting – these may proceed for generations with little apparent change. History, as Braudel says, moves at a thousand different speeds, rates of change 'which bear almost no relation to the day-to-day rhythm of a chronicle or of traditional history.'[6]

---

[4] See Chs 1 and 3, pp. 16–17 and 63–6 above.
[5] Braudel (1975), vol. 2, p. 901.
[6] Braudel (1980), p. 12.

## 7  Continuity and change

Thus history consists of more than the day-to-day activities of rulers and their ministers. We have to see the continuities in history as well as the changes. How can we understand the events of the sixteenth century without knowing about food prices and fairs, firearms and field systems? Braudel speaks of civilizations whose profound structural characteristics endure for centuries – even, we might add, millennia. Would this not be true of Egypt from the Great Pyramid (twenty-sixth century BC) to the Roman conquest (first century BC) or of China from the Emperor Shih Huang Ti (221–210 BC) to the last Manchu emperor, Mo-Ti (1908–12 AD)? To judge from archaeological remains, the bullock carts of rural India to-day are little different from those used at Mohenjo-Daro some 4,000 years ago. Nevertheless, things *do* change; even the most deep rooted of customs do not last for ever.

Historians of Philip II's Spain usually find it necessary to explain the system of long-distance pasturing of sheep which was controlled from the thirteenth to the eighteenth centuries by the syndicate known as the 'Mesta'. Since this endured over five centuries it is hardly an 'event' of the sixteenth; it was a continuity. Why put it into the histories of that period? Because it formed an important part of Spanish life (political, economic and social) in those days. And it is no longer there. For this reason it needs explaining. What is not recorded in the history books is that sixteenth-century Spaniards had two legs, a heart and lungs, loved their wives and children. These facts are omitted, not because they are unimportant, but because they have been true throughout Spanish history. Similar considerations apply to the institutions of Pharaonic Egypt or Imperial China. Thus we see that the conscientious historian records not only the changes in his period but also the continuities, *if* those continuities have not always been there. Perhaps even the longest of continuities, if it has a beginning and an end, can be regarded as an 'event' when it is seen in long perspective. After all, the Nile Valley has been inhabited for some 40,000 years. In that context even the 2,600 years of the Pharaohs can seem only one of several ripples on the surface – i.e. an event, a change in the state of affairs.

Events, I conclude, are not the short-lived flashes of Braudel's 'fire-flies'. They **are changes in states of affairs that both are perceived and are considered (for one reason or another) to be worth recording.** There are no rules about either size or importance, for these vary with the context and the people involved in the perception and the evaluation.

## 8  Events are not objects

Before leaving the subject, it is worth clearing up one or two confusions.

First we must be clear that **events are not objects or things**. Confusion may arise from the fact that events are part of the real world (i.e. not part of our ideas about it). Because every object may be distinguished by its particular situation of time and place – its spatio-temporal location, and because every event also has its own time and place, then it is possible to mistake one for the other. This is particularly easy if one thinks of a piece of historical evidence: a potsherd, a tombstone. When I write a letter I put at the top the address from where I am writing and the date. This is a spatio-temporal location. It is the spatio-temporal location of the sheet of paper lying before me (which is an object). It is also the spatio-temporal location of the act of writing. Which of the two is the event? Obviously the act of writing. The letter may pass on to distant places and ages and become a historical document, a piece of evidence for some future historian. Thus it may have many spatio-temporal locations; the event (my act of writing) has only one. Thus writing a letter may produce simultaneously an object, an event, and a piece of evidence. These three are, nevertheless, quite distinct and are not to be confused.

## 9   Events are not facts

A second confusion is that between events and facts. It is true that 'historic events cannot be compressed into generalities.'[7] Nevertheless, almost all social scientists attempt to do this. Moreover, that it must be done if history is to be explained at all is the contention of 'covering-law' theorists.[8] Again, confusion springs from taking one thing to be another: in this case identifying events with facts.

We have already defined 'event'. **A fact may be defined as 'an event or state of affairs *under a particular description*.'** 'The cat sat on the mat' is only one way of describing a state of affairs. 'The mat lay under the cat' is another. So is 'the cat rested on the mat in a semi-upright posture.' Thus one event or state of affairs is susceptible of many different descriptions. It is the descriptive part of the fact that is sometimes challenged as incorrect. Events and states of affairs, being part of the world, cannot be correct or incorrect; they just are. Disagreement can arise over whether the verbal part of the fact correctly describes the state or event. **Facts are stated; events occur.** One necessarily involves words, the other not.

It may help to make the distinction if we recall that an event has a spatio-temporal location, a fact has not. The Battle of Waterloo was won by Wellington on a muddy field in Belgium on 18 June 1815. The *fact* that Wellington won the battle is not located in that field or in that year. It is always the case, everywhere.

So Veyne is right that events cannot be compressed into generalities.

[7] Veyne (1984), p. 63.
[8] See chapter 8, pp. 214–20 below.

Every event is unique. It is because facts capture only part of the event (or part of all the possible ways of describing it) that they can be so compressed. That Waterloo was a battle enables it to be linked with Thermopylae and Cannae in some generalization about battles. That it was an English victory in the Napoleonic Wars permits a link with Copenhagen, Salamanca and Trafalgar. That it happened in the Regency period belongs to quite a different generalization – perhaps about Jane Austen and the Brighton Pavilion.

Covering-law theorists of explanation should remember that facts lend themselves very well to such laws; events not at all. But the task of historians is to explain what occurred (events) rather than what is stated (facts). Thus covering laws are of no great use to the historian. He has to be sure of both the truth and the relevance of the alleged facts about an event before he may consider explanation of those facts. For him the unique event is always primary.[9]

## B.   The Forms and Structures of History

### 1   Historiography mirrors history

History does not write itself. Every student toiling over an essay, every historian struggling to meet a publisher's deadline knows that. Any work of history is a contrivance, usually a painful one. Even a work as apparently artless as the Anglo-Saxon Chronicle requires some thought: where to begin; what to put in and what to leave out; how to describe the events that need to be recorded. And there must be some relation among the elements of the work, even if only chronological. A first-year essay has to be much more sophisticated than that.

Somewhere behind all these forms of historiography, there is an original past more or less accurately reflected in them. Do the historian's arrangements follow the arrangements of the past? What, in a general way, was history(1) really like?

### 2   Chronology is necessary, but not enough

The first characteristic to be noticed is that the past had a chronological order; things happened either one after another or at the same time. Such an order is the main (sometimes the only) historiographical feature of a chronicle. Yet to maintain this order is quite a disciplined effort. For many people in the Middle Ages (if we may judge from the literature) the past was a remote time when historical figures like Charlemagne rubbed shoulders with classical and biblical characters like Theseus and Joshua. To sort all this out, to determine what were contemporary and what not, what came before and what after, was no mean achievement.

[9] For fuller discussion of covering-law theories, see ch. 8, pp. 214–20.

But what, except for sheer tidiness, is the point? There seems little reason to settle that one thing came before another unless there is some other connection between them. Such other connections are what writers of history try to bring out. The most damning indictment of the unfortunate student essay is to say that it is no more than a list of events. So what sort of connections were there that the writer should bring out? In particular, how are earlier and later events connected?

There may be one of three reasons for emphasizing the order of events. One is that of plot. In telling a story we usually relate the happenings in roughly the order in which they occurred. But this is not always done. Very often (as we saw when looking at narrative) we vary the order for the sake of the plot.[10] Nevertheless, both writer and reader are aware that in this there is a departure from reality. The second reason is that the earlier events caused the later ones. Different opinions may be held as to how far the course of history is determined; we discussed these in chapter 1, pp. 18–21 above. The different kinds of historical causation are discussed below.[11] The third reason is to show that knowledge of the earlier events influenced later actions, thus providing not so much a cause as a reason for those actions. Neither student essays nor major works of historiography always make clear distinctions among these three reasons. The reader is sometimes left in the dark as to which of these three links between earlier and later events the historian thinks he is tracing. The main point here, however, is to note that the past is extended through time. It is important for more than one reason to establish chronological order.

## 3    The 'field of history' and its extent

Chronology orders what may be called 'the field of history'. What are the limits of that field? They may depend upon our definition of history. If we think that history demands written sources, it cannot begin before the invention of writing. That occurred somewhere about 3000 BC, so on this definition there can be no history before that. Another way of defining history is to say that it is the story of identifiable men and women – historical characters. It is not altogether a coincidence that the first individual whom we can name is Nar-mer, king of Upper and Lower Egypt, who reigned shortly before this date. For both reasons 3000 BC is a good date to mark the beginning of history. However, if we accept more modern definitions of history, more independent of documentary sources and of 'great names', then we shall have to look for a much earlier date. For by 3000 BC some of the greatest human achievements were already in hand: fire, religion, art, language, farming, the domestication of animals,

---

[10] See ch. 4, pp. 90–1 above.
[11] See ch. 8, pp. 194–204.

seafaring, pottery, metallurgy, war, dance, song, brewing and quite sophisticated forms of social organization. Of course, we have no written evidence about these developments, nor do we know the individuals involved. Thus they are normally apportioned to the realm of prehistory rather than that of history proper.

Such is the temporal extent of the historical field. What of its spatial extent? At first, one is tempted to answer that it is the whole of the surface of the earth. Roughly, this is correct. But one must not forget that during the last 5,000 years that surface has altered, with some lands rising from the sea and others disappearing into it. It is only in the last tenth of that period that the great oceans have been crossed, and even more recently that the sea-bed has begun to be both explored and exploited. Only in the last twentieth have men ventured into the atmosphere above the surface of the earth, and only in the last hundredth have they left the earth altogether to travel in space and walk on the moon.

## 4  The occupants of the historical field

If those are the dimensions of the historical field, what are its occupants? Men and women, of course, but not only these make up history. There is the world of nature, which is the necessary setting for human existence. However, we record natural events only when they have an important impact upon human life – earthquakes, storms and so on. Otherwise history is not concerned with nature in itself but nature in interaction with humanity: our food, our tools, our clothes, our homes and all our industry from flints to semi-conductors. Moreover, human life has not only a setting in nature; it is also rooted in society. As the Greeks used to say, one who lives by himself is not human, but either a beast or a god. These societies – tribes, villages, cities, nations, empires – are important elements in history. How people live in these societies is what anthropologists call culture. Cultural elements, however, are not confined to any one society. Languages, religions, art forms, tools and all kinds of customs are easily transported across boundaries. Cultural transmission is vividly illustrated in the history of post-Columbus America.[12] The wide expansion of Islam and of the language and literary culture of Arabic during what we call the 'Dark Ages' is no less striking.

Cities, nations and empires have long been subjects of historical study. Clearly they, no less than individual men and women, have always been deemed elements of the historical field ever since Thucydides told the story of the war between Athens and Sparta, or Livy that of the Roman people. But what of the elements of culture – language, art, clothes, religion, and so on? Since these frequently extend far beyond the bounds of any one society, their histories must be different from the traditional kind. The

[12] See, for example, Fischer (1989).

twentieth century has seen a proliferation, first of histories of art, architecture, music, literature and other forms of high culture, and then histories of 'low' culture: child-rearing, death, work practices, games, etc. These also must be regarded as elements of the historical field.

## 5   Organizations and groups

Most human activities throw up organizations and institutions as necessary structures for their support. Among these are courts, governments, judicial systems, public utilities, trading companies, schools and universities, sports clubs, factories and airlines. Many such organizations and institutions have had their historians, and are sufficiently coherent and defined to belong among the elements of the historical field.

A more difficult question arises in relation to groups of people. Some groups, like churches or political parties, are supported and structured by such organizations. They possess their own rules and rituals and visible concomitants in the forms of buildings, land and material equipment – furniture, telephones, vehicles, etc. But perhaps the two most important characteristics are a status at law and a self-conscious membership. With such groups may be contrasted others (sometimes distinguished by sociologists as 'quasi-groups') that lack structure and organization, have no standing at law, and whose members may be unaware of their membership. These include classes, races, and age-, sex-, or blood-groups. It is not to be denied that so-called 'histories' have been written of some such quasi-groups, but when we see that these aggregates are so ill-defined, without structure, regulations or (often) conscious membership, we may question whether they are genuine elements of the historical field or whether they are not constructs of the historian's mind.

## 6   Historical movements

Such doubts are even stronger in the case of great historical movements like the Renaissance, the Reformation, or the Enlightenment. Not only do they, of necessity, lack structure and organization; they also lack a self-conscious membership. Many of the most important figures in each of these movements would have been surprised to learn that he was part of any such thing. Historians are familiar with the idea of 'enlightened despotism' of the eighteenth century, and the 'Great Depression' in the world economy of the late nineteenth. Of the first, one scholar writes: 'The nature of the reality it attempts to describe, its dimensions in space and time, perhaps even its very existence, have all been, and still are questioned by historians.'[13] Of the second, another writes: 'As regards the "Great Depression" itself, surely the major outcome of modern research has been to destroy once and for all the existence of such a period in any

13 Anderson (1979), p. 119.

unified sense . . . the sooner the "Great Depression" is banished from the literature, the better.'[14] How many "historical movements" are actually historians' constructs?

## 7  Combinations and divisions in history

This discussion of so-called 'great historical movements' has brought us from the elements of the historical field to the ways in which these elements may be connected to form larger wholes. The basic elements are human beings. They combine in societies. The societies create cultures. Many parts of these cultures take on an existence of their own by spreading to other societies. Most cultural and social activities create organizations of a semi-permanent, partly material and quasi-personal form – such as the East India Company or the US Presidency. We may be safe in taking all these to be genuine elements of the historical field, though doubts arise about quasi-groups.

Now all these elements are not idle, but, both singly and combinedly, are involved in many kinds of activities – making love, making money, making war, making bread, making music, and so on. The pursuit of all these activities makes the fabric of history(1), as well as the subject matter of history(2). But is history(1) a 'seamless web', a fabric all of one piece?

At first sight, it may seem that it is. We have already seen reason to suspect that some 'historical movements' belong less to the objective course of history than to historians' minds. Similar considerations may make us doubt such discontinuities as Foucault claimed to find. There were 'two great discontinuities in . . . Western culture: the first inaugurates the Classical Age (roughly half-way through the seventeenth century) and the second, at the beginning of the nineteenth century, marks the beginning of the modern age.'[15]

But this is only one of the more recent examples of the ancient game of dividing history into ages or epochs. The Book of Daniel in the Bible (written in the second century BC) speaks of four world empires. This may be an echo of the older eastern tradition of the decline of mankind from the original age of gold, through silver and bronze ages to the present deplorable age of iron.[16] The idea, found in the *Works and Days* of the Greek poet Hesiod (*c.* 700 BC), became familiar through the very popular *Metamorphoses* of the Roman poet, Ovid (written in the first decade AD.) But it was the Bible rather than the classical poets that inspired the various millenarian movements of medieval and early modern times.[17] The belief in the imminent coming of the 'Fifth Monarchy', a belief that inspired

[14] Saul (1972), pp. 54–5.
[15] Foucault (1970), p. xxii.
[16] See Jasper Griffin, 'Greek Myth and Hesiod', in Boardman et al. (1985), p. 96.
[17] See Cohn (1962), pp. 3–4. Also Cohn (1993).

many soldiers of Oliver Cromwell and that influenced even John Milton (perhaps the most learned man of his day), sprang from the four empires of the Book of Daniel.[18] More widely influential were the prophecies of the twelfth-century Italian abbot, Joachim of Fiore. Norman Cohn writes: '. . . in the whole Middle Ages there was scarcely another intellectual who did so much to shake not only the structure of orthodox medieval theology but also the assumptions which must underlie any conceivable Christian faith.'[19] He goes on to find the 'indirect and long-term influence of these speculations' in the 'phantasy of the three ages that re-appeared' in the anti-Christian ideas of Auguste Comte, Karl Marx and Adolf Hitler.[20]

From such heady notions it seems mundane to come down to the familiar division of history into Ancient, Medieval and Modern. Yet a moment's thought will show that these traditional divisions, too, belong to the realm of history(2); they do not exist in history(1).


## 8    States, nations and empires

In our search for larger historical wholes we are on much firmer ground if we look at the subjects of traditional history – cities, nations, empires. When a group of people live together, share a common ancestry (or believe they do) and a common language, intermarry and interact in a thousand different ways in the course of daily life, then those people form a cohesive whole. It is a unit in the historical field. As they become aware of this they usually tell their own histories – at first, perhaps, only in the oral form of folklore, but later (if they rise to that degree of sophistication) in written history – history(2). In so far as they are conscious of having a separate identity they may be regarded as elements in the historical field between which run 'vertical' lines of division. (By 'vertical' I mean 'extended through time' or 'diachronic').

Are there also genuine 'horizontal', or synchronic, divisions, running across time – apart from those artificial divisions that we looked at in the preceding subsection? It would seem that there are: the beginnings and the endings of cities, nation-states and empires. The history of Athens becomes absorbed into that of the Roman Empire, then the Turkish Empire, then the nation-state of Greece; Virginia or Massachusetts into that of the USA, and so on. Sometimes, however, they seem just to disappear: where are the Hittites, the Assyrians, the Aztecs today? Biologically the peoples must go on; their descendants must be still

---

[18] See Firth (1962), pp. 338–9; C. Hill, (1972), p. 96 and passim.
[19] Cohn (1962), p. 100. For a slightly different view of Joachim, see Reeves (1969 and 1976).
[20] Cohn (1962), p. 101.

around somewhere. But the historical entities – the cities, states and empires – have come to an end. At that point a horizontal line has been ruled across the account.

The situation is not always so simple, however. The events of 1989–91 threw eastern Europe and parts of Asia into some confusion. Ancient peoples and former states reappeared. They appealed to history and asserted that, though they had for many years been subjected to Austro-Hungarian, Turkish, Tsarist or Soviet Empires, yet they could trace a continuous history back to some glorious epoch in the remote past when they enjoyed freedom and a historical identity. Hence they claim independence, sovereignty and, eventually, no doubt, a seat at the United Nations. Thus what is a historical whole, an element in the historical field, is no idle question.


## 9    A history for all?

Do all peoples, then, have histories? This is explicitly denied by Hegel, who argued that some peoples are 'destitute of *objective* history' because they have 'no *subjective* history, no annals'. His reasoning is that, unless a people has enough self-awareness to create laws and a state to regulate their common life, they will not think it necessary to make records – the basis of history. Hegel put it thus: 'Only in a State cognizant of Laws can distinct transactions take place, accompanied by such a clear consciousness of them as supplies the ability and suggests the necessity of an enduring record.'[21] In other words, only if a people have what is requisite for history(2) – both self-awareness and written record – can they be an element in history(1). The question for us, then, is whether every human being and every human group that has ever existed constitutes a part of the historical field, or whether that field is to be restricted to those groups who have been aware of themselves as coherent wholes and who have, therefore, made some attempt to record their history. As we saw above, it is possible to live in time without having a sense of history. Can only those who possess historicity be granted a place in history?[22]

Hence our final question: 'Do the various national histories make up one (world) history?' I would suggest this answer: As soon as, and in so far as, historicity is achieved on a world scale, then both world history(1) and world history(2) become realities. Whether you agree with this, or prefer a different answer, will depend very much on what you think about the issues raised in this section.[23]


[21] Hegel (1956), p. 61.
[22] For historicity, see above, 3, pp. 50–1.
[23] For further discussion of the topics in this section ('Forms and structures of history'), see Stanford (1990), chapter 5.

## C.   Time

### 1   *What is time?*

Time is basic to history, so it is time that we had a closer look at it. But is there a problem? We live in time like fishes in water, and we can hardly imagine what it would be to live without or outside it. That is one reason why all ideas of Heaven or Hell are ultimately baffling, though they have long exercised men's imaginations. Unlike our fellow creatures that also live in time, we can think about past and future. Such thinking is, as we have seen in chapters 2 and 5, the essence of action and the essence of history alike.

The Russian language lacks articles (like 'a' and 'the'), so if a Russian asks you 'What is time?' he will probably accept an answer like 'It is ten past three.' But suppose that his English is faultless and he meant just what he said. What will you reply?

If you find yourself at a loss, you are in good company. In his *Confessions* St Augustine (AD 354–430) wrote, 'What, then, is time? If no one asks me I know: if I wish to explain it to one that asks, I know not.'[24] But do you agree with how he goes on? 'Yet I say boldly, that I know that if nothing passed away, time past were not; and if nothing were coming, a time to come were not; and if nothing were, time present were not.' For these remarks commit him to one of two opposing theories of time.

### 2   *Is it the contents or the container?*

There are similar theories about space, and it may be easier to start with the latter. To my right and left are two walls of the room. The space between them is filled by books, furniture, a human body and a lot of air. Suppose all those were taken out and there was nothing at all between the walls. Would they still be twelve feet apart? Or would they touch? Common-sense answers the former (unless we think the vacuum would collapse the walls). Now apply this to time. Between Tuesday and Thursday a lot of things happen on Wednesday. But suppose *nothing* happened on Wednesday. Would Thursday then come immediately after Tuesday? Or would there be an empty section of time between them, like the walls of my empty room? If you give the second answer you are thinking about time and space as Isaac Newton did. He thought that time and space are real things, quite apart from anything they may contain. They are 'the places as well of themselves as of all other things'. On this view time and space are like metal boxes which stay the same size and shape whether they contain anything else or not. By contrast a balloon,

---

[24] Book XI (xiv), 17; (1991), p. 230. Indeed the whole of book XI of the *Confessions* is a profound meditation on time.

not being rigid, derives its size from its contents. Newton, then, thought of space like a huge box of infinite size that contains everything, and he thought of time like an infinitely long straight line. 'I now demonstrate the Frame of the System of the World', he wrote in the *Principia*. The trouble is that physicists and mathematicians no longer hold Newton's view of a universe whose space is described by the geometry of Euclid (that is, the one we all learned at school). They suggest that it is finite (not infinite), and curved, spherical, saddle-shaped or even toroidal (like an American doughnut). Moreover, many of them believe that space expands or stretches rather like the surface of that balloon. There is nothing straight or rigid about it. But not all are agreed whether it is an empty container or something that derives its size and shape, indeed, its very being, from its contents.

Now if we turn to time we see that Augustine did not share Newton's view. He said, 'If nothing passed away, past were not', and so on. He does not think that time *contains* the events of the past; he thinks that time *is* the events of the past; and, of course, the same for the present and the future. What you have is not something that would be there anyhow, even if no events happened: what you have is simply events with temporal (i.e. time) relations between them – relations such as 'six days later' or 'a long time before'.

## 3   *Is time unreal?*

This would suggest that it is not time that is real, but only events. These events are laid out along a certain dimension (so that one can talk of 'before' and 'after' as positions along this dimension). But what is this dimension along which events are arranged? Is it really there? We have just seen reason to suspect it might not be. Then can it be that events only *seem* to be laid out in this way? In Lewis Carroll's *Alice Through the Looking-Glass* you will remember that Alice moves across a chessboard like a pawn. Her moves are actually shown in a diagram at the front of the book. First she meets the Red Queen, then the White Queen, then Humpty Dumpty, then the White King then the Red Knight, then the White Knight; finally she reaches the end and is crowned as Queen. But pieces can move across a board in many ways. If she had met the White Knight before the Red Queen, and so on, the meetings would have been arranged in a different way along the time scale. Do 'before' and 'after' have any real meaning on a chessboard? Do they not designate the course of a series of moves in space? May it be that we appear to move through time, meeting events in a particular order, but that really (as in chess) we could meet them in any order? And in whatever the order we met them, that would seem to be the way they are arranged along the axis of time.

This reminds us of the theories of a great philosopher, Immanuel Kant (1724–1804). In a seminal work, *The Critique of Pure Reason*, he argued that because of the way our minds are made up, we have to perceive the world in certain ways. (A useful analogy is to think of wearing coloured spectacles. If we never removed our blue spectacles we should always perceive the world as bluish.) Kant's arguments need not be given here. All we need note is this: it is impossible to have any experience of the world at all without perceiving the world as extended in three-dimensional space and without the experience being extended in one-dimensional time. Space and time, however, are not qualities of the objects we perceive (as are being green or hot or sticky); they are necessary conditions of such experiences. Similarly, having your eyes open is not part of a visual experience; it is a necessary condition of seeing.[25] It is not something you see; it is *how* you see.

### 4   Modern views

In spite of these doubts, Kant, like Newton, did believe in the reality of space and time.[26] It is just these beliefs that modern science has rejected. According to Einstein's theories of special and general relativity time is not, as we normally suppose, independent of space, but both space and time constitute a four-dimensional whole called space-time. 'The theory of relativity put an end to the idea of absolute time! It appeared that each observer must have his own measure of time, as recorded by a clock carried with him, and that identical clocks carried by different observers would not necessarily agree.'[27] The time measured depends on the speed (strictly, the relative velocity) of the measurer. Since Einstein things have become even stranger: '. . . when one combines general relativity with the uncertainty principle of quantum mechanics, it is possible for both space and time to be finite without any edges or boundaries.'[28] We need not pursue the topic further, fascinating though it is. It is clear that the scientists' views of space and time have departed a long way from the common-sense view.

### 5   What is the speed of time?

But even the common-sense view of time has its problems. For example, we talk of 'the passage of time'. In Samuel Beckett's play, *Waiting for Godot*, Vladimir remarks of something that at least it helped to pass the time, whereupon Estragon retorts that time would have passed anyway. The first speaker is taking a personal or subjective view; he is talking of the experience of happenings in time. The second takes the public or objective view that minutes, hours and days follow each other at a regular

[25] Kant (1963), pp. 74–82; Körner (1955), pp. 33–9.
[26] Körner (1955), pp. 33–4.
[27] Hawking (1990), p. 21.
[28] Ibid., op. cit, p. 44.

pace. The distinction is a convenient and useful one; both private and public time play an important role in history.

Let us return to the word 'pace' that I slipped into the last sentence but one. Does it make sense to talk of the 'pace' of time? 'Time goes so quickly', we say; 'I can't believe it's nearly Christmas.' As Rosalind tells Orlando in the forest of Arden, 'Time travels in divers paces, with divers persons.'[29] There is no problem here, you may say. They are talking about subjective time – as Rosalind makes clear with the examples she gives. But public time, we should surely all agree, passes at the same rate. But what rate? Well, if time passes, flows, goes on etc., it must pass at *some* rate. Anything that moves must have some speed, rate or velocity. How could we measure the speed of time's passing? Two o'clock is approaching, when I shall have to stop writing this. How fast is it approaching? At how many miles per hour? The question makes no sense. Obviously time does not pass in miles; it passes in hours. So must I say it is approaching at so many *hours* per hour? This is like saying that a car moves at one mile per mile. Both are nonsense. The root of the trouble is that the notion of movement implies change of position and change of time. The idea of time is already there in the idea of movement. To use movement to describe time is using time to describe time. And this is as impossible or as meaningless as lifting yourself up by your own bootstraps or seeing your own eye (without a mirror). You can measure the speed of anything except speed or time. A lady can take a tape measure out of her work-box and measure anything with it – except the tape-measure itself.[30] Thus all talk about the passing of time, or the passing of events from the present into the past, or of things passing away – as Augustine did; all this is pure metaphor. But unlike most uses of metaphor (for example, 'the rosy-fingered dawn'), we do not in the least understand the reality of which we speak.

## 6 Why cannot we visit the past?

Another puzzle is the asymmetry of time. This points to the fact that in various ways the future is not like the past. The past seems to be fixed but the future unformed. Then, again, if time is a dimension, why can one move in it (that metaphor again!) in only one direction? A yard to the left is like a yard to the right; a foot up is like a foot down. But not so in time. Bearing in mind that, for modern science, time and space are common dimensions of space-time, should travel in time not be possible – at least, in theory? We cannot today travel to Jupiter or Alpha Centauri, but this is only a practical, and perhaps temporary, impossibility. One day we may. Is the impossibility of visiting the eighteenth century only a practical one

[29] *As You Like It*, Act III, Sc. ii, 1. 301.
[30] I base some of the arguments in this paragraph on Seddon (1987).

like that? Or is it a logical impossibility? And if it is the latter, is that because we cannot go back, or because in no sense is there a past to go back to? If I am riding an Amtrak from New Haven to Boston I cannot logically visit New Haven while I am so travelling. But that logical impossibility does not imply that New Haven is no longer there. It would still be there even if everybody happened to be travelling away from it. Is that our situation with regard to visiting the eighteenth century? Or is there something else that makes it impossible? Is the past still 'there' in any sense? If so, in what?

## 7   The Wheel of Time

Lastly, I will mention the problem of time's cycle and time's arrow.[31] In spite of the fact that we seem to move from the past to the future and not the other way, most early cultures and civilizations took a **cyclical view of time; that is, as a series of repetitions going on for ever, like a wheel.**[32] It is fairly clear that this idea comes from the succession of the seasons, and from the cycle of birth, maturity and death of all animal life. The early riverine civilizations of Sumeria, Egypt, India and China all depended on the seasonal high and low waters of the Euphrates, the Nile, the Indus and the Hwang-Ho.

The alteration of the seasons was observed to correspond to the movements of the heavenly bodies, so that the science of astronomy grew out of the necessity of measuring and anticipating time. This measurement preoccupied all civilizations; for example, it led the peoples of Central America to develop a complicated calendar that is still in use in a few places. Unlike our calendars which repeat every 365 days, the Central American 'Calendar Round' covered 18,980 days, that is, something over fifty years. Nor was this all. Before the birth of Christ the Mayan peoples developed, and inscribed on their still extant monuments, a so-called 'Long Count' which was adequate for dating any event in their history. A Long Count consisted of 1,872,000 days, or approximately 5,100 years. After this the cycle would start again.[33]

## 8   Plato's theory of time

We do not know the thinking behind the Mayan calendar, but a dialogue of Plato, the *Timaeus*, which was written about 360–350 BC, gives a reasoned account of creation. The *Timaeus* was known throughout the Dark and early Middle Ages, and indeed has never ceased to be read. It has not for a long time been taken as literally true, but it has stimulated the imagination and influenced ways of thinking about the universe.

[31] For a good discussion of the importance of both concepts, see Gould (1987).
[32] See Bury (1924), pp. 12–13. Also Trompf (1979).
[33] See Coe (1971), pp. 66–7.

First, Plato begins by stressing the distinction between eternal truths (as those of mathematics seem to be) and contingent facts – things that happen to be the case, but might well be otherwise. The former are to be apprehended by reason, the latter by the five senses. These senses, as we know, can easily be deceived and we can never wholly rely on their deliverances – what is called 'empirical knowledge'.[34] Thus eternal truths are about what never changes – the world of Being, while empirical facts are about the changing – that is, things that never stay the same for long, the world of Becoming.

Nevertheless, although (for Plato) the created universe must be subject to change, it need not be chaotic. So chaos is replaced by order.[35] And to emphasize this order, and to make the created world as close as possible to the uncreated, time was created. Plato's creator-god (or demiurge) made 'time an eternal moving image of the eternity which remains for ever at one.'[36] So he ordered the heavens, and 'as a result of this plan and purpose of god for the birth of time, the sun and moon and the five planets as they are called came into being to define and preserve the measures of time.'[37] It is clear that, on this view, time is a perpetual motion measured by the movements of the heavenly bodies; that is, time is cyclical.

But the cycles are large. Plato points out that only a few men consider the movements of the further planets (Mars, Jupiter, Saturn). They are 'virtually unaware' that the 'wandering movements are time at all', so bewildering and intricate are they. 'None the less', he goes on, 'it is perfectly possible to perceive that the perfect temporal number and the perfect year are complete when all eight orbits have reached their total of revolutions relative to each other.'[38] What he is referring to here is the fact that eventually all these heavenly bodies come back to the same relative positions. Plato does not attempt to calculate how long this takes.[39] But he seems to have in mind a long cycle – quite long enough to accommodate the story of Atlantis, supposedly 9,000 years earlier, which is told (also in the *Timaeus*) by an Egyptian priest. The latter claimed that in Egyptian temples 'we have preserved from earliest times a written record of any great or splendid achievement or notable event.'[40] We can see that Plato was able to take a view of history and historical records very like our own, and yet to believe that the course of human affairs went

---

[34] Plato (1965), p. 40; §§ 27–8.
[35] Ibid., p. 42; § 30.
[36] Ibid., p. 51; § 37.
[37] Ibid., p. 51; § 38.
[38] Ibid., p. 54; § 39.
[39] He is not, as we might suppose, thinking of the precession of the equinoxes – a matter of 26,000 years. Whether or not he is thinking of the 'Great Year' of 36,000 years is a matter of scholarly dispute. See A. E. Taylor (1928), pp. 217–18; Cornford (1941), p. 253, n. 3.
[40] Plato (1965), p. 35; § 23.

round in large circles. This contrasts with our own view that the world began only once, and that affairs proceed steadily on from past to future, so that every event, once happened, is irrevocable. Time, we believe, is a path that can never be retraced.

## 9   More cycles

If we are so firmly committed to the linear view of time, is there any more to be said for the cyclical view? Is there at least poetic truth in the words of the Bible?

> 'The thing that hath been, it is that which shall be; and that which is done is that which shall be done: and there is no new thing under the sun.
>   Is there any thing whereof it may be said, See, this is new? it hath been already of old time, which was before us.'[41]

With every new war or outbreak of senseless violence it is tempting to take this weary view of history. 'When will they ever learn?' one thinks. Perhaps we should look a little more closely at this notion of cycles. There can be four ways of doing so.

The first is to note (with the Preacher) repeated patterns in human behaviour. Of course, these are not all foolish or criminal. Traditions consist of just such patterns, and they form the pillars of any society – even if sometimes they need to be adjusted or changed. Traditions and customs are hardly cycles, but what about trends?

This second kind of repetition refers to certain sets of phenomena often noted in history. Metternich after the defeat of Napoleon based over thirty years of European policy on the belief that the most dangerous moment for an autocracy is when it admits the first reform. Russia seems to have illustrated this twice in the twentieth century. Another is the observation that revolutions devour their children: those who make revolution very rarely remain long in command. These, and other examples, would suggest that events repeat themselves not only singly, but in series.

An even stronger candidate for historical cyclicity is the belief that nations and civilizations follow patterns of growth, maturity and decline similar to those of living creatures. Chad, we may say, is a young country, France is a mature one, China is very old – though not necessarily in decline. The notion of historical cycles has been applied with much learning by Oswald Spengler in *The Decline of the West* (1932) and by Arnold Toynbee's *A Study of History* (1934–61). Both claimed to find a repeated pattern in various civilizations.

---

[41] Ecclesiastes 1. 9–10.

Fourthly, there is the belief in a repetition, not *within* history, but *of* history. This was held, presumably, by the Mayans, and certainly by Plato. We do not believe such things today. But, on a larger scale, the question is still open. In *A Brief History of Time* Stephen Hawking points out that 'the laws of science do not distinguish between the past and the future.'[42] He then considers why the arrows of time (he describes three of them) always point in the same direction – from past to future. 'They will not point in the same direction for the whole history of the universe', he says; but it is only when they *do* that intelligent beings can develop who are capable of asking these questions.[43] The universe is expanding at present, though there is no reason why it should not then contract, and afterwards go on expanding and contracting. However, 'it might seem a bit academic to worry about what would happen when the universe collapses again, as it will not start to contract for at least another ten thousand million years.'[44] How long the contracting phase would last he does not say, but presumably after that we could start all over again.

Finally, to come down to earth, we should note that the laws of nature (or the law-like theories of natural science, to be more precise) certainly guarantee the repetition of similar events – for example, the way money drops out every time I have a hole in my trouser pocket. But these laws contribute nothing to the cyclical view of time unless it can be shown that they actually bring about cycles of or in time. And this has not been done. We must conclude with Stephen Hawking that for us (at least for the next ten thousand million years) time moves in the same direction. So much for the arrow of time. But we must remember that, just as arrows and cycles of time are metaphors, so is talk of the 'movement' of time. We are still far from understanding the true nature of time.

## 10   *Private and public time*

Time is indeed a puzzle. Perhaps the source of the puzzle may be found here: space and time are concepts. As concepts they form part of a model that we construct (voluntarily or involuntarily) to represent the real world. Many of our concepts are very useful, but they do not necessarily have a counterpart in the real world. Not all concepts do – unicorns, for example. Does time?

I have said that time is a concept, but it might be more accurate to say that we have two related concepts of time: private time and public time. Personal or private time is based on our inner experience which varies from one occasion to another – as Rosalind tells Orlando. In sleep or unconsciousness, we are quite unaware of time passing at all. Yet we recognize that it does pass. Sometimes an inner prompting – hunger,

---

[42] (1990), p. 144.
[43] Ibid., p. 145.
[44] Ibid., p. 149.

thirst, weariness – reminds us of it. Sometimes the movements of the moon, the sun or the stars tell us of it. Nowadays, however, we are less aware of these natural measures of time than of artificial ones.

As our societies have become more complex we have had to co-ordinate our actions with others and to live by an agreed timetable. To do this – ensuring for example that trains and planes leave on time – we have to be constantly aware of the exact hour and minute. Even for the most hardened city-dweller it is not always easy to make one's inner, personal time fit with these public demands. For less sophisticated people the problem can be almost insuperable. There was a marked change in town life in the later Middle Ages when clocks began to replace bells: 'one of the major events in the history of these centuries.'[45]

Similar problems were met in the early days of the Industrial Revolution when home-workers in domestic industries had to become factory hands and submit to the tyranny of factory time.

Over longer periods, too, we find it difficult to adjust our memories to the public calendar. The keeping of diaries, journals and memoirs are attempts to do so.

The various methods that have been employed to measure, establish and record a common public time of hours, days and years is a vast study in itself, ranging over nearly five millennia from Egyptian temples to atomic clocks. This is not our business here. It is enough to recall a few points important for the historian.

## 11    Five points for the historian

The first is to remember that most people in the past had not our awareness of the hour and date when things were happening. Still less did they have any accurate idea of how long ago other things had occurred. Phrases like 'time out of mind', 'beyond the memory of man' or 'once upon a time' were normal.[46]

The next point is to remember that for historians an accurate chronology *is* important. We are much concerned with cause and effect. We also know that the effect cannot come before the cause. Thus our decision whether or not an event A might have been a cause of event B can be made by finding out the relative times of A and B. For example, if A was a movement of armies by the White King and B was a decision for war by the Red King, it is important to know which happened first. Although we are in these cases concerned with relative, not absolute times, it soon becomes clear that we cannot establish the sequence of events until we can establish the exact date and, in some cases, the hour.

This reminds us of a third point. It is not only in Einsteinian physics but

---

[45] Le Goff (1980), p. 30. See also 'Clocks and Culture', in Cipolla (1970) for the impact upon China.
[46] See Le Goff (1988), pp. 174–83. Also Febvre (1962), pp. 426–34.

also in history that time is relative to space. Just as Einstein had to allow for the speed of light in his space-time calculations, so the historian has to remember speed of communication in his period. If the sun had ceased to exist five minutes ago we should still be tanning ourselves on the beach in happy ignorance. If all the silver mines in Peru had collapsed in 1600, the king of Spain would have been calculating and spending his revenues in sublime ignorance weeks later.[47] Thus, in the case given in the last paragraph, our decision whether the White King's action caused the Red King's or vice versa, depends not on whether A happened absolutely before B, but on whether the Red King could have known of the White King's actions, given the distance and communication time between them.

A fourth reminder for the historian is that past events for us lay in the future for the people most concerned. When we try to understand why the Red King acted as he did, we have to forget that we know the consequences of his actions; *he* didn't. It is important to remember, too, that people sometimes act under the pressure of very great hopes and fears — hopes and fears that are hidden in an unknown future. The historian can totally fail to see that these hopes (or fears) were ever held, and hence can be quite wrong about the conditions under which the Red King acted. This is because the hopes (or fears) were never realized; the historian, knowing what *did* subsequently happen, may lose sight of them altogether.

My final point is less obvious, though no less important. It is this. We read novels, see plays, films, etc. In these the narrator lives in one world, his characters live in another. But in the case of history the narrator and his characters live in the *same* world. To a large extent they share the same past. They live under the same constraints of time and space; they have the same ignorance of the future; their whole lives are bound and embedded in the culture of their age. In fiction the narrator can control the lives of his characters; they cannot alter his. In history it is largely the other way round. A historian, writing about Oliver Cromwell or George Washington, cannot shape his subject's life as a novelist can. He has to be faithful to the evidence. But Cromwell and Washington have certainly had a great deal to do with shaping the modern world in which the historian lives. Thus it is not enough to say that narrator and characters both live in history under historical conditions. We must recognize that they live in the *same* history. Our future will be partly shaped both by the historian and by Cromwell and Washington. We share with Oliver and George not only a common humanity, but a common past and a common future.

## Conclusion

After several chapters on how history-as-account is made, we have returned in this one to history-as-event — the material with which

---

[47] See Stanford (1990), p. 29.

historians claim to be dealing. Yet if we go back, behind the works of historians, to reach their subject matter, we cannot stop at events. For 'event' is a man-made concept. The universe is the scene of ceaseless flux, of constant change. Only a few of these innumerable changes are perceived by man, and only a few of those perceived are considered so worthy of remark and remembrance as to be called 'events'. So if the material of history is events we must remember that they are partly the product of human thought. As material they are not raw but are already processed. Moreover, they are neither objects nor facts, and should not be confused with either.

Nevertheless, some of the changes that constitute this raw material seem to be linked together. These assemblages constitute objects in what we call the historical field – the spatio-temporal region in which historical events occur. These objects are: first, human beings; second, societies of human beings; and, third, such ideas and behaviour of these beings as are linked to their society – to which ideas and behaviour we give the name of cultures. Such occupants of the historical field are the subjects of historical research and writing. There is doubt, however, as to whether some of these subjects may not be constructs of the historians' imaginations (e.g. the 'Great Depression') rather than anything that actually existed as object in that field.

All things change. Like everything else under the sun (or, as the ancients would say, under the moon), the objects of the historical field, the subjects of historical study, are not eternal; they come to be and they pass away. Time, therefore, is basic to them. Questions of date, of 'before' and 'after', are essential to the historian's thinking. So we, like St Augustine, have to ask: What is Time? We may never know the answer to the question, or even whether there is one correct answer. But the idea of time is of such fundamental importance to the historian that she should be aware of some of the difficulties involved in this familiar notion, and preferably should be clear about her own standpoint. Nor should she forget that we, the students of history, share much of a common past and a common future with the historical figures whom we study. We are all alike creatures of time.

## Suggested Reading

Braudel 1975; 1980
Burke, P. 1990
Danto 1965
Duby 1985
Hegel 1956
Hexter 1979
Le Goff and Nora 1985
Marrou 1966
Nisbet 1969

Oakeshott 1983
Plato 1965
Ricoeur 1984
Seddon 1987
Stanford 1990
Stoianovich 1976
Trompf 1979
Veyne 1984
Whitrow 1972

# 8

# History as Sequence

An instructor is one who explains the causes of a thing ... and the most knowable things are first principles and causes, for it is through and from these that other things are known.

Aristotle, *Metaphysics*

Felix qui potuit rerum cognoscere causas (Happy is he who has come to know the causes of things).

Virgil, *Georgics*

How small, of all that human hearts endure,
That part which laws or kings can cause or cure!

Goldsmith, *The Traveller*

Never explain, never apologize.

attributed to Lord Curzon

## Introduction

There is a clear distinction to be drawn between the notion of cause and that of explanation. They are frequently connected, because most explanations (though not all) seek for a cause, and causes are identified usually in respect of an explanation. Nevertheless, they are quite distinct, for they belong to different orders of being. To quote a modern philosopher, 'But if causality is a relation which holds in the natural world, explanation is a different matter ... it is not a natural relation ... It is an intellectual or rational ... relation. It does not hold between things in the natural world, things to which we can assign places and times in nature. It holds between facts or truths.'[1] Thus a cause is something that operates in the real world; it is what it is, whether people understand it or not. The milk turns sour because of the presence of certain bacteria. The fact that everyone believes it is sour because a witch put a curse on it affects the milk not at all. An explanation, on the other hand, belongs to the realm of ideas. It has psychological force (not physical), because it has

---

[1] See Strawson, 'Causation and Explanation', in Vermazen and Hintikka (1985), p. 115.

to satisfy its seekers. The witch explanation was a good one in the seventeenth century, because it fitted everybody's beliefs. Cause, let us be clear, belongs to history(1), explanation to history(2).

*Questions about causes in history; how things come about; explanations*

1   Why do things happen as they do?
2   Why do things happen at all?
3   What is a cause?
4   Can there be more than one kind of cause?
5   Can there be more than one kind of explanation?
6   What is meant by 'counter-factual'?
7   Do some things happen by chance?
8   If we know the cause do we know the explanation?
9   If we know the explanation do we know the cause?
10   What is a good explanation?
11   How do historians explain?
12   How can we explain unique events?
13   Does understanding another's feelings provide an explanation?
14   Is there any difference between reasons and causes?

This chapter begins with a discussion of the idea of causation as used by historians (Section A). Since causation is a problem of the real world (history-as-event), we are then led on to a brief discussion of how that world runs: (Section B). Only after this are we in a logical position to look at the ways in which historians explain events. This (as Strawson insists) is a different order of being; it is part of history-as-account. Causes operate in a dynamic universe, whether we understand them or not. But our explanations of history *may* be as fallacious as that for sour milk quoted above. Section C discusses the best we can do at present by way of explaining the past. Section D glances briefly at three related themes.

A   Causation in History
B   The Dynamics of History
C   Explanation
D   Other Relevant Topics

## A.   Causation in History

The basic problem of this (Eleatic)school. . . . was that of the rational understanding of *change* . . . I think . . . that it still remains the fundamental problem of Natural Philosophy.

Karl Popper, *Conjectures and Refutations*

The study of history is a study of causes.

E. H. Carr, *What Is History?*

## 1   *The forces of nature and their directions*

As we have remarked, the world does not stand still. The whole universe is in ceaseless motion, and change is the order of the day. History is the story of some of the important changes during the last 5,000 years. First, we may ask of these changes what we ask about any particle in motion: velocity? direction? Of every event we may ask: What is the force for change? To what end?

Physicists tell us that there are only four kinds of force in the universe: gravitational, electro-magnetic, weak nuclear and strong nuclear. Of these only two were known before the twentieth century. Electromagnetic radiation from the sun has supplied most of the energy, directly or indirectly, for the dynamics of history, though gravitation has also played some part. So much for the sources of energy.

Of more concern to historians is why these forces have moved in the ways they have. If we study the long history of life on earth we shall notice two things: there has always been energy available for the creatures that inhabit it; but they have evolved in particular ways that fix the channels along which that energy must flow. For example, both humans and fish need oxygen, but the methods that the one uses are not available to the other. (The fish gasps out its life in the bottom of the boat while the fisherman falls overboard and drowns). You can scratch the back of your neck with your fore-limb, but a horse cannot. Such fixed channels for the flow of energy are called the laws of nature. These channels determine the structure and possibilities not only of living beings but also of the inanimate parts of the earth – rocks, soil, waters and atmosphere.

## 2   *Uses of nature: rules of society*

A new factor comes into play with human beings. A very long time ago our ancestors realized that they could make changes in the natural world. That is to say, they could make energy flow along new channels. Purposely chipped flints are the first evidence of this. How our technology has developed from that to the exploration of space is not a story to be told here. Natural forces are still used to provide the dynamics even of space travel.

History, however, consists of more than technology. We live in societies, and social life has produced elaborate systems – political, economic, cultural, linguistic, aesthetic, religious. Just as nature has evolved along certain lines (so that fish cannot breathe air), so societies have developed in distinct ways so that energy flows in some directions rather than others. There is a difference, however, in that the flows of energy directed by human systems are rather less determined than the laws of nature. Thus I have the energy but I *cannot* (like some birds) see 360° around my head; I have the energy but I *may* not dance on the President's breakfast table. There are laws, rules and customs of societies that resemble but are weaker than the laws of nature. Yet the former can mould one's personality so much that people are often said to have a 'second nature' (created by society) which can seem almost as strong as their 'first nature'.

### 3   Four courses of energy

Questions about the channelling of energy in history are usually put in terms of cause. What caused the Reformation, the repeal of the Corn Laws, the Vietnam War? To such questions it would be pretty pointless to answer in terms of the electro-magnetic and gravitational forces that ultimately supplied the necessary energies.

Thus when we ask of any occurrence what was its cause, we mean to ask why things took this particular course. Why did this little piece of a universe that is always and everywhere in motion, on this occasion move in this particular direction? We may seek the answer in four areas.

The first is that of pure nature: that is, nature untouched by man. Questions about acorns and earthquakes and butterflies belong here. The answers are given in accordance with the theories of the natural sciences. The second area is that of nature in the service of man. Questions like 'Why did the match burst into flame when it was struck on the box?' belong here. Matches and match-boxes are not found in nature. Nevertheless, the answer to a technological question like this is given largely in terms of natural forces governed by natural laws. (In this case, in terms of oxygen, friction, phosphorus and so on.) Yet these situations (unlike those in the first area) arise only as a result of human intentions.

The third area is that of human societies with their laws, rules, customs, traditions and skills. Questions like 'Why does traffic in Britain drive on the left?' or 'Why had Milton a choice of either the Petrarchan or the Shakespearean sonnet form?' must be answered in terms of the arrangements of society rather than the laws of nature.

The fourth area is the most familiar and at the same time the most puzzling. This is the area of intention: familiar every time my finger presses a key on the typewriter, puzzling in that changes in the world (the domain of our first three areas) are initiated by changes in the mind. Whether the material is really moved by the immaterial, as it appears, has long been a problem for philosophers and is still unsolved.

Very often the answer to why-questions is given in terms of what somebody wished, decided or intended to do. If we ask about the match not 'Why did it light?' but 'Why was it struck?' the answer is 'Because

Mary wanted to light the fire'. Intention also answers the question 'Why *did* Milton use the Petrarchan form of the sonnet?'

## 4   *Four types of causation*

Sometimes the answer draws upon more than one area of causation. Thus to the question 'What caused him to break his leg?' we find that a complete answer involves the following: (1) He wanted to catch the post – Area 4. (2) The time was 8.57 and the post went at 9.00 – Area 3. (3) He had to go down a steep flight of steps – Area 2. (4) There had been a sudden drop in temperature and the steps were covered with black ice – Area 1. Yet any one of the four might be called *the* cause.

We notice two things about these many types of cause. The first is that human intentions are normally exercised in the other three areas; rarely are they confined to the realm of pure thought. The second is that predictability is found in all four areas. The ceaseless motions of the universe (both human and natural) show a sufficient degree of regularity for human intentions to be turned into human actions. It is only because we can count on plants normally growing from seeds that we have developed agriculture. It is only because I expect all other vehicles to drive on the left that I venture to use my car at all.

What makes history possible, as well as what makes it unfailingly interesting, is a paradox. The paradox is that human actions are intended to make changes in an already changing universe; yet they can be planned only on the assumption that everything else will remain the same. But of course it doesn't; unforeseen changes also occur. We all know the result: 'The best-laid schemes o' mice and men / Gang aft agley.' Yet we have to go on making the assumptions that fire burns, bread nourishes, traffic stops at the red lights, and so on. In short we have to rely on a high degree of predictability in the world, whether natural, technological or human. Life would otherwise be impossible. Our intentions have to take effect in the outer world over which we have less power than we have over our own minds. Living is a risky business.

## 5   *Picking the cause*

The second thing to notice about the multiplicity of types of cause is that it offers a wide choice in answer to the question 'Why?' And, let us remember, these four areas are only for answering the question about direction: the energy involved in any change (perhaps even a change of mind) has to be supplied by one or more of the physical forces. For example, in the case of the broken leg, in addition to the four areas of cause that I cited, I could have added an account of the electro-magnetic, the gravitational (and possibly the weak nuclear) forces that came into play. But when we ask for the cause, or the causes, we do not usually require a complete list of *all* the contributory causes. We want only the cause that interests us or that would be of advantage. As Gardiner puts it, 'For common-sense, the cause of an event is frequently conceived of as being a kind of handle, an instrument for achieving, or helping to achieve, an end that we desire.'[2]

'Why did the car stop?' you ask. 'Because you neglected to fill the tank', I reply. I could have given an answer involving loss of momentum, lack of petrol vapour, and much more. But the helpful answer I gave was what it was useful for you to know. It gave you a 'handle' on the situation so that you might avoid a repetition.

## 6   Finding causes in history

The historian, however, does not normally seek such a 'handle' when he asks about causes in history. He is concerned rather to understand the past than to influence the future. Statesmen and diplomats, though, do want a 'handle'. For example, they inquire into the causes of a war and then try to remove such causes in order to avoid another such. Believing that weak states on the borders of France tempted French aggression, the victors at the Congress of Vienna in 1814–15 established stronger states on those borders. The victors at the Paris Conference in 1919 believed that suppressed nationalities had been one of the causes of the late war. Therefore they broke up empires and founded a number of new small states, thus reversing the policies of a century before. It is for the historian to explain why the policy of 1815 was markedly more successful in securing a long peace than that of 1919.

If the historian does not seek a 'handle' on events, neither does he attempt to list everything that might conceivably be a cause. Most elements, whether natural, technological, social or psychological, he takes for granted. It is departures from the norm that he notices. For example, governments normally rule their peoples. It is when a government is overthrown by revolutionary action that the historian's interest is aroused and he seeks an explanation. To account for this unusual event he looks for unusual precedents. The French monarchy that fell in 1792 had lasted a thousand years. Among the unusual precedents were a series of costly wars and the consequent bankruptcy of the government, the widespread dissemination of ideas hostile to that type of rule, popular unrest over high food prices, and so on.

The line of thinking here was systematized by John Stuart Mill in his *System of Logic* (1843), though it is much older. It goes like this. There are two situations: one, where conditions A, B, C, D, E are always present and R never happens. The other is where A, B, C, D, E and F are present and R does happen. Common-sense would suggest that condition F has

[2] See Gardiner (1952), p. 11.

something to do with the occurrence of R. Hence it is among the unusual characteristics of pre-revolutionary France that historians look for the causes, not among those that had continued for a long time without a revolution.

## 7 *What is necessary or sufficient to bring things about*

It is these combinations of causes that are so puzzling. Let us look first at the idea of 'bringing something about'. Causes may be either necessary or sufficient, or both. (Strictly these terms apply to conditions rather than causes, but the distinction is not needed here.) **A cause is *necessary* for a certain effect if that effect never comes about without it.** Flour is necessary for bread; air temperature below zero is necessary for a frost, and so on. **A cause is *sufficient* if the effect always follows from that cause.** A brick thrown at a pane of ordinary glass is sufficient to break it.

However, what is necessary is not always sufficient. Flour is not all we need to make bread. Equally a pane of glass can be broken by other things than a brick. So what is sufficient is not always necessary.

Unfortunately the historian usually deals with situations more complex than these simple examples. At first sight it may seem that what he is seeking is the necessary cause, which is defined as 'that without which the effect never comes about'. There are two problems here. The first is that more than one thing may be necessary. To strike a match, both box and match must be firmly held, and the match must be drawn across the side of the box. We may be aware of these conditions. What we are likely to overlook are other conditions, like the necessities that box and match be dry, that oxygen be present, that the match be tipped with phosphorus, and so on. When a match fails to strike, or a car to start, we probably know from experience which necessary conditions are likely not to have been fulfilled – a dry match box or a fully charged battery. Having found which it is, we say: 'That was the cause. That's why the car did not start [or the match did not strike].'

## 8 *Necessary causes in history*

In history, however, it is more difficult to be certain that we have found all the necessary conditions. Can we be sure that Paul Revere's ride or Burgoyne's surrender at Saratoga was necessary for American victory? Might the colonial revolt still have succeeded without them? While we may safely ignore some of the necessary conditions for that victory (like the availability of weapons or the presence of oxygen in the North American atmosphere), there may be others (such as the greater literacy of the colonial troops or the devotion of American women) which were necessary for that victory (for it would not have happened without them), yet which have been overlooked by historians. If we do not know in regard to any particular event what conditions were necessary and what not, then we can hardly be said to have understood how it came about. We don't know 'what made the difference.'

Thus there is a problem with the plurality of necessary conditions. But there is also the problem of experience. We have had so much of it in striking matches or starting cars that we can be reasonably successful in identifying what is and what is not necessary. The historian has the twin problem of a comparatively limited experience (for example, of colonial revolts) – and that at second hand, and also an insufficiency of reliable information. Thus, if he should suspect that either literacy or women held the key to the success of the American revolution, he might well discover that there is not nearly enough evidence available for any firm conclusion to be reached. Most historians know such frustration.

### 9    Sufficient causes in history

Let us now turn to sufficient causes. Whenever this sort of cause occurs the result always follows. On the other hand, the same result may be achieved in other ways; if so, the cause is sufficient but not necessary. Of any particular historical event or situation we may ask, 'What brought it about?' (as distinct from, 'What is it without which the event would not have occurred?'). We know what is sufficient to break a pane of glass or kill a man, though there are many alternative ways of doing so. What is sufficient to start a revolt, defeat an enemy, win an election? It is not easy to answer such historical questions with any certainty. In practice it would seem that any answer you give admits of some exception. For example, it was supposed in 1991 that a heavy bombardment and overwhelming military disaster would be sufficient for the fall of Saddam Hussein in Iraq – just as defeat had put an end to Mussolini and Hitler and many another dictator. The supposition was disappointed; overwhelming defeats do not always dislodge dictators.

In practice historians often take refuge in plurality; that is, failing to find any single condition that can with certainty be said to have sufficed for a given result, they talk of a *set* of conditions that *jointly* were sufficient to bring about the effect, though none would have done so by itself. Often this approach seems more convincing, for it avoids a generalization ('X is the sort of thing that always starts a revolt, wins an election, etc.') which can usually be disproved by counter-instances. (It is enough to say, 'But in this case it didn't.'). For example, while the historian can admit that Washington's generalship, British naval weakness, French help, colonial resentment of arbitrary taxation were none of them *singly* sufficient for American victory, yet *taken together* they sufficed.

Two problems arise here. One we have already noticed in regard to necessary causes. Since such revolts are not everyday occurrences like breaking windows, we do not have enough experience to be sure that we have correctly identified what is and what is not sufficient. This, again, is magnified by the historian's doubts about the adequacy and reliability of the available evidence.

But the greater problem about citing a set of jointly sufficient causes is to know where to stop. More than one philosopher has remarked that the true cause of any event is the whole previous history of the world. This, though correct, is not helpful. But where do we draw the line? Do we not concentrate on causes that may afford us a 'handle' on events, or that interest us for one reason or another, or that seem to have a convincing air of inevitability? Yet can the conscientious historian be sure that she has omitted nothing relevant?

## 10   Proximate causes

Now relevance is related to proximity. We feel that the closer the cause is to the effect the more certain is the result. Experience teaches that the longer is the chain of events by which we plan a desired result, the less certain is that result. (Mate in two moves is easier than mate in ten.) Too many unexpected things can happen if there is a wide gap between initial cause and intended result. Hence when we look at chains of causation we often stress **the last in that chain (called the 'proximate cause')** and label that as *the* cause; for that seems the one from which the effect must inevitably follow. Yet citing the proximate cause can seem unsatisfactory. The fall of the headsman's axe in Whitehall on 30 January 1649 was the proximate and quite sufficient cause of King Charles's death (though by no means a necessary cause). But as an explanation it is inadequate. We want to know how a king came to be in the position of a condemned criminal. The answer must partly lie in his defeat in the Civil War. This defeat, though perhaps a necessary, was not a sufficient, cause of his condemnation. But it is certainly one of a set of jointly sufficient causes. (Others may have included his failure to hold to his agreements, frustration among his captors, and the 'purging' of the House of Commons by Colonel Pride.)

However, there would have been no defeat had there been no war. And it is an attempt to take 'a more sophisticated view of the causes of the English Revolution' by a modern historian, Lawrence Stone, that well illustrates the problems of relevance. A conscientious student who is determined to include everything that may have 'causal force' must go far back from the proximate cause. 'To make sense of these events,' he writes, '. . . has necessitated the construction of multiple helix chains of causation more complicated than those of DNA itself.'[3] It is impossible, he says, to

---

[3] Stone (1972), p. 146.

pick out any one cause as decisive, or even the most important. 'The ultimate causes ... have to be traced far back into the early Tudor period.'[4] That he goes no farther back than 1529 shows that he thinks that nothing before that is to his purpose. Now he probably would not deny that some earlier events (like the development of parliamentary politics in the fourteenth and fifteenth centuries) were relevant to the events of 1640–2. Clearly they were. Probably he picked 1529 as a starting-point because he thought that from then on there was a certain inevitability, whereas before that date things might well have turned out otherwise. Nevertheless, there are varying degrees of inevitability; there is an increase of 'causal force' as we approach nearer and nearer to the climax. In order to illustrate these degrees Stone develops what he calls a 'multi-causal' approach. He arranges the causes under three headings: 'The preconditions, 1529–1629'; 'The precipitants, 1629–39'; and 'The triggers, 1640–42'. Thus he believes that he avoids having to decide 'whether or not the obstinacy and duplicity of Charles I was more important than the spread of Puritanism in causing the Revolution'.[5]

## 11   What is an 'important' cause?

This remark of Stone's raises the question of what historians mean when they say that one cause was more important than another. What can 'importance' mean in causation? One thing it could mean is inevitability: that the results of this cause flowed more certainly, more ineluctably, than the results of that cause. Arguing like this, one can assert that the German attack on the USSR on 22 June 1941 was a more important cause of the downfall of Nazism than Hitler's plans for eastern conquest in his *Mein Kampf*. Again, one could argue that the defeat of the German armies at Stalingrad in the winter of 1942–3 was more important for that downfall than the invasion of June 1941. These arguments, like Stone's, come close to equating inevitability to proximity: the nearer the cause lies to the effect, the more certain is its outcome. But Stone, we observe, explicitly denies that proximity (or any other single concept) will suffice to measure the importance of a cause.

So what else might 'importance' mean? It could mean **causal force – the power to override other causal factors**. Hence it is possible to judge that an earlier event is more important than a later one. For example, let us suppose that a soldier is badly wounded in battle. While crawling towards his unit he falls into a shell-hole. His wounds prevent him from climbing out and he dies. We judge that his being shot was the more important cause of his death than the later event of his fall. Why? Because being

[4] Ibid.
[5] Ibid. p. 58.

badly wounded is a much more probable cause of death than merely falling into a hole, from which a healthy man could easily climb out. But please notice that the last nine words make a supposition about what did not, in fact, occur. The fact is that, having been wounded, he fell. If we decide that the former was a more important cause of his death than the latter, it is because we can evaluate separately the likely consequences of being wounded and of falling into a hole.

In this way historians often assert that one thing was a factor of greater importance than another, even though the greater one occurred earlier. In doing so they judge that proximity is not the measure of causal force. We must note that such judgements (as in the case of the soldier) involve a supposition about what *might* have happened, as distinct from what *did* happen. We evaluate one cause in a sequence of events as more important because of the greater probability of its consequences. Now we are able to make judgements of probability only in the light of our experience. This has taught us the way things usually turn out. We feel safe in assuming that they would have turned out like this if such and such had not occurred. (The soldier would have climbed out of the hole had he not been wounded). Thus our labelling a cause or condition as 'necessary' (defined as 'that without which not') implies that we know what would have happened had that cause not occurred, or that condition not obtained. For example, if the historian of the American revolution judges that Washington's leadership was necessary for American victory, then he makes an assumption about what would have happened without that leadership – i.e. no victory. Indeed, a large number of historical judgements about significance or importance rest on the assumption that we know what would have happened otherwise. Such **assumptions of possibilities contrary to the facts are known as 'counter-factual conditionals'.** Thus 'Germany lost the Second World War' is a fact; therefore 'Germany won the Second World War' is a counter-fact. We may speculate on the basis of such a counter-fact. Usually we begin with a condition – e.g. 'If Germany had won . . .' Hence such speculation or assumption or guess is called a 'counter-factual conditional'.

## 12  *Counter-factual conditionals*

The familiar sing-song of childhood – 'For want of a nail the shoe was lost; for want of a shoe the horse was lost', and so on to 'for want of the battle a kingdom was lost' – is based entirely upon counter-factual speculation. Indeed, without deciding what is significant the historian can hardly write at all; he does not know what to put in and what to leave out. Yet all judgements about significance, importance, necessity, causal force and so on involve assumptions about what did not happen – assumptions about what would have happened if . . .; in short, counter-factual assumptions. Thus counter-factual conditionals are quite indispensable for the historian, and yet they must remain mere suppositions. They are no more than estimates of probability. Why use them at all?

We sometimes speak of an event as being a 'watershed' in history. This reminds us of streams in the hills. Most, we observe, follow the same slope to the valley below. One, however, meets an obstruction and is deflected away from the others. It begins to fall in a different direction, enters another valley and eventually becomes another river. Hence the importance of the watershed. If it had not met that obstacle it would have followed the same course as the other streams. This is the counter-factual assumption. How do we know 'what would have happened if . . .'?

Without making judgements about the significance of events, without judging the nature of causal forces in history, of necessity and sufficiency, of the relative importance of this or that causal factor, the historian cannot work at all. Such judgements constitute the very essence of history. Otherwise it is no more than 'a tale told by an idiot . . . signifying nothing'. But how can such judgements be justified? Only on the basis of our understanding of how the world runs – that is, of the dynamics of history. Then we can estimate and compare the probabilities that underlie our counter-factual judgements.

## B. The Dynamics of History

L'amor che move il sole e l'altre stelle (The love that moves the sun
and the other stars)
The closing line of Dante's Divine Comedy

### 1 Chance?

When I remarked to a friend that I was writing about the moving forces of history, he replied, 'Don't forget chance!' He was echoing the thoughts of the ancients who personified Chance, or Luck, and made her a goddess under the name of Fortuna. Of course, many things happen that we have not foreseen; this is a not surprising consequence of our ignorance or lack of attention. More puzzling are the things that cannot be explained in retrospect. The historian, wishing to make an intelligible story, is often reduced to speaking of chance or hazard to account for them. In July 1944 a group of German officers attempted to end the Nazi regime by assassinating Adolf Hitler. A brief-case containing a bomb was placed under the table at Hitler's feet. Just before it exploded a totally unsuspecting but tidy-minded aide-de-camp noticed it and moved it to the other end of the room. Hitler lived. The war, which was to have ended there and then, continued for another ten months – the most destructive period of the whole conflict. We cannot estimate the immense losses that Europe and civilization suffered in those ten months; we note only that they all seem to have stemmed from the moving of that little leather case.

## 2    No. Only nature and man

In reviewing the dynamics of history must we then find room for chance or fate among the moving forces? I believe not.

The forces of history stem from two sources only: nature and man. At this point I mention, but only to put aside, two great questions. The first is whether there is, behind nature and man, a God or Absolute Spirit who created them and who works through them. This is a matter of faith that the historian is not required to decide upon; it does not affect his account. The second question is whether my two sources are, not too few, but too many. Is there only nature, within which man is completely included? In that case nature provides the only source for the forces of history. This, too, is a question that lies outside the historian's field. It is sufficient to agree with a modern philosopher 'that one ought to separate, as being utterly distinct, causation in nature and causation, if we are to use that name, in the realm of individual or collective human action.'[6]

## 3    The forces of nature

The forces of nature, as we noted on p. 195 above, are the four fundamental forces of the physicists (electro-magnetic etc.) channelled by the evolution of the universe. Many apparently necessary features of the natural world are actually contingent. All mammals have five digits because we are all descended from a Devonian fish that had five phalanges in its fins. If it had had six we should probably count in twelves, not tens. If gravity on Earth were less than 1g, plants and animals would be more long and spindly like giraffes or Lombardy poplars; if more than 1g, we should all be built like rhinoceroses or Japanese wrestlers. When we try to explain why the so-called 'laws of nature' should be as they are, we can find causes in the history of the universe.

But whether the universe *had* to develop as it has, or whether it is all a matter of pure chance (and the further question of what 'chance' and 'had to' can mean in this context), is not a matter for the historian. He takes nature as he finds it. It is not for him to explain why water consists of oxygen and hydrogen and freezes at 0°. It is enough to remember that it always does. Such is the 'law-like' or 'covering-law' type of explanation that some people think is the appropriate answer to the historian's question about the cause of a particular event.

## 4    Human intentions

Thus a natural event is the result of a combination of natural forces. But is a historical event also such a result? I believe not. There is another element

6 Von Wright (1971), pp. 160–1.

here whose source is not nature but the human mind. **Such forces are called 'intentional' because they spring from a human purpose, usually a purpose to bring about a change in the world.** Now such a result certainly makes use of the forces of nature – they provide the mechanical power for our own bodies and for the machines that we have invented. Yet poems and interplanetary rockets are not products of natural forces alone.

When human intentions employ the forces of nature we call it technology. But how do human intentions work upon other humans? Kant taught that 'man (and every rational being) is an end-in-himself, i.e. he is never to be used merely as a means for someone (even for God) without at the same time being himself an end . . .'[7] On Kant's principle we should never force, but only persuade, other people (manipulation is out). Strictly speaking, however, we *can* never force another person to act. If a man of great strength seized your hand and smacked my face with it, the action would be not yours but his. This is why R. G. Collingwood argues that there is a difference in the meaning of 'cause' depending on whether it applies to nature or humanity. We 'cause' an event in nature by striking a match or catching a fish. We brought these about by moving a match against a match-box or baiting a line and putting it in the water. But this is not how we act when we 'cause' someone to do something (like lending us money or running away to sea). 'Here', says Collingwood, 'that which is "caused" is the free and deliberate act of a conscious and responsible agent, and "causing" him to do it means affording him a motive for doing it.'[8]. There are, of course, marginal cases. If we beat a man half-senseless till he signs a document, does that count as his action? Or have we 'caused' it in the technological sense? If we threaten his wife and children unless he signs, have we forced him? That is the term we normally use. But, strictly, his signing would still be the free act of a conscious and responsible agent, though one with a very strong motive. Phrases like 'we made him do it', 'circumstances compelled him to do it', are frequently used metaphorically rather than literally. What we understand in such cases is that he was afforded a very strong motive, usually because the alternative was so unpleasant. The fact that occasionally the subject proves obstinate (goes to the stake for his beliefs, or forfeits a fortune) shows that he is not literally forced. After all, the struck match and the caught fish had no choice at all.

## 5   From the past, or towards the future?

The distinction that Collingwood makes so clearly is the difference between something coming about because of a preceding event and its coming about because of some envisaged future. Thus, if you ask why I am writing at this moment, it is not an adequate explanation to refer to

[7] Kant (1956), p. 136; part I, ch. II, 6.
[8] Collingwood (1940), p. 285.

preceding events, such as my getting out of bed. Although these may be necessary, they do not account for my action. The reason for writing is my intention of completing the book. The finished book is the envisaged future event that accounts for my typing. This is called **a teleological or final explanation, from the Greek 'telos' or the Latin 'finis', both meaning 'an end'**. It is this type of explanation that is more appropriate to human affairs rather than the natural kind, where events are accounted for by preceding events and the operation of natural laws.

This distinction, clear in theory, is less clear in worldly affairs, which is the arena of the historian. Here laws of nature and human intentions are almost inextricably mixed in historical events, great and small. Suppose that we ask, 'Why is the barn on fire?' The answer may be either, 'Because wood and straw are highly combustible' or 'Because someone set fire to it'. A full causal account would include all the natural and all the human elements; in practice, we confine ourselves to picking out the one that seems relevant to the present inquiry. Historians differ in the kind of explanation they prefer. One will say that the battle was lost because the victors had better tanks, another because they had better generals. People argue whether this or that was the 'real' cause. Certainly there is some mileage in either argument, but does not the question ultimately come down to individual preferences and philosophies of life?

## 6   Laws of nature and laws of humanity

The problem becomes more difficult when we move into the realm of the social sciences. These sciences are concerned, not with natural objects, but with human behaviour in society. Economics, sociology, political science, individual and social psychology, anthropology, linguistics all find regularities and predictabilities in human affairs which are similar to those found in nature. Such regularities lie at the base of the social sciences. The point was clearly put more than two centuries ago by Kant: 'Thus marriages, births, and deaths do not seem to be subject to any rule by which their numbers could be calculated in advance, since the free human will has such great influence upon them; and yet the annual statistics for them . . . prove that they are just as subject to constant natural laws as are the changes in the weather . . .'[9] Yet are these human regularities attributable to 'constant natural laws'? Or is human behaviour in society free from natural laws? Some people argue that there is only Science, and that all sciences have the one subject matter, nature; and the one method, that of establishing theories and making deductions, known as the hypothetico-deductive method. It is not for historians to attempt to resolve this long-standing debate. They should know of it, however, and

[9] Kant (1784), in Reiss (1977), p. 41.

should be aware of their own (perhaps subconscious) tendencies towards one or the other side, as well as the tendencies of their colleagues.[10]

Where do the moving forces of history come in? For these regularities of society are very like the laws of nature. Are we, then to account for social events in terms of cause (i.e. brought about by natural laws) or of intention (i.e. brought about by human will)? In other words, is our explanation **law-like (or nomological – from Greek 'nomos' – a law)** or is it to be a teleological explanation? We have already suggested (p. 205 above) that most laws of nature took on their present form through the long development of the earth and life upon it. On earth the fundamental forces of the universe are now channelled in certain ways. But they do not *have* to be like that. The earliest stages of life were based on methane not oxygen. Animals and plants might have been made of silicon, not carbon as they are now. Animal life might well have evolved along quite different lines.[11]

Similarly, human societies have developed in a large number of different ways (as anthropologists have demonstrated), and yet there remain many unrealized possibilities. Within societies certain systems – economic, cultural etc. – have been developed. Such systems seem to take on a reality of their own and mould the behaviour of men and women accordingly. The presence or absence of slavery, or of tribal possession of land, or of a free market greatly influences how people behave. Indeed, they not only regulate what people do; they regulate how they think. Thus, for me, marriage to three or four women simultaneously has never entered my calculations; it is almost literally unthinkable. Yet in some societies it would be commonplace. Such instances could be endlessly enumerated. The point (as we saw on pp. 195–7 above) is that the various systems of society make the behaviour of our fellows quite regular, and hence predictable and reliable. How could we drive a car, post a letter, buy the groceries otherwise? Society gives us each 'second nature'. But, again, we do not *have* to be like that. We are not slaves to our social systems. Hence the historian must allow for those determined characters who, in one way or another, break out of them. They, like unexpected events in nature, upset his estimate of probabilities.

## 7   Intentional systems

Then are social systems (unlike social actions) not intentional? If I write to a friend, I use material objects (pen, paper, stamp) as tools for my purpose. But then I entrust my letter to the servants of the Post Office. I use this organization as an instrument for my purpose, just as I use pen and paper. Am I then (contrary to Kant's dictum) using other people instrumentally? Not really: first, because the Post Office is established to

[10] For more on this debate, see ch. 3, pp. 69–70 above.
[11] See Gould (1991).

serve the ends of its users; second, because the Post Office employees have a double purpose – that of conveying letters (the common purpose) and that of earning a living (their private purpose). Social systems, then, like private actions, embody human intentions. What is of particular interest to historians is that such systems do not always work in the ways intended; sometimes the private interests of their servants conflict with the public interest. Corruption in political life is a familiar instance. Such vagaries do not, however, alter our main point: that social systems are intentional.

Nor are social systems found only within societies. Some, like trade and diplomacy, exist between them. Indeed, international war and commerce are almost as old as history. The main point is the same: across national boundaries, as well as within them, there have grown up intentional systems – laws, customs, habits, traditions – which channel behaviour and mould character.

## 8 No mysterious forces of history

When we consider the many natural and human means that we employ in seeking our ends, it is not surprising that things sometimes go wrong. Neither nature nor technology has been completely mastered. As for other human beings, we try to secure their co-operation, but do not always succeed. They have ideas and wills of their own. Sometimes unintentionally, sometimes casually, sometimes intentionally they set their wills against ours. The result, very often, is what none of us wants. There is no need to postulate witchcraft or evil spirits or the Devil to explain these misfortunes, though that has often been done. Nowadays it is more common, though scarcely more rational, to blame some designated group – communists, Jews, Arabs, liberals – in explanation of why things go wrong. The combination of hatred, ignorance and wanton stupidity in these resentments is enough to make the angels weep. Perhaps some knowledge of history coupled with a sane and balanced outlook can mitigate at least the ignorance and the stupidity. A rational understanding of the complex processes of human affairs, a grasp of the true causes and of the moving forces in history – in these lies hope for a better world.

If you go up in a helicopter and look down on the traffic flow of a road system at rush hour you may well have the impression of a steady force driving streams of metal, much as gravity drives water between rocks in a river bed. You will be wrong; there is no such force. There are only human intentions making use of explosions of vaporized petrol. Similarly, in looking at the course of human affairs in politics or history, many people have had the illusion of seeing great, non-human forces at work which they variously labelled Necessity, Determinism, Fate, Luck, Fortune, History, Absolute Spirit, the Life Principle and so on. All talk of 'the great, underlying forces of history' is of so much illusion. There are only the objects of nature and human beings. The only forces in history are the four fundamental forces of the physicists plus human intentions.

# C. Explanation

## (i) THE NATURE OF EXPLANATION

### 1 *When do we explain?*

'Now then! What's going on here?' asks the policeman, and every one hastens to explain. Not only to extricate ourselves from an embarrassing situation but for many other reasons do we engage in explanation every day: it may be a practical problem ('Why did the light go out?'); we may want to help another's understanding by simplifying what is complex or by making familiar what is strange; we may want to confer meaning and significance ('That is the very axe George Washington used to chop down the cherry tree'), and so on.

Many, but by no means all, explanations are made in response to the question 'Why?' These are frequently answered, 'Because . . .' There is a hidden trap here. Not all explanations do explain by citing causes. To the child's question 'Why is it bed-time?' the answer 'Because it is eight o'clock' is a proper explanation. Yet it is not a causal explanation. Nothing can be a cause of itself. Briefly, we may state that a 'because-type' answer may refer to causes – for example: the heat caused the butter to melt; to reasons – for example: he rose at 5.30 because he wanted to catch an early train; or to dependencies (logical, mathematical, conventional or otherwise) – for example: 'because it is eight o'clock'. Most dependency relations rest on some kind of identity, though they do not have to. Examples are: 'Because I am married I cannot be a bachelor' (logical); 'Because this is a plane triangle the sum of its angles is 180°' (mathematical); 'Because the lights were red, he could not lawfully proceed' (conventional). Thus to give a cause is only one of many ways of answering 'Why?' by using an explanation that begins 'Because . . .' This is a snare set by language.

### 2 *How and what do historians explain?*

So what sorts of explanation do historians engage in? As we have seen, they frequently explain *why*; but they also explain *how* and *what*, or occasionally, *when, where* or *who*. Consider the problem that the defeated powers of the second World War – Germany and Japan – became, in little more than a generation, nearly the greatest economic powers in the world, while the victors – the USSR, the USA and Great Britain – became mired in economic difficulties. The historian feels constrained to address herself, not so much to the question 'Why?' as to the question 'How did it come about?' As to explaining-what, one recalls the story of Louis XVI in July 1789 receiving the news of the taking of the Bastille and exclaiming: 'Mais, c'est une révolte!' 'Sire', answered a courtier, 'it is not a revolt. It is a revolution.' So a doctor may explain that my pain is not appendicitis but indigestion. Showing *what* something is often makes the best explanation.

## 3  What requires explanation?

If these are the sorts of explanations that historians engage in, what, precisely, are the sorts of things that have to be explained? First are events. An event (as we saw in chapter 6) is a change in a state of affairs. We must remember that a failure to change (especially when one might be expected) should also count as an event; the historian needs to account for unchange as well as change. Other candidates for explanation are actions and series of actions (like policies, programmes or campaigns), texts (which may be anything from a single sentence to a whole compilation like the Bible), and objects. Here, as with events, it is the absence of an expected object that sometimes calls for explanation. One recalls the strange behaviour of the dog in the night in Conan Doyle's story, 'Silver Blaze':

> 'Is there any point to which you would wish to draw my attention?'
> To the curious incident of the dog in the night-time.'
> 'The dog did nothing in the night-time.'
> 'That was the curious incident', remarked Sherlock Holmes.

Other things to be explained are ideas of all kinds, but especially political and religious doctrines which have long lives and wide influences. Lastly, practices – habits, customs, traditions, rituals and ceremonies – all call for explanation. Explaining all these things requires insight into human behaviour. But many of them also call for some understanding of the natural world. This is true, for example, in the explanation of the dog's behaviour in the night-time, which turns out to be the key to the whole mystery.

## 4  Is there a special kind of explanation for history?

After the different sorts of things that have to be explained, we ask what sort of explanation can be used? Is there a special kind of explanation for historians? If so, how does it differ from ordinary, everyday explanation? And is it different, again from scientific explanation? These questions have given rise to lengthy controversies over the last fifty years.[12] In these, many historians, as well as philosophers sympathetic to history, have argued that proper methods of explanation in history are quite different from those used in science. However, the philosopher David-Hillel Ruben is

[12] See pp. 214–26 below.

surely right when he says, 'The only distinction that can usefully be drawn is that between full and partial explanations . . .'[13] Rather than bother with distinctions between scientific and historical explanations, or between either of these and the everyday type, we should look for complete or full explanations of anything that needs to be explained. On any particular occasion it may not be necessary to give more than a partial explanation, for some parts can be taken for granted. But a complete explanation should always be in the background.

## 5   *Full explanations and good explanations*

This last consideration leads us to the distinction between a *full* explanation and a *good* explanation. **A full or complete explanation is one that meets all possible questions. A good explanation is one that meets the purpose for which a particular question was asked.** Different people want different explanations. For example, if the car stops, the explanation for the mechanic is that there is no petrol in the tank, the explanation for the driver is that her husband failed to fill the tank when he last used the car, and for the husband that his wife never looks at the petrol gauge. Of course, a full explanation would include all these, and many more. A good explanation is usually a partial explanation, but it meets the needs of the case and could, if necessary, be expanded into a full one. (The needs of the enquirer are not always met, however. When the priest asked a certain bank robber why he robbed banks, the latter replied, 'Because that's where the money is.')[14]

Yet explanation in history does raise problems of its own. As we have seen, A. C. Danto points out that a full description of any historical event is always impossible in principle, for fully to describe it requires knowledge of its significance for future times: 'a complete account of an event would have to include every true historical description of that event.'[15] The question arises, if we can never give a complete account of an event, is it equally impossible to give a complete explanation of it? A similar doubt springs from what F. W. Maitland called 'the seamless web' of history. He is remarking that in history everything seems to be connected to something else in a way that leaves no natural seams or divisions. If this is really so (or anything like it), then how can we give a complete explanation of any event in history without reciting the whole of what went before? As we shall see, this is not the only reason for doubting the possibility of full historical explanation.

One thing is certain: an explanation, whether full or only partial, must rest on reality. Politicians, journalists and parents are often tempted to offer explanations that seem good (in the sense that they satisfy the

[13] Ruben (1990), p. 17.
[14] See Putnam (1979), p. 42.
[15] See Danto (1965), pp. 18, 148ff.

questioner) but are not strictly true. Ruben rightly insists that 'explanation is an epistemological concept', but it has 'a solid metaphysical basis'.[16] He means that a proper explanation, in history as in science, must not only be **a part of our system of knowledge and beliefs (that is, be epistemological)**; it must rest on **a metaphysical basis (that is, upon how the world really is, or was)**. A merely *good* explanation, however plausible, may not be enough. Any explanation must be more than just words and ideas; it must include some truthful account of the real world. This reinforces the distinction between cause and explanation made at the beginning of this chapter.

The distinction between full explanation and good explanation is particularly relevant to history. All too often the historian is satisfied with what he believes to be a good explanation. Now a good explanation is **audience-relative; it varies with the audience to whom the explanation is offered**. It is often, rather smugly, asserted by historians that the important thing in history is to ask the right questions. But there are no right questions as such. There are only the questions that it is useful for the student to ask at each point of her investigations. Any explanation that meets the question put is, to that extent, a good explanation. But if the historian is doing original work, then he may claim that the explanations he seeks are not merely audience-relative. They are part of a full explanation – an explanation so complete that it satisfies all possible questioners, covers all points and meets all reasonable objections. Here, we may say, he is seeking to discover the whole truth.

## 6   Are full explanations possible in history?

We have already seen reasons (arising from Danto's and Maitland's remarks) for doubting the possibility of full explanation in history. Indeed historians rarely attempt them – though not for the reasons already cited. For one thing, a great deal can taken for granted between narrator and audience. We do not need to have explained that men feel fear in the face of an enemy or that politicians seek power. A full explanation along these lines might well be a bad one, for it could easily send the audience to sleep and thus fail to explain anything.

But historical explanations are partial for another reason also: sheer ignorance. In almost no case do we know the whole story. (This, by the way, is not Danto's point, which is about description not evidence). Of even such well-reported events as the assassination of President Kennedy there is much yet to be known. So no one can be confident that further knowledge would not alter our explanation of these events. Like all good narrators, historians omit what is tedious. But they also omit what they do not know. Both audience and historian can easily mistake one reason for omission for the other.

<hr>

[16] See Ruben (1990), pp. 2, 232.

Yet would it not be salutary for any historian to submit himself from time to time to an exhaustive questioning, so that he is forced to make explicit all his assumptions, guesses and evasions? Having to face just what a full explanation would be like would search out his sources, his reading, his methods of procedure and his ways of thinking. It would also expose his moral, religious and political beliefs. Finally, if the questioning were rigorously continued, it would lay bare his metaphysical beliefs: beliefs about how the world runs, beliefs about causation, determinism, action, decision, event, particular and universal, oneness and plurality, coherence and separateness, process and progress, individualism and holism. It may well be that, for the reasons given, any full explanation in history is unattainable. But the possibility of a full explanation should be held before historians as an aim and a guide – like the Pole Star.

Now we turn to look at the hotly contested debate about explanation in history.

## (ii)   EXPLANATION IN HISTORY

### 7   *The Covering Law Debate: Hempel's theory*

The debate begins with the theory that 'explanation is achieved, and only achieved, by subsuming what is to be explained under a general law.'[17] This theory was put forward by a philosopher of science, C. G. Hempel.[18] Hempel's basic assumption is that history is one of the empirical sciences, like physics, biology or geography. Speaking of history and the natural sciences he asserts, 'Both can give an account of their subject matter only in terms of general concepts.' In his examples historical and natural events are lumped in together: 'For the object of description and explanation in every branch of empirical science is always the occurrence of an event of a certain *kind* (such as a drop in temperature of 14°F., an eclipse of the moon, a cell-division, an earthquake, an increase in employment, a political assassination) at a given place and time . . .'[19] Although in a certain sense all such events are unique, their uniqueness plays no part in their explanation. What explains them is that they are instances of a certain *kind* of occurrence. Thus an eclipse of the moon at a particular date is explained by the laws (relating to the respective movements of the earth and the moon around the sun and the light rays coming from the sun) that govern lunar eclipses in general. The particular date of this or that eclipse fixes *what* is to be explained; but is no part of the explanation proper. The important part of the explanation is the law that *whenever* sun, moon and earth are in a certain alignment there will be an eclipse.

Thus the second thing to note about Hempel's theory is that all explanation, whether historical or scientific, deals with 'kinds or proper-

[17] Dray (1957), p. 1.
[18] See Hempel (1942), in Gardiner (1959) pp. 344–56.
[19] Ibid., p. 346.

ties of events, not ... individual events'.[20] This may seem strange to historians, who tend to concentrate not so much on similarities as on dissimilarities.[21]

The third thing to notice is that Hempel puts forward an ideal pattern of explanation. This is the pattern:

1   a set of statements asserting the occurrence of certain events $C_1 \ldots C_n$ at certain times and places.
2   a set of universal hypotheses.[22]

Provided that the two sets are 'reasonably well confirmed by empirical evidence', and provided that the occurrence of an event E can be logically deduced from (1) and (2), then we have the explanation of event E. We may apply this to the eclipse of the moon thus: (1) on such a day the earth moved between the sun and the moon; (2) whenever the earth moves between the sun and the moon there will be a lunar eclipse.

From (1) and (2) taken together we may deduce that there was an eclipse of the moon on the day stated. Can we agree with Hempel that 'historical explanation, too, aims at showing that the event in question was not 'a matter of chance', but was to be expected in view of certain antecedent or simultaneous conditions.'?[23]

## 8   Why is Hempel's method uncommon in history?

Such a procedure is not familiar to history students. The explanations offered by historians are rarely like these. For this Hempel suggests two reasons. The first is that general laws used in many historical explanations relate to the sort of 'truths' of human nature that I referred to above (pp. 207–8). They are supposedly so familiar that they do not need to be stated explicitly.[24] Hempel's second (and less convincing) reason is that it would often be difficult 'to formulate the underlying assumptions explicitly with sufficient precision' and 'in agreement with all the relevant empirical evidence available.'[25] To illustrate this he suggests that we may explain a revolution by the growing discontent of many of the people, but we cannot put our fingers on handy general laws for this.[26]

Hempel meets these difficulties by suggesting that historians use an *explanation sketch*. 'Such a sketch consists of a more or less vague indication of the laws and initial conditions considered as relevant ...'[27]

[20] Ibid.
[21] See also Dray (1957), pp. 47–9.
[22] In Gardiner (1959), p. 345.
[23] Ibid, pp. 348–9.
[24] See also Popper (1962), vol. II, pp. 264–5. Popper argues that 'the host of trivial, universal laws we use are taken for granted.'
[25] In Gardiner (1959), p. 349.
[26] Ibid., p. 350.
[27] Ibid., p. 351.

This sketch, he adds, can be filled out by further research, for which it suggests the direction and indicates the sort of evidence applicable. By this he intends to exclude explanation by such 'empty' notions as racial destiny or historical justice.

## 9   Arguments in support of Hempel

What do we make of Hempel's argument? First we must recognize the valuable service he performs by insisting that what is offered as an explanation in history must really *explain*. This agrees with my suggestion (pp. 213–4 above) that any explanation should be capable of being expanded at need into a full explanation; and, moreover, that we should have a good idea of what a full explanation would, in principle, be like even if we do not or cannot offer one in practice. All too often, as Hempel says, words like 'therefore' conceal quite unacceptable and ill-founded assumptions.

Second, we must recognize that his appeal to general laws in history is not so bizarre as may at first appear. History involves natural events as well as human actions. Our actions always take place in a natural context where we are subject to well-established laws of nature. Like other things we can be burnt, or shattered by a fall. Thus many historical explanations rightly appeal to such laws. Again, a great deal of human behaviour, especially in the mass, can be explained by appeal to similar hypotheses in the social sciences – that is, to what may be called economic, sociological or psychological laws. Historians frequently appeal to observed regularities of human behaviour.

Let us examine a suitable case. In *The Making of Victorian England* G. Kitson Clark discusses the rapid growth of population in the first half of the nineteenth century.[28] How is it to be explained? Immediate explanations point to a rise in the birth rate and a fall in the death rate. But why these? The greater availability of medical facilities, increase in medical skills, improvements in hygiene and widespread vaccination are among the reasons put forward for the latter. The former can be accounted for by a lowering of the marriage age for women and a higher proportion of marriageable women actually marrying. These, in turn, can be explained by a slackening of customary precautions against early or foolish marriages because fewer employees lived in the households of their masters. This, both in town and country, results from changes in industrial and agricultural techniques. Thus suggested explanations make use of natural (especially biological) laws, and also refer to widespread changes in technology, in the economy, in society and in customs. Here, I think, Hempel's case is made: that historians frequently appeal to

[28] 'The difficulty is to account for the increase' (Kitson Clark, 1965, p. 66).

empirically established laws or regularities by way of explanation. Or, at least, they offer explanation sketches along these lines.

## 10   Criticisms of Hempel's approach

Why, then, have so many historians and philosophers of history challenged Hempel's argument? One reason is that historians use many types of explanation. That only one model of explanation is valid and that all the other ways of explaining things are invalid seems improbable. But there are more. The 'covering-law' argument of Hempel (and others) is challenged on the grounds that it is useless for many historical explanations. W.H. Dray takes the (oft-quoted) example of a historian's writing: 'Louis XIV died unpopular because he pursued policies detrimental to French national interests.'[29] Dray shows that to explain this on Hempel's lines would lead to the absurdity of explanation by a general law with only one instance.[30] The consequences follow (a) that the law can hardly be called general if it has only one instance; (b) that the empirical substantiation that any law requires (see Hempel above, p. 215) would be none other than the sort of evidence that led to the historian's conclusion in the first place. In such a case the covering-law model is useless.

## 11   The unique in history

This reminds us that many historians see it as their business to be concerned with the unique. It is true that the historian could hardly write at all if he did not use general terms or, as the grammars say, 'common nouns'. But the use of everyday language does not justify the belief that history is concerned solely with general phenomena. Historians are concerned with the particular much more often than with the typical or general. To note that the war in the USA of 1861–5 was a civil war tells us something about it, but not very much compared with all the particular things that we want to know.[31] But we can go further. It is often said that historians study not merely the particular but the unique. Although scientists may be much concerned with the particular – e.g. the eruption of Krakatoa in 1883, yet their interest is primarily in what they can learn in general about volcanoes, the earth's structure, the movement of the upper air, and so on. What fascinates a historian about, say, the assassination of Kennedy is its uniqueness – in spite of the fact that Kennedy is only one of several American presidents to have been murdered. As Paul Veyne puts

[29] Dray (1957), p. 25.
[30] Ibid. 25–39.
[31] 'As the definite article indicates in the French Revolution, historians do not proceed from the classificatory term toward the general law, but from the classificatory term toward the explanation of differences' (Ricoeur, 1984 vol. I, pp. 124–5).

it, 'There is indeed a "field" of physical phenomena . . . But it is not enough for the reality of a phenomenon in that field to be recognized for it to become ipso facto part of the corpus of physics, save as a problem. In contrast, this would be fully sufficient if a historical fact were involved.'[32] A similar point was succinctly made by Oakeshott: 'The moment historical facts are regarded as instances of general laws, history is dismissed.'[33]

There is another good reason why historical events are unique. It is because past events shape future events, though not vice versa. Thus the pattern of history is cumulative (like a widening spiral), not successive (like a circle) (see above, chapter 1, p. 18). Events are rarely repeated exactly; not only because the circumstances are different the second time, but also because the actors are often aware of what happened the first time.

Historical events are unique in an important sense. Any happening may be seen as unique in a trivial sense. Every time my pen falls off my table as I am working a unique event occurs. Its only interest may be that it instantiates the law of gravity. But suppose that the hundredth time the pen falls off I bend down to pick it up, jog the table and spill coffee all over my work. As a result of the accident I have to rewrite the chapter, thus delaying publication by some weeks. Then the incident of the falling pen would have significance in the history of this book and of my life. Thus history is concerned not just with what is unique, but with what is judged to be importantly unique. History in many ways is a matter of judgement.

## 12   The importance of judgement

Indeed, judgement will play an important part in historical explanation, whether covering-law theories are employed or not. Hempel specified for his ideal explanation, first, a set of initial conditions ($C_1 \ldots C_n$), and, second, a set of universal hypotheses (see above pp. 214–5). Even when they employ this model of explanation (as I suggested might be the case with the problem of English population growth – pp. 216–7 above), historians have to use their judgement in selecting the relevant initial conditions and the relevant hypotheses. As with the population problem, historians are by no means agreed as to what relevant conditions they should list as ($C_1 \ldots C_n$). Each historian thinks over the problem to the best of her ability and then submits her conclusions to her colleagues. In our present (and perhaps permanent) state of ignorance of all the relevant

---

[32] See Veyne (1984), p. 12
[33] See Oakeshott (1933), p. 154; quoted by Dray (1957), pp. 49–50.

facts, personal judgement, not logical deduction, must be the deciding factor in this – as in most other historical problems.

The necessity of judgement does not, then, invalidate the covering-law model of explanation. Even the considerations adduced above in relation to the unpopularity of Louis XIV do not actually invalidate it, though they do render it useless. There remain, however, other questions that have to be asked – about events, about causes, and about explanations. The first and second are discussed elsewhere.[34] The third I will discuss here.

## 13    The need to explain 'how'

The covering-law model, whatever its logical validity, is not always satisfactory *as an explanation*. And this for two reasons. One is that often an explanation in a historical narrative does not answer the question 'Why?' but the question 'How?'.[35] Sometimes in history we ask 'How could it possibly have happened that . . .?' How could the civilized nations of Europe after a century of peace and unprecedented progress have plunged into the barbarities of war and revolution in 1914–18? How could the rival superpowers have avoided conflict between 1950 and 1990 when the mere touch of a button could have unleashed a war? (Note that here a non-event requires explanation.) Such cases cannot be met by the covering-law model.

## 14    Do general laws explain?

A second defect of this model is that even when we do ask 'Why?' it doesn't yield the sort of answer we want. In one of Mozart's operas the two heroes find that their beloveds have been unfaithful to them. When Ferrando and Guglielmo are bursting with indignation, Don Alfonso assures them that 'all women behave like this – così fan tutte.' But if Ferrando wants to know why Dorabella has betrayed him, is it any use to try to explain it by . . . 'così fan tutte?' Ferrando doesn't care about *all* women; he agonizes only over betrayal by *one* woman. To subsume the lovely Dorabella under a general law is no help at all.

The truth is that there is a hidden assumption in the covering-law model of explanation. This is, that when you have shown that the thing to be explained is an instance of a general law, then there is no more to be said. It is assumed that if something always happens, then it has to happen; regularity implies necessity. Why? Simply because that is how the world is.

[34] See pp. 169–75, 194–204.
[35] See pp. 210–11 above. Also Dray (1957), p. 158.

## 15    Prediction

This assumption of unbreakable regularity leads some covering-law theorists to argue that explanation and prediction go together. Hempel says that an explanation 'is not complete unless it might as well have functioned as a prediction.'[36]

Any historian must be struck by the strangeness of the idea that an explanation offered in history could equally well be used for the purposes of prediction. Historians are almost unanimous in holding that historical prediction is a very doubtful and chancy business indeed. They would be very surprised to learn that their explanations gave them the power to predict.

This casts further doubt on whether covering-law theory is properly applicable to history. For, if a covering-law explanation may also function as a prediction, and if successful prediction rarely occurs in history, then we must conclude that successful covering-law explanations are also rare in history.[37]

## 16    Making sense

So far we have been talking about explanation largely in its **logical and epistemological aspects – that is, how it relates to the sciences of thinking and knowing.** But we must remember that there is a human dimension to the act of explaining. When I write or speak to another, I want my ideas to make sense to her.

So, in telling a story (as in narrative history) we want it to make sense to our audience. Therefore, we explain those parts of the story not immediately self-evident. But we seldom make use of Hempel's model. For example, if asked why Little Red Riding Hood went to visit her grandmother, we could reply (invoking the covering-law) that little girls often visit their grandmothers. But that rarely needs explaining. We are more likely to be asked why she mistook a wolf in bed for her grandmother. ('Little girls usually mistake wolves for grandmothers?'). Rather, the explanation (if any) would be given in *particular* terms of Little Red Riding Hood's short sight, or the darkness of the room, or the excellent histrionic powers of the wolf.

Let us take an example from history. Wellington won the Battle of

---

[36] Hempel in Gardiner (1959), p. 348. See also Karl Popper: 'The use of a theory for the purpose of *predicting* some specific event is just another aspect of its use for the purpose of *explaining* such an event' (162), vol. II, pp. 262–3).

[37] It seems that Hempel and Popper are wrong in identifying explanation and prediction in at least some areas of science. A zoologist writes of 'the "pageant" of evolution as a staggeringly improbable series of events, sensible enough in retrospect and subject to rigorous explanation, but utterly unpredictable and quite unrepeatable'. See Gould (1991), p. 14.

Waterloo. Why? Again, covering-law answers of the type 'It is the better general who wins' or 'It is the side with the larger army that wins' do not help. For Napoleon was the better general and the French army was larger. It turns out that the question is not of the 'Why must?' type that the covering-law model answers, but of the 'How possibly?' type. *How* did an inferior general with a smaller army win this decisive battle? Explaining how involves studying the course of events. It seems that what decided the battle was the failure of the Imperial Guard to charge the British lines. A British officer, right in the path of the charge, reported;

> They continued to advance until within fifty or sixty paces of our front, when the [British] Brigade was ordered to stand up. Whether it was the sudden and unexpected appearance of a Corps so near to them, which must have seemed as starting out of the ground, or the tremendously heavy fire we threw into them, *La Garde*, who had never before failed in an attack, *suddenly* stopped.[38]

Almost at once, the Guard turned about and fled. Napoleon had lost.

He lost, not because of something that generally occurs, but precisely the opposite: 'who had never before failed in an attack'. As so often in history, the point of interest is not what generally happens (in accordance with a covering law), but the unusual and unexpected. Notice, too, the explanation offered by the British officer. He tries to understand how the situation appeared to the Imperial Guard and thus to explain their actions.

## 17 *Explanation by empathy*

This bring us to another model of explanation – that of empathy. As Herbert Butterfield put it, 'The story cannot be told correctly unless we see the personalities from the inside, feeling with them as an actor might feel the part he is playing – thinking their thoughts over again and sitting in the position not of the observer but the doer of the action.' He goes on to grant at once that this is impossible (in any complete way), but it remains 'the thing to aspire to'.[39] This is obviously true, not only of history, but of all tales since the world began; for nearly 3,000 years Homer's audiences have had no difficulty in following the tale of Troy. As Gallie says, to understand history is to be able to follow a story. This is just the sort of explanation given by the British officer at Waterloo, as his use of the phrase 'must have seemed' shows. Where could one look for a better account, short of interrogating the French soldiers themselves? An officer of the line taking part in the battle at Waterloo is likely to understand infantry better than any historian. Need we look further for an explanation – given that we have no account from the French side?

[38] See Keegan (1978), p. 169.
[39] Butterfield (1951), p. 146.

## 18    *Is empathy an adequate way of explaining?*

To these questions Hempel gives a firm 'No'. The method of empathy, he insists, merely suggests where to look for an explanation. Proper explanation must depend 'upon the factual correctness' of certain 'empirical generalizations'.[40] In our example of the behaviour of the Imperial Guard at Waterloo it is not easy to find an 'empirical generalization' that would explain the mystery. Clearly 'Élite bodies of troops always obey orders' will not do, for in this one case – the very one that needs explaining – they didn't. Can one amend it to 'Élite bodies of troops always obey orders except when they come under extremely heavy fire'? This would seem to apply, but does it tell us any more than the British officer did? If we are to establish an empirical generalization of that kind we must do so by assembling a number of instances. At best this offers an explanation of the 'così fan tutte' type. It brings us little nearer to the sort of explanation that Napoleon doubtless demanded. ('Why did the Guard fail me *now*?') Like Napoleon we may want to probe more deeply. Perhaps the Guard had empty stomachs, perhaps they had not had their usual preliminary swig of brandy, perhaps they were battle-weary, having fought for the emperor one time too many. If we found that they had missed their brandy we might conclude that that had something to do with it. But it would not satisfy the covering-law logician. Hempel would presumably insist that we investigate further in order to establish an empirical generalization like 'Élite troops always obey orders except when they come under heavy fire *and* have missed their customary swig of alcohol.' Is a covering-law explanation really necessary? Does it make the best sense of the story?

Nevertheless, the empathy type of explanation is not without its problems. In the Waterloo example we may surmise that the British officer correctly understood the thoughts and feelings of the Imperial Guard. It is conceivable that, in similar circumstances, his own men might have done the same. But most explanations in history are not like this; in most cases the historian has to explain the actions of men and women very different from himself, who lived in another age, perhaps in another country, and certainly in different circumstances. In these cases one cannot be confident that the empathy is correct; thus Hempel's insistence on a more objective and reliable way of explaining has some substance.

## 19    *Assumptions made in explanation by empathy*

How far do you believe in a common human nature? As we saw above, a typical Enlightenment thinker like David Hume made that belief a principle of historical understanding. If the historian wanted to know

---

[40] Hempel, in Gardiner (1959), pp. 352–3.

what ancient Greeks and Romans were like he had only to study Englishmen and Frenchmen (see above ch. 3, pp. 63–4). Even if one accepts this view, there is still the objection that not all contemporary Frenchmen behave in the same way. You cannot make the same assumptions about a Provençal peasant as about a graduate of one of the Grandes Écoles, nor about an anticlerical as about a devout Catholic. Did Hume, who knew France well, really believe that all Frenchmen and Englishmen behaved on the same principles – not to mention Scotsmen like himself?

Another easy assumption about the empathy model of explanation is that the historian explains by what he himself would do in a particular situation. But this is palpably wrong. What you or I would do on the field of Waterloo or in the councils of Philip II must be a very bad guide to understanding or explaining what was done there. Empathy may be valid for the British officer at Waterloo; he could easily put himself in the French soldiers' position. But I doubt whether I could; still less could I see myself as an SS officer at Auschwitz. Here, as in many other historical cases, one's imagination fails.

## 20  *Dray and principles of behaviour*

A more convincing answer to the problem is suggested by Dray. In place of asking what he himself would have done, the historian may explain by means of the sensible or reasonable thing to do. He gives as example a quotation from G. M. Trevelyan's *English Social History* about the smoke-cloud that used to hang over London: 'There is no wonder that King William with his weak lungs had lived at Hampton Court when he could, and at Kensington then he must.' This explanation cites not a covering law but what any sensible person would do in the circumstances.[41] Here is an advance in objectivity upon the 'what I would do' type. This explanation is justified on grounds of what it would be *reasonable* to do.

Here again, however, one can see objections. There are three. The first is that not all actions are done on principle. Sometimes we act in a muddled or foolish or untypical way. The second is that what seems rational to one person or, still more, in one type of society, may not seem rational to another person or in another society. One has only to remember that in the seventeenth century an explanation in terms of the supernatural would have been perfectly acceptable. Sweeping the house for the sake of the sixpence left in your shoe by a fairy was done on rational principles – if we may believe Bishop Corbet's delightful poem, 'Farewell, rewards and Fairies.'[42] A third objection (and this is a powerful

---

[41] Dray (1957), pp. 134–5.

[42] The problem of rationality as a social variable has provoked much debate. See, for example, Wilson (1970); Putnam (1981); MacIntyre (1988).

one against any type of explanation based on human intentions) is that it fails to account for those occasions when human actions bring about what *nobody* intends. A bank crash is one example, and perhaps the First World War is another.

## 21   *Disposition and typical behaviour*

Dray discusses another way of dealing with *un*reasonable behaviour – by citing disposition. Sometimes we account for another person's action by saying, 'That was typical of him. He always behaves like that.' Thus irrational behaviour is accounted for in a way that meets Hempel's demand that the event be shown to be what 'was to be expected in view of certain antecedent or simultaneous conditions'.[43] Presumably among these conditions was the doer's known disposition to behave in this particular way. This is called 'the logic of dispositional characteristics'.[44]

Dray rightly dismisses this model of explanation. It 'may alleviate surprise', but it does not reveal 'the point or rationale' of the action. 'Disposition' is a spectator's word.[45] When asked for an explanation of his behaviour, the agent is not likely to say, 'I always act like that, being a bad-tempered/impulsive/jealous/foolish sort of person.' He is likely to reject our (the spectator's) dispositional type of explanation in favour of a rational one: something like 'I did what any one else would have done in the circumstances.' The dispositional model is unsatisfactory, then, from the empathy angle; it fails to give an explanation 'from the inside'. But it is also unsatisfactory from the covering-law angle. Could we provide an empirically established law of *this person's* behaviour? Perhaps his psychoanalyst might oblige, but it is too much to ask of a historian.

## 22   *Rethinking the thought*

A variation of the empathy model was put forward by the philosopher-historian, R. G. Collingwood, in a posthumous work *The Idea of History*. 'What must the historian do in order that he may know them?' he asks of historical facts. To which he gives the surprising answer that 'the historian must re-enact the past in his own mind.'[46] He does not mean that the historian must survey a sort of stage performance in his own head. He means that the past must be literally acted over again. This seemingly impossible injunction is made clear by Collingwood's further insistence that all history is the history of thought. 'Of everything other than thought there can be no history.'[47] He explains it thus: the past has left relics

[43] Hempel in Gardiner (1959) pp. 348–9.
[44] See Dray (1957), p. 145.
[45] Ibid., p. 149.
[46] Collingwood (1961), p. 282.
[47] Ibid., p. 304.

behind it: these relics are often written words. The historian has to discover what the writer of those words meant by them. 'This means discovering the thought ... To discover what this thought was, the historian must think it again for himself'.[48]

This seems to be yet another statement of the familiar empathy theory. But not quite so. For Collingwood insists that the re-enactment applies only to the intellectual side of consciousness; it applies to thoughts, but not to feelings. There cannot be 'a history of memory or perception'.[49] 'But if there are ways of perceiving which ... have prevailed here and there in the past, and are not practised by ourselves, we cannot reconstruct the history of them, because we cannot re-enact the appropriate experiences at will.'[50] The bodily life of man is a framework of natural process. 'Through this framework ... the tides of thought, his own and others', flow crosswise, regardless of its structure, like sea-water through a stranded wreck.'[51]

## 23   Do feelings matter?

This striking simile of the tides washing through the bare bones of an old boat brings home to us the clear distinction that Collingwood makes between thought and feeling. However, he escapes one pit only to fall into another. By separating thought from feeling he meets the objection to the empathy model. This is that, although I can re-enact (say) Euclid's thought when he worked out the proof of the square on the hypotenuse, I cannot re-enact his accompanying feelings – which were, perhaps, of intellectual satisfaction, an aching head, cold feet, and an irritation with the constant interruptions of his wife asking what he was going to say when the tax collector called. Collingwood's argument is plausible because on his theory we have only to re-enact the *rational thought* of the historical agent. His feelings, though unknown, are irrelevant. As Collingwood puts it, '... this character in this situation cannot but act in this way, and we cannot imagine him as acting otherwise.'[52] But by making feelings quite irrelevant to explanation, is he not excluding a very important factor? Sometimes we cannot understand why another did not do what seems to us the sensible thing in the circumstances. Only when we realize that he was pressed by a powerful emotion can we understand the action. That is why both assessment and driving force are important factors in the analysis of action.[53] Knowing the agent's assessment of the situation allows for his or her (perhaps distorted) perspective of the

[48] Ibid., pp. 282–3.
[49] Ibid., p. 307.
[50] Ibid., pp. 307–8.
[51] Ibid. p. 304.
[52] Ibid., p. 245.
[53] See ch. 2, pp. 23–7 above.

situation, and knowing the driving force allows for whatever emotion was moving him or her. This analysis covers irrational as well as rational actions in a way that Collingwood's 're-enactment of thought' and Dray's 'principles of action' fail to do.

## 24    The study of cultures

At this point we come back to the difficulty that Collingwood was trying to avoid: how can we know what the historical agents *felt*? By insisting that we must take account of the non-rational factors, have I not made explanation all but impossible? Fortunately, help is at hand. It comes from an unexpected direction – the study of culture and cultures. This includes linguistics, aesthetics, semiology (the science of signs) and, especially, anthropology. It tackles in various ways our problem of how to understand other people. If you and I both agree that $2 + 2 = 4$, we may share the same thought, but how do we share anger, lust or terror? And meanings are no easier than feelings. A person or a place or a line of poetry may mean a lot to me; you are indifferent to them. How can you share my experiences and so share my sense of meaning?[54] Thus our problem of understanding, and hence explaining, the actions of people in the past is similar to that encountered by translators, art historians and aestheticians, travellers and anthropologists. In all these cases we are both helped and hindered by a human nature that in some respects is common and in others is wildly divergent. But which, and how much, and in what ways is never easy to determine. Yet in all these directions we make progress. My contention is that the problems of historical explanation by means of empathy can best be tackled along lines similar to those in the study of cultures. That is partly why so many historians are now writing cultural history.

# D.   Other Relevant Topics

Explanation is not only a large topic in itself, but one that has generated a good deal of debate, both within and without history. It is also, especially in the study and writing of history, closely bound up with other concepts like 'understanding', 'cause' and 'knowledge'. Thus it is very easy to stray into other topics when one thinks one is discussing explanation. Three topics that I have not opened up are the questions of social meaning, of individualism or holism, and of ideal types. Here, again, it seemed better to restrict myself to making clear a few major considerations, rather than trying to include many others at the imminent risk of causing confusion.

---

[54] For more on meaning, see ch. 10, pp. 280–5.

These three topics are, however, discussed in collections edited by Patrick Gardiner in 1974 and Alan Ryan in 1973 which are listed in the bibliography below.

## Conclusion

In this chapter we have tried to see why historical events have come about. We drew an analogy with the movement of particles as analysed in elementary physics, where we seek to know the forces acting upon them and their directions of movement. It is wrong to think of the universe as naturally at rest, so that it is motion that calls for explanation. Rather it seems that change and movement are normal. We have still to ask, in any particular case, what are the relative powers of the forces and their respective directions. So we do not ask why things change, but why do (or did) they change in this way and not in that. Thus, in this chapter we have first examined what may be meant by 'cause' in history, and then have gone on to look at the forces that are the agents of change. In the third section we turn from what actually happens (whether or not we understand such happenings) to our attempts to explain the changes, how we try to make sense of them. It is important to remember that causes and forces operate in the 'real' world; explanations operate only in and on our minds. Distinguishing partial from full explanations, we notice that in practice the latter are only rarely called for. Partial explanations (of the same phenomenon) may vary. Which parts are given in a partial explanation and which parts are omitted (but tacitly assumed) depends on the question and the questioner. In theory every partial explanation should be capable (if required) of expansion into a full explanation. In history, however, full explanations are rarely if ever possible because of the gaps in historical knowledge.

The sort of explanation that historians favour usually depends upon their outlook or 'philosophy' – how they see the the world as a whole. In the next chapter we look at what may be involved in a philosophy of history.

**Suggested Reading**

Atkinson 1978
Benson and Strout 1965
Carr E. H. 1964
Collingwood 1961
Danto 1965
Dray, 1957; 1959; 1964; 1966; 1974; 1980

Gallie 1964
Gardiner 1959; 1974
Hempel 1959
Hume 1975
Kant 1977
Lukes 1973
Mandelbaum, 1977

Martin, 1977

Nadel 1965

Popper 1959; 1962

Reiss 1977

Ruben 1990

Ryan 1973

Stone 1972

Veyne 1984

Walsh 1958

Watkins 1973

von Wright 1971

# 9

# History as Theory

'All theory, dear friend, is grey;
But Life's gold tree is ever green.

(Grau, teurer Freund, ist alle Theorie
Und grün des Lebens goldner Baum.)

Goethe, *Faust*

I am no believer in what is called the philosophy of history.
Bishop William Stubbs, Regius Professor of Modern History at Oxford

## Introduction

In China old people have always been accorded great respect, for they have lengthy experience. One of the compensations for growing old (it is said) is that one learns about life. And it has been remarked that those who do not know history are condemned to repeat it. In short, whether we consult personal memory or the social memory that we call history, experience is a great teacher.

If we learn from the past (and from where else should we learn? The present is gone in a flash and the future is not yet), must we not organize and systematize what we have learned? Should there not be guesses, calculations, hypotheses, theories sufficiently articulated for them to be weighed and tested in criticism and discussion? Further, should we seek help from philosophers, the experts in this sort of rational winnowing?

'The only Thought which Philosophy brings with it to the contemplation of History, is the simple conception of Reason', wrote Hegel.[1] Can we use our faculty of reason to make sense of the past? And not only make sense of it, but draw the same sort of practical conclusions that mature practitioners of any craft (farmers, sailors, carpenters, journalists) have gained from experience? In short, can we usefully apply reason to history?

In the last chapter we asked some fairly searching questions about the ways the world runs, and about how we try to account for them. In this

[1] See below, p. 240.

one we look at more extended and coherent attempts to make sense of our common experience of the past, and to learn something useful from it.

*Questions about making sense of history; analytical and speculative approaches; theories in history*

1 Can we learn anything useful from history?
2 Can we make sense of history – of all that has happened?
3 What is philosophy of history?
4 Have philosophers anything to teach historians?
5 Have historians anything to teach philosophers?
6 What is analytical philosophy of history?
7 What is speculative philosophy of history?
8 Has speculation any place in a factual subject like history?
9 Is philosophy of history of any practical use?
10 Are there any patterns of history?

## A. Speculative Philosophy of History

### 1 *What is philosophy of history?*

In all subjects the way to make progress (as every teacher knows) is to ask questions. Philosophy arises from a sense of wonder. Most of the questions that arise in, say, mathematics or biology or geography can, in principle, be answered within the subject by the methods normally used. If we want to know the height of a mountain, the sort of eggs a salmon lays, or the expansion of $(x - 1)^n$ we can learn from a textbook or teacher how we set about finding out. But there are some questions arising from the study of a subject that cannot be answered within that subject. What do we mean by 'height'? What is a 'metre'? Can we assume that the number of eggs laid by the salmon we have observed is correct for all salmon?

Similarly, historical research might lead a historian to write: 'The fundamental causes of the French revolution were the bankruptcy of the royal government and the high price of bread in Paris.' Though other historians might agree or disagree, they would know what he meant. But a philosopher might want to ask such questions as: 'What exactly do you mean by "cause"? Is it the same thing as saying that the lack of petrol caused the car to stop? And how can we tell that one cause is more fundamental than another? What is a revolution? How do we recognize one? If we know what caused the French one, can we tell when another one is going to occur – in China, or in Russia, or in Britain, say? If the French revolution was a very significant event, may I ask "Significant of, or for, what?" And what exactly is an "event"? Is it any kind of happening or a special kind? How many people must it involve, how long must it last to count as an "event"?'

And there are other questions that have often been asked, such as 'Does history repeat itself?' 'Can we learn from history?' 'Is there, must there be, real progress in history?' 'Does history reveal any pattern?' 'Is there a purpose in history?' 'Can we find the meaning of history?' and so on. It is difficult to believe that any amount of historical research is going to answer any of these questions, or others like them. These questions belong not to history but to the philosophy of history. As with most philosophical questions, the problem is not just finding the answer. It is rather a problem of which way to go in order to find it. We may not succeed in measuring the mountain, but we know the sort of things to do. We can count the eggs of any number of particular salmon, but what certainty have we that another salmon that we have not observed will behave in the same way? This is a logical, not a biological problem. Historians have written histories of morals. Yet even if they manage to avoid making judgements about whether one age was more or less moral than another, can they be sure of identifying moral questions? Was infanticide a moral issue for a primitive society living at the limit of natural resources and without knowledge of conception and contraception? Was vegetarianism a moral question for a people that lived by hunting or herding? Or slavery in ancient Athens? These are questions that arise from history, but must be settled outside history (if settled at all) by philosophical thinking, not by historical research.

## 2  Two sorts of philosophy of history

You may notice that the philosophical questions I have just listed fall into two different categories. The first lot – about cause, significance etc. – are really about how historians think. The second lot – about pattern and progress and repetition – are about the course of history itself. This corresponds to the distinction already drawn between history-as-account and history-as-happening. The former kind belong to what is called analytical or critical philosophy of history; the latter to speculative or substantive philosophy of history. It happens that most of the age-old questions belong to the speculative kind; the analytical kinds of question are the ones that have predominated in the twentieth century. Here we look at speculative philosophy of history.

## 3  Speculative philosophy of history

Such questions (about patterns and purpose and meaning) have been raised over the past twenty-five centuries not only by historians but also by poets, dramatists, novelists, theologians, politicians and philosophers. In all this time no generally acceptable answers have been produced. This may be because the questions are inherently unanswerable, or it may be that they have not been pursued with sufficient rigour and historico-philosophical skills. Clearly it is not because the questions themselves are trivial. Of course, there are certain obvious difficulties. One is the vast and varied extent of the historical field; another is the difficulty (perhaps impossibility) of obtaining reliable data for much of that field. But if the extent of our ignorance is daunting, that has not hindered the advance of such sciences as physics or astronomy. The historical field looks positively cosy compared to a universe that contains 100 billion stars. So why should we give up?

Indeed, a large number of people are interested in these questions. Effective work in, say, astronomy, nuclear physics or marine biology calls for a fairly high intelligence, a long training and access to expensive instrumentation. This imposes drastic limitations on the number of scientists working in those fields. But to have ideas about history requires little more than the ability to read, a lively curiosity and a certain amount of time. Indeed, not even books are essential. It may be surmised that any European over the age of sixty has lived through so many terrible and strange events that his or her life experience alone furnishes enough material to raise many of the big questions of the philosophy of history – especially those about causation and meaning. Why did it happen like this? Did it have to happen? What does it all mean? Since the invention of nuclear warfare have we all been living in the most appalling danger? Or have those weapons been a better guarantee of peace than has ever been found before? What should we do now? The twentieth century has raised more than enough problems for the philosopher of history. And, of course, they are problems that concern every one of us. With some exaggeration it could be said that every thoughtful person has his own (more or less crude) philosophy of history. We might echo Lloyd George (who said that war is too important to be left to the generals) and assert that the philosophy of history is too important to be left to the philosophers and the historians.

So what do we find if we pursue the speculative philosophy of history? Until about 150 years ago most writers on the subject attempted to survey the whole course of world history (or as much of it as they knew) and to find therein certain patterns of regularity, of causation and of meaning. Famous examples of these are Bossuet in the seventeenth, Voltaire (who invented the term 'philosophy of history'), Herder and Condorcet in the eighteenth, Hegel and Marx in the nineteenth, and Spengler and Toynbee (latecomers these) in the twentieth century, though St Augustine in the fifth and Ibn Khaldun in the fourteenth century also have a claim.

## 4   Arguments against such speculative philosophy

For a number of reasons speculative philosophies of history are in rather bad odour. One reason, as we have pointed out, is that no one can ever hope to be adequately acquainted with all societies and all ages. Inevitably he lays himself open to attack by the specialists in the various smaller fields. Toynbee's fate at the hands of the Dutch historian, Pieter Geyl, is a good example.[2] Bishop Stubbs, quoted at the head of this chapter, went on: '... I am opposed to the school of thinkers which exalts the generalizations of partially informed men into laws, and attempts out of those laws to create a science of history.'[3] Such is the typical reaction of historians.

Another reason is that some of the ugliest political practices of this century have been based on philosophies of history. Eberhard Jäckel said that 'Hitler ... achieved a view of history and he ... constructed from it a *Weltanschauung* from which he could then proceed to deduce logically all of his political demands.'[4] Hitler claimed that his theories about race, blood and soil, *Lebensraum* ('living-space'), the extermination of the Jews and the conquest of the world – theories that the Nazis later attempted to put into terrible practice – were founded on his reading of history. Theories of history may be sound or unsound, but they are not negotiable, nor are they confined to armchair theorists.

Thirdly, Karl Popper has argued that the search for inherent laws that determine the course of history is contrary to reason, to morality and to religion.[5] Indeed, he demonstrated that the theory of history that claims to foretell the future must be fraudulent.[6] Is it not a claim of megalomaniac arrogance that one should pretend to grasp the hidden structures and meaning of the whole of human experience – past, present and future?

These might well seem sufficient arguments against the speculative philosophy of history. But there is yet another, a methodological argument. Most such philosophies have been built around some governing idea drawn from another sphere of thought. Some, like Montesquieu or Mackinder, and, to some extent, Lucien Febvre, Fernand Braudel and others of the *Annales* school, have found in geography the causes and explanations of the course of history. Others have found the clue to history in economics (Marxists) or in race, like Gobineau or the Victorian historian E. A. Freeman.[7] Others have looked to the will of God – St Paul, Orosius, Augustine, Joachim of Fiore. A similar example of invasions from other disciplines has been observed in literary criticism. Northrop Frye in *An Anatomy of Criticism* remarks how 'a scholar with a special interest in geography or economics expresses that interest by the rhetorical device of putting his favorite study into a causal relationship with what

[2] See Geyl (1962).
[3] See Stubbs (1906), p. 194.
[4] See Jäckel (1981), p. 106. *Weltanschauung* is roughly 'world-outlook'.
[5] See Popper (1962), ch. 25.
[6] See Popper (1961), pp. v–vii. The book is dedicated to 'the countless men and women of all creeds or nations or races who fell victims to the fascist and communist belief in Inexorable Laws of Historical Destiny.'
[7] For Freeman see C. Parker (1990), pp. 44–6.

interests him less.' It would be easy, he goes on 'to compile a long list of such determinisms in criticism, all of them whether Marxist, Thomist, liberal-humanist, neo-Classical. Freudian, Jungian, or existentialist, substituting a critical attitude for criticism; all proposing, not to find a conceptual framework for criticism within literature, but to attach criticism to one of a miscellany of frameworks outside it'.[8]

The same condemnation can be applied to most philosophies of history. They do not arise from within the discipline of history, but attempt to attach it to an external and alien system. Should theories of history be written by historians, not by biologists, economists, geographers, theologians or even philosophers?

## 5    An example of speculation by a historian

An interesting example of such theorizing by a historian is Paul Kennedy's book *The Rise and Fall of the Great Powers* (1989). The author's theme is wide but still limited. Studying the great powers since the early sixteenth century, he finds that the military strength of nations rises and falls with their economic power. In his words: 'The history of the rise and later fall of the leading countries in the Great Power system ... shows a very significant correlation *over the longer term* between productive and revenue-raising capacities on the one hand and military strength on the other.'[9] But he goes on from observing the correlation to perceiving causal relationships: 'there is detectable a causal relationship between the shifts which have occurred over time in the general economic and productive balances and the position occupied by individual powers in the international system.' Again, the close connection between economic success and military power 'is hardly surprising, since it flows from two related facts'.[10] Having found the links and put forward causal explanations, Kennedy is led to speak of the military/economic connection in the present rather than the past tense. For example, he writes: 'If, however, too large a proportion of the state's resources is diverted ... then it is likely to lead to ...'; and again: 'if a state overextends itself strategically ... it runs the risk ...', and so on.[11] This usage would imply that the generalization is valid beyond the instances examined, and actually constitutes a general rule. We note that he is here making an induction from few examples, but from a large sample of the relevant cases. And indeed, the peculiar interest of this work (which accounts for a lot of its commercial success as a bestseller) is that it goes beyond the usual historian's generalizations; it attempts some prediction of the future – albeit a cautious and limited prediction. As Kennedy puts it: 'What follows, then, can only be

[8] Frye (1971), p. 6.
[9] Kennedy (1989), p. xvi (author's italics).
[10] Ibid., pp. xxiv–xxv.
[11] Ibid., p. xvi.

provisional and conjectural, based upon a reasoned surmise of how present tendencies in global economics and strategy may work out – but with no guarantee that all (or any) of this will happen.'[12] In spite of this very proper disclaimer, what we have here is something like a scientific theory, based upon the examination of certain selected examples. There is the perception, first, of a correlation, then of causal connections that account for the correlation. This in turn leads to the tentative formulation of a hypothesis that goes beyond the instances examined. Historians do sometimes theorize in this way and even surmise that any other historical instances yet to be examined will be found to conform to their theory. This is often called retrodiction. But Kennedy is doing more; he is suggesting what may be the future course of history, and doing so on the basis of a sufficiently substantiated theory. Thus he is making predictions. Now, according to the well-known arguments of Karl Popper about scientific method, a hypothesis can never be proved by any number of positive results; it can, however, be disproved by one negative.[13] Hence a good scientist seeks the falsification of his theory. Kennedy wisely guards against counter-examples by issuing a caveat: 'Unforeseen happenings, sheer accidents, the halting of a trend, can ruin the most plausible of forecasts; if they do not, then the forecaster is merely lucky.'[14] And of course it is true that his theory would not be totally invalidated if things were to turn out otherwise, if a great power were to enjoy a long period of military supremacy coupled with marked economic inferiority. But his theory would be weakened. He might then have to face one or the other of two unpleasant alternatives: either to build so many qualifications into his theory that it became almost unfalsifiable (but then it would lose its predictive value); or to demote it from a respectable theory (applicable to all cases past, present and future) to a mere generalization that was limited to the small number of instances already examined. Kennedy prefers not to discuss theory and methodology, protesting that he is not a political scientist.[15] Nevertheless, if we are to take his predictions seriously we can hardly avoid examining the logic of his argument. Kennedy concludes 'The above analysis has tried to suggest what the prospects are likely to be for each of those polities and, in consequence, for the Great Power system as a whole. But that still leaves an awful lot depending upon the "skill and experience" with which they manage to sail on "the stream of Time" '.[16]

This final appeal to experience suggests that Kennedy believes that the past does have a vital connection with the future, and hence that a proper understanding of the former may be a guide to finding our way in the

[12] Ibid., p. 565.
[13] See Popper (1972a), p. 33. See also above, ch. 3, p. 74.
[14] See Kennedy (1989), p. 565.
[15] Ibid., p. 693.
[16] Ibid., p. 698.

latter. I believe that to be true. As I reiterate throughout this book, men and women are at every moment called upon to make decisions for the future, and usually the best guide to action is our considered experience of the past. That is why a critical understanding of history (past, present and future) is so important. Kennedy's book is a worthy attempt to meet our continuing practical needs.

## 6   Do we need the philosophy of history?

If historians are unwilling and philosophers unfitted, who is to do philosophy of history? One can, of course, conclude that it is better not done, it is better to abandon the attempt altogether. And yet the problems remain: just what are historical facts? What are the really significant events? What things do cause historical change? Can we really learn from the past? How is the course of history to be understood? How is it to be explained honestly to eager young minds? What meanings can we find in it, or do we impose upon it? All these and others like them are not esoteric questions. They arise in the minds of millions of thoughtful people as they look at a television bulletin or open a newspaper or read any literary text written in or treating of the past. Moreover, as remarked above, we need some understanding of past history because we have to make decisions and to act in present history. If we are to learn from experience, there in history is our experience. And those who do not learn from experience are condemned to make the same mistakes over and over again.

In other areas where genuinely pressing, if apparently insoluble, problems arise, scientists and philosophers do not give up and cease to speculate. To think one knows all, or even one, of the answers may be arrogant and foolish, but that should deter no one from working toward greater understanding. After all, men and women have looked at the stars and speculated about them for thousands of years. We now know a lot more about the physical universe than our ancestors, but we are still very ignorant; we are nowhere near a conclusion of our astronomical studies. We have hardly begun to explore even the other planets of our own system. Should we not admit that we have attained to our present state of knowledge only as a result of the patient work of innumerable predecessors? As Newton said, we see so far only because we stand on the shoulders of giants.

So if the average man or woman often asks questions in the philosophy of history (though they might be surprised to be told that that was what they were doing), then this is not a subject that can be ignored or abandoned. And the main reason is not merely that intellectual hunger has a right to some substance; it is the danger that if good men ignore this need, bad men easily step in to supply it with mean and cruel falsehoods, as has already happened in this century. 'The hungry sheep look up and are not fed', as Milton complained.

## 7   'Making sense' of history

In spite of the fact that speculative, or substantive philosophy is rather ill thought of today, there is a widespread need to make some sense of the apparently infinite succession of recorded happenings in the human past. The subject is rejected in almost any philosophical text that mentions it at all For one example: 'It [i.e. substantive philosophy of history] tends to be condemned both by analytical philosophers and practising historians, and for much the same reason, namely, that evidential support is lacking for its sweeping generalisations.'[17]

We shall look at some of the ways of doing so in a moment, but first let us contemplate some definitions. Patrick Gardiner writes: 'What projects customarily referred to as "philosophies of history" frequently have in common is the aim of giving a comprehensive account of the historical process in such a way that it can be seen to "make sense".'[18] Karl Löwith defines philosophy of history as 'a systematic interpretation of universal history in accordance with a principle by which historical events and successions are unified and directed toward an ultimate meaning'.[19] Arthur Danto says that 'Substantive philosophy of history is an attempt to discover a kind of theory concerned with the, as yet unclarified, notion of the whole of history.'[20] William Walsh is clear that 'If the philosopher can be said to have any specific concern with the course of history, it must be with that course as a whole, i.e. with the significance of the whole historical process.'[21] It is clear that they all see substantive philosophy of history as being concerned with the whole of history, with seeing it as a unified whole (not a series of random and unconnected happenings), and as being capable of interpretation in terms of some theory, or significance, or meaning. Some or all of these are implied in 'making sense' of history.

I have suggested above that the day-to-day experience of historical events in the twentieth century has been quite sufficient to provoke the man or woman in the street to ask profound philosophical questions about cause, significance and meaning. They do not need to contemplate, let alone possess, fully-fledged philosophies to do so; nor do they need to be able to survey the whole course of history. But they do question what causes, meanings or purposes may lie behind what they have seen and, perhaps, suffered. And the word 'purpose' reminds us that we are not, nor do we see ourselves as, the blind playthings of fate. Most of the evils that we have seen had a human origin. If men do wrong, other men can stop them. Such was the conviction behind the British defiance of Nazi

[17] Atkinson (1978), p. 9
[18] Gardiner (1959), p. 7.
[19] Löwith (1967), p. 1.
[20] Danto (1965), p. 2.
[21] Walsh (1958), p. 27.

Germany in 1940 and behind the popular revolutions in central and eastern Europe in 1989. So, as well as asking 'Why has this happened?' we also ask 'What can we do about it?' Therefore the concept of purpose is applicable to history not only in the theological sense. Löwith sees it this way when he writes: 'It is not by chance that we use the words "meaning" and "purpose" interchangeably, for it is mainly purpose which constitutes meaning for us. The meaning of all things . . . created either by God or by man, depends upon purpose.' Hence he argues 'History, too, is mean-ingful only by indicating some transcendent purpose beyond the actual facts.'[22]

But might it not be argued that the meaning of history is also very much the concern of human purposes? Not only do they go far to account for the past; they are of vital concern for the present, for we are always faced with the practical question 'What shall we do now?' History can help us to answer that question by giving us an understanding of the past, the context of the present and the probable limitations on that future to which both our hopes and our fears are directed. In short, making sense of history is part of making sense of where we are now and what we may do next.

## 8   The need for a practical philosophy of history

The pressure of the future upon present action, however, has not always been so great. Why this is so is interestingly connected with the rise of the philosophy of history itself. The seventeenth century, as we all know, saw the rise of modern science with Kepler, Harvey, Galileo, Newton and Boyle, and the rise of modern philosophy with Bacon, Hobbes, Descartes, Spinoza and Leibniz. But it did not see a new dawn in the philosophy of history. Attempts at making sense of the whole past were still theological, not philosophical. The outstanding work in this genre was Bishop Bossuet's *Discours sur l'Histoire Universelle*, written about 1679 for the instruction of his pupil, the Dauphin. His argument, against the freethinkers of his day, was that the whole course of history is guided by divine providence. Among such freethinkers he might have classed the members of the Royal Society in London, who, good Christians all and by no means opposed to the notion of divine providence, were yet subtly undermining old beliefs by their faith in new, empirical scientific methods. Now until that time the one belief universally held about the course of history was that it was a story of decline from a distant golden past – for men of letters a Golden Age of Greece and Rome, for theologians biblical, and especially New Testament, times.[23] But at the end of the seventeenth century the learned world was riven by the Battle of the Ancients and

---

[22] Löwith (1967), p. 5. For a non-theological view of purpose, see Popper (1962), ch. 25, concluding paragraphs.

[23] Bossuet himself admirably illustrates the latter point. See Hampson (1968), p. 18.

Moderns; by the early eighteenth century the issue was decided in favour of the latter, and the way was open for the Enlightenment. By this time reason was beginning to displace revelation, knowledge (or at least the way to it) was conquering ignorance, and pessimism about human affairs was giving way to optimism: Newton had, it seemed, demonstrated the fundamental laws of the physical universe, and Locke those of the mind. It was then that Vico, Voltaire, Montesquieu, Ferguson, Diderot, Turgot and even Rousseau gave those rational accounts of human affairs, accounts devoid of any dependence upon revelation or divine providence, which mark the beginnings of the philosophy of history, as distinct from the theology of history. Fully developed philosophies had to wait a little longer for the great German thinkers of the period c.1780–1830; these included Kant, Herder, Schelling, Fichte and Hegel. Yet it is not these thinkers who demand our attention at the moment, but the men of action. For it was at this very time that the American colonists were in revolt, that Jefferson and others were drafting the immortal words of the Declaration of Independence, and a new society with new constitutions (both federal and state) was emerging on the western shores of the Atlantic. The example was infectious. Soon France was in revolution and the *ancien régime* in the melting-pot. A few years later the armies of France were carrying the new ideas to the rest of Europe. Among these ideas, those of the sovereign people and of the rights of man were startling enough, but I believe that even more revolutionary was the notion (first acted on by the Americans) that the societies in which people lived, the laws which regulated their lives together and the kings and bishops who imposed these laws were by no means divinely appointed fixtures; they could be swept away at will and be replaced by better ones. For the first time in history men and women believed that the sort of society in which they lived was a matter of their own choice. To this extent they had become masters of their own fate. Today we accept that we live in a changing world and we expect to change it. And we look to a critical understanding of history to help us to do so.

## 9   Classical philosophy of history a retrograde step

It was therefore something of a retrograde step when philosophers, mostly German, tried to identify hidden forces that rule history. The greatest of these were Kant and Hegel. As we have seen, Kant thought that the solution lay in nature: 'The only way out for the philosopher ... is for him to attempt to discover a purpose in nature behind this senseless course of human events ...[24]

In other words the course of history is explained not by the foolish and senseless acts of men and women, but by the (concealed) wisdom of

[24] See Reiss (1977), p. 42. Quoted in full above, p. 62.

nature. A similar 'hidden hand' directs the course of history for Hegel. In a famous passage he asserts:

> The only Thought which Philosophy brings with it to the contemplation of History is the simple conception of *Reason*; that Reason is the Sovereign of the World; that the history of the world, therefore, presents us with a rational process . . . That this 'Idea' or 'Reason' is the *True*, the *Eternal*, the absolutely *powerful* essence; that it reveals itself in the World, and that in that World nothing else is revealed but this and its honour and glory – is the thesis which, as we have said, has been proved in Philosophy, and is here regarded as demonstrated.[25]

But this all-powerful idea, or reason, works in history (like Kant's 'nature') without the knowledge of even the leaders of the age – Hegel's famous 'world-historical' individuals. 'Such individuals had no consciousness of the general Idea they were unfolding . . .' in spite of the fact that they, 'World-historical men – the Heroes of an epoch, must, therefore, be recognised as its clear-sighted ones . . .'[26] All unknowing, they are driven on by their passions. 'This', says Hegel, 'may be called the *cunning of reason* – that it sets the passions to work for itself'[27]

It is clear that Kant and Hegel, like many lesser philosophers of history, were writing a sort of secular theology of history. History relates so much suffering: for Gibbon it is 'little more than the register of the crimes, follies and misfortunes of mankind', and Hegel speaks of it as 'the slaughter-bench' of happiness, wisdom and virtue.[28] It has always seemed to most people of any sensitivity or imagination that so much evil requires some justification. The problem offers the greatest difficulty for Christian theology – how to combine the existence of manifest evil with belief in an all-powerful, all-loving God. Philosophers of history, replacing theologians of history, still felt the urgency of the ethical demands and tried to find some hidden force or purpose that could explain apparent evil and answer the anguished cry of 'Why?' Today philosophers have given up even trying to solve the problem. Perhaps they are right. Today faith in God is, to say the least, less implausible than a blinder faith in Nature, Reason or Absolute Spirit. Today even the most successful of philosophies of history, Marxism, is not in the best of health, yet it has made a much bigger impact on the world than any of its predecessors. The common fault of them all, as we have remarked, is that they brought philosophical ideas of history from the outside. Marx did this better than the others. It is still rewarding (some people would insist that it is still necessary) to read

[25] Hegel (1956), pp. 9–10.
[26] Ibid., p. 30.
[27] Ibid., p. 33. For further discussion of Hegel, see ch. 10, pp. 262–4 below.
[28] Gibbon (1910), vol. I, ch. 3, p. 77; Hegel (1956), p. 21.

and write history in the light of Marxism, but who reads Kantian or Fichtean or Hegelian history? This seems to point to the conclusion that a philosophy, a search for the causes and meanings and plot and, perhaps, purpose of history, is better if it is based on a close study of history and rises from within that study. Just how this might be done is not yet clear, though Paul Kennedy's book, discussed above, may suggest a possible direction. Other nineteenth-century movements – Positivism, Historicism, Idealism – were to attempt different approaches (as we shall see in chapter 10 below). Toynbee's ten-volume work, entitled in these very words *A Study of History* and published in the mid-twentieth century, ended as more of a theology than a philosophy of history. Yet it did exhibit a great deal of historical knowledge (though not enough for its critics) and it did attempt to trace the patterns of history.

## 10   History is for living

Before turning to the topic of patterns of history we may conclude this section by insisting again that philosophy of history is not a dry-as-dust business of draping more cobwebs round the lumber of a useless past. Like history itself, it is concerned with the present and the immediate future – with the world as it is in which we find ourselves here and now, where we have upon us the desire and the need to act. One of the acutest critics of historians, Friedrich Nietzsche, begins his essay *The Use and Abuse of History* by asserting that we need history for life and action, and adds, 'We would serve history only so far as it serves life . . .'[29]

## B.   Patterns in History

### 1   The attempt to make sense by finding regularities and patterns

To find regularities and patterns in history would seem to be the preliminary and necessary steps to making any sense of it at all. Almost any branch of science would seem to begin like this. Then it may proceed to the search for causes, structures, underlying unities and explanatory theories. I have already likened the study of the past to that of the physical universe. And astronomers with their 'Doppler effects' and 'Big Bang' theories do just this. But, it may be objected, the analogy does not hold: astronomy is dealing with blind, regular and (supposedly) predictable physical forces – so predictable, some claim, that the future may be mapped, as well as the past.[30] History, on the other hand, is concerned with human actions (as well as blind physical forces) and is by no means

[29] See Nietzsche (1957), p. 3.
[30] See, for example, Hawking (1990).

predictable. Hence the analogue is to be found in artefacts rather than in nature. The point was made long ago by Giambattista Vico who (as we have seen) distinguished the works of God from the works of man, and argued that we can properly know only what we create.[31] Our preference for the made rather than the discovered, because of our greater familiarity with it, is also evidenced by the popularity of narrative history. We all know how to follow a story, just as we all know how to make one up and tell one (indeed, telling stories is a nursery euphemism for lying). Narrative, it is often held, is central to history.[32] It may be, then, that the philosophy of history should look at least as much in the direction of aesthetics as in that of the sciences.

However, before we consider the relevance of aesthetic considerations, we must turn to the question of regularities and patterns in history. Nor must we forget the ever-present problem of whether these things are really present in the course of history or whether they have been put there by historians.[33]

## 2   Regularities

Let us look first at regularities. That one thing resembles another is fundamental to human activity of all kinds; if we did not realize that the bread before us today is essentially like the bread we ate yesterday we should not know what to eat. Nor could we name it. A moment's thought shows that language depends on the identifiability of objects, qualities and actions to which can attach words like 'ball', 'red' and 'catch'. Thus a historical account contains words like 'king', 'sword', 'ship', which we instantly recognize, and which thus cause no difficulty. Other words used by historians – for example battle, massacre, defence, aggression, revolution, rebellion, democracy, development, victim, ally – raise problems. Does the term correctly identify the object? (Was Culloden a battle or a massacre? When does a food shortage constitute a famine?) Does the use of certain terms presuppose a moral or political judgement – for example, massacre, democracy, victim, hero, puppet, leader? If so, should the historian avoid the use of these terms in the interest of historical science? How far could biology have got if scientists could never have agreed about whether they had a dandelion or a buttercup before them, a rhinoceros or a giraffe? Unless and until it becomes possible for historians to agree in the use of a neutral and accurate terminology, we may wonder how useful it is to talk of regularities in history. There are

---

[31] See p. 67 above.
[32] See Gallie (1964) and Ricoeur (1984), quoted on p. 95 above.
[33] For a fuller study of those patterns in history that may be defined as structures, see Stanford (1990).

serious implications here for, among other things, the notion and practice of comparative history.[34]

## 3   Patterns

The finding of patterns in history is characteristic of philosophy in history – and it is this that is most frequently attacked by its opponents. Two questions arise: one (already noted) asks, 'When any pattern is found in history, was it really there or was it put there by the historian?' The other asks whether any particular pattern in the past has any bearing on the future. For example, historians tend to see the history of the nineteenth and twentieth centuries as dominated by nationalism. Is this true? They have certainly found a pattern in the events of those years. But did they read it into the evidence? Even if they are innocent and nationalism really was dominant, is there any guarantee that the next two centuries are going to be like that? They would not say so, for a study of the past provides little warrant for foretelling the future. Many philosophers of history, on the other hand, have believed that a study of the past reveals patterns and causes which must continue in the future because they are fundamental to all history. Marx, for example, believed that class conflict would continue into the future until the triumph of the proletariat brought about the first wholly free, because the first wholly classless, society. That would be the end of history as we know it; or, as he picturesquely put it, the end of the prehistory of man. Beyond that he wisely declined to go. Thus the general view is that it is quite acceptable for historians to discern patterns in the past, but that only philosophers of history attempt to prophesy the future on that basis, and that they are foolish to do so.[35] However, Paul Kennedy's work inclines the other way.

## 4   The historian's search for patterns

Yet perhaps the activity of the normal historian is not beyond question, either. On the face of it this seems harmless enough. The very act of writing any history involves some sort of patterning. No work of history can hope to record everything that happened, however restricted the scope of that work – for example, the history of one regiment in one campaign or one village in a visitation of plague. The historian selects some facts for inclusion and rejects others. The grounds for his selection are that the favoured facts are the most significant and that they constitute a

[34] For further discussion of terminology and comparison in history, see ch. 3, pp. 72–3 above.
[35] For example, see Atkinson (1978) and Popper (1962) quoted above, pp. 237 and 233.

recognizable pattern. He believes in addition that, taken together, they correctly represent the course of events rather as a map represents, in miniature, a given tract of land.

The chosen pattern is most frequently a narrative. However, it need not be; it could be a description – for example Jacob Burckhardt's *The Civilisation of the Renaissance in Italy*. Or it could be analysis like Marc Bloch's *Feudal Society*, or it could set forth an argument, like Alan Macfarlane's *The Origins of English Individualism*. Whatever the form of the work, the big question remains: Did the historical reality that the history purports to describe actually bear the shape ascribed to it? In short, does it fit the facts? Is it an accurate map? Did the Roman Empire really decline, as Gibbon said, or were the first Christian centuries an era of steady improvement? The question is most pertinent in relation to the most popular form, narrative history. Did the events really have the cohesion and recognizable shape – the beginning, the development, the conclusion, together with the inherent meaning – that belong to a story?[36] Leaving this problem aside, let us stick to the general question of a pattern. Some patterns in the past are hallowed by tradition and long usage. History books are full of them: the Roman Empire, the rise of Christianity, the Crusades, the Renaissance, the Reformation, the Enlightenment, the American revolution, etc. We do not question them until, perhaps, we come to study other histories. For example, the Crusades, the papal/imperial conflict, the Renaissance, the Reformation and the discovery of America played almost no part in the story of Russia. When we move further east, to Persia, India, China and Japan, the patterns of history become, to us, stranger.

The point here is that these historical patterns had been completed by the time that they were recognized. As A. C. Danto points out,

> Petrarch's brother witnessed Petrarch's ascent of Mt. Ventoux. Historians might say that when he climbed Mt. Ventoux, he opened the Renaissance. But his brother could not have witnessed Petrarch's opening the Renaissance . . . Not unless he knew what was going to happen in the future and knew, in addition, what historians were later going to say was the significance of what he saw.[37]

It is true that a movement may be recognized as very significant before it is completed: Thucydides saw the importance of the Peloponnesian War as it took place, Vasari spoke of a rebirth of art while the Italian Renaissance was still in progress, and it was in July 1789 that Fox wrote of the French Revolution: 'How much the greatest event it is that ever happened in the world! and how much the best!' These prophetic remarks showed insight into the nature of contemporary affairs. But Thucydides, Vasari and Fox

[36] For further discussion see ch. 4, pp. 88–92 above.
[37] Danto (1965), p. 61.

would surely have admitted that they did not, could not, know the whole story. For the movement whose importance each acknowledged had not at that time come to a conclusion, the pattern had not been completed. For the historian, Hegel's words are as true as for the philosopher: 'The owl of Minerva spreads its wings only with the falling of the dusk.'[38] We cannot grasp the full significance till we can tell the whole story – when we employ the wisdom of hindsight.

## 5   Historians' patterns commonly useless for practical purposes

Now if patterns in history can be correctly described only with hindsight they can have no part in the ever-moving present. Doubtless the events in which we now find ourselves form part of patterns that future historians will recognize and describe. Some of them will probably write narrative histories in which these passing moments find a place. But what such patterns may be, what stories they will find to tell of us, we cannot now possibly know – though we are free to guess.

## 6   Are historians' patterns invalid?

It has been argued that the philosophy of history is useless because it cannot foretell the future, that part of history which is yet to unfold. Hence such philosophers make claims that cannot be met. And I have just argued that a philosophy that purports to perceive the patterns of historical events cannot even refer to the present; it is therefore incapable of helping us with our present needs. Yet more devastating is Danto's argument: we cannot give a complete description of the past (or any part of it) unless we can perceive the significance of the events we describe – as in the case of Petrarch climbing Mont Ventoux. How long must we wait before we can be sure that we grasp the full significance? Is it not possible that events in the twenty-first century may alter the significance of those of the fourteenth and fifteenth? A history of the historiography of the Renaissance (like Wallace Ferguson's *The Renaissance in Historical Thought*) shows that each subsequent generation has found meanings in it that their predecessors had missed – or rather, were never in a position to perceive. And it is likely that we have not yet exhausted its significance. Suppose that Europe in the late twenty-first century were to become a congeries of city-republics, or that men adopted the fashion of short doublets and tight hose, would that not add to our descriptions of fifteenth-century Italy? Would not historians of the twenty-second century describe fifteenth-century Italy as the society that set the political or

---

[38] Hegel (1967), p. 13.

sartorial fashions for the twenty-first? This may seem a little fanciful. A more sombre, and profoundly moving, example is found in a little book, *The German Catastrophe*, written, in 1946 immediately after Germany's defeat, by the German historian Friedrich Meinecke. He was old enough to have watched the return of the victorious armies from the Franco-Prussian War of 1870–1. He had made a profound and sympathetic study of the revival of Prussia after its defeat by Napoleon. Now he looks back on his work half a century later and asks rather ruefully:

> But does it not happen in the case of all great and fruitful ideas in world history that in the course of their historical evolution both good and evil can develop out of them? One effect of what we have experienced is that the demonic element hidden in human and historical life rises before our eyes more clearly and disturbingly than previously.[39]

Here is a true historian who, even at the age of eighty-four, is prepared to rethink his evaluations of past events.

But if we cannot now give a complete characterization of the events of the past, still less of their inherent pattern, what could justify a belief that we can find the plot and meaning of history? It seems that such a belief could be based only on one of two things: either that there is some, as yet to be discovered, underlying cause which shapes all things into a given pattern, rather as a packet of genes is transferred through successive generations more or less intact and so shapes each generation in much the same mould; or that there is some external or, better, transcendent force (like Hegel's Absolute Spirit or the Judaeo-Christian God) working in and through history. These are still open questions.

A famous negative answer to them was given by H. A. L. Fisher:

> One intellectual excitement has, however, been denied me. Men wiser and more learned than I have discerned in history a plot, a rhythm, a predetermined pattern. These harmonies are concealed from me. I can see only one emergency following upon another as wave follows upon wave, only one great fact with respect to which, since it is unique, there can be no generalizations, only one safe rule for the historian: that he should recognize in the development of human destinies the play of the contingent and the unforeseen.[39]

That he did discern patterns seems undeniable; among his chapter

[39] Meinecke (1963), p. 105.
[39] See Fisher (1936), Preface. Also below, ch. 10, p. 282.

headings we find 'Strands of History', 'The New Europe' and 'Menacing Tendencies in Germany and Russia' and so on. What Fisher would presumably deny is that such patterns were predetermined. But this is perhaps beyond the power of any historian to affirm or deny. What any historian can be asked is whether the patterns are inherent in the subject matter or (possibly unconsciously) imposed upon it.

## 7  Are patterns imposed? The need for a more critical approach

Thus we may turn to the surmise that the patterns and meanings that men and women find in history are not inherent in the events, but rather arise from the nature of whatever account we give of them. Do we impose patterns and meanings of our own invention upon the past? It has often been suspected that we do. This suspicion is one of the reasons for the important change in the meaning of 'philosophy of history' that occurred between the nineteenth and the twentieth centuries. Put at its simplest, this is a change from philosophizing about history (1) to philosophising about history (2), from history-as-event to history-as-account. One, you might say, is philosophy of history with all the facts put in, the other is philosophy with all the facts left out. The one is what philosophers call a first-order discipline – one that studies the world or reality; the other is a second-order study – one that studies that discipline, and so is not directly concerned about the world at all.

Moreover, this same suspicion requires us to look very carefully and critically at every aspect of the historian's activity. Hence this book.

## Conclusion

In the first part of this chapter we looked at speculative philosophy of history. Though once widely practised, in this century it has been comprehensively condemned and rejected. Yet, on further thought, we concluded that the questions it attempts to answer remain pertinent. They will not go away. We must face them.

In the second part we looked at the question of patterns in history. Here again is a problem. On the one hand, it seems impossible to make sense of history without patterns of some sort. On the other hand, any pattern is suspect as an invention of the historian rather than a part of history itself. We have no hope of a solution without looking critically at the work of the historian – which constitutes much of the purpose of this book. Yet as well as taking a close look at history, we may also benefit from standing well back and taking a distant view to get things into better perspective. Can we take a transcendental view of history? The next (and last) chapter looks at some attempts to do so.

## Suggested Reading

Berlin 1980
Collingwood 1961
Geyl 1962
Hegel 1956
Kant 1977
Kennedy 1989

Löwith 1967
Manuel 1965
Marwick 1989
Popper 1961, 1962
Reiss 1977
Walsh 1958

# 10

# History Transcended: Metaphysics, Marx, Myth and Meaning

To-morrow, and to-morrow, and to-morrow,
Creeps in this petty pace from day to day,
To the last syllable of recorded time;
　　　　　. . . It is a tale;
Told by an idiot, full of sound and fury,
Signifying nothing.

*Shakespeare, Macbeth*

Homo non potest icedicare nisi humaniter (human beings can make none but human judgements).

*Nicolas of Cusa*

Time [is] the moving image of eternity.

*Plato, Timaeus*

## Introduction

In the last chapter we saw that the philosophy of history studies problems that arise when we try to make sense of the past. In this final chapter we look first at some of the external ideas that have been brought to history in an attempt to solve such problems.

To conclude, we consider how history relates to our central concerns as human beings. Of course, a greater knowledge of history gives us a greater knowledge of ourselves. But in saying that, people usually mean a greater knowledge of history(1), of what happened. It is no less important to see that a greater understanding of our thinking about history – history(2) – is essential to our self-knowledge. To be human is to be confronted with time and death. To every historical manifestation we may say:

Thou, silent form! dost tease us out of thought
As doth Eternity.

*John Keats, 'Ode on a Grecian Urn'*

But what has eternity to do with the historian, that toiler in the fields of time? Do not suppose that eternity is merely a religious concept. It belongs equally to philosophy and to science. As some have argued, it lies at the heart of narrative, whether fictional or historical.[1] In our lives we are the slaves of time, bound hand and foot to the passing hours and years. In our minds we are free – free to range into the past, the future, the eternal, the impossible. Among these freedoms is the study of history – an attempt to overcome the tyrant, time. History belongs with the other supreme efforts of the human spirit – religion, philosophy, mathematics, science, music and, as Keats perceived, art and literature. All these are attempts (who knows how successful?) to break our bondage to time. ' "The question is", said Humpty Dumpty, "which is to be master – that's all." '

*Questions about philosophy and history; rationality and myth; meaning and truth*

1   What assumptions underlie the writing of history?
2   How have philosophical ideas affected the writing of history?
3   How do we distinguish history from myth?
4   Have myths any value or are they just falsehoods?
5   Can we make rational sense of history?
6   What did Marx teach?
7   What can we learn from Marx?
8   Who was the greatest philosopher of history?
9   What sort of meaning, if any, can we find in history?
10   What do we mean by 'meaning'?

As the title implies, this chapter looks at various ways of going beyond history, or standing outside it, in order to view it in the right perspective. The sections are

A   Metaphysics: Historicism, Positivism and Idealism
B   Marx
C   Myth and Truth
D   Meaning
E   Other Relevant Topics

## A.   Metaphysics: Historicism, Positivism and Idealism

**Metaphysics studies the nature of reality – or, as the Greeks said, the nature of being.** Different views about this affect the ways people perceive history. Here we look briefly at three ways of doing so: historicism,

---

[1] See Ricoeur (1984), vol. I, pp. 22 ff. and H. White (1987), pp. 183–4.

positivism and idealism. All three flourished in the nineteenth century. Though none of them today is to be found in its original form, they are still influential – often as unconscious assumptions. They are worth a little study, not only for their intrinsic interest, not only as episodes in the history of historiography, but because only when they are clearly seen can they be consciously accepted or rejected. Otherwise, one can hold such a point of view subconsciously and uncritically, believing it is only 'common-sense'.

## (i)  HISTORICISM

### 1  *The particular and the general*

We have already come across the Greek beliefs (ideas which long dominated European thought) of the distinction between Being and Becoming; the former is eternal and the latter merely transient; truth belongs only to Being, and mere half-truth to Becoming; the realm of Being and Truth is the heavens, but in this world (sublunary, under the Moon) things are ceaselessly coming into being and passing away, and therefore cannot be fully and properly known; knowledge is appropriate to that world, confused and uncertain opinion to this.[2] As a relic of these ideas science seeks to discover, or to establish, laws or theories, that is, statements of universal application whose truth is independent of time or place. Natural scientists pride themselves on their empirical methods: they study only what can be observed. They are not always aware that their aim is to move from the observable (the plant or chemical before them) to the unobservable (some law or formula). This is Greek thinking.

The contrary attitude is roughly that of **historicism. This is the belief that truth is found in the single, particular object or event, something with its own spatio-temporal location in this 'sublunary' world, rather than in universal but abstract and unobservable theories.**

Such a view is particularly congenial to poets. Wordsworth wrote sadly:

> A primrose by the river's brim
> A yellow primrose was to him,
> And it was nothing more.

> 'Peter Bell'

William Blake scribbled in the margin of Reynolds's *Discourses* (on art) 'To Generalize is to be an Idiot. To Particularize is the Alone Distinction of Merit.' And in 1780 Goethe wrote to a friend: 'Have I not already written to you, "Individuum est ineffabile [The particular thing is inexpressible]", from which I derive a whole world?' (The ambiguity here is worth noting. To the scientist the particular is inexpressible because,

---

[2] See, for example, ch. 6, p. 136 above.

taken by itself, it says nothing useful to him. To Goethe, as to Wordsworth, the particular could speak volumes.)

However, it was not poetry that brought Germans of the late eighteenth century to historicism. It was rather a revulsion against the assumption of the Enlightenment that human beings are part of nature. Consequently, they may be brought under general laws and their behaviour thus explained, much as Newton had done with moving bodies. Indeed, **the whole Enlightenment can be seen as an attempt to do for human affairs what Newton had done for physics.** The enemy these Germans identified was not only the French *philosophes*, however, but also the Stoic philosophers of the third and second centuries BC and their theory of natural law. The Stoics believed in a world-state, of which both gods and men are citizens. They believed that both God (or the gods) and men are rational beings; that by this divine faculty of reason men can grasp the perfect laws of morality and nature that govern the whole created universe. **For every man there are two laws, the law of his city and the law of the world-city, the law of custom and the law of reason – sometimes known as positive law and natural law.** The latter has greater authority than the former; hence it is the duty of every ruler to endeavour to bring the laws of the state into closer conformity to the divine law. 'Historicism', its German defenders held, 'liberated modern thought from the two-thousand-year domination of the theory of natural law, and the conception of the universe in terms of "timeless, absolutely valid truths . . ." '[3] Today, perhaps, we need the ideal of a rational and universal law to bring greater justice to world affairs through the United Nations.

## 2   *Historical individuals are unique*

Yet one can understand how people who valued history and tradition were antagonized by the Enlightenment insistence that men and their affairs, like the phenomena of nature, follow set patterns. (One recalls David Hume's insistence that ancient Greeks and Romans behaved exactly like modern Englishmen and Frenchmen).[4] Newton is said to have been inspired by observing apples falling from a tree. There was no distinction to be made between apple and apple; each obeyed the law of gravitation. But what of Newton himself and his great work? That was not one among a myriad examples of some universal law; the man and his achievements were unique. Human affairs and men and women (so it has appeared not only to poets and artists but also to historians) have an individuality and an importance each of their own. 'The core of the historicist outlook lies in the assumption that there is a fundamental difference between the phenomena of nature and those of history, which requires an approach in

---

[3] Iggers (1983), p. 5.
[4] See above, pp. 63–4. For further discussion see Pompa (1990).

the social and cultural sciences fundamentally different from those of the natural sciences'[5]

As we have seen, Giambattista Vico in the early eighteenth century argued that we have an inside knowledge of human institutions (law, the arts, politics etc.) because they were made by men like us, while we can have only an external knowledge of things of nature because they were made by God.[6] And (it has seemed to many) the more we bring our human insights to understanding human affairs, the more we see the individuality and the unique significance of men and women and of their actions. Paradoxically, this appreciation was helped by the work of the great Enlightenment historians themselves – Voltaire, Montesquieu, Gibbon and even Hume. For these works demonstrated the variety of human institutions and led to the suspicion that people who lived in such different ways from ours, under different laws and customs, must have had different thoughts, habits and values. It was not only in their dress and their architecture that Romans were not like Englishmen; their minds were differently furnished.[7]

## 3   Nations

Such perceptions were put forward in 1774 by Johann Gottfried Herder in a book entitled *Also a Philosophy of History*. From this notion of the uniqueness of historical individuals it is clear that two things immediately follow: one is that comparisons cannot be made, and so unique individuals cannot be brought into classes and subsumed under general laws; the other is that it is difficult to talk about progress, for to do so involves just such comparisons. So far the historicist argument appears not unreasonable. We have already seen that human actions have to be treated differently from the blindly repetitive phenomena of nature, because to understand action means grasping the thoughts and intentions involved.[8] Herder, however, drew rather more disputable conclusions: one about knowledge, the other about values. At the root of these lay an emphasis on the nation. The *philosophes* of the Enlightenment, like all natural-law thinkers since the Stoics, were guided by the ideals of reason and law. As ideals, reason and law have no material form, no spatio-temporal location. They exist only in the mind (as we would say) or in the heavens (as the Greeks said). In contrast to this, historicists like Herder point to the world around us where they discern in the flux of history some things that possess at least relative stability. These are nations; entities that are alive, dynamic, growing. As Herder put it, they are not

---

[5] Iggers (1983), pp. 4–5.
[6] See above, pp. 67 and 242.
[7] We have already touched on this argument in a different form in ch. 3, pp. 63–4.
[8] See pp. 23–7 and 67–70.

mechanical assemblages of units like machines; they are organisms, like men and beasts. In them both life and culture are handed on through the generations, the one biologically, the other by tradition. Men and women are not bricks of standard size and shape that can be made indifferently into any building – a house, a church, a palace or a pig sty. They fit into the nation of their birth and derive both their life and their values from it. Rejecting the disembodied reason of the Enlightenment, he insisted that the nation is the source of all truth; for there are no objective and external criteria of truth to be brought to a nation's knowledge. The nation is also the source of all values, so that each nation has to judge for itself what is good for it; outsiders do not understand and so cannot criticize.

## 4 Historicism and the German nation

Such views, unconvincing as they may appear to us, are not without merit. They emphasize what is empirically present in the world (instead of just an idea); they appreciate the intrinsic value of every human being, as well as of their extended families (the nations). It is, perhaps, unfortunate that further experiences of history (the French revolution and the Napoleonic Wars) brought some alteration to historicism in Germany. There were three changes: a largely cultural view of the nation (which is, literally, a group sharing a common birth or origin) gave way to the ideal of the nation-state; next, the stress on individuality shifted from the intrinsic value of the man or woman to that of the collective; third, it followed that the nation-state was entitled to express its own identity in the rather amoral pursuit of power politics – a manifestation of the 'higher morality'. As a distinguished historian of ideas wrote: 'Morality has not only a universal but also an individual side to it and the seeming immorality of the state's egoism for power can be morally justified from this perspective. For nothing can be immoral which comes from the innermost, individual character of a being.'[9] The effect of these nineteenth-century views became apparent in the course of the subsequent history of Germany, particularly in the Second Reich (the Empire of 1871 to 1918) and Hitler's Third Reich of 1933 to 1945. They also shaped the way most German history was written in that century, with a concentration on nations and upon political and diplomatic history, almost to the exclusion of economic, social or cultural history. Leopold von Ranke (1795–1886) was the chief of such historians.[10]

[9] Friedrich Meinecke, quoted in Iggers (1983), p. 9.
[10] For a survey of the development of German historiography, see Iggers (1983) and Mandelbaum (1971). Also *History and Theory*, Beiheft 14, *Essays on Historicism* (1975) and Meyerhoff (1959), Preface.

## 5  Historicism defined

Although historicism arose and was most influential in Germany, it was by no means confined there, but rather spread over Europe. The Italian historian of ideas, Carlo Antoni, thinks that historicism can be regarded 'as the common denominator for a Europe-wide "reaction and revolt of national traditions against French Reason and the Age of Enlightenment" '.[11] Therefore many other disciplines – such as law, economics, philosophy – were studied in terms of their internal and historical development. Thus a useful definition is offered by Mandelbaum: 'Historicism is the belief that an adequate understanding of any phenomenon and an adequate assessment of its value are to be gained through considering it in terms of the place which it occupied and the role which it played within a process of development.'[12] In a looser sense, we can say that **historicism is the recognition that all social and cultural phenomena are historically determined**. These things belong each to their own age and their own socio-cultural complex. On these grounds one may talk of a national spirit and a spirit of the age (or *Zeitgeist*). Hegel put the idea neatly when he wrote that philosophy is its own time expressed in thoughts.[13] But it inevitably follows from this that no philosophy (or religion or science), however profound, can exceed the limitation of its age. As Wilhelm Dilthey put it: 'Every world-view is conditioned historically and therefore limited and relative.'[14] Though not so intended by its founders, historicism leads to a position of relativism in knowledge and in ethics: in our judgements we, too, are prisoners of our age. In cases of disagreement why should only we be right? Historicism has never quite solved this dilemma, though historicists have wrestled long with it.

## 6  Popper's variant

The subject is important, the literature is voluminous and the definitions (precisely what we are to understand by the term 'historicism') are not wholly consistent. One disagreement is sufficiently important to be worth clearing up. Any discussion of the subject sooner or later turns to Karl Popper's work, *The Poverty of Historicism*, written in 1935 and first published in book form in 1957.[15] This book, like his greater work, *The Open Society and Its Enemies* (1962) is an attack upon Hegel and Marx, whose writings did, to some extent, justify the lethal belief of Popper's dedication.[16] By way of explanation of his title, Popper writes in his

[11] See Iggers (1983), p. 6.
[12] Mandelbaum (1971), p. 41.
[13] Hegel (1967), p. 11.
[14] 'The Dream' (1903), in Meyerhoff (1959), p. 41.
[15] See Popper (1961).
[16] See ch. 9, p. 233 n. 6 above.

Introduction: '. . . I mean by "historicism" an approach to the social sciences which assumes that *historical prediction* is their principal aim, and which assumes that this aim is attainable by discovering the "rhythms" or the "patterns", the "laws" or the "trends" that underlie the evolution of history . . . (For this) I have deliberately chosen the somewhat unfamiliar label "historicism".'[17]

It has often been pointed out since 1957 that the term was far from unfamiliar, that it already had an established meaning, and that that meaning was quite different from Popper's definition. Nowadays dictionaries tend to give Popper's as an alternative definition of the term. 'Historism' is often an alternative form in other languages of what in English is 'historicism'. In German we have *Historismus*, in French both *historisme* and *historicisme*, in Italian *storicismo*. Except for Popper's confusing usage, there is no need to bother with whether we use 'historism' or 'historicism'.[18]

## 7 Ten points of historicism

To clear up any remaining confusion here are the salient points of historicism:

1 The contrast of nature and history
2 The uniqueness and incomparability of historical phenomena
3 The importance of volition, or will, and of intention
4 Men, groups, institutions and, above all, nations seen as centres of identity and stability
5 The existence within these of inner forces and principles of development
6 The vital unity of each age or epoch
7 The belief that criteria of judgement are local and temporal rather than universal
8 The conclusion that the methods and logic of the historian herself are likewise time-bound
9 The need for understanding and insight, rather than reasoning
10 The insistence that all ranks and aspects of a society must be studied.

As Erich Auerbach puts it in a thorough definition of historicism (which is well worth reading but too long to quote in full), it is 'the conviction that the meaning of events cannot be grasped in abstract and general forms of cognition . . .' This meaning lies not only 'in the upper strata of society and in major political events, but also in art, economy, material

---

[17] Popper (1961), p. 3.
[18] Popper (1961), p. 17. Also Meyerhoff (1959), pp. 299–300)

and intellectual culture, in the depths of the workaday world and its men and women . . .'[19]

Briefly put, historicism finds reality and vitality in the particular and the local.

## (ii)  POSITIVISM

### 8  *The Enlightenment lives on*

We have seen how the ideas of the Enlightenment were challenged by historicism – 'the highest stage in the understanding of things human attained by man'.[20] They were challenged, but by no means defeated. Indeed, for some time historicism made little impact outside Germany. The Enlightenment approach to human affairs still found many adherents in France and Britain. In spite of the reaction against the French revolution and the advent of Romanticism, the idea that there could be a science of society as rigorous as the science of physics still had its appeal in the early nineteenth century.

It found its fullest expression in the philosophy of Positivism. Its greatest exponent was Auguste Comte (1798–1857); his chief work was *Cours de Philosophie Positive*, published between 1830 and 1842. In this he anticipated the 'covering-law' theorists we have already discussed.[21] Comte's definition of **positivism** is that it **regards all phenomena as subjected to invariable natural *Laws*.** His concern is not with the Why? of things. It is solely 'to analyse accurately the circumstances of phenomena, and to connect them by the natural relations of succession and resemblance'. His aim is to bring every occurrence under some natural law and to reduce these laws to the smallest possible number.[22] We need not go into the implications of Comte's very influential views for science and philosophy: here we are concerned only with how they relate to the study of history.

### 9  *A science of society?*

All existing sciences consist of Astronomy, Physics, Chemistry and Physiology (arrived at in that order). Now, he says, 'there remains one science . . . Social Physics. This is what men have now most need of . . .' By 'Social Physics' he means what we call history and the social sciences. He divides it into two parts: Social Statics and Social Dynamics. '. . . social dynamics studies the laws of succession, while social statics inquires

---

[19] See Auerbach (1968), p. 391.
[20] Meinecke quoted in Iggers (1983), p. 5.
[21] See pp. 214–24 above.
[22] The quotations are taken from the extracts from this work printed in Gardiner (1959), pp. 75–82.

into those of coexistence.' These laws 'furnish the true theory of progress' and that of social order.[23]

It is striking to find here, confidently expressed long ago, many of the beliefs about history and society that are frequently encountered today. If we have so far mastered the laws of nature that we can put men on the moon, cannot we also master the laws of human nature, both individual and collective, to make happier and more successful societies? Why do we still endure crime, poverty, famine and war? Cannot scientists find the answers here, too? It is my own conviction, in which faith I write this book, that an understanding of history can contribute at least as much as science to the solution of these problems.

**Comte's views add up to this: there are fixed laws governing the behaviour of men and women; there are fixed laws controlling the arrangement and functioning of the groups and societies made up of these men and women; there are fixed laws governing the development in history of all these groups and societies.** To some people these propositions have an instant appeal; to others they seem manifestly false. What is your reaction?

### 10   A model for historians?

The effect on historians and their work has been varied. Let us take his chief precepts and examine them in order.

(i)   **Everything is to be examined externally, with no thought for 'inwardness' – its cause or reason or meaning.** The same method is applied to human beings as to earthquakes and earthworms. This view, known as **'Behaviourism'** is not popular among historians.[24] I think that they can hardly avoid describing human behaviour with some insight into its motivation and meaning. The reason is that nearly all the evidence comes in verbal form from the historical agents or their contemporaries who *already* describe with insight the actions they have performed or observed. Interpretation *precedes* the historical evidence in nearly every case.

(ii)   **Facts are to be established exactly, objectively and conclusively.** How far this can be done in the natural sciences I do not know. But the three great twentieth-century revolutions in physics (relativity theory, quantum theory and chaos theory) suggest that it is not nearly as simple a matter as Comte and other nineteenth-century positivists supposed. As for facts in history, we have already seen that only a limited number have been established exactly and beyond dispute, or, perhaps, ever could be.[25]

(iii)   **In the study of society it is the collective rather than the individual**

---

[23] Comte in Gardiner (1959), pp. 77, 79.
[24] See pp. 68–9 above.
[25] See ch. 5, pp. 124–5, 128–9 above.

that is to be regarded as the primary datum: that is, that there are social facts quite distinct from facts about the individuals who make up society. This view was basic to the ideas of one of the founders of modern sociology, Émile Durkheim (1858–1917), who was much influenced by Comte. Maurice Mandelbaum puts it thus: '. . . one cannot understand the actions of human beings as members of a society unless one assumes that there is a group of facts which I shall term "societal facts" which are as ultimate as are those facts which are "psychological" in character.'[26] Comte put the same point when he said that a society is 'no more decomposable into individuals than a geometric surface is into lines, or a line into points.'[27] Unlike the first two points, this one has had considerable appeal for historians. To be sure, traditional history concentrated on individuals, but more recently, as we have seen, it is collectives (classes, parties, churches, trades, institutions) that historians have taken for their subjects. Just as most sociologists accept Comte's and Durkheim's emphasis on societal facts, so many social historians (especially historians of cultures and *mentalités*) have borrowed concepts and methods from their sociological colleagues. Comte must be allowed to have made his point here.

(iv) **Our task is to discover the laws of the make-up of societies ('Social Statics') and the laws of their progressive development ('Social Dynamics') – laws which are valid for all societies, irrespective of time and place.** Hence, Comte makes no distinction between the sociologist and the historian. Both study the same subject (i.e. society), using the same methods.

Historians are much less inclined to follow Comte on these points. Few sociologists and fewer historians would agree with his statement that we can foretell the future, because 'social phenomena are subject to natural laws, admitting of rational prevision'. Even sociologists are rarely prepared to admit there are laws of the *development* of societies, though they take more kindly to the idea that there is some regularity in the *make-up* of societies. Indeed, structural-functionalists, who regard societies as working systems, echo Comte's insistence that what he calls 'social elements' have to be considered 'in mutual relation, and forming a whole which compels us to treat them in combination'. Where nearly all historians would disagree is with the notion that there are laws of progress – or even of process.

## 11   *Positivist history*

In the nineteenth century, however, a few historians of ability made brave efforts to write history on positivist lines – that is, to discover the

[26] 'Societal Facts', in Ryan (1973), p. 107.
[27] See Lukes, in Ryan (1973), p. 119.

underlying laws of human society, just as scientists revealed the laws of nature. Among the most noted were Henry Thomas Buckle (1821–62), Hippolyte Taine (1828–93), Leslie Stephen (1832–1904) and W. E. H. Lecky (1838–1903). A few sentences from Buckle will reveal his aims:

> In regard to nature, events apparently the most irregular and capricious have been . . . shown to be in accordance with certain fixed and universal laws . . . advancing civilization . . . strengthen (s) our belief in the universality of order, of method, and of law . . . Are the actions of men, and therefore of societies, governed by fixed laws . . .? I entertain little doubt that before another century has elapsed [Buckle was writing in 1856], the chain of evidence will be complete, and it will be as rare to find an historian who denies the undeviating regularity of the moral world, as it is now to find a philosopher who denies the regularity of the material world . . . It might seem a simple matter to . . . ascertain the whole of the laws which regulate the progress of civilization.[28]

We note the contrast with historicism of these significant words: 'The real history of the human race is the history of tendencies which are perceived by the mind, and not of events which are discerned by the senses.'[29]

## 12  Building knowledge

We shall return to this point later.[30] First, let us note that, while few historians today follow Comte and Buckle in their belief in laws of human progress (similar to science's 'laws of nature'), many more have followed them in their belief in unquestionable historical facts – little building blocks, or atoms, of knowledge which, themselves solid and certain, may be assembled to construct the edifice of history. Buckle scolds historians for not working like scientists: 'In other great branches of knowledge . . . first the facts have been registered, and then their laws have been found.' The historian, he continues, must first quarry the facts and then 'scheme the edifice'.[31] Some half-century later we find J. B. Bury using the same architectural metaphor. He describes the historian's task: '. . . the patient drudgery in archives . . . may seem like the bearing of mortar and bricks to the site of a building . . . This work . . . has to be done . . . in the faith that a complete assemblage of the smallest facts of human history will tell in the end.'[32] Yet, as we have seen, few historical 'facts' are completely

---

[28] Buckle (1903), quoted in Stern (1970), pp. 125–33.
[29] Ibid., p. 136.
[30] See below, p. 261.
[31] Buckle in Stern (1970), p. 133.
[32] Bury (1903), reprinted in Bury (1930), p. 17 and in Stern (1970), p. 219.

invulnerable to criticism; the majority cannot be treated as solid, four-square building-blocks.[33]

## 13   Science and history

The irony is that the positivists who urged historians to emulate the methods of the natural scientists had no better understanding of science than they had of history. Today both scientists (natural or social) and historians find that their methods are not at all like the construction of edifices out of blocks of solid fact. Both history and science are more like the reading of an obscure text or the solving of a puzzle, where clues and hypotheses do and undo each other as the scholar gradually gropes towards a solution.[34]

## (iii)   IDEALISM

## 14   Does mind matter?

**Idealism may be defined as the philosophical theory that the only things that really exist are minds, or mental states, or both.** Just to get it into perspective, we may contrast Idealism with the more familiar approach of **Empiricism. This is the thesis that all knowledge is based on experience – and usually sensory experience at that.** Roughly, we could say that empiricists hold that we experience a real world of matter in time and space, which is primary, and that from that experience we form ideas, which are secondary. Idealists, on the other hand, hold that thought (= ideas) is the primary reality of the universe, and that the apparent world of time, space and matter is secondary – in some ways, a product of the first. But what, you may ask, has so improbable a theory to do with the study of history? Strangely enough, there is a clue in the extract quoted above from that convinced positivist, H. T. Buckle. Real history, he said, is the history of tendencies which are perceived by the mind. While he would not have denied reality to 'events which are discerned by the senses', he did believe that what matters in history is not what our eyes see and our ears hear but what our minds make of it. In spite of the fact that most historians today consider themselves empiricists rather than idealists, many of them are still concerned to get at what people thought and felt and believed. This involves the history of ideas, the role that beliefs play in economic and social history, the studies of popular attitudes to such things as birth, marriage, death, witchcraft and so on. But it goes deeper than that. For thought is involved, and is present already, in almost all of the evidence that historians use. Most of historical evidence is in verbal form, spoken or written, which means (as I said above) that

[33] See above, ch. 5, pp. 124–5.
[34] Cf. Cipolla (1991), p. 52.

interpretation precedes the evidence. The historian's aim is in part to get inside his subjects, to see the world through their eyes, to understand their ideas, feelings and beliefs, and to read the thoughts of the people who produced the documents and other evidence on which history is based. Thus the Idealist approach to history has more to it than may appear at first sight. The empiricist approach, which works well enough for dandelions and dust-storms, seems ruled out for history by the fact that the historian can have no sensory experience of the past, but only of the evidence for it.

## 15　Hegel's philosophy

There are, moreover, two good reasons for considering Idealism in connection with history. For the greatest of Idealist philosophers, Hegel, excelled all other philosophers in the importance that he gave to history in his philosophy. A second reason is that Karl Marx derived a great deal of his, more successful, philosophy of history from Hegel. So let us take a quick look at Hegel.

'Man is only a reed, the weakest thing in nature', wrote Blaise Pascal, 'but he is a thinking reed.' More than one philosopher has remarked that the physical universe can easily snuff out the life of a man, yet the man still has the advantage that he can think about the universe but the universe cannot think about him. So much for the primacy of mind, the basic tenet of Idealism. But how can this connect with history? Hegel saw the connection in a familiar human experience: how we get to know something. For **cognition, the activity of knowing,** lies at the root of his philosophy of history. We certainly do not know everything, and what we do know cannot be known all at once; learning takes time. Nevertheless, we nearly all assume that everything is, in principle, knowable. It is striking to see how scientists and mathematicians working in the fields of genetics or quantum physics or chaos theory or astronomy take this assumption into the most remote and almost impossible areas. They refuse to admit that anything is beyond the reach of the human mind. Idealists, too, make this common assumption. But they then go further than most scientists. They argue that if something is knowable, that means it must be rational – for if it were not we could never hope to know it. And if it is rational it must share with our minds (and we with it) at least one common quality – i.e. rationality. This suggests that the whole universe (being knowable and rational) is, in one sense, like a huge, all-embracing mind. But in another sense it is not the least like a mind. When I stub my toe or cut my finger I realize that the universe is full of hard, unsympathetic facts. Nevertheless, I can avoid some of the pains of life if I take more care (i.e. get to know) about rocks and knives. The learning process consists of my mind making rational contact with the knowable (= rational) aspects of part of the universe.

## 16   *The universe gets to knows itself*

Hegel now proceeds to another step. This learning process (that I have just described) is typical of the process of the universe. The rock and I are not identical; we are different parts of the same universe. But the universe includes everything. Therefore, if the universe is a rational whole (like a super-mind), it includes all knowers and everything that they know. Indeed, it *is* all knowers and all knowables. **Hence the universe (which Hegel calls the Absolute or World Spirit) may be seen as thought thinking itself** – for there is nothing else it can think. 'Thought thinking thought' is not so far-fetched a notion as it seems. It is an everyday experience that we call self-consciousness. Yet our self-consciousness, like our consciousness of the rest of the universe, is incomplete. We do not know everything, even about our own thoughts (as Freud was to show later on). To get to know anything we have to go through a learning process. Hegel thought the same applied to the Absolute. Only potentially is the Absolute all thought thinking all thought. In actuality, it is only some thought thinking some thought: it has to acquire knowledge by going through a rational process. One is tempted to say that it has to do this 'just like us'. But that would be wrong. It is not like us, it is us – at least, as far as learning goes. Although the Absolute contains everything, it does not know everything. By a steady process it has to get to know itself. ('To know itself', I repeat, because there is nothing else for it to know.) Thus the progress of human knowledge is the Absolute getting to know itself. Now, perhaps, you can see why history is so important for Hegel's theory.

Hegel also has a theory of how this progress occurs. It is like the three-step pattern of a waltz: left–right–together. (Is it pure chance that this dance was invented in his lifetime?). For in the process of knowing, you have first the inquiring mind, then you have the puzzling object, thirdly (if the learning is successful) you have the completed knowledge, which links the first and the second. This is the familiar pattern: What (inquiring mind) is this (puzzling object)? Ah, now I understand (knowledge). **This process of coming to the truth by question and answer is found at the beginnings of western philosophy in the method of Socrates; it is known as the dialectic.** For Hegel, this is how the Absolute comes to know itself – by gradual self-disclosure or self-unfolding.

## 17   *History is the process of the universe*

There is another notion to notice here, for Marx makes a lot of it. I said above that knowledge results if the learning is successful. But before learning occurs, or if the attempt is unsuccessful, then the object confronting the mind is, or remains, a puzzle – often a threatening one, for we tend to fear the unknown. **This is called 'alienation' – the sense** that what confronts us is strange, incomprehensible, other, alien. We shall meet the term again. Meanwhile it serves to remind us that the whole cosmic process of absolute mind coming to know itself is still not completed. And, amazingly, this cosmic process takes place in human history; in fact, strictly speaking, this *is* human history.

History, therefore, is of prime importance. It is, as we can now see, central to Hegel's philosophy. That is why he worked out a philosophy of history to explain in detail how this self-realization of the Absolute actually comes about in the course of human affairs over the ages. It is not necessary here to follow this working out – his *Lectures on the Philosophy of World History* [35] are easy to read and, in spite of much prejudice and many inaccuracies, are worth the reading. It is necessary here only to note that he begins with the assertion that the 'history of the world presents us with a rational process', that 'the History of the World is none other than the progress of the consciousness of freedom', and that the state is fundamentally necessary to the achievement of freedom – hence that 'the State is the Divine Idea as it exists on Earth'.[36]

Needless to say, there is a great deal more to be said (and much has been said) about Hegel's philosophy of history, but it is time to go on to Karl Marx.

## B.    Marx

### 1    *'The point is to change it'*

In this book I have distinguished the acting of history – history (1) – from the writing of history – history (2). In this chapter we are looking at a third aspect, **the philosophy of history: that is, what we make of both history (1) and history (2) considered as a whole.** Karl Marx (1818–1883) massively contributed to all three. Nor is his influence by any means at an end.

Unlike other thinkers we have looked at, Marx was an activist. All his life he was true to an early saying of his: 'The philosophers have only *interpreted* the world, in various ways; the point is to *change* it.'[37] Before he was thirty he had ceased to study philosophy and devoted himself to economics, history and politics. His ideas were formed from a mixture of German Idealist philosophy, French rationalism and socialism, and British political economy. Thus the philosophy of history was not his main concern. Nevertheless, in his attempts both to interpret and to change the world, he developed a set of ideas that constitute perhaps the only comprehensive philosophy of history that is taken seriously today. Not

[35] Hegel (1975; also in 1956).
[36] Hegel (1956), pp. 9, 19, 39.
[37] 'Theses on Feuerbach' (1845), in Marx (1975), p. 423.

that it is universally accepted; only that most critics of Marxism have nothing to match it. ('But we do not need a philosophy of history', they explain. 'Sour grapes', retorts the Marxist.)

## 2   Five questions for the philosopher of history

Marx's philosophy of history answered five big questions:

1   *What is the content of history?* What elements make it up? Which are the more important ones?
    What are the relations between the parts?
2   *How does the course of history run?* What are the mechanics of the process? (For, like Hegel, Marx saw history as a process.) What forms the drive? How do the parts act upon each other? How does development occur?
3   *Where is history going?* What is the aim of the course of events? What is its meaning?
4   *Where do we stand in history?* How are we caught up in it? How are we to understand ourselves in the light of history?
5   *What ought we to do?* If the point is to change the world, how do we try to do so? What meaning can be given to our lives by the part that we play?

Most of these questions, as we have seen, could be answered from Hegel's philosophy. Was Marx merely repeating his predecessor? By no means. Marx was a very different sort of man with a very different life and purpose. He was deeply influenced by people, ideas and events of which Hegel, predeceasing Marx by over fifty years, could know nothing. Moreover, Marx explicitly criticized and disagreed with Hegel early in his career. Nevertheless, a good deal of Hegel was left in Marx, who for many years remained 'a convinced, consistent and admiring follower of the great philosopher'.[38]

## 3   Problems with Hegel

Where, then, did they differ? First, it was about religion. Not that that ever meant much to Marx. He came from a Jewish family, though both Karl and his father were baptized. The father, Heinrich, was a gentle soul who held the Enlightenment beliefs about the inherent goodness of man and the force of rational argument. Karl was never as optimistic, but he shared his father's cool rationalism and belief in progress. This essentially eighteenth-century attitude, together with his piercing intelligence and biting wit, stood him in good stead in the age of Romanticism and nationalism whose cloudy notions – mystical, metaphysical, irrational – gained no purchase on him. Marx encountered Hegelianism at the

[38] Berlin (1948), p. 60.

University of Berlin where he studied law, philosophy and history from 1836 to 1841. Immersing himself in Hegel's writings, he was simultaneously overwhelmed by their power and ill at ease with the cloudy concepts of Idealism. Relief came from two quarters. Becoming involved in 1842 in political journalism, he made a close examination of Hegel's philosophy of law. He discovered that 'legal relations as well as forms of state' are not part of 'the so-called general development of the human mind' (a dig at Hegel), but 'rather have their origins in the material conditions of life . . .'[39] About this time (1842–3) there was implanted in his mind the seed of his theory of historical materialism. This theory is outlined below.

## 4 *The influence of Feuerbach*

The second source of relief for the tension between admiration and distaste was his discovery of Feuerbach. Ludwig Feuerbach was an atheist, who published in 1841 *The Essence of Christianity*, and in 1843 *Preliminary Theses for the Reform of Philosophy*, which Marx was asked to review. Feuerbach's message was simple: 'Consciousness of God is self-consciousness, knowledge of God is self-knowledge.' For theology (the study of God) read anthropology (the study of man). In short, he was repeating the old objection to religion: namely that men made God in their own image. It was in the sixth century BC that Xenophanes pointed this out, adding that if cows and horses had hands they would doubtless depict their gods as cows and horses. Nevertheless, the notion came as a revelation to Marx and his neo-Hegelian colleagues – including Karl's future friend and collaborator, Friedrich Engels. Marx declared, 'there is no other path to truth and freedom except that through the fiery stream' (the literal meaning of Feuer-bach).[40] In particular Feuerbach wanted to reverse Hegel's mistake of confusing man with God. 'It suffices', he wrote, '. . . to turn speculative philosophy upside down, and we arrive at the truth in its unconcealed, pure, manifest form.'[41] As Engels recalled Feuerbach's impact, 'It placed materialism on the throne again. Nature exists independently of all philosophy. It is the foundation upon which we human beings, ourselves products of nature, have grown up . . . Enthusiasm was general; we all became at once Feuerbachians.'[42]

## 5 *'The prerequisite of all criticism'*

But Marx saw that Feuerbach's criticism of Hegel did not go far enough; Feuerbach was only substituting one set of ideas for another. What was

---

[39] See Marx (1975), p. 425.
[40] Marx (1975), p. 434.
[41] Quoted in Walker (1978), p. 74.
[42] Ibid.

needed was not ideas but activity; not to interpret the world, but to change it. It is true that 'the *active* side was developed abstractly by idealism', but Hegel talked only of the progress of ideas, not of 'sensuous human activity, practice'.[43] Hegel's philosophy pictured thought developing, by a dialectical process, towards the truth; this both abstractly (as outlined in his *Logic*) and over time (as outlined in his philosophy of history). Marx wanted to replace this development of ideas with a development of sensuous human practice – the harsh and earthy conditions of daily life, especially of the poor. So the overthrow of religion must lead straight on to the overthrow of laws and customs of human society which are sanctioned and supported by religion. Thus he wrote:

> *Religious* suffering is at one and the same time the *expression* of real suffering and a protest against real suffering. Religion is the sigh of the oppressed creature, the heart of a heartless world and the soul of soulless conditions. It is the *opium* of the people. Thus the criticism of heaven turns into the criticism of earth, the *criticism of religion* into the *criticism of law* and the *criticism of theology* into the *criticism of politics.*[44]

## 6 The proletariat

This criticism of politics is primarily in the interests of the common people, living under conditions 'in which man is a debased, enslaved, neglected and contemptible being – conditions that are best described in the exclamation of a Frenchman on the occasion of a proposed tax on dogs: 'Poor dogs! They want to treat you like human beings!'[45] This sudden social awareness on Marx's part had not come from rubbing shoulders with the poor (as later in exile he had to), but from reading French socialists and from a deep study of the French revolution.[46] However, it was not so much the common people as the industrial proletariat on whom he was to pin his theories and his hopes. 'The proletariat', he wrote (in 1843–4), 'is only beginning to appear in Germany as a result of the emergent *industrial* movement. For the proletariat is not formed by *natural* poverty but by *artificially produced* poverty . . .' It was not so much the misery of these wretched people that moved him (poverty was no new thing), but the fact that they had no place in society. He describes the proletariat as 'the dissolution of all classes . . . When the proletariat proclaims the *dissolution of the existing world order*, it is only declaring the secret of its own existence, for it *is* the

---

[43] See 'Theses on Feuerbach' (1845), in Marx (1975), p. 421.
[44] See Introduction to 'A Contribution to the Critique of Hegel's Philosophy of Right' (1843–4) in Marx (1975), pp. 244–5.
[45] Marx (1975), p. 251.
[46] See McLellan (1976) pp. 96–7.

*actual* dissolution of that order. When the proletariat demands the negation of private property, it is only elevating to a *principle for society* what society has already made principle *for the proletariat* . . .'[47] It may seem an exaggeration to claim that the creation of a propertyless proletariat is a destruction of the structures of society, a dissolving of all the bonds that hold society together. But Engels's description of the working class in England in 1844 shows that it is not much exaggerated. As he pointed out, in the Middle Ages, 'the serf had a guarantee for the means of subsistence in the feudal order of society in which every member had his own place. The free working-man has no guarantee whatsoever, because he has a place in society only when the bourgeoisie can make use of him; in all other cases he is ignored, treated as non-existent.'[48]

In sum, **the proletariat for Marx is a class of industrial workers who have neither property nor any place in society.** Of Weber's three social pillars – wealth, status and power, the proletariat entirely lacked two: Marx promised them the third. He hoped that German philosophy would work hand in hand with the German workers to put an end to what he saw (in 1843) as the still medieval condition of Germany. 'Just as philosophy finds its *material* weapons in the proletariat, so the proletariat finds its *intellectual* weapons in philosophy . . .' But he acknowledges the debt to the French: 'When all the inner conditions are met', he concludes, 'the *day of the German resurrection* will be heralded by the crowing *of the Gallic cock*.'[49]

## 7   *1848 and the Manifesto*

Less than five years later, in February 1848, some French troops fired upon a Parisian mob. The city rose in revolution; the king (Louis-Philippe) abdicated and fled to England; the second French Republic was declared. The Gallic cock had crowed. Was not this the signal that Germany had awaited? Indeed, it seemed so, for revolutions broke out all over Europe. With notable foresight, Marx and his friend Engels had anticipated the event and composed that classic Marxist text, *The Manifesto of the Communist Party*. It was published in London on 24 February 1848, the same day that Louis-Philippe fled his capital. In form and purpose it is no more than a political pamphlet written to meet an immediate occasion, yet it contains much of Marx's philosophy of history. (Paradoxically, it was hardly read in the 1848 revolutions; its real impact began in the 1870s.) But it begins with the living moment: 'A spectre is haunting Europe – the spectre of Communism.' Written on the eve of the Year of Revolutions, it could not have been more timely.

Marx was correct in forecasting revolution; he was quite wrong in

[47] Marx (1975), p. 256.
[48] Engels (1969), p. 212.
[49] See Marx (1975), p. 257.

forecasting successful revolutions. By the end of 1849 they had all failed. Marx's assessment of the economic and political state of Europe in 1847 was surprisingly accurate; his theoretical conclusions drawn from it are readily comprehensible if we think ourselves back to that year. Unfortunately he did little to revise his theories during the rest of his life, as the course of history increasingly diverged from the course he expected.[50] Not until the appearance of Lenin (born thirteen years before Marx's death) was Marxism adapted to the practical ends of revolution. Now that Lenin's great seventy-year experiment has failed, one must ask whether communism has any future. On the other hand, one must recognize in the *Manifesto* the shrewd perception of many truths about capitalism that have no less force a century and a half later. No capitalist could have praised the triumphs of capitalism more eloquently than Marx does in the opening pages, but when he proceeds to list its destructive effects upon traditional societies he hardly exaggerates. Indeed, even greater indictments could be levelled at it today; namely, its careless destruction of the planet's irreplaceable natural resources, its pollution of air, sea, earth and stratosphere, and the trillion-dollar trade in arms that ceaselessly supplies the governments of the world with means for the destruction of their own and other nations' subjects. It is true that many communist governments were also guilty of these crimes, but they have in no way ceased with the fall of these governments.

## 8   Marx's answer to the first question

Now let us turn from the history of Marxism to Marx's philosophy of history. We take the questions listed above.

(1)   *What is the content of history?* 'The history of all hitherto existing society is the history of class struggles.'[51] The clue is his remark (quoted above) that the material conditions of life are what Hegel calls 'civil society', and that 'the anatomy of this civil society . . . has to be sought in political economy.'[52] We approach the question via 'political economy', or (as we now say) economics. It is clear that human beings have material needs – food, shelter, clothing. These they have to make by some means or other. **These means Marx calls 'material forces of production'. Basically, they consists of land, tools and raw materials, together with the labour.** This production of necessities takes place within organized society, in which the most important consideration is who owns, or controls access to, the requisite land, tools and raw materials. (These things do not come freely. We can imagine that even the most primitive of men treasured their

---

[50] But see pp. 274–5 below.
[51] See *The Manifesto of the Communist Party*, in Marx (1973a), p. 67.
[52] See Preface to 'A Contribution to the Critique of Political Economy', in Marx (1975), p. 425.

own, or their tribe's, crude tools and their own hunting and food-gathering territory.) These questions of property are very important; they do not stay the same, but alter as the methods of production alter – i.e. as new lands, new materials, new implements and new techniques are brought in. As this economic basis grows more complex, involving more and more specialized skills, techniques and sciences, so arise questions of property, of **who owns or has access to these things. These are 'relations of production'**. Considerations of ownership and access create **classes – i.e. groups of people who relate to this economic basis in various ways, but primarily in respect of property**. This is what Marx means when he says, 'The totality of these relations of production constitutes the economic structure of society, the real foundation . . .'[53] **This economic foundation of society is sometimes called the 'substructure'. It is distinguished from the 'superstructure' of society, which is its institutions and ideas**. On the foundation, says Marx, 'arises a legal and political superstructure', with its corresponding forms of social consciousness.[54] By contrast with Hegel, who believed that thought was of fundamental importance in human affairs, Marx insists that the economy (i.e. the satisfaction of our material needs) 'conditions the general process of social, political and intellectual life.' As he puts it in his most challenging vein. 'It is not the consciousness of men that determines their existence, but their social existence that determines their consciousness.'[55] Now we have the answer to our questions about **what Marx considered to be the elements of history, which were the more important ones, and what were the relations between them. This is the theory of historical materialism.**

## 9   . . . To the second

(2)   *How does the course of history run?* As these economic processes advance they outrun the social arrangements, particularly in respect to property, so that the weight of the latter impedes the advances of the former. In Marx's words: 'At a certain stage of development, the material forces of society come into conflict with the existing relations of production or – this merely expresses the same thing in legal terms – with the property relations within the framework of which they have operated hitherto.'[56] The sort of thing that happens is that new inventions occur which threaten existing methods of manufacture. Because much capital has been invested in the old method, owners will ignore, or even buy up and destroy, inventions that render those methods out of date. (This practice was much more common in the early days of the Industrial Revolution than now.) Thus property relations conflict with the pro-

[53] Ibid.
[54] Ibid.
[55] Ibid.
[56] Ibid.

ductive forces. Moreover, the conflict occurs in another way also: namely, in class conflict. In this, the workers, ever better organized and more aware of their situation, represent the expanding *forces* of production, while the owners represent the established and unmoving *relations* of production. (Here again, Marx is describing the capitalism of his day rather than of ours.)

Now we come to a particular Marxist notion which he drew from Hegel. **This is the concept of advance through contradiction – the dialectic.** In explaining Hegel's ideas, I described it as like the dance-steps of a waltz. Frequently it happens that we seize upon a particular notion. Then, when we expound it to a friend or test it against reality, we find that it is not satisfactory, it doesn't quite fit. Rather, the opposite seems to assert itself. From the ensuing consideration or discussion we often arrive at a more satisfactory concept that embodies much of the truth of each of the first two and yet is superior to either. Thus, believed Hegel, thought progresses towards the truth. The German word for this is 'aufheben', which has the dual sense of 'to annul or abolish' (negative) and 'to supersede or transcend' (positive). Both Hegel and Marx used this word in a technical sense because of its combination of two meanings. For both Hegel and Marx, progress arises from contradiction. While for Hegel what matters in history is the progress of thought, for Marx the course of history demonstrates material progress. **For both, 'Aufhebung' (in the sense of transcendence, and hence progress, via contradiction) is the driving force of history, but ideal for the one and material for the other.** One can see how useful a dynamic philosophy like Hegel's is for a thinker like Marx, whose primary concern is with historical change, not to say revolution.

This, then, answers our questions about the driving forces, the interaction of the elements, and methods of development in history. For Marx, **history is progress by the supersession of material contradictions.**

## 10   ... To the third

(3)   *Where is history going?* 'All previous historical movements', wrote Marx in *The Manifesto of the Communist Party*, 'were movements of minorities, or in the interest of minorities. The proletarian movement is the self-conscious, independent movement of the immense majority, in the interest of the immense majority.'[57] The bourgeois (or capitalist) society has produced this immense class of propertyless, exploited men and women. The advance of industry brings them together in larger and larger factories, in greater and greater cities. Thus they become aware of their exploitation and they organize. They will begin to resist the conditions of their exploitation. But they cannot do this without first the alteration, and

[57] Marx (1973a), p. 78.

then the destruction of all the arrangements of society – legal, political, religious – that combine to oppress them. As Marx puts it, 'The proletariat, the lowest stratum of our present society, cannot stir, cannot raise itself up, without the whole superincumbent strata of official society being sprung into the air.'[58]

The bourgeoisie cannot avoid its fate and does not deserve to, for all earlier forms of exploitation have at least been able to 'assure an existence to its slave within his slavery ... Society can no longer live under this bourgeoisie ... What the bourgeoisie therefore produces above all are its own gravediggers. Its fall and the victory of the proletariat are equally inevitable.'[59]

What happens then? In the *Manifesto* Marx outlines the preliminary measures necessary for the creation of **the new propertyless and classless society of communism – abolition of property, heavy progressive income tax, centralization of credit, communication and transport, free universal schooling, etc.**[60] With the fall of the bourgeois state what Marx calls 'the prehistory of human society' comes to an end.[61] There will be no further need of government as an instrument of power, for with the disappearance of classes there will also go the need for class oppression. 'In place of the old bourgeois society, with its classes and class antagonisms, we shall have an association, in which the free development of each is the condition for the free development of all.'[62] Along with the antagonism of classes there will also be an end to the oppression of women and to war. 'In proportion as the antagonism between classes within the nation vanishes, the hostility of one nation to another will come to an end.'[63]

Moreover, man's relation to his work will undergo a profound change. Marx puts his finger on a serious defect of the capitalist system: what he calls **the 'alienation' of the worker. The nature of the work and working conditions of the proletarian inflict upon him a fourfold separation – from the products (which belong to his employer), from other men (the community), from the satisfaction of work (the sort of satisfaction that comes in doing useful jobs about the house and garden), and from his own essential nature, his humanity.** One aspect of this alienation is found in the division of labour – something that ties a man for life to one job (or even, when working on a conveyor belt, to part of a job). Such labour many people find boring and soul-destroying. Under this system, says Marx, a man

> is a hunter, a fisherman, a shepherd, or a critical critic, and must remain so if he does not want to lose his means of livelihood; while

[58] Ibid.
[59] Ibid., p. 79.
[60] Ibid., pp. 86–7.
[61] Preface to *A Contribution* ... in Marx (1975), p. 426.
[62] See *Manifesto* in Marx (1973a), p. 87.
[63] Ibid., p. 85.

in communist society . . . society regulates the general production and thus makes it possible for me to do one thing today and another to-morrow, to hunt in the morning, fish in the afternoon, rear cattle in the evening, criticize after dinner, just as I have a mind . . .[64]

It is clear that Marx did not give much practical thought to the construction of post-revolutionary society. He concentrated on achieving revolution. When the Bolsheviks in Russia achieved power almost bloodlessly in November 1917 they had to face the problem of constructing a communist society, for which Marx had given them very little help. But such a society, for Marx, was the aim of history.

## 11   . . . To the fourth

(4)  *Where do we stand in history?* We stand on the eve of the inevitable proletarian revolution. If you are already a worker, a member of the proletariat, you join your fellows in 'the ever-expanding union of the workers . . . The organization of the proletarians into a class, and consequently into a political party . . .'[65] If you are not already a proletarian, you may soon become one: 'The lower strata of the middle class – the small tradespeople, shopkeepers and *rentiers*, the handicrafts-men and peasants – all these sink gradually into the proletariat . . .'[66] But at least these fallen elements 'supply the proletariat with fresh elements of enlightenment and progress'. Moreover, as the struggle warms up, some members of the bourgeoisie will abandon their side and join the triumphing proletariat – in particular those who are intelligent enough to have understood the inevitability of the workers' victory.[67]

## 12   . . . To the fifth

(5)  *What ought we to do?* Only in reply to this question is there some uncertainty. For, on the one hand, a person's beliefs are shaped by the course of economic history: 'man's consciousness changes with every change in the conditions of his material existence, in his social relations and in his social life . . . The ruling ideas of each age have ever been the ideas of its ruling class.'[68] On the other hand, where can the intellectual leaders of the proletariat come from (the Bolsheviks are a case in point), unless non-proletarians can transcend the (economically determined)

[64] See *The German Ideology* (1846) in Marx (1977), p. 169. The *German Ideology* gives a fuller account of Marx's historical materialism, but I have normally used the *Manifesto*, which is much more accessible.

[65] The *Manifesto*, in Marx (1973a), p. 76.

[66] Ibid., p. 75.

[67] Ibid., p. 77.

[68] Ibid., p. 85.

notions of their class and support the cause of the workers? As we saw above, p. 273, Marx anticipated this in the *Manifesto*. But are his ideas consistent? Strictly, if history is determined by its material basis, if it is people's 'social existence that determines their consciousness' (p. 270 above), then it is pointless to ask what we *ought* to do. If our ideas and actions are determined we can have no choice. Some have argued (citing other Marxian texts) that Marx is not to be held to this rigid determinism; that he believed that our ideas are only *influenced*, not determined, by the nature of the economic base of our society. Thus it is possible to explain the many non-proletarians who have become devoted communists and have, indeed, led the cause for a century and a half. This concession to common-sense, however, rather spoils the elegant simplicity of the theory of economic determinism, which has appealed to many of his followers.

## 13   Marx and history

This is not, perhaps, the place to trace the continuing influence of Marx, either upon the course of 150 years of history or upon the study of history. I will restrict myself to a few brief comments.

First, with respect to Marx's theory of historical development, he was not as dogmatic as is often supposed – or as many of his followers became. For example, in later life he seriously considered the possibility of a revolution in Russia which could avoid the (supposedly necessary) capitalist stage altogether and pass from the peasant commune directly to communism. 'I have arrived at this conclusion', (he wrote to a Russian in 1877): 'If Russia continues to pursue the path she has followed since 1861, she will lose the finest chance ever offered by history to a nation' of escaping capitalism. He goes on to insist that any application of his theories must take account of historical circumstances. One will never learn why events happen if one uses 'a general historico-philosophical theory, the supreme virtue of which consists in being super-historical'.[69]

Second, with respect to the course of events, it is a pity that, influenced by Feuerbach, he made atheism an essential part of his theories. The result has been a series of violent and bloody conflicts and a wall of fear and misunderstanding between his followers and religious believers. Many of the horrors of the civil wars in Russia (1918–21), in Spain (1936–9), in China (1927–49), as well as in other countries in Asia, Africa and America, could have been avoided. Similar hostility served to fuel the Cold War between East and West (1947–89). To attack Hegel's philosophy of Idealism was necessary for his political and philosophical purposes, but the insistence on militant atheism was not needed for his arguments. This was to do untold harm to his, and the workers', cause.

---

[69] Letter to the editor of *Otyecestvenniye Zapisky* in Marx and Engels (1934), pp. 353–5. See also Marx (1977), pp. 576–84.

Third, with respect to the study of history, I would make two remarks. The first is that in the opening pages of *the Manifesto*, as in *The German Ideology*, Marx gave an inspired account of the development of capitalism. **His whole theory, based upon the two concepts of historical process and the fundamental importance of economics,** imparted a sharp stimulus to the study of economic and social history, from which we have all profited. That he was wrong in many details matters little; his ideas have yielded a rich historiographical harvest.[70]

My second remark on Marx and history(2) is that in many Marxists, though not in Marx himself, we have a clear demonstration of the unfortunate effects of a lack of historical sense. In all that he wrote, Marx was limited to the knowledge available to him at the time. (That he sometimes recognized this we have just seen in the case of Russia.) The capitalism, the industry and the political and social forms that he described were those of his day. But when he made generalizations, like 'the history of all hitherto existing society is the history of class struggles', he was going beyond his knowledge. In his economic and political philosophy he generalized about the past and the future on the basis of contemporary conditions. To do so may have been foolish, but it was forgivable. What is less forgivable is the number of people who have since taken his works as holy writ and have held distorted views of both past and future on the basis of what Marx wrote. Had they enjoyed a historical education (or, in the most blameworthy cases, had they not ignored such an education), they would have grasped that the writings of Marx, like every other historical document, have to be placed in their setting and interpreted in the light of what the writer knew at the time of writing. No man can foresee the future, and none can be certain of the past, so much of which must be hidden from us. Within the limits of the knowledge of his age, Marx was brilliant, but he was not superhuman.

## C.   Myth and Truth

'What is truth?' said jesting Pilate, and would not stay for an answer.
Francis Bacon, Essays

### 1   Popular stories

What is myth? 'A purely fictitious narrative, usually involving supernatural persons, actions, or events, and embodying some popular idea concerning natural or historical phenomena', answers the *Shorter Oxford English Dictionary*. The dictionary is doing its duty in giving the general

---

[70] See, for example, Hobsbawm, 'Karl Marx's Contribution to Historiography', in Blackburn (1972); also Iggers, 'Marxism and Modern Social History', in Iggers (1975); and Kaye (1984).

usage of the word, but this definition is far from applying to all myths. Many of these involve human (not supernatural) persons, and many are not 'purely fictitious', but contain some truth. In practice, the problem for the scholar is often that of distinguishing truth from falsehood in each case. A general study of **myths** is not our concern here. We are interested only in myths as they relate to history; only in so far as they **are narratives 'embodying some popular idea concerning . . . historical phenomena'.**

Now, at first sight, it may seem that the tales which we learned in the nursery of gods and heroes and monsters endowed with impossible powers can have no place in this book. Nevertheless, we must recognize that the myths of the ancient Greeks (popularized in Ovid's *Metamorphoses* and made available to children in countless bowdlerized versions) have been part of the furniture of the European mind for over 2,000 years. The whole history of European art and literature bears witness to their vitality. Who can forget the story of Perseus who slew the Gorgon and released Andromeda, the maiden chained to a rock? Or Jason and the Argonauts, Theseus and the Minotaur, Orpheus and Eurydice, the Labours of Hercules? Indeed, Karl Marx, as we noted, is an unexpected witness to the everlasting charm of these stories.[71]

## 2   *The magic of mythical time*

The characteristic of myth, fictitious or not, is the hold that it has on our minds. As Kelley remarks in this connection: 'The study of history, like the human condition it affects to portray, cannot entirely disengage itself from the irrational and the subconscious . . .'[72] Anthropologists know that every society, primitive or developed, has its own powerful myths. We may define **a myth as an account of the past that does popular service in the present.** The question of truth is hardly relevant, for myths appeal to the imagination rather than to the intellect: hence, perhaps, their power. Modern nations, no less than ancient peoples, have their myths – popular beliefs about the past that suit some present purpose. Among these are (for the United States) the Pilgrim Fathers in the *Mayflower*; (for the English) the navy ruling the seas; (for the French) the liberating revolution; (for the Protestants of Northern Ireland) King Billy and the Battle of the Boyne; and many, many more. The question presses: Why, if truth is irrelevant, do myths take so firm a grip? To understand our modern myths it is helpful to look at the myths of older societies, like the Greeks or the Indians of North America. Myths are about the past but are important in the present. Now most older societies knew little history. In some cases, they even feared and rejected history, because it involved

---

[71] See above, ch. 1, p. 19.
[72] Kelley (1991), p. 3.

change and a departure from the sacred order of things.[73] Nevertheless, their myths were set in the past – often in **a time of creation (when the gods walked with men and men talked with birds and beasts) – a sacred time that had no continuity with the 'profane' time of normal human existence.** About such a time the myths were not, as *we* think, false. They told absolute truth, narrating sacred history – a model for all future generations.[74] Such an age, redolent of the biblical myth of the Garden of Eden, is called by Australian aborigines the 'Dream Time', for it is visited now only in dreams. We, however, have reconciled ourselves to living only in profane time. Yet even we who have elaborated detailed and continuous histories – we still reckon our years from some divine or semi-divine event: the exodus from Egypt for the Jewish calendar, the birth of Christ for the Christian, and the migration of Mohammed from Mecca to Medina for the Islamic.

## 3    *The functions of myths*

One contrast between myth and history is that a myth is full of meaning but may contain little or no (historical) truth, while a history is supposed to be true, but often has little meaning for us. What sort of meanings do myths have? They may serve to express the values of a society; they may sustain authority (as of a king or priesthood); they may explain some of the phenomena of the natural world; they may validate or authorize some custom, ritual or procedure; or they may justify whatever seems irrational or incomprehensible. Except for the third (explaining natural phenomena) we can see that modern myths may still fulfil such functions. These are sociological functions. Many myths also perform the psychological functions of releasing tension or repression – this is 'catharsis' – and of wish-fulfilment or creating a desirable state of emotion – this is day-dreaming or fantasizing.[75] To these functions one may also add the insight of Roland Barthes, that myth is a mode of communication, a language or even a 'metalanguage' – that is, a language for talking about language.[76] The idea of myth as an expression of thought has been thoroughly explored by Claude Lévi-Strauss in a number of well-known books.[77] Whatever their function, myths are perceived by their believers as important; they nearly always imply some sort of evaluation, showing how people think about the world they live in. Often they are what R. G. Collingwood calls 'encapsulated history'.

[73] See Eliade (1968) and (1989).
[74] Eliade (1968), p. 23. Cf. Christian use of the New Testament.
[75] See, for example, Kirk (1970; 1974).
[76] See 'Myth To-day', in Barthes (1973), pp. 109, 115.
[77] Lévi-Strauss (1969–81).

## 4  Historical myths

History as myth is something that historians always suspect. Just as certain episodes in an individual life stick in the memory, so, it seems, do groups (especially nations) have traditional accounts of important episodes in their communal life.[78] These help both to motivate and to direct their common actions. (Think how in times of war peoples have been called upon to emulate the brave deeds of earlier generations.) Such versions of history play the same roles as the myths of more primitive peoples. The social function of history is by no means limited to the educational and the academic. Unfortunately for the historian, history as myth is strong on meaning and weak on truth – though rarely quite false. But the establishment of historical truth is the aim of the historian. So what can we say about truth?

## 5  Truth in history

It has been remarked that myths proclaim great truths by telling great lies.[79] Is it possible for historians, by avoiding the fictitious and the fanciful, to tell equally great truths? Perhaps not, unless the truths that they tell are as significant and as full of meaning as myths.

So what is truth? **'Agreement with reality'** answers the dictionary (*The Shorter Oxford English*); **conformity with fact'**. This seems simple enough – until we come to historical truth. What are the facts with which a historical account must conform? What was the historical reality? Here we have a problem; not a historical problem but a logical one. If I say, 'The cat is on the mat', the statement can be checked against reality by my senses, looking to see if the cat really is on the mat. But let us take the statement, 'Brutus stabbed Caesar'. Doubtless there once was, over 2,000 years ago, a reality with which the statement might agree, But no longer. Our belief that Brutus stabbed Caesar rests upon various pieces of evidence, evidence so convincing that nobody doubts it. Yet that belief is not verifiable through the senses. If I am told, 'Caesar stabbed Brutus', I may retort that the statement is false. But I cannot *point* to reality to back me up – as I could do if he said, 'The cat is not on the mat.' I have to appeal, in justification, to the belief of all competent historians, a belief that is based on certain pieces of evidence. Nevertheless, 'Caesar stabbed Brutus' and 'Brutus stabbed Caesar' are held to be false or true because they agree with the beliefs of historians. Thus we check thoughts against thoughts, not against present reality (as in the case of the cat).

Does not this seem unsatisfactory? As the philosopher J. L. Austin, remarked, 'When a statement is true, there is, *of course*, a state of affairs

[78] See discussion on pp. 12 and 54–5 above.
[79] Lewis (1976), p. 121.

which makes it true and which is *toto mundo* distinct from the true statement about it; but equally of course, we can only *describe* that state of affairs *in words* (either the same or, with luck, others).'[80] The difficulty with truth in history is that there *was* a state of affairs which makes the true statement true, yet now all that we have is a description of that state in words – i.e. the considered judgement of historians upon the evidence. And that is if we are lucky; in very many cases we are not so fortunate, for there is not sufficient evidence to secure an agreed judgement. But if there was once a state of affairs that makes a present statement true or false, we have to acknowledge that there is no way of getting at that state except by means of the surviving evidence and of the judgements made from it. The only criterion we have for the truth of a historical statement (or of the thought behind it) is a set of other statements (or the thoughts, judgements, behind them).

## 6  Coherence or correspondence?

Now this conclusion has brought us to a peculiar position. There are two common definitions of truth in philosophy: one is based on **the *correspondence* theory of truth; i.e. a statement is true if it corresponds to the facts (or reality).** The other rests on **the *coherence* theory; i.e. a statement is true if it coheres with other statements which are known to be true.** The anomaly is that, however much one favours the correspondence view, which is the one put forward by Austin, in the case of historical statements one seems to be forced to hold the coherence view of truth. There is no existent state of affairs, or reality, to correspond with the statement.

Now, apart from any natural prejudice that one may feel against the coherence theory as an account of truth, there are further difficulties. Every statement is couched in words. And every historian knows that a set of words has to be understood in the context of the place, the age, the situation, the intention and the basic assumptions of the speaker (or writer). If one wishes to compare, say, a statement made in Chinese in Beijing to the emperor in the eighteenth century about the current political state of the country, with a late twentieth-century American writing in English for his students about the same subject, can one be certain of making all the necessary allowances for differences of language, place, age, intention, culture, and so on? Can one be sure of perceiving how far their statements do or do not cohere?

Furthermore, one must remember that much of the past must remain for ever unknown because we just lack the evidence for it. If we knew a little more than we do, might we not find that our judgements of coherence (and hence of truth) had to be revised?

[80] Austin (1970), p. 123.

There is more. As the American philosopher, A. C. Danto, has pointed out, it is impossible to give a full description of any event until the end of time. This is not for lack of evidence (my last point), but because we do not yet know all the consequences of an event, and those consequences are part of a full description.[81] Neither of these two objections would be so damaging to the correspondence view of truth (if one could only make this theory work for history), but raise serious difficulties for the coherence view of historical truth.

It seems that the best we can do is to say that the preferred view (the correspondence theory of truth) can be applied to present evidence. But when we proceed to making deductions from that evidence, then we are thinking and talking about what is past (hence, is not present). Here we cannot use the correspondence theory, but only the coherence theory. Truth in history, we must conclude, is the goal to be aimed at. It is the magnetic north to which our compasses point. But like the early navigators, we can hardly hope ever to arrive there.

> It is the star to every wand'ring bark,
> Whose worth's unknown, although his height be taken.

## D.   Meaning

> The summer's flower is to the summer sweet,
> Though to itself it only live and die.
> Shakespeare, Sonnet 94

### 1   The Meaning of 'meaning'

We have seen that myths have a strong hold upon the minds of those who believe in them. We have also noted that the strength of this hold has little to do with truth – hence the problem that current historical myths pose for the historian. The power of the myth, then, lies in its meaning rather than its truth. But surely the historian, however conscientious in pursuit of truth, is not indifferent to meaning? We have already seen (in chapter 2, p. 29 above) how contexts give historical meaning. But what *is* meaning?

'Meaning' is one of the most complex of concepts, one that has given rise to a vast amount of philosophical discussion. Let us skirt round this particular morass. **The verb 'to mean' is generally used either in the sense of 'to signify' (a red traffic light means Stop!) or 'to intend' ('What do you mean by that?' or 'What do you mean to do now?').** Of course, the historian, like every one else, frequently makes use of both these senses, in

---

[81] See above, pp. 92 and 244–5.

what he reads and in what he writes. There is, however, a third and more elusive sense of the word, and it is this that we must consider here. Sometimes we speak of a meaningful experience or relationship. Occasionally we ask what is the meaning of life or (not the same thing) of the universe. We may find that an activity we once enjoyed has become meaningless. What is this kind of meaning? Why do we feel put out when it seems to be lacking? It is in this (third) sense that I want to consider meaning *in* history and the meaning, or meanings, *of* history. The one clue that these examples offer us is that **what is meaningful to us is enlivening, enriching and positive; on the other hand, what we find meaningless is depressing, dispiriting and negative.**

## 2  *Meanings in history*

Let us consider several examples of meaning in history to see if they can provide further clues to this (perhaps the most important) kind of meaning.

(i)  *History as myth*   This we discussed in the preceding section. The importance of this is that it offers a connection with a past that (unlike the 'dream time' or 'creation age' of primitive peoples) is continuous with our present. For them it was an eternal model for life; for us the past is an earlier stage of life.

(ii)  *History as sacred*   This, the biblical or Judaeo-Christian view of history, holds that God reveals himself in history. It differs from history-as-myth in that historic truth is of first importance. This is because the providence and purpose of God is revealed in the events. The chief characteristics of the Old Testament doctrine are these:

(a)   That God did not merely create the universe in the beginning; he also sustains it at every moment and works out his purposes in it.

(b)   That the purpose of God was revealed to the people of Israel, but they disobeyed their God and came under moral judgement.

(c)   That God is not just their own tribal god, but the God of all nations; hence that his purpose for the Jews is a missionary one.

(d)   That for these reasons it is essential both to establish historical facts and to reach a correct interpretation of history.

Therefore, the study of history has bulked large in western civilization, based as much of it is upon Jewish and Christian religious culture. If history-as-myth lends itself to distortion and manipulation, history-as-sacred requires a serious pursuit of the truth. It is this view, perhaps more than any other, that gives a profound meaning to history.

(iii)   *History as tradition*   Tradition, too, has a peculiar authority. The very word indicates a handing-over (to the next generation) of what is worth preserving. A modern philosopher argues that we are too preoccupied with change, and too little with 'the traditions in which we stand ... Hence the perspectives which come from the experience of historical change are always in danger of distortion because they forget the hidden constants.'[82] A famous justification of political tradition is Edmund Burke's *Reflections on the Revolution in France*, written in 1790. If those who hold temporary power, he urges, were to be 'unmindful of what they have received from their ancestors, or what is due to their posterity ... the whole chain and continuity of the commonwealth would be broken ... Men would become little better than the flies of a summer.'[83] Many other things can give this sense of continuity through the generations – a family, a house, a book or work of art, even a game like chess or cricket. In every case, the awareness of this continuity adds meaning.

(iv)   *History as contingency*   Some people, however, have professed to find little meaning in history. The historian of Europe, H. A. L. Fisher, wrote that he could see in history no plot or rhythm or predestined pattern: 'There can be no generalizations, only one safe rule for the historian: that he should recognize in the development of human destinies the play of the contingent and the unforeseen.'[84] For Gibbon, we recall, history is little more than 'the register of the crimes, follies and misfortunes of mankind.'[85] We have seen the positivist belief that history is a science to be understood in terms of general laws and solid facts. Even J. B. Bury, one of the few British historians to think seriously about the philosophy of history, was compelled to recognize the dominance of 'the contingent and the unforeseen'. Another historian tells us that Bury

> could explain why a Prime Minister happened to be walking down a street, and he could explain the scientific laws which loosened a tile on a roof so that it fell down at a particular moment; but he could not explain the conjuncture of the two – the fact that the Prime Minister should just be there to be killed by the falling tile – and yet it was just this *conjuncture* of the two things which was the most important feature of the story.[86]

R. G. Collingwood discusses the same point in *The Idea of History*.[87] If

[82] Gadamer (1979), pp. xiii–xiv.
[83] E. Burke (1910), pp. 91–2.
[84] Fisher (1936) Preface.
[85] Gibbon (1910), vol. I, ch. 3, p. 77.
[86] Butterfield, 'God in History', in McIntire (1977), p. 198. See also Bury, 'Cleopatra's Nose' (1916) in Bury (1930).
[87] (1961), pp. 149–51.

one concludes, with Bury and Fisher, that the course of human affairs is governed chiefly by chance, then how can we recognize a meaning?[88]

(v) *History as Narrative*   In spite of the fact that a good deal of history is no longer written as narrative, it may yet be that all history has an ultimately narrative character. Paul Ricoeur argues that even history 'most removed from narrative form continues to be bound to our narrative understanding'. It still involves 'our basic competence for following a story'. The reason is that understanding history and following a story require some of the same '**cognitive operations' – i.e. ways of coming to know something.**[89] Frederick A. Olafson has argued for 'the notion of the centrality of narrative within history as a whole'. As we have seen, he thinks that 'the rational structure of action is the structure of narrative.'[90] Narrative, some hold, occurs not after, but *with* the action. We tell ourselves stories to give meanings to our actions.[91] Hence historical narrative gives to the events it narrates a meaning – whether or not it is that given by any of the agents.

(vi) *History as Structure*   This view of history is roughly the opposite of history-as-narrative. It owes much to the social sciences and to the *Annales* school of historians. With them it often involves taking a 'horizontal' view, rather than narrative's 'vertical' view: not so much seeing a sequence of happenings through time, but rather a number of states of affairs existing at the same time. However, the concept of history as structure involves more than this. It is a big subject and I have already written a book on structures in history.[92] A dictionary definition is: '**structure: an organized body or combination of mutually connected parts or elements'.** One obvious analogy is that of the human body. Thus for proper structural history, the following conditions apply: **one, the subject should be a coherent whole; two,** *all* **the parts should be described, not only those that the historians find convenient; and, three, it should be clear how each part is related to the rest.** Bearing these in mind it is possible to see as a structure any given part of history. And this is the sort of meaning that, on this view, history might have – that of a structured whole. History-as-narrative gives the meaning from the inside, history-as-structure the meaning from the outside. We recall Barthes's remark that intelligibility is the keynote of structural history.[93]

(vii) *History as evolution*   The word can mean no more than 'unrolling' or 'unfolding', but here **by 'evolution' I understand 'the doctrine according to which higher forms of life have gradually arisen out**

---

[88] For my own view of chance, see ch. 8, pp. 205, 210 above.

[89] Ricoeur (1984), vol. I, p. 91.

[90] See Olafson (1979), pp. 133, 151.

[91] See D. Carr (1986a) p. 125 and Dennett (1991), pp. 412–18. Also see above, ch. 4, pp. 100–2.

[92] See Stanford (1990).

[93] See above, ch. 4, p. 107.

**of lower'.** Both the biological and the historical applications of this idea are very old, but the notion in its modern form comes from Charles Darwin and his book, *On the Origin of Species* (1859). Biology apart, however, it is still open to question whether history reveals an evolution in the sense defined. The answer would seem to be that human evolution of the biological kind is clearly established over the 40 or 50 million years between the first apes and the first men, some 40,000–50,000 years ago. Since then the biological forms have changed little if at all, but there has been very considerable evolution of societies from less to more complex forms. Two questions follow: (1) Does this process have to pass through similar stages in all cases, or may some stages be omitted or by-passed? (2) Is this process in all cases inevitable, or can there be halts, regressions or terminal breakdowns? For many people, the view of history as evolution, either of mankind as a whole, or of one particular nation, is what gives it meaning for them. But it is worth considering carefully what sort of evolution one believes in.

(viii)  *History with a determined future*  Although history is a subject directed towards the past, we must not forget the importance of the future. Now many have believed (and some still do) that the future is already determined; that there is an inevitable end to which all things are approaching. There are two roots for this. One is the Bible, especially the Old Testament prophets and the Book of Revelations (a vision, not a prophecy). The other is German philosophy, best known in Marx and Engels. Although their views were formed before Darwin's book, they saw in his theory of biological evolution a welcome reinforcement of their ideas of historical evolution.[94] In 1888 Engels wrote that class struggles formed 'a series of evolutions'. 'This proposition', Engels went on, '. . . is destined to do for history what Darwin's theory has done for biology . . .'[95] As we saw above, for Marxist theory the future is certain; it is the triumph of communism.

(ix)  *History with an open future*  The idea that, whatever the trials and tribulations of humanity, we shall at last come to a happy ending has appealed to many. Others, however, have found the idea repulsive. The prospect of a fixed ending seems to them to subtract from our freedom. Like children, we may always be overruled by a kindly but firm nurse called God or History or Fate or the Absolute. Another objection is that it detracts from the importance of historical events. If the future is determined, it matters not whether we fight or surrender. Why make any effort? We lose all dignity if our actions have no effect upon the course of history. The authors of the Declaration of Independence (1776) and of the Rights of Man and of the Citizen (1789) believed that their efforts were

---

[94] See above, pp. 270–1.
[95] Preface to the English edition of the *Manifesto of the Communist Party* (1888), in Marx and Engels (1969), p. 46.

creating a better society and a better world. They did not expect some mystical, disembodied force to do it for them. The view that history must have an open future was, as we have seen above, vigorously defended by Karl Popper.[96] Strictly he does not *prove* that history has an open end, but by pointing out the calamitous effects of the opposite theory, he persuades us to believe it. And in this respect it is belief that counts – we cannot *know* the truth. Thus those who believe that history is not determined but is made by the efforts of men and women find in it a very different meaning from that of the opposite party.

## 3   *Conclusion*

Can we find any common thread in all the various meanings of 'meaning' that we have discussed? Perhaps it is that of 'connection'. When we find a meaning (of this third kind), it is because we feel that it connects – intellectually, emotionally or spiritually – with something deep but central within us. Connection is also a characteristic of the other two (more common) uses of 'meaning'. For the symbol connects with reality and the intention connects with the action. **Meaning, I conclude, is a sense of vital connection.**

Yet I cannot agree with the much-quoted definition of the anthropologist, Clifford Geertz: **Believing . . . that man is an animal suspended in webs of significance he himself has spun, I take culture to be those webs . . . and the analysis of it to be therefore . . . an interpretive one in search of meaning.**[97] For I do not think that culture, either for the anthropologist or for the historian, is (as Geertz claims) a matter of semiotics. (**Semiotics is the theory of signs**). The meanings to be found therein (Geertz's 'webs of significance') certainly do link man with man. However, I cannot believe that the whole of history, still less one human life, consists entirely of mankind communicating with itself – any more than that it is only Gibbon's 'crimes, follies and misfortunes'. For it is characteristic of any meaning that it points away from itself to something other (as C-A-T points to the feline on your lap). To what 'other' does human history point? If the spirit of man is at one end of the linkage that we call meaning, who or what is at the other?

# E.   Some Other Relevant Topics

The whole complex question of meaning in its various relations to history needs a lot more thought. A useful starting-point is William Bouwsma's essay, 'From History of Ideas to History of Meaning' in Rabb and Rotberg (1982).

[96] See above, pp. 255–6.
[97] Geertz (1975), p. 5.

The collapse of communism calls Marxism into question. Far from being totally discredited, Marx's ideas can be re-examined with less prejudice. He was far from infallible either as a prophet or as a historian, but he was almost unparalleled in his understanding of Europe and the European mind of, at least, the 1840s. Furthermore, both the understanding and the misunderstanding of Marx by successive generations teach us a lot about the last 150 years. One might make a start with Carver (1992), Graham (1992) or Kolakowski (1981).

Thirdly, we have not yet done with Hegel, in spite of Popper's attempt in 1945 to discredit him in *The Open Society and Its Enemies*. An idea, it has been said, is not responsible for the people who hold it. In spite of the materialism, utilitarianism and empiricism in the dominant modes of our contemporary thought and practice – all part of the heritage of the Enlightenment, many of us are still concerned with the issues of freedom and of nature (now called 'the environment') that we inherit from the French revolution and the Romantics. Hegel understood these issues in ways that Marx did not. Further consideration might begin with Charles Taylor (1979).

# Conclusion

This chapter has tried to look at history as a whole and to see what meanings it has had from various viewpoints. In particular, we have seen how different beliefs about reality (or metaphysics) have influenced what people make of it. These have included historicism, positivism, idealism and materialism.

The difficult problem of meaning (and its meanings) comes up first in relation to myths (full of meanings) and to historical truth – the apparent enemy of myths. Some other possible meanings of history have been sketched, and we conclude with an attempt at discovering the elusive but important third meaning of 'meaning' – as in the 'meaning of life'. Can history as a whole have such a meaning?

## Suggested Reading

Berlin 1948; 1980  
Bury 1930  
Gardiner 1959  
Hegel 1956  
Hughes 1959  
Iggers 1975; 1983  
McLellan 1976  
Mandelbaum 1971  

Marwick 1989  
Marx and Engels 1969  
Marx 1973a; 1975; 1977  
Meyerhoff 1959  
Stern 1970  
Taylor C. H. 1979  
Walker 1978  
Walsh 1958

# Bibliography

The date given before the title is that of the edition consulted. The date of first publication (if different) follows in brackets.

Acton, Lord, 1960. 'Inaugural Lecture on the Study of History' delivered at Cambridge (June 1895), in *Lectures on Modern History*, Fontana

Acton, Lord, 1970. 'Letter to the Contributors to the *Cambridge Modern History*' (1898) in Stern

Anderson, M. S., 1979. *Historians and Eighteenth-Century Europe 1715–1789*, Clarendon Press

*Anglo-Saxon Chronicle*, 1953. tr. and intro. by G. N. Garmonsway, Dent/Everyman

Aristotle, 1965. 'On the Art of Poetry', in *Classical Literary Criticism*, tr. T. S. Dorsch, Penguin

Ash, Timothy Garton, 1990. *We, The People: The Revolution of '89 Witnessed in Warsaw, Budapest, Berlin and Prague*, Granta-Penguin

Atkinson, R. F., 1978. *Knowledge and Explanation in History. An Introduction to the Philosophy of History*, Macmillan

Auerbach, Erich, 1968. *Mimesis: The Representation of Reality in Western Literature*, tr. Willard R. Trask, Princeton University Press (1957; 1946)

Augustine of Hippo, 1907. *Confessions*, tr. E. B. Pusey, Dent/Everyman; also tr. Henry Chadwick, Oxford University Press, 1991 (AD 397)

Austin, J. L., 1970. *Philosophical Papers*, Oxford University Press (1961)

Ayer, A. J., 1956. *The Problem of Knowledge*, Penguin

Bann, Stephen, 1990. *The Inventions of History: Essays on the Representation of the Past*, Manchester University Press

Barnes, Harry Elmer, 1962. *A History of Historical Writing*, Dover Publications (1937)

Baron, H., 1966. *The Crisis of the Early Italian Renaissance*, Princeton University Press

Barthes, Roland, 1970. 'Historical Discourse' in Lane

Barthes, Roland, 1973. *Mythologies*, selected and translated by Annette Lavers, Paladin

Barthes, Roland, *Image-Music-Text* 1984. essays sel. and tr. by Stephen Heath, Fontana/Flamingo (1977)

Bauman, Zygmunt, 1978. *Hermeneutics and Social Sciences: Approaches to Understanding*, Hutchinson

Bendix, Reinhard, 1967. 'The Comparative Analysis of Historical Change' in Burns and Saul

Benson, Lee, and Strout, Cushing, 1965. 'Causation and the American Civil War: Two Appraisals' (1960), in Nadel

Berlin, Isaiah, 1948. *Karl Marx: His Life and Environment*, Oxford University Press (1939)

Berlin, Isaiah, 1980. *Vico and Herder: Two Studies in the History of Ideas*, Chatto and Windus (1976)

Blackburn, Robin (ed.), 1972. *Ideology in Social Science: Readings in Critical Social Theory*, Fontana/Collins.

*The Blackwell Dictionary of Historians, see* Cannon (1988)

Bloch, Marc, 1949. *Strange Defeat: A Statement of Evidence*, tr. Gerard Hopkins, Oxford University Press

Bloch, Marc, 1954. *The Historian's Craft*, tr. Peter Putnam, Manchester University Press.

Bloch, Marc, 1967. 'A Contribution towards a Comparative History of European Societies' (1928), in *Land and Work in Medieval Europe*, Routledge and Kegan Paul

Boardman, John et al., 1986 *The Oxford History of the Classical World*, Oxford University Press

Bock, Kenneth, 1979. 'Theories of Progress, Development and Evolution' (1978), in Bottomore and Nisbet

Bottomore, T. B., 1971. *Sociology: A Guide to Problems and Literature* (rev. edn), George Allen and Unwin

Bottomore, Tom, and Nisbet, Robert, (eds), 1979. *A History of Sociological Analysis*, Heinemann

Bouwsma, William J., 1982. 'Intellectual History in the 1980s: From History of Ideas to History of Meaning', in Rabb and Rotberg

Braudel, Fernand, 1975. *The Mediterranean and the Mediterranean World in the Age of Philip II*, 2 vols, tr. Siân Reynolds, Fontana/Collins (1949)

Braudel, Fernand, 1980. *On History*, tr. Sarah Matthews, Weidenfeld and Nicolson (1969)

Braudel, Fernand, 1981–4. *Civilization and Capitalism 15th–18th Century*, 3 vols, Collins (1979)

Buckle, Henry T., 1903. *The History of Civilization in England*, 2 vols, Grant Richards, (1857–61)

Burckhardt, Jacob, 1945. *The Civilization of the Renaissance in Italy*, Phaidon (1860)

Burke, Edmund, 1910. *Reflections on the French Revolution and Other Essays*, Dent/Everyman (1790)

Burke, Peter, 1969. *The Renaissance Sense of the Past*, Edward Arnold

Burke, Peter, 1974. *Tradition and Innovation in Renaissance Italy: A Sociological Approach*, Fontana (1972)

Burke, Peter, 1980. *Sociology and History*, George Allen and Unwin

Burke, Peter, 1990. *The French Historical Revolution: The 'Annales' School, 1929–89*, Polity Press

Burke, Peter, (ed.), 1991. *New Perspectives on Historical Writing*, Polity Press

Burke, Peter, 1992. *History and Social Theory*, Polity Press

Burns, Tom, and Saul, S. B. (eds.), 1967. *Social Theory and Economic Change*, Tavistock Publications

Burrow, John, 1981. *A Liberal Descent: Victorian Historians and the English Past*, Cambridge University Press

Bury, J. B., 1903. 'The Science of History', Inaugural Lecture at Cambridge, repr. in Stern (1970), and in Bury (1930)

Bury, J. B., 1916. 'Cleopatra's Nose', in Bury (1930)

Bury, J. B., 1924. *The Idea of Progress: An Inquiry into its Origin and Growth*, Macmillan (1920)

Bury, J. B., 1930. *Selected Essays*, ed. Harold Temperley, Cambridge University Press

Butterfield, Herbert, 1950. *The Whig Interpretation of History*, G. Bell (1931)

Butterfield, Herbert, 1951. *History and Human Relations*, Collins

Butterfield, Herbert, 1957a. *George III and the Historians*, Collins

Butterfield, Herbert, 1957b. *The Origins of Modern Science, 1300–1800*, G. Bell (1949)

Butterfield, Herbert, 1960. *Man on His Past: The Study of the History of Historical Scholarship*, Beacon Press (1955)

Butterfield, Herbert, 1968. 'Narrative History and the Spadework Behind it', *History*, 53, no. 178

Butterfield, Herbert, 1977. 'God in History' (1958), in McIntire

Canary, Robert H. and Kozicki, Henry, (eds), 1978. *The Writing of History: Literary Form and Historical Understanding*, University of Wisconsin Press

Cannon, John (ed.), 1980. *The Historian at Work*, George Allen and Unwin

Cannon, John et al. (eds), 1988. *The Blackwell Dictionary of Historians* Blackwell

Carbonell, Charles-Olivier, 1976. *Histoire et historiens: une mutation idéologique des historiens français, 1865–1885* Privat

Carlyle, Thomas, 1893. *Oliver Cromwell's Letters and Speeches with Elucidations*, Chapman and Hall

Carlyle, Thomas, 1899. 'On History' (1830), in *Selected Essays*, T. Nelson (n. d.) and in *Critical and Miscellaneous Essays*, vol. II, Chapman and Hall

Carr, David, 1986 a. 'Narrative and the Real World', *History and Theory*, vol. 25

Carr, David, 1986 b. *Time, Narrative and History*, Indiana University Press

Carr, E. H., 1964. *What is History?* Penguin (1961)

Carroll, Noël, 1990. 'Interpretation, History and Narrative', *The Monist*, 73, no. 2 (April)

Carver, Terrell, 1992, *The Cambridge Companion to Marx*, Cambridge University Press

Chatman, Seymour, 1980. *Story and Discourse: Narrative Structure in Fiction and Film*, Cornell University Press

Cherry, Colin, 1966. *On Human Communication*, MIT Press

Chisholm, Roderick M., 1966. *Theory of Knowledge*, Prentice-Hall

Cipolla, Carlo M., 1970. *European Culture and Overseas Expansion*, Penguin

Cipolla, Carlo M., 1991. *Between History and Economics: An Introduction to Economic History*, Blackwell

Clark, G. Kitson, 1965. *The Making of Victorian England*, Methuen (1962)

Clark, G. Kitson, 1967. *The Critical Historian*, Heinemann

Clark, Stuart, 1990. 'The "Annales" Historians', in Skinner

Clive, John, 1990. *Not by Fact Alone: Essays on the Writing and Reading of History*, Collins Harvill (1989)

Coe, Michael D., 1971. *The Maya*, Penguin (1966)

Cohn, Norman, 1962. *The Pursuit of the Millennium*, Heinemann/Mercury (1957)

Cohn, Norman, 1993. *Cosmos, Chaos and the World to Come: The Ancient Roots of Apocalyptic Faith*, Yale University Press

Collingwood, R. G., 1940. *An Essay on Metaphysics*, Clarendon Press

Collingwood, R. G., 1961. *The Idea of History*, Oxford University Press (1946)

*Comparative Studies in Society and History*, 1958 (Cambridge University Press)

Cornford, F. M., *see* Plato (1941)

Coser, L. A., and Rosenberg, B. (eds), 1969. *Sociological Theory: A Book of Readings*, Macmillan (New York), 3rd edn. (1957)

Dalzell, Charles (ed.), 1976. *The Future of History*, Vanderbilt University Press

Danto, Arthur C., 1965 *Analytical Philosophy of History*, Cambridge University Press

Danto, Arthur C., 1968. *Analytical Philosophy of Knowledge*, Cambridge University Press

Davis, Natalie Zemon, 1975. *Society and Culture in Early Modern France*, Duckworth

Dawkins, Richard, 1983. *The Extended Phenotype: The Gene as the Unit of Selection*, Oxford University Press

Dawkins, Richard, 1991. *The Blind Watchmaker*, Penguin (1986)

Dawkins, Richard, 1989. *The Selfish Gene*, Oxford University Press (1986)

Denley, Peter, and Hopkin, Deian (eds), 1987. *History and Computing*, Manchester University Press

Dennett, Daniel C., 1991. *Consciousness Explained*, Little, Brown

Dilthey, Wilhelm, 1959. 'The Dream' (1903), in Meyerhoff

Dilthey, Wilhelm, 1976. *Selected Writings*, ed. H. P. Rickman, Cambridge University Press

Douglas, David C., 1943. *English Scholars 1660–1730*, Eyre and Spottiswoode (1939)

Drake, Michael (ed.), 1973. *Applied Historical Studies: An Introductory Reader*, Methuen/Open University

Dray, W. H., 1957. *Laws and Explanations in History*, Oxford University Press

Dray, William H., 1959. ' "Explaining What" in History', in Gardiner (ed.), 1959

Dray, William H., 1964. *Philosophy of History*, Prentice-Hall

Dray, William H. (ed.), 1966. *Philosophical Analysis and History*, Harper and Row

Dray, William H., 1974. 'The Historical Explanation of Actions Reconsidered' (1963) in Gardiner (ed.), 1974

Dray, William H., 1980. *Perspectives on History*, Routledge and Kegan Paul

Duby, Pierre, 1985. 'Ideologies in Social History' (1974), in Le Goff and Nora

Eagleton, Terry, 1983. *Literary Theory: An Introduction*, Blackwell

Eliade, Mircea, 1968. *Myths, Dreams and Mysteries: The Encounter between Contemporary Faith and Archaic Reality*, tr. Philip Mairet, Collins/Fontana (1957)

Eliade, Mircea, 1989. *The Myth of the Eternal Return, or Cosmos and History*, tr. Willard R. Trask, Arkana (1954)

Elliott, J. H., 1986. *The Count-Duke of Olivares: The Stateman in an Age of Decline*, Yale University Press

Elton, G. R., 1969. *The Practice of History*, Fontana/Collins (1967)

Elton, G. R., 1970. *Political History: Principles and Practice*, Allen Lane, Penguin Press

Elton, G. R., 1983, in Fogel and Elton

Elton, G. R., 1991. *Return to Essentials: Some Reflections on the Present State of Historical Study*, Cambridge University Press

Engels, Frederick, 1969. *The Condition of the Working Class in England*, Panther/Granada (1845; English translation 1892)

Engerman, Stanley L., 1977. 'Recent Developments in American Economic History', *Social Science History*, 2, no. 1

Evans, R. J. W., 1984. *The Making of the Habsburg Monarchy 1550–1700: An Interpretation*, Clarendon Press (1979)

Febvre, Lucien, 1962. *Le Problème de l'incroyance au XVIᵉ siècle: La religion de Rabelais* (L'Évolution de l'humanité), Albin Michel

Fehrenbacher, Don E., 1963. 'Disunion and Reunion', in Higham (ed.), 1953

Fejtö, François, 1974. *A History of the People's Democracies*, tr. Daniel Weissbort, Penguin (1969)

Ferguson, Wallace K., 1948. *The Renaissance in Historical Thought: Five Centuries of Interpretation*, Houghton Mifflin

Ferro, Marc, 1984. *The Use and Abuse of History – or How the Past is Taught*, Routledge and Kegan Paul (1981)

Finberg, H. P. R. (ed.), 1965. *Approaches to History: A Symposium*, Routledge and Kegan Paul (1962)

Firth, C. H., 1962. *Cromwell's Army*, Methuen (1902)

Fischer, D. H., 1989. *Albion's Seed: Four British Folkways in America*, Oxford University Press (New York)

Fisher, H. A. L., 1936. *A History of Europe*, Edward Arnold

Fletcher, Anthony, 1968. *Tudor Rebellions*, Longman

Flinn, M. W., and Smout, T. C. (eds), 1974. *Essays in Social History*, Clarendon Press

Floud, Roderick (ed.), 1974. *Essays in Quantitative Economic History*, Clarendon Press

Floud, Roderick, 1979. *An Introduction to Quantitative Methods for Historians*, Methuen (1973)

Fogel, R. W., and Elton, G. R., 1983. *Which Road to the Past?: Two Views of History*, Yale University Press

Foucault, Michel, 1970. *The Order of Things: An Archaeology of the Human Sciences*, Tavistock Publications (1966)

Frye, Northrop, 1971. *Anatomy of Criticism: Four Essays*, Princeton University Press (1957)

Fueter, Eduard, 1936. *Geschichte der Neueren Historiographie*, Oldenbourg (Munich)

Furet, François, 1981. *Interpreting the French Revolution*, Cambridge University Press. (ET of *Penser la Révolution Française*, 1978)

Gadamer, Hans Georg, 1979. *Truth and Method*, tr. William Glen Doepel, Sheed and Ward (1965, German 2nd edn)

Gallie, W. B., 1964. *Philosophy and the Historical Understanding*, Chatto and Windus

Gardiner, Patrick, 1952. *The Nature of Historical Explanation*, Oxford University Press

Gardiner, Patrick (ed.), 1959. *Theories of History*, The Free Press

Gardiner, Patrick (ed.), 1974. *The Philosophy of History*, Oxford University Press

Gay, Peter, 1975. *Style in History*, Jonathan Cape

Geertz, Clifford, 1975. *The Interpretation of Cultures*, Hutchinson (1973)

*Gender and History*, 1989 – (Blackwell)

Geyl, Pieter, 1962. *Debates with Historians*, Collins/Fontana (1955)

Geyl, Pieter, 1965. *Napoleon: For and Against*, tr. Olive Renier, Penguin (1949)

Gibbon, Edward, 1910. *The Decline and Fall of the Roman Empire*, 6 vols, Dent/Everyman (1776–88)

Gibbon, Edward, 1911. *Autobiography*, Dent/Everyman (1796)

Giddens, Anthony, 1976. *New Rules of Sociological Method: A Positive Critique of Interpretative Sociologies*, Hutchinson

Gilbert, Felix and Graubard, S. R., (eds), 1972. *Historical Studies To-day*, W. W. Norton and Co.

Goldstein, Leon, 1976. *Historical Knowing*, University of Texas Press

Goubert, Pierre, 1968. *Cent Mille provinciaux au XVIIᵉ siècle: Beauvais et le Beauvaisis de 1600 à 1730*, Flammarion (1960)

Gould, Stephen Jay, 1988. *Time's Arrow, Time's Cycle: Myth and Metaphor in the Discovery of Geological Time*, Penguin (1987)

Gould, Stephen Jay, 1991. *Wonderful Life: The Burgess Shale and the Nature of History*, Penguin (1989)

Graham, Keith, 1992. *Karl Marx, Our Contemporary*, Harvester-Wheatsheaf

Griffin, Jasper, 1986. 'Greek Myth and Hesiod', in Boardman et al.

Hale, J. R., 1971. *Renaissance Europe 1480–1520*, Fontana/Collins

Haley, Arthur, 1976. *Roots*, Doubleday

Hamlyn, D. W., 1971. *The Theory of Knowledge*, Macmillan

Hampson, Norman, 1968. *The Enlightenment*, Penguin

Hanson, Norwood Russell, 1965. *Patterns of Discovery: An Enquiry into the Conceptual Foundations of Science*, Cambridge University Press (1958)

Hart, H. L. A., and Honoré, A. M., 1959. *Causation in the Law*, Clarendon Press

Harte, N. B., 1971. *The Study of Economic History: Collected Inaugural Lectures 1893–1970*, Cass

Hawking, Stephen, 1990. *A Brief History of Time: From the Big Bang to Black Holes*, Bantam Books (1988)

Hegel, G. W. F., 1956. *The Philosophy of History*, tr. J. Sibree, Dover Publications (1831); also published as *Lectures on the Philosophy of World History*, Cambridge University Press (1975)

Hegel, G. W. F., 1967. *Philosophy of Right*, tr. T. M. Knox, Oxford University Press (1821)

Hempel, Carl Gustav, 1959. 'The Function of General Laws in History' (1942) in Gardiner (ed.), 1959

Henige, David, 1982. *Oral Historiography*, Longman

Herodotus, 1954. *The Histories*, tr. Aubrey de Sélincourt, Penguin

Hexter, J. H., 1972. *The History Primer*, Allen Lane, Penguin Press

Hexter, J. H., 1979. *On Historians: A Scrutiny of Some of the Makers of Modern History*, Collins

Higham, John (ed.), 1963. *The Reconstruction of American History*, Hutchinson (1962)

Higham, John, 1965. *History*, Prentice-Hall

Hill, A. O., and Hill, B. H., 1980. 'Marc Bloch and Comparative History', *American Historical Review*, 85, no. 4

Hill, Christopher, 1975. *The World Turned Upside Down*, Penguin (1972)

*History and Computing*, 1989– (Oxford University Press)

Hobsbawm, Eric J., 1972. 'Karl Marx's Contribution to Historiography' (1968), in Blackburn

Hobsbawm, Eric J., 1974. 'From Social History to the History of Society', (1971) in Flinn and Smout

Hobsbawm, Eric J. and Ranger, Terence (eds), 1984. *The Invention of Tradition*, Cambridge University Press (1983)

Hofstadter, Richard, 1970. *The Progressive Historians: Turner, Beard, Parrington*, Vintage Books (1968)

Holborn, Hajo, 1972. *History and the Humanities*, Doubleday

Hoskins, W. G., 1955. *The Making of the English Landscape*, Hodder and Stoughton

Hoskins, W. G., 1959. *Local History in England*, Longman

Hughes, H. Stuart, 1959. *Consciousness and Society: the Orientation of European Social Thought 1890–1930*, MacGibbon and Kee

Hume, David, 1975. *An Enquiry concerning Human Understanding*, ed. L. A. Selby-Bigge, Clarendon Press (1748)

Iggers, Georg G. 1975. *New Directions in European Historiography*, Wesleyan University Press

Iggers, Georg G., 1983. *The German Conception of History: The National Tradition of Historical Thought from Herder to the Present*, Wesleyan University Press (1968)

Iggers, Georg G., and Parker, Harold T., 1980. *International Handbook of Historical Studies: Contemporary Research and Theory*, Methuen

Jäckel, Eberhard, 1981. *Hitler's World View: A Blueprint for Power*, Harvard University Press (1969)

Jenkins, Keith, 1991. *Re-Thinking History*, Routledge

Joinville, John, Lord of, 1908. *Chronicle of the Crusade of St. Lewis*, Dent/Everyman (1309)

Jones, Gareth Stedman, 1972. 'History: The Poverty of Empiricism', in Blackburn

Kann, Robert A., 1968. *The Problem of Restoration: A Study in Comparative Political History*, University of California Press

Kant, Immanuel, 1956. *Critique of Practical Reason*, tr. L. W. Beck, Bobbs-Merrill (1788)

Kant, Immanuel, 1963. *Critique of Pure Reason*, tr. Norman Kemp Smith, Macmillan (1781)

Kant, Immanuel, 1977. 'Idea for a Universal History with a Cosmopolitan Purpose', (1784), in Reiss

Kaye, Harvey J., 1984. *The British Marxist Historians: An Introductory Analysis*, Polity Press/Blackwell

Keegan, John, 1978. *The Face of Battle*, Penguin (1976)

Kelley, Donald R. (ed.), 1991. *Versions of History from Antiquity to Enlightenment*, Yale University Press

Kennedy, Paul, 1989. *The Rise and Fall of the Great Powers: Economic Change and Military Conflict from 1500 to 2000*, Fontana/Collins (1988)

Kenyon, John, 1983. *The History Men: the Historical Profession in England since the Renaissance*, Weidenfeld and Nicolson

Kermode, Frank, 1967. *The Sense of an Ending: Studies in the Theory of Fiction*, Oxford University Press (New York)

Kirk, G. S., 1970. *Myth. Its Meaning and Functions in Ancient and Other Cultures*, Cambridge University Press

Kirk, G. S., 1974. *The Nature of Greek Myths*, Penguin

Kolakowski, Leszek, 1981. *Main Currents of Marxism*, 3 vols, Oxford University Press (1978)

Körner, Stefan, 1955. *Kant*, Penguin

Kuhn, Thomas, 1970. *The Structure of Scientific Revolutions*, University of Chicago Press (1966)

Lane, Michael (ed.), 1970. *Structuralism*, Jonathan Cape

Langlois, C. V., and Seignobos, C., 1898. *Introduction to the Study of History*, tr. G. G. Berry, Duckworth

Le Goff, Jacques, 1980. *Time, Work and Culture in the Middle Ages*, tr. Arthur Goldhammer, University of Chicago Press

Le Goff, Jacques, 1988. *Medieval Civilization, 400–1500*, tr. Julia Barrow, (1964)

Le Goff, Jacques, and Nora, Pierre (eds), 1985. *Constructing the Past: Essays in Historical Methodology*, Cambridge University Press

Le Roy Ladurie, Emmanuel, 1978. *Montaillou: Cathars and Catholics in a French Village 1294–1324*, tr. Barbara Bray, Scolar Press (1975)

Le Roy Ladurie, Emmanuel, 1979. *The Territory of the Historian*, tr. Ben and Siân Reynolds, Harvester Press (1973)

Le Roy Ladurie, Emmanuel, 1980. *Carnival: A People's Uprising at Romans 1579–1580*, tr. Mary Feeney, Scolar Press (1979)

Le Roy Ladurie, Emmanuel, 1981. *The Mind and Method of the Historian*, tr. Ben and Siân Reynolds, Harvester Press (1978)

Levine, Joseph M., 1987. *Humanism and History: Origins of Modern English Historiography*, Cornell University Press

Lévi-Strauss, Claude, 1969–81. *Mythologiques: Introduction to the Study of Mythology*, tr. John and Doreen Weightman, 4 vols, Jonathan Cape

Lewis, I. M., 1976. *Social Anthropology in Perspective: The Relevance of Social Anthropology*, Penguin

Lipset, S. M., and Hofstadter, R. (eds), 1968. *Sociology and History: Methods*, Basic Books

Lloyd, Christopher, 1993. *The Structures of History*, Blackwell

Lloyd-Jones, Hugh, et al. (eds), 1981. *History and Imagination: Essays in honour of H. R. Trevor-Roper*, Duckworth

Löwith, Karl, 1967. *Meaning in History*, University of Chicago Press/Phoenix Books (1949)

Lukes, Steven, 1973. 'Methodological Individualism Reconsidered' (1968), in Ryan (ed.), 1973

Macaulay, Lord, 1931. *The History of England from the Accession of James II*, 5 vols, Oxford University Press

McCullagh, C. Behan, 1984. *Justifying Historical Descriptions*, Cambridge University Press

McIntire, C. T. (ed.), 1977. *God, History and the Historians: An Anthology of Modern Christian Views of History*, Oxford University Press (New York)

MacIntyre, Alasdair, 1981. *After Virtue: A Study in Moral Theory*, Duckworth

MacIntyre, Alasdair, 1988. *Whose Justice, Which Rationality?* Duckworth

McLellan, David, 1976. *Karl Marx: His Life and Thought*, Paladin (1973)

McPherson, James M., 1990. *Battle Cry of Freedom: The American Civil War*, Penguin (1988)

MacRae, Donald G., 1974. *Weber*, Fontana/Collins

Maitland, Frederick William, 1960a. *Domesday Book and Beyond: Three Essays in the Early History of England*, Fontana/Collins (1897)

Maitland, Frederick William, 1960b. *Frederick William Maitland, Historian: Selections from his Writings*, ed. Robert Livingston Schuyler, University of Chicago Press

Mandelbaum, Maurice, 1971. *History, Man and Reason: A Study in Nineteenth-Century Thought* Johns Hopkins University Press

Mandelbaum, Maurice, 1973. 'Societal Facts', in Ryan (ed.), 1973

Mandelbaum, Maurice, 1977. *The Anatomy of Historical Knowledge*, Johns Hopkins University Press

Mandrou, Robert, 1978. *From Humanism to Science 1480–1700*, (Pelican History of European Thought, vol. III), tr. Brian Pearce, Penguin (1973)

Manuel, Frank E., 1965. *Shapes of Philosophical History*, George Allen and Unwin

Marrou, Henri-Irénée, 1966. *The Meaning of History*, Helicon Press (1954)

Marsh, Robert M., 1967. *Comparative Sociology: A Codification of Cross-Societal Analysis*, Harcourt, Brace and World

Martin, Rex, 1977. *Historical Explanation: Re-enactment and Practical Inference*, Cornell University Press

Marwick, Arthur, 1989. *The Nature of History*, Macmillan (1970)

Marx, Karl, 1973a. *The Revolutions of 1848*, ed. David Fernbach, Penguin

Marx, Karl, 1973b. *Surveys from Exile*, ed. David Fernbach, Penguin

Marx, Karl, 1975. *Early Writings*, Penguin

Marx, Karl, 1976. *Capital: A Critique of Political Economy*, Vol. I, tr. Ben Fowkes, Penguin

Marx, Karl, 1977. *Selected Writings*, ed. David McLellan, Oxford University Press

Marx, Karl, and Engels, Friedrich, 1934. *Correspondence 1846–1895*, and ed. V. Adoratsky, Lawrence and Wishart

Marx, Karl, and Engels, Friedrich, 1969. *Basic Writings on Politics and Philosophy*, ed. Lewis Feuer, Collins/Fontana

Meiland, Jack W., 1965. *Scepticism and Historical Knowledge* Random House

Meinecke, Friedrich, 1963. *The German Catastrophe*, Beacon Press, (1946)

Meyerhoff, Hans (ed.), 1959. *The Philosophy of History in our Time*, Doubleday

Mill, John Stuart, 1973. *A System of Logic*, in *Collected Works of John Stuart Mill*, vol. VII, University of Toronto Press (1843)

Mink, Louis O., 1966. 'The Autonomy of Historical Understanding' (1965), in Dray (ed.), 1966

Mink, Louis O., 1978. 'Narrative Form as a Cognitive Instrument', in Canary and Kozicki

Momigliano, Arnaldo, 1966. *Studies in Historiography*, Weidenfeld and Nicolson

Moore, Barrington, 1969. *Social Origins of Dictatorship and Democracy: Lord and Peasant in the Making of the Modern World*, Penguin (1966)

Mousnier, Roland, 1973. *The Assassination of Henry IV: The Tyrannicide Problem and the Consolidation of the French Absolute Monarchy in the Early 17th Century*, Faber (1964)

Munz, Peter, 1977. *The Shapes of Time: A New Look at the Philosophy of History*, Wesleyan University Press

Nadel, George H. (ed.), 1965. *Studies in the Philosophy of History: Selected Essays from* History and Theory *(vols I–IV)*, Harper Torchbooks

Nagel, Thomas, 1979. *Mortal Questions*, Cambridge University Press

Nagel, Thomas, 1986. *The View From Nowhere*, Oxford University Press (New York)

Namier, Sir Lewis, 1961. *England in the Age of the American Revolution*, Macmillan (1930)

Namier, Sir Lewis, 1965. *The Structure of Politics at the Accession of George III*, Macmillan (1929)

Nietzsche, Friedrich, 1957. *The Use and Abuse of History*, tr. Adrian Collins, 2nd edn, Bobbs-Merrill (1874)

Nisbet, Robert A., 1969. *Social Change and History: Aspects of the Western Theory of Development*, Oxford University Press (New York)

Nisbet, Robert, 1980. *History of the Idea of Progress*, Heinemann

Norman, Andrew, 1991. 'Telling It Like It Was: Historical Narratives on their own Terms', *History and Theory*, 30, no.2

Novick, Peter 1988. *That Noble Dream: The 'Objectivity Question' and the American Historical Profession*, Cambridge University Press

Oakeshott, Michael, 1933. *Experience and Its Modes*, Cambridge University Press

Oakeshott, Michael, 1967. *Rationalism in Politics, and other Essays*, Methuen (1962)

Oakeshott, Michael, 1983. *On History and other Essays*, Blackwell

O'Hear, Anthony, 1988. *The Element of Fire: Science, Art and the Human World*, Routledge

Olafson, Frederick, A., 1979. *The Dialectic of Action: A Philosophical Interpretation of History and the Humanities*, University of Chicago Press

Oral History, 1970 – (University of Essex)

Oral History Review 1966 – (Oral History Association, Los Angeles)

Parker, Christopher, 1990. *The English Historical Tradition since 1850*, John Donald

Parker, Geoffrey, 1979. *The Dutch Revolt*, Penguin (1977)

Perrot, Michelle, (ed.), 1992. *Writing Women's History*, Blackwell (1984)

Perrot, Michelle, and Duby, Georges, 1990. *Histoire des femmes*, Plon (ET 1992. *A History of Women in the West*, Belknap Press)

Pitcher, George, (ed.), 1964. *Truth*, Prentice-Hall

Plato, 1941. *The Republic of Plato*, tr. Francis Cornford, Clarendon Press

Plato, 1965. *Timaeus*, tr. H. D. P. Lee, Penguin

Plumb, J. H. 1973. *The Death of the Past*, Penguin (1969)

Plutarch, 1910. *Lives*, Dent/Everyman

Pocock, J. G. A., 1971. *Politics, Language and Time: Essays on Political Thought and History*, Methuen

Pocock, J. G. A., 1975. *The Machiavellian Moment: Florentine Political Thought and the Atlantic Republican Tradition*, Princeton University Press

Pollard, Sidney, 1971. *The Idea of Progress: History and Society*, Penguin (1968)

Pompa, Leon, 1990. *Human Nature and Historical Knowledge: Hume, Hegel and Vico*, Cambridge University Press

Popper, Karl R., 1959. 'Prediction and Prophecy in the Social Sciences' (1948), in Gardiner; also in Popper (1969)

Popper, Karl R., 1961. *The Poverty of Historicism*, Routledge and Kegan Paul (1944–5)

Popper, Karl R., 1962. *The Open Society and its Enemies*, Routledge and Kegan Paul (1945)

Popper, Karl R., 1969. *Conjectures and Refutations: The Growth of Scientific Knowledge*, Routledge and Kegan Paul (1963)

Popper, Karl R., 1972a. *The Logic of Scientific Discovery*, Hutchinson (1959)

Popper, Karl R., 1972b. *Objective Knowledge: An Evolutionary Approach* Clarendon Press

Powicke, F. M. 1955. *Modern Historians and the Study of History: Essays and Papers*, Odhams

Prawer, S. S., 1978. *Karl Marx and World Literature*, Oxford University Press (1976)

Prins, Gwyn, 1991. 'Oral History', in P. Burke (ed.), 1991

Putnam, Hilary, 1979. *Meaning and the Moral Sciences*, Routledge and Kegan Paul (1978)

Putnam, Hilary, 1981. *Reason, Truth and History*, Cambridge University Press

Rabb, Theodore K., and Rotberg, Robert (eds), 1982. *The New History: The 1980s and Beyond*, Princeton University Press

Ranke, Leopold von, 1970. Preface to *Histories of the Latin and Germanic Nations* (1824), in Stern

Ranke, Leopold von, 1973. *The Theory and Practice of History*, tr. Wilma A. Iggers, Bobbs-Merrill

Reeves, Marjorie, 1969. *The Influence of Prophecy in the Late Middle Ages: A Study in Joachimism*, Clarendon Press

Reeves, Marjorie, 1976. *Joachim of Fiore and the Prophetic Future*, SPCK

Reiss, Hans (ed.) 1977. *Kant's Political Writings*, Cambridge University Press (1970)

Renier, G. J., 1965 *History: Its Purpose and Method*, George Allen and Unwin (1950)

Ricoeur, Paul, 1984–5. *Time and Narrative*, tr. K. McLaughlin and D. Pellauer, 2 vols, University of Chicago Press (1983–4)

Rigby, S. H., 1987. *Marxism and History: A Critical Introduction*, Manchester University Press

Rigney, Ann 1990. *The Rhetoric of Historical Representation: Three Narrative Histories of the French Revolution*, Cambridge University Press

Roberts, David D., 1987. *Benedetto Croce and the Uses of Historicism*, University of California Press

Robinson, James Harvey 1965. *The New History: Essays Illustrating the Modern Historical Outlook*, Free Press (1912)

Rogers, Alan 1977. *Approaches to Local History*, Longman

Rorty, Richard, et al. (eds), 1984. *Philosophy in History: Essays on the Historiography of Philosophy*, Cambridge University Press

Ross, Charles, 1975. *Edward IV*, Book Club Associates/Eyre Methuen (1974)

Ruben, David-Hillel, 1990. *Explaining Explanation*, Routledge

Runciman, Steven, 1965. *A History of the Crusades*, Penguin (1951–4)

Russell, Bertrand, 1978. *Autobiography*, George Allen and Unwin (1967–9)

Russell, Conrad, 1990. *The Causes of the English Civil War*, Clarendon Press

Ryan, Alan, 1970. *The Philosophy of the Social Sciences*, Macmillan

Ryan, Alan (ed.), 1973. *The Philosophy of Social Explanation*, Oxford University Press

Sacks, David Harris, 1991. *The Widening Gate: Bristol and the Atlantic Economy 1450–1700*, University of California Press

Samuel, Raphael, and Thompson, Paul, (eds), 1990. *The Myths We Live By*, Routledge

Saul, S. B., 1969. *The Myth of the Great Depression*, Macmillan

Schutz, Alfred, 1972. *The Phenomenology of the Social World*, tr. George Walsh and Frederick Lehnert, Heinemann (1932; English translation 1967)

Seddon, Keith, 1987. *Time: A Philosophical Treatment*, Croom Helm

Seldon, Anthony (ed.), 1988. *Contemporary History: Practice and Method*, Blackwell

Seldon, Anthony, and Pappworth, Joanna, 1983. *By Word of Mouth: 'Élite' Oral History*, Methuen

Sellar, W. C. and Yeatman, R. J., 1931. *1066 and All That: A Memorable History of England*, Methuen (1930)

Shafer, R. J., 1974. *A Guide to Historical Method*, Dorsey Press (1969)

Shapiro, Barbara J., 1983. *Probability and Certainty in Seventeenth-Century England*, Princeton University Press

Skinner, Quentin, 1974. ' "Social Meaning" and the Explanation of Social Action' (1972) in Gardiner (ed.), 1974

Skinner, Quentin (ed.), 1990. *The Return of Grand Theory in the Human Sciences*, Cambridge University Press (1985)

Skocpol, Theda (ed.), 1984. *Vision and Method in Historical Sociology*, Cambridge University Press

Spengler, Oswald, 1932. *The Decline of the West*, 2 vols, George Allen and Unwin (1918–22)

Stanford, Michael, 1962. 'The Raleghs Take to the Sea', *The Mariners' Mirror* (Cambridge University Press), 48, no. 1

Stanford, Michael, 1990. *The Nature of Historical Knowledge*, Blackwell (1986)

Stern, Fritz, (ed.), 1970. *The Varieties of History: From Voltaire to the Present*, Macmillan (1956)

Stoianovich, Traian, 1976. *French Historical Method: The 'Annales' Paradigm*, Cornell University Press

Stone, Lawrence, 1972. *The Causes of the English Revolution, 1529–1642*, Routledge and Kegan Paul

Stone, Lawrence, 1987. *The Past and the Present Revisited*, Routledge and Kegan Paul

Strassburg, Gottfried von, 1960. *Tristan*, tr. A. T. Hatton, Penguin

Strawson, P. F., 1950. 'Truth', in Pitcher (ed.)

Strawson, P. F., 1985. 'Causation and Explanation' in Vermazen and Hintikka

Stubbs, William, 1906. *Lectures on Early English History*, ed. Arthur Hassall, Longmans, Green

Sutherland, Lucy S. (ed.), 1966. *Studies in History: British Academy Lectures*, Oxford University Press

Taylor, A. E., 1928. *A Commentary on Plato's Timaeus*, Oxford University Press

Taylor, A. J. P., 1964. *The Origins of the Second World War*, Penguin (1961)

Taylor, Charles H., 1979. *Hegel and Modern Society*, Cambridge University Press

Taylor, Charles H., 1984. 'Philosophy and Its History' in Rorty et al.

Temin, Peter (ed.), 1973. *New Economic History: Selected Readings*, Penguin

Thomas, Keith, 1978. *Religion and the Decline of Magic: Studies in Popular Beliefs in Sixteenth- and Seventeenth-century England*, Peregrine/Penguin (1971)

Thompson, Edward P., 1968. *The Making of the English Working Class*, Penguin (1963)

Thompson, J. W., 1942. *A History of Historical Writing*, 2 vols Macmillan (New York)

Thompson, Paul, 1988. *The Voice of the Past: Oral History*, Oxford University Press (1978)

Thucydides, 1954. *History of the Peloponnesian War*, tr. Rex Warner, Penguin

Tosh, John, 1984. *The Pursuit of History: Aims, Methods and New Directions in the Study of Modern History*, Longman

Toynbee, Arnold, 1934–61. *A Study of History*, Oxford University Press

Trevor-Roper, Hugh R., 1962. *The Last Days of Hitler*, Pan (1947)

Trevor-Roper, Hugh R., 1967. *Religion, the Reformation and Social Change and Other Essays*, Macmillan

Trevor-Roper, Hugh R., 1981. 'History and Imagination' in Lloyd-Jones et al.

Trompf, G. W., 1979. *The Idea of Historical Recurrence in Western Thought: From Antiquity to the Reformation*, University of California Press

Vandecasteele-Schweitzer, Sylvie, and Voldman, Danièle, 1992. 'The Oral Sources for Women's History', in Perrot (ed.), 1992

Van der Dussen, W. J., and Rubinoff, L., (eds), 1991. *Objectivity, Method and Point of View: Essays in the Philosophy of History*, E. J. Brill (Leiden)

Vansina, Jan, 1973. *Oral Tradition: A Study in Historical Methodology*, Penguin (1961)

Vansina, Jan, 1985. *Oral Tradition as History*, University of Wisconsin Press

Vermazen, Bruce and Hintikka, Merrill B. (eds), 1985. *Essays on Davidson: Actions and Events*, Clarendon Press

Veyne, Paul, 1984. *Writing History: An Essay on Epistemology*, tr. Mina Moore-Rinvolucri, Wesleyan University Press (1971)

Vico, Giambattista, 1970. *The New Science of Giambattista Vico*, tr. T. H. Bergin and M. H. Fisch, abridged 3rd edn of 1744, Cornell University Press (1961)

Wainwright, F. T., 1962. *Archaeology and Place-Names in History: An Essay on Problems of Co-ordination*, Routledge and Kegan Paul

Walker, Angus, 1978. *Marx: His Theory and its Context: Politics as Economics*, Longman

Walsh, Kevin, 1992. *The Representation of the Past: Museums and heritage in the post-modern world*, Routledge

Walsh, W. H. 1958. *An Introduction to Philosophy of History*, Hutchinson

Watkins, J. W. N., 1973. 'Ideal Types and Historical Explanation' (1953) in Ryan

Watson, James D., 1970. *The Double Helix: A Personal Account of the Discovery of the Structure of DNA*, Penguin (1968)

Weber, Max, 1949. *The Methodology of the Social Sciences*, tr. and ed. Shils, Edward A. Shils and Henry A. Finch, Free Press

Weber, Max, 1964. *The Theory of Social and Economic Organization*, ed. Talcott Parsons, Free Press (1947)

Weisman, Richard, 1984. *Witchcraft, Magic and Religion in 17th-century Massachusetts*, University of Massachusetts Press

White, Alan R. (ed.), 1968. *The Philosophy of Action*, Oxford University Press

White, Hayden, 1973. *Metahistory: The Historical Imagination in Nineteenth-Century Europe* Johns Hopkins University Press

White, Hayden, 1975. 'Historicism, History and the Figurative Imagination', *History and Theory*, Beiheft 14

White, Hayden, 1978a. *Tropics of Discourse: Essays in Cultural Criticism*, Johns Hopkins University Press

White, Hayden, 1978b. 'The Historical Text as Literary Artifact', in Canary and Kozicki

White, Hayden, 1987. *The Content of the Form: Narrative Discourse and Historical Representation*, Johns Hopkins University Press

White, Morton 1965. *Foundations of Historical Knowledge*, Harper and Row

Whitrow, G. J., 1972. *What is Time?* Thames and Hudson

Wilson, Bryan R. (ed.), 1970. *Rationality*, Blackwell

Winch, Peter, 1958. *The Idea of a Social Science and Its Relations to Philosophy*, Routledge and Kegan Paul

Wittgenstein, Ludwig, 1968. *Philosophical Investigations*, tr. G. E. M. Anscombe, Blackwell (1953)

Woodham-Smith, Cecil, 1953. *The Reason Why*, Constable

Woodward, E. L., 1966. 'Some Considerations on the Present State of Historical Studies' (1950) in Sutherland

Wright, G. H. von, 1971. *Explanation and Understanding*, Routledge and Kegan Paul

Wrigley, E. A. (ed.), 1966. *An Introduction to English Historical Demography from the Sixteenth to the Nineteenth Century*, Weidenfeld and Nicolson

Wrigley, E. A., 1969. *Population and History*, Weidenfeld and Nicolson

Wrigley, E. A., and Schofield, R. S., 1981. *The Population History of England 1541–1871: A Reconstruction*, Edward Arnold

Zeldin, Theodore, 1973–7. *France 1848–1945*, 2 vols, Oxford University Press

# Index